AGING AND DEMOGRAPHIC CHANGE IN CANADIAN CONTEXT

Edited by David Cheal

The Canadian population is aging. As the 'baby-boom' generation reaches retirement age, policy-makers have begun to fear the economic and demographic challenges ahead. *Aging and Demographic Change in Canadian Context* responds to this alarmist view. Cautioning that exaggerated concerns about population aging can be harmful to rational policy-making, the contributors present several alternative perspectives and question whether an aging society is as problematic as it is commonly assumed to be. 'Old age' is a slippery concept, and the effective boundaries between it and 'middle age' are not always clear. The contributors argue that it is important to develop forward-looking programs that may influence life-course trajectories in favourable directions, and that these new policies should be developed with respect to the life course considered as a whole. The essays in *Aging and Demographic Change in Canadian Context* address these challenges and seek to broaden public discussion on aging and Canadian public policy.

(The Trends Project Series)

DAVID CHEAL is a Professor of Sociology at the University of Winnipeg.

Policy Research: The Trends Project Series

The Trends Project is a result of the Government of Canada's Policy Research Initiative, an undertaking that seeks to strengthen the Government of Canada's policy capacity and ensure that policy development benefits from the work of researchers and academics. The Policy Research Initiative, in cooperation with the Social Sciences and Humanities Research Council of Canada, developed a new model for academics and government to collaborate on policy research. Teams of academics examined the forces that are driving change in Canada and identified the potential implications for public policy. This collaboration came to be known as the Trends Project. Under the Project, academics, research institutes, and government officials worked in partnership to build a better knowledge base on longer-term issues to support policy development and identify knowledge gaps requiring further research. The Trends Project includes the following books:

Gordon Smith and Daniel Wolfish, editors
Who Is Afraid of the State? Canada in a World of Multiple Centres of Power
(2001)

Edward A. Parson, editor
Governing the Environment: Persistent Challenges, Uncertain Innovations
(2001)

George Hoberg, editor
Capacity for Choice: Canada in a New North American (2002)

Neil Nevitte, editor
Value Change and Governance in Canada (2002)

David Cheal, editor
Aging and Demographic Change in Canadian Context (2003)

Danielle Juteau, editor
Social Differentiation: Patterns and Processes (2003)

AGING AND DEMOGRAPHIC CHANGE IN CANADIAN CONTEXT

Edited by David Cheal

UNIVERSITY OF TORONTO PRESS
Toronto Buffalo London

© University of Toronto Press Incorporated 2002
Toronto Buffalo London
Printed in Canada

ISBN 0-8020-8505-9

Printed on acid-free paper

National Library of Canada Cataloguing in Publication

Aging and demographic change in Canadian context / edited by David Cheal.

(The Trends Project series)
Includes bibliographical references.
ISBN 0-8020-8505-9

1. Aging – Social aspects – Canada.   2. Age distribution (Demography) –
Canada.   I. Cheal, David J.   II. Title.   III. Series: Trends project series.

HA1064.C2A3485 2002   305.26′0971   C2002-903315-2

The University of Toronto Press acknowledges the financial assistance to its
publishing program of the Canada Council for the Arts and the Ontario
Arts Council.

The University of Toronto Press acknowledges the financial support for its
publishing activities of the Government of Canada through the Book
Publishing Industry Development Program (BPIDP).

Contents

List of Tables and Figures

Foreword

Aging and Demographic Change in Canadian Context is one of a series of books sponsored by the Trends Project. The Trends Project, a collaborative effort of the Policy Research Initiative and the Social Sciences and Humanities Research Council of Canada, was conceived as a means of providing a new model for academics and government to collaborate on policy research and as a means of feeding the policy development process. Exchanging ideas, perspectives, frameworks, and data between academics and government is, at once, necessary for the development of innovative and effective public policy and difficult to accomplish in times of constant change.

Three goals lie at the heart of the Policy Research Initiative and the Trends Project. They are:

- Supporting the creation, sharing, and use of policy research knowledge
- Strengthening policy research capacity in departments through the recruitment, development, and retention of people
- Building a policy research community through networks, vehicles, and venues

In the past, the government has usually either commissioned research to address government-identified knowledge gaps, or the federal granting councils have funded an academic-led research agenda. Under the Trends Project, academics, think tanks, and government officials worked in partnership to identify the knowledge gaps requiring further research. The objective of this governmental and academic collaboration was to identify what we do and do not know, and to understand how we know it. The research undertaken by the Trends Project teams looked forward to the medium- to long-term rather than addressing immediate policy concerns.

The makeup of the teams themselves was unique. The project brought together some of Canada's leading academics to head eight teams made up of over fifty researchers from universities across the country. The researchers participating in the project were selected through a call for proposals administered by the Social Sciences and Humanities Research Council of Canada. By creating multidisciplinary teams consisting of participants from across Canada, the Trends Project succeeded in bringing together people who would normally not interact with one another. The result of this multidisciplinary, cross-Canada approach has been that we now have a greater depth and breadth of understanding of the emergent policy areas Canada is likely to confront in the coming years.

The Trends Project research essays have been presented on several occasions at workshops and conferences across the country where Canadian researchers and government officials provided insightful comments and useful feedback. Finally, each of the essays published under the Trends Project has been through the process of anonymous peer review.

The Trends Project was also innovative because it provided a means for academics to have their ideas and research circulated widely throughout government. The overall product was not simply the production of research papers, but also the process of continual collaboration between governmental and academic communities. The second annual National Policy Research Conference in November 1999 enabled the researchers to showcase their work to over 800 policy developers and experts in the federal and provincial governments.

Commentaries and research excerpts have been featured regularly in *Horizons*, the Policy Research Initiative's newsletter. *Horizons* targets a broad policy audience throughout the Canadian policy research community, both inside and outside of government, with over 8,400 people on its distribution list. By bringing governmental and academic communities together on an ongoing basis, they were exposed to each other's research needs, perspectives, and constraints. The Trends Project is one part of a larger effort to build Canada-wide policy research capacities. It is a model that we would like to build on in the future.

Laura A. Chapman
Executive Director
Policy Research Initiative

Acknowledgments

Producing the present book has been a team effort at every stage. It began with a shared vision, held by the Trends Project team on Aging and Demographic Change, led by Verena Haldemann. The team is committed to the idea that important aspects of an "aging society" are being under-communicated, and they set out with the aim to correct that situation. The team was fortunate to benefit in their endeavour from the support of Vasanthi Srinivasan and Michael Carley. Together, Vasanthi and Michael worked hard to ensure that the topic of aging and demographic change was included in the publication agenda for the Trends Project. Subsequently, practical assistance with administrative and technical details of bringing the work to completion was provided by Jeffrey Frank, Daniel Wolfish, and Louise Boyer. The editor also wishes to acknowledge the support and assistance of Dr. Sandra Kirby and the University of Winnipeg.

The quality of the present book is ultimately the result of the work of the contributors themselves. However, acknowledgment of the influence of advice provided by the Trends Project Adjudication Committee for this publication should also be made. The Adjudication Committee stressed the importance of integrating the individual chapters into a coherent collective work. The contributors and the editor have collaborated in an effort to realize that aspiration, and we hope that all those who have supported the project along the way will find the results worthwhile.

The authors wish to acknowledge permission to reproduce the following:

Reprinted by permission of Doubleday Canada, a division of Random House of Canada Limited.

Excerpt from *Aurora Leigh* reprinted from Elizabeth Barrett Browning, *Aurora Leigh* edited by Kerry McSweeney (Oxford World's Classics, 1998). Editorial matter © Kerry McSweeney 1993. Reprinted by permission of Oxford University Press.

Excerpt from *Blue Marrow* by Louise Bernice Halfe. Used by permission, McClelland and Stewart Ltd. *The Canadian Publishers.*

'The Macroeconomic Implications of Ageing in a Global Context,' *Economics Department Working Paper*, No. 193. Copyright OECD, 1998.

'The Transition From Work to Retirement,' *Social Policy Studies*, No. 16. Copyright OECD, 1995.

Statistics Canada information in Chapter 2 is used with the permission of the Minister of Industry, as Minister responsible for Statistics Canada. Information on the availability of the wide range of data from Statistics Canada can be obtained from Statistics Canada's Regional Offices, its World Wide Web site at http://www.statcan.ca, and its toll-free access number 1-800-263-1136.

Contributors

Krista Abbott holds a Bachelor of Arts Degree in gerontology and sociology from McMaster University, in Hamilton, and a Master of Science degree in family relations and human development from the University of Guelph. She is currently employed as a senior researcher at the Earlscourt Child and Family Centre in Toronto. Her earlier research explored life satisfaction among the never-married elderly as well as familial relationships across aging generations.

David Cheal is a professor of sociology at the University of Winnipeg. He has published nationally and internationally on a variety of issues in the social sciences. In recent years he has focused mainly on the study of family relationships and on aspects of economic well-being. Relevant policy research in the latter area includes analyses of survey data on income poverty and the Employment Insurance Family Supplement. Current projects include a book on Sociology of Family Life (Palgrave) and a four-volume set of edited papers on Family: Critical Concepts (Routledge).

Ingrid Arnet Connidis is professor of sociology at the University of Western Ontario in London. Her primary research area is aging, with particular interests in family ties including intergenerational relations, sibling ties in middle and later life, informal support, and policy-related issues. Her work has appeared in a variety of journals and her most recent book is entitled *Family Ties and Aging* (Sage). She is currently exploring multigenerational families, the negotiation of family ties over time and across generations, and continuity and change in social trends and family life.

Susan A. McDaniel is professor of sociology at the University of Alberta. She is working on studies of intergenerational transfers/linkages, gendering demographics, and family/social policy challenges in a reconstructing Canada. Her recent publications include *Close Relations* (with Tepperman, Prentice-Hall), '"What Did You Ever Do For Me?": Intergenerational Linkages,' in Gee and Gutman, *The Overselling of Population Aging* (Oxford), '"Born at the Right Time?" Gendered Generations and Webs of Entitlement and Responsibility,' Canadian Journal of Sociology, "Generational Consciousness of and for Women," in Turner and Edmunds, eds., *Narrative, Generational Consciousness and Politics* (Rowman Littlefield). She is a Fellow of the Royal Society of Canada and president of the Canadian Sociology and Anthropology Association.

Joan E. Norris received Bachelor's, Master's, and doctoral degrees in psychology from the University of Waterloo. She is a professor in the Department of Family Relations and Applied Nutrition, and the Associate Dean of Graduate Studies, University of Guelph. Norris is the co-author of two books on aging, *Among Generations: The Cycle of Adult Relationships* and *The Social Psychology of Aging: A Cognitive Perspective*, as well as of many papers on intergenerational family relations.

Joel Prager is a political economist. He received a Master of Arts degree from Brooklyn College, City University of New York, as well as Master's and doctoral degrees from Princeton University. Until his recent retirement, he was Director of Planning for Saskatchewan Finance. Prager was the first fellow in the newly established Saskatchewan Institute of Public Policy. He was technical adviser to the intergovernmental task force that reformed the Canada Pension Plan, served on the parliamentary task force examining the Canadian labour market and employment opportunities, and advised the Progressive Conservative Party during the patriation of the Canadian Constitution. He also taught at Brooklyn College, Princeton University, Fordham University, and the University of Calgary where he is currently adjunct professor of history.

Marty Thomas joined the Department of Applied Human Sciences at Concordia University in Montreal as an assistant professor in 1998. Prior to academic work, Thomas worked as a private and governmental consultant in leisure planning throughout Ontario. In 1992, she returned to graduate study, completing a Master's degree in environmental planning at York University prior to doctoral work in leisure studies at the Pennsylvania State University. Thomas's doctoral dissertation focused on Thorstein Veblen's theory of leisure. Her current research is in the areas of leisure futures, work/leisure balance, and community development.

Douglas Thorpe is associate professor of English at the University of Saskatchewan, where he teaches courses in nineteenth-century literature, literary theory, and literature and aging. He has published in the *Dickens Studies Annual, Victorian Review,* and *Canadian Children's Literature.* Recent conference papers have turned increasingly to interdisciplinary work in the history of discourses of aging. He is completing a book on competing representations of aging in nineteenth-century culture.

Joseph A. Tindale received Bachelor's and Master's degrees from McMaster University and a doctoral degree from York University. He is a professor and chair of the Department of Family Relations and Applied Nutrition at the University of Guelph. Tindale is the co-author of *Among Generations: The Cycle of Adult Relationships,* and of various articles concerning health promotion and policy among older persons as well as those addressing intergenerational relations.

Rosemary A. Venne received a Bachelor's degree from University of Windsor, two Masters' degrees from Queen's and a doctorate from the University of Toronto. She is an associate professor in the Department of Industrial Relations and Organizational Behaviour at the College of Commerce at the University of Saskatchewan. Her research interests include hours of work, alternative worktime arrangements, and demography as it relates to human resource topics, in particular to career patterns, labour force supply, and labour force demand issues.

AGING AND DEMOGRAPHIC CHANGE IN CANADIAN CONTEXT

1. Introduction: Contextualizing Demographic Concerns

David Cheal

Introduction: Population Aging

Demographic aging is a process of population change in which the population of a country progressively contains larger proportions of people in older age groups. This process is projected to have a huge impact on the population of Canada over the next forty years. In 1998, about 3.7 million Canadians were 65 years of age or over, and they made up 12.3 per cent of the population. According to the National Advisory Council on Aging, their numbers will increase to 6 million in 2016, when the baby boomers begin to turn 65, making up 16 per cent of the population at that time.[1] The proportion of older people will continue to increase to 19 per cent in 2020, and 22.6 per cent in 2041, when there will be 10 million people over 65 in Canada.

It is important to keep in mind that a growing proportion of people who are age 65 or older and who are likely to be retired is not the only feature of population aging. In an already aging society the average age of people who are still considered to be of 'working age' is rising. In Quebec, for instance, people who are aged 45 to 59 are projected to comprise 54.7 per cent of all people who are of working age by 2008.[2] The aging of the working population is identified as an issue that deserves attention, partly because older workers who become unemployed tend to remain unemployed longer than younger workers.[3]

Demographic projections for Canada, and for other countries, are frequently the basis for rising concerns about negative futures of 'aging societies.'[4] These concerns are often intensely debated, and arguments and counter-arguments abound in and around the academic discipline of demography. It is therefore not surprising that aging and demo-

graphic change was selected as a topic for the Project on Trends sponsored by the Social Sciences and Humanities Research Council of
Canada and the Policy Research Initiative.

Each theme in the Project on Trends highlights a challenge faced by
Canada during the present decade, and possibly beyond. Over the next
three decades, a growing proportion of the Canadian population will
comprise older people.[5] These groups have traditionally had low levels
of labour force participation and high levels of dependence on public
income transfer programs. The declining health of older people with
their advancing years places increasing demands on medical systems
and social support networks. Issues such as these are part of a complex
network of demographic concerns that we will explore in this book.

Demographic Concerns

Concerns about negative consequences of population aging fall into six
main groups:

1 that escalating costs of providing public pensions to a growing
   population of older people will place a heavy financial burden on
   people of working age;
2 that a growing volume of older people with heavy health care needs
   will create a huge and unsupportable demand for costly medical
   services;
3 that if current trends continue, personal assistance with daily activities may not be available in the future to all elderly people who
   need it;
4 that reduced labour force participation, and an older workforce, may
   hinder current efforts to increase the economic output of Canada's
   population;
5 that more economic and social responsibilities for supporting both
   children and older people is falling on a narrower section of the population, defined as the 'sandwich generation';
6 that if more resources are shifted towards older people, existing
   intergenerational inequities may worsen, possibly contributing to a
   breakdown in social cohesion.

In Quebec, concern about these issues is accompanied by the additional concern about the linguistic future of that province. Some people
are afraid that current demographic trends may lead to the decline of

French as a vital working language.[6] Together, all of these concerns about possible future consequences of demographic aging constitute a challenging view of the issues to be addressed by policy makers and social researchers.[7]

Before allowing ourselves to be stampeded into an alarmist stance, however, it might be useful to pause and consider some alternative points of view. Individually, the contributors to this book present such alternative perspectives. Collectively, they question whether an aging society necessarily presents greater problems than those facing society in the recent past. They warn that exaggerated concerns about population aging, or in other words demographic fears, can be harmful to rational policy making. The following chapters substantiate these claims by drawing our attention to a variety of factors beyond the proportion of the population in older age groups – factors that the authors believe carry considerable weight.

For example, in Chapter 2 Susan McDaniel observes that the overall proportion of the population that is calculated to be economically dependent (i.e., the 'dependency ratio') is at a historically low level today, and it should continue to fall over the next two decades. This is because the increasing proportion of the population over the age of 65 is currently being more than compensated for by the decreasing proportion of the population under the age of 18.

Clearly, to understand what is happening in an aging society it is not enough to look only at the aged themselves, or even to compare them with the overall society. It is also necessary to analyse how different groups, and different factors, are related within a complex system of action. The purpose of this book is therefore to show how the implications of demographic projections need to be examined within a larger context. That larger context is economic, political, social, familial, cultural, and temporal.

Susan McDaniel takes a broad look at many of these issues in her chapter. She introduces a theme that we will take up again later, namely, the necessity for a multidimensional approach to the study of aging and the place of older age groups in society. She highlights this theme by dropping the conventional terminology of intergenerational relations in favour of a new term: intergenerational interlinkages.

Terms such as intergenerational relations, intergenerational ties, or intergenerational transfers refer to specific connections between the members of different generations and their interactions. This conceptualization tends to overlook the multiple connections between generations, some direct and some indirect, that can be interwoven in complex ways. To take just one example, which is relevant to the controversial issue of intergenerational equity, McDaniel notes that the older generations have borne a share of the cost of recent debt reduction policies through tax increases and reduced medical services. However, since some of them are close to the end of their lifespans, they are unlikely to reap many of the subsequent benefits of this 'fiscal dividend.' Younger generations, on the other hand, presumably will have a longer period in which to enjoy some of the fruits of deficit and debt reduction.

The general point to make here is that in addressing issues of an aging population, it is not enough to pay attention only to the factor of age itself. It is also necessary to take into account the individual's position in the life course, including the length of the lifespan. We will see below that the nature of the life course is an important factor to consider in more than one context.

In Chapter 3, Douglas Thorpe introduces two additional factors, language and culture. Thorpe shifts the context from demographic structures to cultural meanings. The particular meaning that Thorpe is most interested in is that of old age as a period of decline. He problematizes this taken-for-granted meaning in several ways. Notably, he reports that Alzheimer's disease was first observed – that is, first became 'observable' – when it was manifested in people in their fifties. Otherwise it was just felt to constitute normal behaviour in elderly people.

Thorpe's analysis of this example puts an interesting twist on concerns about expensive medical treatments for an aging population. He points out that medical treatment is provided only when a set of presenting symptoms is categorized as a treatable disease. Since conditions of many kinds are viewed as 'normal' in elderly people, rather than as symptomatic of a specifiable medical condition, he argues that there is an age-based discrimination in diagnostic practice. It is presumably consistent with this line of argument that a recent analysis of medical procedures in Quebec found that health costs during the last year of life do not increase with age.[8] The medical costs studied were surgical, diagnostic, and therapeutic procedures, which accounted for 26 per cent of the cost of physician services received during the last year of life. According to this study, middle-aged persons are somewhat more likely to receive aggressive medical treatment than older persons – and considerably more than the very elderly – in the last year of their lives.

Thorpe has a serious reason for drawing our attention to the social construction of concepts of disease. He wants to show us that normative images about aging can control public perceptions of needs and capacities, and therefore shape the forms of social institutions. For example, he shows that in the late nineteenth century concerns about an additional burden of dependants produced by an aging population led to panicky cuts in public income supports for aged persons in Canada. Similar worries recurred in the 1930s. Then, concerns about declining fertility rates precipitated debates about population decline and its implications for the wealth and power of nations. Viewed in a historical context, the total effect of an aging population lies in certain phenomena of demographic change and in the social responses to them. In a contemporary context, this points to a rationale for a diversity of policy responses to support an aging population, given the complexities of the actual aging process.

Aging and Demographic Change

Population aging refers to the increase of the average age of a population as measured on a calendrical scale of 'societal time.' This shift manifests itself in the emergence of a greater proportion of older people in a society's population. The number of older people at any given time is actually the result of a series of individual processes of transition into old age, each one taking place in a life course of 'personal time.' It is therefore necessary to examine both the demographic processes that occur in societal time and that occur in individual life courses that take place in personal time. Long-term processes of change in individual life courses have been conceptualized as trajectories that define a broad pattern of events across the life course.[9]

Life-course trajectories are especially relevant when considering the capacity of families to provide informal social supports for older people. This capacity is often considered to be crucial for the ability of a society to sustain more older people. Families help to provide services that would otherwise have to be provided at public expense, and they help to sustain the emotional and physical well-being of older people who need assistance with daily living.[10]

Ingrid Connidis takes up the question of the supply of family caregivers as a central policy issue. The factors involved here turn out to be more complex than might be supposed. One of Connidis's more intriguing findings is that although fertility rates have been falling in

Canada, it is not the case that there will be more elderly Canadians without children in the next two decades. Women who enter into old age at the beginning of the twenty-first century are, in fact, less likely to be childless than women in preceding cohorts. That is, although the average completed family size has been shrinking, more women are now more likely to have had at least one child than was the case with women born at the beginning of the twentieth century. It is therefore not necessarily the case that more women who are entering into old age now will lack family caregiving.

Multidimensional Demography

Demography is a more complex field of study than is often acknowledged. A complete demographic assessment of an aging population involves more than just a description of an increasing average age as a result of declining fertility rates and greater longevity. In addition to describing the proportion of the population in older age groups, it is also necessary to take into account other demographic dimensions of the lives of older persons, such as their earlier marital history and their completed fertility.

In Chapter 4, Ingrid Connidis reminds us that a good demographic study is multidimensional. The question of potential familial support for older people, for instance, is best addressed by looking at trends in family composition for multiple age groups. As well as knowing whether the availability of the support of their children to older parents has changed over time, as a result of fertility trends, one must also know about the social situations of these parents' children (Do they have young children of their own? Are they employed full-time? Are they lone parents?). Therefore, it is necessary to examine trends across time for several age groups, not just for older cohorts. For example, studies in the United States confirm the idea that living arrangements of older parents are affected by the circumstances of their adult children. The proportion of older widows who are either living alone or with kin is influenced not only by the number of surviving children that they have, but also by the number of children who are unmarried and therefore more available for co-residence.[11] As Tindale, Norris, and Abbott note in Chapter 7, adult children in these circumstances are more likely to co-reside with parents than are children living in stable relationships.

Another interesting insight from multidimensional demography comes from a focus on familial support that is shifted from looking only at vertical ties, especially those of parents and children, to include lateral ties such as relations between siblings. Connidis shows that for elderly persons age 80 and over, three-quarters have at least one living sibling and over half have two or more living siblings. Interestingly, there are more older people with a surviving sibling than with a surviving spouse. This shows the availability of siblings as a potential source of support to most older Canadians, including the very old. It is too often assumed that social support can be provided only by a spouse or a child. Of course, these particular, intimate family members are usually the preferred source of help. However, if they are not available, for reasons either of death or geographic mobility, then available siblings may be called on to fill the breach.

The crucial point here is that in the context of family ties, and probably in other contexts, too, there is often more than one option. If one particular option, such as children, becomes less viable, for example, because of declining fertility rates, then in the short term, at least, siblings could provide a viable alternative for some older people to receive the support they need for daily living. Furthermore, there is no reason to suppose that social supports must be provided only by kin, although there are some important cross-cultural variations in this respect. In a comparative study conducted in Odawara, Japan, and West Haven, Connecticut, in the United States, Akiko Hashimoto found that whereas elderly Japanese rely heavily on close family members, especially their eldest son, North Americans are more likely to believe that when they need help in old age they can rely on community resources.[12] People in West Haven believe they can draw on a wide pool of goodwill among their family members, other relatives, friends, neighbours, and even complete strangers who live in their communities. That belief is realistic and based on a high level of community involvement. It is also based on a tendency to form social bonds primarily with one's generational peers, rather than with one's parents or one's children. These important members of an individual's support network include, especially, one's spouse, but also friends of the same age.

Having this kind of choice means that an individual's degree of enjoyment or lack of informal social support is hard to predict in practice. It follows that average levels of social support in a population cannot be estimated precisely by knowing only the average number of children of people in older age groups. In that sense, demography is clearly not destiny.

Demography Is Not Destiny

Demographic projections, based on assumptions of constant factors, are not hard to produce. Realistic predictions of outcomes, however, are not so easy to produce. In addition to the interplay of multiple factors already considered, this is partly because the future quantity of elderly people tells us nothing about their personal qualities. Tomorrow's older Canadians will not be the same as today's older Canadians because they will have had different life histories. Pierre-Joseph Ulysse and Frédéric Lesemann have expressed this point in the following way: 'On ne vieillit plus aujourd'hui de la même façon qu'hier' (People are not aging today in the way that they did before.)[13]

If future populations of older people will have aged differently than the current population of older people, then they may behave differently too. For example, Joel Prager in Chapter 5, and Marty Thomas and Rosemary Venne in Chapter 6, suggest that in the future the current trend towards earlier retirement among older people might reverse because of changing distributions of social characteristics. In particular, it is expected that the gap in educational attainment between older and younger workers will decrease.[14] Rising levels of education, and a greater share of workers in professional occupations, may encourage some older people to remain in the workforce longer.

In addition, the social history of societal time suggests that the society in which tomorrow's older people live will not be the same as the current society of older persons. There are, therefore, both micro- and macro-processes to be taken into account in contextualizing the effects of demographic change.

Macroprocesses

At the macrolevel, the future outcomes of an older population will inevitably be influenced by major factors of political economy. These include developments in governmental programs as well as changes in technology and in market relationships. Any of these factors could potentially evolve in ways that override purely demographic factors. One need only look back to the recent past to see how limited the influence of demographic trends can be, as noted by Thomas and Venne.

Thomas and Venne observe that reports on current demographic trends indicate that there may be a shortage of young people in the labour force in the future, contributing to a tight labour supply. They also point out that similar predictions of labour force shortages were previously made for the late 1980s and into the 1990s, when the 'baby bust' generation was entering the labour force. Those predictions largely did not materialize in Canada, since other factors such as economic restructuring and the recession of the early 1990s had a bigger impact.

Prager is more concerned about predictions of declining productivity in an aging society, based on beliefs that older workers are a comparative liability and that a relative increase in their numbers could undermine Canada's competitive advantage. Once again, Prager notes that this is not a new argument, although reasons for it have changed somewhat over time. In the past, emphasis was placed more on beliefs of declining physical strength and mental quickness in old age. Today, attention is focused more on assumptions about a lesser willingness of older workers to invest in their human capital and to move occupationally and geographically to new jobs.

Prager points out that, in fact, there have not been many rigorous studies that examine the relationship between aging and productivity. The conventional wisdom is not well supported, he believes, and he states that the few studies that do exist are dated. They were based upon work patterns and organizational structures that have changed significantly in recent years. Finally, Prager claims that the variance in output within older age groups is greater than the variance between age groups. Susan McDaniel makes a similar observation in chapter 2, although in this case she is referring to a variance in income.

McDaniel is concerned that a variety of events are conspiring to draw public attention away from the problems of the needier older Canadians. The increasing average income of older people obscures the fact that not all older Canadians are well-off, especially some older women. She claims that intragenerational polarization is more important than intergenerational polarization. In this connection it is important to note the following conclusion from a report on social trends in Quebec: 'Elderly and retired persons no longer form a relatively homogeneous group. The trend is toward much greater diversity in their standard of living. On the one hand are those who are able to maintain a comfortable life-style even after retirement; these people most often live in couples. On the other hand are the more underprivileged, especially among very elderly women living alone and the elderly living in large urban centres, particularly in Montréal, where the cost of living is the highest.'[15]

McDaniel claims that age is less important than cohort in shaping later life circumstances.[16] That is, she believes that an individual's chronological age is less important than the experiences that individual shares with other people who were also born at the same time and who have therefore aged together. For example, the current cohort of older people is better off on average (though with wide variations) compared with older people in the past, because of the governmental programs and market opportunities that were available to them when they were younger. In contrast, she observes that future generations of older people have not been enjoying the same favourable environment and they could have a greater need for public transfers in their old age.

A good illustration of McDaniel's points about intragenerational differences between women and men and the shifting experiences of different cohorts can be seen in recent changes in pension coverage.[17] Pension coverage rates fell substantially among men age 17 to 24 between 1984 and 1994, and also declined among men age 25 to 34, although the decrease was not as great. Among men age 25 to 34 employed full-time in the private sector, about 46 per cent were covered by a registered pension plan in 1994, down from 51 per cent a decade earlier. In contrast, pension coverage among women increased, especially among women age 35 to 54 who were moving up into better jobs. In 1994, about 47 per cent of women were covered by a registered pension plan, up from 40 per cent a decade earlier.

McDaniel is concerned that a variety of events are converging to lessen the effectiveness of the welfare state as the main instrument for addressing the problems of needier older Canadians. This trend is most evident in the retreat from universality in social policy, introduced first in reforms to income support programs and later in the erosion of public health care in provinces such as Alberta. McDaniel points out that in this context we need to know more not only about the effects of these changes, but also about how they are perceived. Different age groups, and different cohorts, may perceive these changes in different ways, which can make it hard to predict how much public support for making major changes to Canadian public policies there really is.

Microprocesses

Future developments at the microlevel of action are even harder to predict than macrolevel changes, in light of the sweeping shifts in personal lifestyles that have occurred over the past four decades. It is not surprising, then, that in Chapter 7 Joseph Tindale, Joan Norris, and Krista Abbott choose to focus on one of the most stable and enduring properties of family relationships, namely, reciprocity in intergenerational relationships. They respond to negative views on aging by contending that notions of the 'caregiver burden' in an aging society are exaggerated. Supports flow both ways between the generations, over long periods of time, and as a result adult children rarely experience the help they give to elderly parents as a burden.

In this context, it should be pointed out that grandparents are an important social resource in many Canadian families.[18] In particular, grandparents often take a great deal of interest in their grandchildren. They are often the preferred caregivers for children of employed mothers, and under certain circumstances grandparents can play an important role in raising children. However, the role of grandparents has been largely ignored by social researchers and family policy specialists. It deserves more attention at a time when public policy makers increasingly recognize the importance of child development for the future of Canadian society.

A noteworthy feature of Tindale, Norris, and Abbott's chapter is that they discuss the influence of culture on the strength of standards of intergenerational contact and support. In the North American context they see the influence of culture in contrasts between people of different ethnic origins, as well as between people of different generations within a given immigrant group.[19] This leads them to emphasize the relevance of diversity in intergenerational support systems involving older people. One of the biggest population changes affecting Canada today is an enormous increase in ethnic diversity. As Canada is becoming more ethnically diverse, it is highly desirable to find out more about cultural norms of various intergenerational systems.[20]

The desirability of gaining a better understanding of the effects of ethnic differences within Canada is accentuated by the fact that one response to population aging in the future may be to deliberately increase the scale of immigration. If the natural rate of population increase is not sufficient to fill all of the jobs that are created by a growing economy, then we can expect to hear a growing chorus of demands from employers to make immigration easier. Immigration policy, and its anticipated consequences, is therefore likely to contribute to a volatile mix of policy issues that may arise in an aging Canadian society.[21]

Towards a National Longitudinal Survey of Later Life Transitions

Several of the chapters in this collection attest to research deficits on issues of aging and demographic change in Canada. If Canada is entering into an era with more older people, then we need to know more about how they are approaching, entering into, and passing through their later years. The necessity for studying demographic change in relation to individual aging leads to a general recommendation about research directions that is worth considering. Joel Prager concludes his essay on productivity issues by stating that, in order to examine the impact of an aging labour force, 'a longitudinal study tracking workers of different age groups, their career paths, expectations, and ... "the microeconomics of the retirement decision" should be commissioned' (p. 176). It should be added that similar information needs exist for persons who are not currently in the labour force. It is therefore recommended that there should be a new National Longitudinal Survey of Later Life Transitions. In case that project seems overly ambitious, let us recall that there is already a National Longitudinal Survey of Children and Youth (NLSCY) for which there is as yet no parallel in the study of later life.

Data collection in Canada has improved greatly in recent years, especially with the introduction of major longitudinal surveys on children and youth and on labour and income dynamics (SLID). However, neither the NLSCY nor the SLID were designed with the express purpose of observing the progress of older people. A new longitudinal survey of older people, that combines the strong emphasis on health of the NLSCY with the strong emphasis on income and occupation of the SLID is needed.

Health and income adequacy of older people are likely to continue to be major preoccupations of public policy makers in an aging society. Although these concerns are reflected in discrete programs, each with its own distinctive policy-making process, they are interconnected issues and careful attention needs to be paid to the linkages between them. Declining physical and mental health in the latter part of the life course can lead to reduced hours of employment or early exit from work, resulting in lower income.[22] Conversely, higher incomes are generally associated with better health, and this association may delay the need for expensive medical treatments in some people. Clearly, it is desirable to know more about the precise linkages between occupation, income, and health insofar as they affect the retirement decisions of older people as well as the income supports and health services that they need.

There are other reasons for wanting to know more about the connections between occupation, income, and health. In particular, we need to have a better understanding of the relevance of occupational changes in the process of population aging. It is well known that mortality rates differ substantially from occupation to occupation.[23] Although changing fertility rates seem to have a larger affect on population aging in the long run, changing mortality rates are also a contributory factor. It is therefore important to understand how the changing distribution of occupations that occurrs as a result of the shift towards a 'knowledge society' may affect future demographic trends.

Health, income, and occupation issues are only three of many things we need to know more about as the population of Canada ages. The following chapters address the diversity of subjects that exist at the interface between academic and governmental research into aging and demographic change. The next linkage that needs to be considered, therefore, is the linkage between the researchers in universities and those in governmental departments.

Collaboration between university and governmental researchers is presently most common and most successful in analysing data from large-scale surveys that only national governments can afford to carry out. Such work tends to focus on demographic population characteristics, work patterns, and financial transactions such as income earning and income supports. In this volume, the chapters by Susan McDaniel, Ingrid Connidis, Joel Prager, and Marty Thomas and Rosemary Venne reveal the depth of work in this area. To a lesser extent, collaborative research is also conducted on aspects of social structure and social relationships, notably through the General Social Survey.[24] However, the many-sided features of relationships over time, that are discussed by Joseph Tindale, Joan Norris, and Krista Abbott, and especially the cultural meanings stressed by Douglas Thorpe, are not so easily captured in quantitative surveys. Nor are these subjects usually of as much interest to policy makers, who are often looking for specific policy levers through which they might guide the behaviour of large numbers of people into a particular direction. In the long run we will probably still need to pay more attention to these areas.

Cultural constructions of the meaning of old age are likely to be of greater importance in the future, in an 'era of old age' (ère de la géritude), as Michel Loriaux refers to the future society that will consist of more older people.[25] That is also the main implication of the chapter by

Douglas Thorpe, who wants us to re-examine both common and professional assumptions about older people, especially concerning what they can and cannot do.

This is a challenge that others seem likely to take up in the future, especially if the number of younger workers proves to be insufficient for acceptable rates of economic growth. In that event, there may be pressure on older workers to work longer and to invest more in their human capital to maintain and increase their productivity. For that to happen, some older workers would have to change their attitudes towards continued education and retraining. As well, some employers would have to adopt a more positive approach to older employees than they do at present. More carefully targeted government programs are needed to address the particular needs of older workers who have been laid off and who are seeking re-employment, including outreach to employers.[26] It is important to ask: Can attitudes to older workers change in the future, so that greater emphasis is placed on their retention in the labour force rather than on their accelerated replacement?

Attitudes probably can change, if the need for them to do so is strong enough. In that case, we will need to pay more attention to aspects of the workplace that either facilitate or hinder contributions made by older workers. This includes, in some cases, a 'business culture' (*cultures d'enterprise*) that tends to devalue the contributions of older workers, and which therefore makes few or no modifications to working practices in response to individual changes that occur as workers get older.[27] New research programs would seem to be needed to stimulate new thinking in this area and to draw attention to 'best practices.' Relevant academic disciplines, such as industrial gerontology, need more investment if the potential that exists in an aging workforce is to be fully realized.[28]

Culture is malleable, and creative reconstructions of new meanings for old age are conceivable. Arguably, one of the most difficult questions for the future is how new meanings of old age that might emerge from a public discourse on aging will be connected to individuals' private expectations. An important issue here is age of retirement. Older workers developed their ideas about expected retirement age at an earlier stage in their lives, under different social and economic conditions than seem likely to prevail in the future. Their expectations about the timing of retirement, and about the balance between work and leisure in old age, may not be easily altered.

Today, people age 65 and over clearly have more leisure time than younger age groups. Thomas and Venne point out that many older people are also more affluent consumers than used to be the case in the past. With both time and money on their hands, leisure activities, including often extensive travelling, have become fundamental to the lifestyles of older people.[29] Whether, and under what conditions, older Canadians could be persuaded to give up some of their new-found freedoms to take on more work in a future round of economic restructuring is an interesting question.

Conclusion: Policy Implications

The policy implications of the analyses presented in this book lie mainly at the level of conceptualization rather than practical recommendations. The authors want to remind policy makers about the internal diversity of older people as a population category, and about the complex factors that affect their lives and their relationships with others. Above all, a common theme of many of the chapters in this volume is that older people should not be separated out from other age groups and treated as a special target for policy reform. That is because there are multiple interlinkages, in McDaniel's terminology, between different age groups. These interlinkages exist both synchronically (i.e., between contemporaries of different age groups) and diachronically (i.e., over time, especially in the consequences of experiences early in the life course for the quality of life in old age).

The first general policy implication of this book is, therefore, that great care must be taken whenever older people are identified as a distinct population category having unique criteria for policy development. We have learned that 'old age' is a slippery concept. The effective boundaries between 'old age' and 'middle age' are not always clear, and indeed, they may shift over time. For example, most statistical studies continue to use age 65 as a conventional boundary for marking the entry into old age, because at one time that was regarded as the normal age of retirement. However, the recent trend towards earlier retirement is making that yardstick increasingly irrelevant as an indicator of the transition from income earning to reliance on other financial resources. Georges Mathews has argued that for purposes of economic analysis age 60 should now be taken as the boundary of old age.[30] For other purposes, such as the analysis of population health, a different criterion might be preferable, as people are now living longer, and in better health than used to be the case.

The second general implication of this book is that policies need to be more clearly articulated with reference to the full range of current transactions between people in different age groups. Some of these transactions are organized in a formal way by public institutions, such as government taxation and income transfer programs. Other transactions are informal and are organized by local social norms such as obligations of reciprocity, especially between family members.[31] The overall well-being of Canadians is a result of the conjunction of both sets of transactions.

The third general policy implication is that new policies should be developed with the life course considered as a whole. This is already done to some extent, notably, in the area of financial provision for retirement. Policies on pensions, and on Registered Retirement Savings Plans, are clearly based on the idea that certain features of old age must be considered as consequences of events at earlier stages in the life course. In other areas, such as medical policy and policies on social supports, the idea of policy making with the life course as the unit of analysis has been slower to take hold. Nevertheless, some important steps have been taken in this direction, notably the development of a 'children's agenda.' Although this policy initiative is framed in a questionable conceptualization of children as a distinct population category, it is nevertheless based on the assumption that what happens to someone in childhood influences what that person becomes in later life.

It is important to develop forward-looking programs that may influence life-course trajectories in directions that are socially preferred. This idea can easily be generalized beyond its inception in childhood studies. In fact, Canada's principal survey in this area began as the National Longitudinal Survey of Children, but it has since been renamed the National Longitudinal Survey of Children and Youth. That shift can only be regarded as favourable to the line of policy development and policy research recommended here.

Notes

1 See National Advisory Council on Aging, *1999 and Beyond: Challenges of an Aging Canadian Society* (Ottawa: Health Canada, 1999).
2 See Normand Thibault and Hervé Gauthier, 'Perspectives de la population du Québec au XXIᵉ siècle: Changement dans le paysage de la croissance,' *Statistiques: Données sociodémographiques en bref* 3, no. 2 (1999): 1–8.
3 See Hélène David, 'Rapports sociaux et vieillissement de la population

active,' *Sociologie et sociétés* 27, no. 2 (1995): 57–68; Martine D'Amours and Frédéric Lesemann, *La sortie anticipée d'activité des travailleurs et travailleuses de 45 à 64 ans* (Montreal: Institut national de la recherche scientifique, 1999).

4 Organisation for Economic Co-operation and Development, *Maintaining Prosperity in an Ageing Society* (Paris: OECD, 1998).

5 See Bertrand Desjardins, *Population Ageing and the Elderly* (Ottawa: Statistics Canada, 1993); Marc-André Delisle, *Aspects démographiques, économiques et sociologiques du vieillissement* (Sainte-Foy, Que.: Les Éditions La Liberté, 1996); Frank Denton, Christine Feaver, and Byron Spencer, 'The Future Population of Canada: Its Age Distribution and Dependency Relations,' *Canadian Journal on Aging* 17, no. 1 (1998): 83–109; Peter Hicks, 'The Policy Challenge of Ageing Populations,' *OECD Observer*, no. 212 (1998): 7–9.

6 See Marc Termote and Jacques Ledent, *L'avenir démolinguistique du Québec et de ses régions* (Quebec: Le Conseil de la langue française, 1994). An issue that is specifically relevant to population aging concerns the potential effect of increased reliance on immigration on the linguistic, and therefore social marginalization of older francophones living in Montreal.

7 See David Cheal, 'Aging and Demographic Change,' *Canadian Public Policy* 26, suppl. 2 (2000): S109–S122; Ellen M. Gee and Gloria M. Gutman, eds., *The Overselling of Population Aging: Apocalyptic Demography, Intergenerational Challenges, and Social Policy* (Don Mills, Ont.: Oxford University Press, 2000).

8 See Marie Demers, 'Age Differences in the Rates and Costs of Medical Procedures and Hospitalization during the Last Year of Life,' *Canadian Journal on Aging* 17, no. 2 (1998): 186–96.

9 See Eliza Pavalko, 'Beyond Trajectories: Multiple Concepts for Analyzing Long-Term Process,' in Melissa Hardy ed., *Studying Aging and Social Change* (Thousand Oaks, Calif.: Sage, 1997), 129–47.

10 See Kelly Cranswick, 'Canada's Caregivers,' *Canadian Social Trends*, no. 47 (1997): 2–6; and Norah Keating, Janet Fast, Judith Frederick, Kelly Cranswick, and Cathryn Perrier, *Eldercare in Canada: Context, Content and Consequences* (Ottawa: Statistics Canada, 1999).

11 See Diane Macunovich, Richard Easterlin, Christine Schaeffer, and Eileen Crimmins, 'Echoes of the Baby Boom and Bust: Recent and Prospective Changes in Living Alone among Elderly Widows in the United States,' *Demography* 32, no. 1 (1995): 17–28.

12 See Akiko Hashimoto, *The Gift of Generations: Japanese and American Perspectives on Aging and the Social Contract* (New York: Cambridge University Press, 1996).

13 Pierre-Joseph Ulysse and Frédéric Lesemann, 'On ne vieillit plus

aujourd'hui de la même façon qu'hier,' *Lien social et politiques* 38 (Autumn 1997): 31–49.

14 See Hervé Gauthier and Louis Duchesne, *Le vieillissement démographique et les personnes âgées au Québec* (Quebec: Bureau de la statistique du Québec, 1991).

15 See Simon Langlois, Jean-Paul Baillargeon, Gary Caldwell, Guy Fréchet, Madeleine Gauthier, and Jean-Pierre Simard, *Recent Social Trends in Québec 1960–1990* (Montreal and Kingston: McGill-Queen's University Press, 1991), 57–8.

16 For discussions of cohort analyses of population aging, see Leroy Stone, ed., *Cohort Flow and the Consequences of Population Ageing: An International Analysis and Review* (Ottawa: Minister of Industry, 1999).

17 See Statistics Canada, 'Pension Coverage among Young and Prime-Aged Workers,' *Statistics Canada Daily,* 22 Dec. 1999.

18 See James Gladstone, 'Factors Associated With Changes in Visiting between Grandmothers and Grandchildren Following an Adult Child's Marriage Breakdown,' *Canadian Journal on Aging* 6, no. 2 (1987): 117–27; James Gladstone, 'An Analysis of Changes in Grandparent–Grandchild Visitation Following an Adult Child's Remarriage,' *Canadian Journal on Aging* 10, no. 2 (1991): 113–26; Jean-Guy Darveau, *Familles et grands-parents* (Quebec: Conseil de la famille, 1994).

19 There are also considerable differences among Aboriginal peoples, derived from a variety of factors such as residence on or off a reserve. The life expectancy of First Nations members living on reserves is nine years less than other Canadians, but the gap is half that among Status Indians living off reserve. See National Advisory Council on Aging, *1999 and Beyond: Challenges of an Aging Canadian Society* (Ottawa: Health Canada, 1999).

20 See, e.g., Verena Haldemann, 'La solidarité entre générations: Haïtiennes âgées à Montréal,' *Sociologie et sociétés* 27, no. 2 (1995): 43–56.

21 See Roderic Beaujot, 'Immigration Policy and Sociodemographic Change: The Canadian Case,' in Wolfgang Lutz ed., *Future Demographic Trends in Europe and North America* (London: Academic Press, 1991), 359–77.

22 See David Cheal and Karen Kampen, 'Poor and Dependent Seniors in Canada,' *Ageing and Society* 18, no. 2 (1998): 147–66.

23 See Otto Andersen, 'Occupational Impacts on Mortality Declines in the Nordic Countries,' in Wofgang Lutz, ed., *Future Demographic Trends in Europe and North America,* (London: Academic Press, 1991), 41–54.

24 The General Social Survey (GSS) regularly collects cross-sectional data that allow monitoring social trends, as well as providing information on current

and emerging social policy issues. See Statistics Canada, *General Social Survey: An Overview*, cat. no. 89F0115XIE (Ottawa: Statistics Canada, 2001).

25 Michel Loriaux, 'Les conséquences de la révolution démographique et du vieillissement sociétal,' *Sociologie et sociétés*, 27, no. 2 (1995): 9–26.

26 See Susan Underhill, Victor Marshall, and Sylvie Deliencourt, *Options 45+: HRCC Survey* (Toronto: Institute for Human Development, Life Course and Aging, University of Toronto, 1997); Martine D'Amours, Frédéric Lesemann, Stéphane Crespo, and Julie Beausoleil *La sortie anticipée d'activité des travailleurs et travailleuses de 45 à 64 ans* (Montreal: Institut national de la recherche scientifique, 1999).

27 D'Amours and Lesemann, *La sortie anticipée*.

28 See Hélène David, 'Le vieillissement au travail et en emploi,' *Lien social et politiques* 38 (Autumn 1997): 51–61.

29 See Langlois et al., *Recent Social Trends*; and Marc-André Delisle, 'Les changements dans les pratiques de loisir des Québécois âgés 1979–1989,' *Canadian Journal on Aging* 12, no. 3 (1993): 338–59.

30 Georges Mathews, 'L'avenir démographique des régions: analyse critique et implications des plus récentes perspectives démographiques du BSQ,' *Recherches sociographiques* 37, no. 3 (1996): 411–37.

31 Agnès Pitrou, 'Vieillesse et famille: qui soutient l'autre?' *Lien social et politiques* 38 (Autumn 1997): 145–58.

2. Intergenerational Interlinkages: Public, Family, and Work[1]

Susan A. McDaniel

Introduction: Intergenerational Interlinkages

Nothing has affected our lives and policies as much since the Industrial Revolution as the doubling of life expectancy, accelerating particularly since the Second World War, and the concomitantly rapid social (including family and gender), economic, political, and technological changes. Intergenerational interlinkages lie at the heart of profound, but sometimes hidden, changes in our lives, and challenges to our policies. More of us live among more generations than ever before, and more of us experience the challenges of aging and relating to elders in our families and communities. As well, intergenerational interlinkages lie close to the heart of social solidarity and cohesion. What is actually known about intergenerational interlinkages from existing data and research is suprisingly less than might be anticipated given the level of public interest.[2] This conclusion is supported to varying degrees by other chapters in this book, including the introductory chapter by David Cheal.[3]

'Generation' has emerged recently as a social category and as an identity, both of which shape social cohesion and public policy,[4] as well as the ways in which individuals create lives in family and work.[5] Yet most social research either ignores generation or equates it simply with birth cohort.[6] The latter is analytically imprecise since it confounds historical period with life-course stage. Policy tends towards seeing generation in 'still-life' as if the old/young today are the same as the old/young of tomorrow,[7] or radically different, transformed but bearing their birth cohort (Boomers, aging Gen Xers) on their backs like snails – 'still-life' that moves. In this overview and assessment of existing knowledge on intergenerational interlinkages, there are three objectives: (1) bringing together existing data and research on intergenerational interlinkages to assess what is known; (2) developing a conceptual framework for analysing intergenerational interlinkages as an aid to clarifying crucial policy questions and directions; and (3) specifying questions, including new avenues of research and policy, that not only remain to be answered, but remain to be asked, and specifying what data/research are needed to provide appropriate answers to frame policy-relevant responses. The particular focus for each of these objectives is on public, family, and work intergenerational interlinkages, and how they fit together.

Turning first to why this chapter prefers 'intergenerational interlinkages' rather than the more common 'intergenerational relations' or 'intergenerational transfers,' we then consider why the concern about, and policy interest in, intergenerational matters has become a current issue. This is followed by the exploration of five dimensions of intergenerational interlinkages, each of which is used as an analytical lens to consider public, family, and work intergenerational interlinkages in relation to the three stated objectives of the chapter. An assessment is made of what is known, and what needs to be known, for policy. In conclusion, we look at connections and interconnections among the three spheres examined (public, family, and work), and what next steps are needed in research and in policy.

Why 'Intergenerational *Interlinkages*'?

The existing literature on generations commonly uses keywords such as intergenerational relations or intergenerational transfers, with the former typically referring to relations among parents and children, often adult children in families,[8] and the latter referring largely to public sector transfers from one demographic cohort or large age group to another. Neither captures the breadth and complexity of intergenerational, particularly policy-relevant, issues, as is compellingly argued in the chapter by Tindale, Norris, and Abbott.[9] A central theme of this chapter is that it is insufficient to build policy on narrowly conceptualized intergenerational relations or transfers that artificially circumscribe the contexts in which lives are made and in which policies are built. This conclusion is echoed by other chapters in this book as well.[10] It is also made by Martel and Legaré, as well as by McDaniel elsewhere.[11]

The concept *intergenerational interlinkages* (IGILs) captures a dynamic, interactive, and more realistically accurate set of social and economic processes taking place among generations in different contexts.[12] As St Exupéry in *Le Petit Prince* so wisely tells us, the planet is borrowed from our children, not given by our parents. Or, the receipt of a gift from a previous generation compels us to return something back to society.[13] The concept of IGILs does not presume that transfers occur only in one direction or in a single context, or that the linkages are of any particular kind. The concept is an inclusive and dynamic one that enables the posing of useful research and policy questions. Assumptions and presumptions about how generations relate, about equities or inequities a priori, or about levels of transfers as opposed to other kinds of social linkages, are set aside in favour of evidence-based examinations of how generations link and interlink in families, at work, and in the public sphere.

Why the Interest Now in Intergenerational Issues?

Intergenerational issues, along with population aging, seem to be much on the public mind in Canada as the twenty-first century begins. References to population aging as related to social policy, education, and health care are commonplace in the popular press and are increasingly expressed as a concern. More myth and mysticism than reality characterize these concerns, as shall be seen, in light of existing research.

However, not everyone sees population aging as a large policy challenge. Demographic analysts in Europe, with the demographically oldest of the world's populations, are not worried: 'it is not the aging of populations which primarily pose a threat to social protection systems. Rather, the finance principles on which those systems are based are flawed or not entirely shockproof. Aging populations are therefore no insurmountable threat, they merely lay bare the weaknesses of social arrangements in correcting market failures.'[14]

The latter conclusion is revisited later in this chapter. Analysts in Quebec[15] take similar non-alarmist views, based on careful analyses of demographic trends over time. Hervé Gauthier[16] reaches two conclusions important to the context of this chapter: First, he finds that diminishing labour force participation is more of a worry for the future than is population aging per se; and second, he reports that the aged in society are an asset because they pay taxes and contribute in other ways, and are not only a burden to the public purse. This is supported by other research as well.[17]

If the demographically oldest region of the world, as well as many demographic analysts in Quebec, do not see population aging as an insurmountable challenge,[18] why does Canada (at least in some popular thinking and some policy arenas), one of the youngest of the industrialized countries? There may be a very simple answer: Canada may be concerned about population aging not because Canada is demographically old, but, paradoxically, because it is not.[19] Canada's self-image is of a young country, with new frontiers and eager immigrants keen to settle and establish new lives. Fear of aging is a powerful force. It is associated with denial of decline and denial of death, about which North Americans seem to have particular anxieties; anxieties allayed by consumer products that promise us that we can look younger and stem the tide of aging. Witness the immense popularity of Viagra, the drug for impotence that already has become the fastest-selling drug of all time, outselling even Prozac. Fear of population aging may be similar. We may worry that our society is losing youthful potency, becoming less dynamic and less economically aggressive,[20] more feminized, and perhaps poorer. Canadians may worry about living in an aging society that they fear may be less vibrant.[21] Personal fears of aging, decline, and death can be linked to fears of social and/or economic decline. Denial of death – as wishing that aging, personal or demographic would not occur, can be reflected in denial by policy makers of ecological realities, because accepting those realities means accepting the notion of limits and finiteness. The guiding image of the women's movement, that the personal is political, can be easily applied to fears of personal aging, which then become societal and political apprehensions, framing policy as reaction, in part, to those personal concerns.

Curiously, Canada's overall 'dependency' ratios – that is, ratios of older (typically over 65) to those of working ages (typically 18–64), and younger (0–17) to working age groups – have never been lower than they are now, as shown in Table 2.1. The balance of old and young in the overall ratios has shifted, of course, with declining birth rates and increased life expectancies. Concern about dependency of older generations on younger ones, however, has peaked at the very moment in Canada when overall 'dependency' is at a historical low, as Cheal points out (in this book).[22] The hypothesis that loss of Canada's youthful self-image may be as, or more, important than realities revealed by analysis of 'dependency' ratios appears to have some support. Dependency ratios, it must be remembered, are not measures of actual dependency at all. They are demographic proxies only, necessitating

TABLE 2.1
Youth, old age, and total dependency ratios – Canada, from 1971 and projected to 2031
(Low growth scenario)

	Youth dep. ratio (0–17/18–64)	Old age dep. ratio (65+/18–64)	Total dep. ratio (0–17, 65+/18–64)
1971	63.4	14.4	77.8
1981	45.2	15.6	60.8
1991	37.1	21.6	58.7
2001	30.9	24.4	55.2
2011	25.3	27.4	52.7
2021	25.2	37.8	63.0
2031	25.0	51.6	76.6

Note: Low growth scenario is based on an assumption of 1.4 children per woman in 1996.
Source: Susan A. McDaniel, *Canada's Aging Population* (Toronto: Butterworths, 1986), 113. Based on Statistics Canada, *Population Projections for Canada, Provinces and Territories, 1984–2006*. Catalogue no. 91-520-DPT (Ottawa: Statistics Canada, 1995), Table 18, p. 55.

extreme caution in policy application, unless actual dependencies of people or groups are assessed by age.[23]

Shifts in overall dependency ratios, from young to old, have caused fear that 'the aging population will exert increasing pressure on the working-age population to support its needs, tilting the intergenerational equity balance towards older Canadians.'[24] However, the opposite case has been compellingly made: that the growing political power of seniors has resulted in reduced poverty among the older population at the cost of increasing poverty among children and young people.[25] This is borne out in family income trends over the past quarter century, from 1970 to 1995, as shown in Table 2.2. Looking only at the lowest decile (10 per cent) of family income over the 25-year period, lone parents who are differentially younger have increased among the poorest, while older families in the poorest 10 per cent of the population, have sharply declined. The same declines in poverty, however, are not apparent among unattached elders, particularly older women not in families who remain among the poorest, at levels comparable to those of lone mothers.

Canadian policy seems to have seized on demographic aging as a force in policy formulation, a tendency begun in the mid-1980s, but

TABLE 2.2
Family income in Canada, 1970–1995 (lowest decile)[a]

	Percentage	
	1970	1995
Lone parents	25	40
Older families	27	6

[a]Family income groups are divided into ten equal groups. This is the lowest of the ten income groups.
Source: Adapted from Abdul Rashid, 'Family Income: Twenty-Five Years of Stability and Change,' in Perspectives on Labour and Income, cat. no. 75-001-XPE (Ottawa: Statistics Canada, 1999), table 2, p. 13.

accelerated since.[26] The self-image of Canada as safe, caring, and having a social safety net superior to that of the United States, may have led to a need for justification, additional to fiscal responsibility, for sharply cutting social programs. Population aging becomes a policy paradigm.[27] The script of 'voodoo demographics,' a term coined by U.S. economist James Schulz[28] to describe demographic alarmist scenes of pensioners and sick elders taxing delivery systems, writes our future. It is not evidence-based, but emotionally and perhaps politically compelling.

Generational equity, however, has been a much hotter issue (Greedy Geezers/Grannies) in the United States than in Canada.[29] Indeed, explicit attention to potential intergenerational conflicts was raised in Canada only in the mid-1990s,[30] as noted by Eric Moore and Mark Rosenberg.[31] Phillip G. Clark draws a crucial contrast between the U.S. and Canadian approaches to population aging:

The highly individualistic nature of the United States promotes an apocalyptic view of the nature of population aging: conflict between individuals and age groups against a backdrop of shrinking social resources is seen as nearly inevitable ... Empirical data are presented in such a way as to reinforce this construction, and assumptions about the proper primacy of the traditional familial model and the secondary responsibility of the government in addressing social problems are unquestioned ... In Canada, by contrast, aging tends to be a more social issue, with the government response embodying collectivist principles set forth in such policies as universal health insurance. Greater reliance on social solutions defuses the apocalyptic aura of aging ... The definition and solution to the 'aging problem' is perceived within this collectivistic framework, undercutting the social polarization and the 'zero sum' thinking common south of the border.[32]

There is sentiment in these generalized comparisons but also policy possibilities on which Canada might build by relying more on its traditional collectivistic and social cohesion building approaches.

Dimensions of IGILs

This chapter examines IGILs through a conceptual typology with five dimensions, extending a typology previously developed.[33]

A crucial dimension of IGILs is *the aperture through which we view the issues*. The usual script of intergenerational issues in the public realm is written about transfers only, not social relations, interrelations, or exchanges (although at times this is what it is called), and about public transfers only. The justifications are good ones. Good data exist on public transfers; far less complete data exist on private transfers; and only sketchy and limited data exist on social relations and interrelations among generations. What data exist on social relations and private transfers come largely from small or regional surveys, case studies, or simulations, although Statistics Canada has made important contributions with national representative samples, notably the cycles of the General Social Survey (SGS) on families, aging, and caregiving.[34] Policy decisions most often take place in the realm of public transfers, among generations and among groups in society as part of redistribution of socioeconomic resources. For the redistributive function of policy to work effectively, analyses of intergenerational transfers must include the full range of transactions, including social transactions.

A second dimension of IGILs is *the direction of the transfers and the nature of those transfers*. In a three-generation typology of intergenerational transfers[35] (see Table 2.3), prototypical children, parents, and grandchildren exist in both receiving and giving generations. Transfers are extended beyond the monetary or the public (either redistributive

TABLE 2.3
A typology of intergenerational transfers.

Giving generations	Receiving generation		
	Children	Parents	Grandparents
Children			
Private		Social joys, continuity, community links	Social joys, continuity
Public		Public debt[a] Support, transfer. potential	Support, transfer potential
Parents			
Private	Child support, attention, care, socialization	Security, attention, care	Attention, care, support
Public	Education, health, care, transfers, i.e. social assistance, public health, etc.	Transfers, i.e., employment insurance, regional equities, social assistance, etc.	Pensions, health care, public debt[a]
Grandparents Private	Attention, care bequests, gifts, values, heritage	Attention, bequests, gifts, support, values, heritage	Attention, care, pooling resources
Public	Public infrastructure, societal wealth	Public infrastructure, societal wealth	Transfers from well-off to less well-off

[a]Cremer, Kessler, and Pestieau treat public debt as a transfer from children to parents, or from parents to grandparents, because they see the latter benefiting from taxes and the former paying taxes without benefiting as much from public expenditures.
Source: Adapted from Helmuth Cremer, Denis Kessler, and Pierre Pestieau, 'Public and Private Intergenerational Transfers: Evidence and a Simple Model,' in John Ermisch and Naohiro Ogawa, eds., *The Family, the Market and the State in Aging Societies* (Oxford: Clarendon, 1994), 216–31.

or entitlement transfer) to include social transfers such as care, as well as intangibles such as attention and joy. This dimension fits well with the concept of 'global reciprocity' developed by Tindale, Norris, and Abbott in this book.[36]

A third dimension of relevance is *the cohort/period conundrum*, long perplexing to demographers and policy analysts. Change is occurring in at least two dimensions simultaneously. The clock of biographical pacing is ticking, as is the clock of historical change, with interactions and intersections of the two. Individuals born at a specific time see their lives intersect with historical changes. Generation changes as we age but birth cohort remains the same. What a function of birth cohort is, what a function of period effects that cut across birth cohorts is, and what a function of generational change over the life course is, are difficult to ascertain. Generation per se is seen as a neglected feature of social stratification.[37] As with biography and history, there is the clock of social hetero- or homogeneity and an increasing similarity or difference within cohorts and/or generations, which interact with both history and biography, but in cross-hatching and, at times, contradictory ways. Analysing intergenerational interlinkages in a historically changing Canada opens a means by which we can begin to detect and assess changes along several dimensions separately and in unison.

A fourth dimension of interest is *the multiple and layered interlinkages* among the various dimensions of intergenerational relations and transfers. Public intergenerational transfers may be connected with private transfers in ways as yet unknown.[38] Janine Brodie,[39] among others, argues that the boundaries between private and public are being radically adjusted in Canada. Both the domestic and the market itself are being privatized, the latter through deregulation, the former through diminishing state apparatus to promote gender and family equality and the growing demands on families to do more work that was previously public.[40] The implications for IGILs and equity of these changes are massive and yet mostly unassessed, although some are now being explored.[41] This is but one linkage of many among generations. All the possibilities in a quilt of intergenerational interlinkages have yet to be explored, but here we focus specifically on public, family, and work IGILs.

A fifth dimension of intergenerational issues is *the ongoing tension between perceptions and realities of intergenerational issues.* This tension often veils infrastructural aspects of interlinkages that are not as visible, as well as unexpected directions of IGILs. One example is the unfunded liability of Workers' Compensation which de facto transfers costs from present-day governments and employers to future workers.[42] Other examples include the third party public health insurance in Canada that makes transfers from those in the middle to the young and the old. Canadian health care also serves an important redistributive function in transferring resources from the well-off to the less well-off.[43]

These five dimensions worked through, insofar as existing research permits, in the realms of public IGILs, family IGILs, and work IGILs, provide an organizational framework by which to assess what is known, what needs to be known for policy, and what gaps in knowledge exist. These dimensions pull the pieces of the picture of IGILs together, so that the interrelationships among public, family, and work IGILs can be detected.

Public IGILs

In the realm of public IGILs, gaps between perceptions and realities tend to be pronounced. Perceptions about public transfers matter to Canadians. Social transfers in Canada, particularly public health insurance, seem to be intertwined with Canadian and Québécois national identities. In reference to social policy shrinkage in Eastern Europe, Guy Standing[44] argues that 'The threshold of tolerance of impoverishment may have been higher than some expected, but the longer term consequences for social cohesion and distributive justice could be ugly.' In Canada, as the twenty-first century opens, concerns about social cohesion are indeed growing louder[45] with a high-level federal interdepartmental group identifying it as a key policy concern, and the Social Sciences and Humanities Research Council of Canada (SSHRCC) initiating 'Social Cohesion in a Globalizing Era' as a new strategic research focus.

A look at dramatic recent social policy shifts in Canada, described by John Ralston Saul[46] as a 'coup d'état' in slow motion, is revealing. In terms of an agenda to improve economic growth and international trade with the presumption of benefits for future generations, the reality of these dramatic shifts and their intergenerational implications have been substantial and not fully examined by research.[47] Marcel Merette examines the intergenerational effects of policies of debt reduction in Canada[48] and states that 'old generations bear the cost of the debt reduction policy, but cannot completely reap the subsequent benefits [of deficit and debt reduction], while the opposite applies for future generations' Merette[49] concludes. 'The higher the weight of future generations in the social welfare function, the faster the debt should be reduced.'

Much more research is needed on the social implications of policies of debt reduction and social policy restructuring on IGILs and the intergenerational compact, including diverse ways to measure and capture the shifting direction and nature of IGILs.[50]

An international comparative analysis of public spending inequalities on old and young[51] finds that Canada is not tilting its social transfers towards the elderly more than the young. Based on a spending index for pensions and for transfers to younger families, each as percentages of the Gross Domestic Product (GDP) divided by, in the case of pensions, those 65 and over, and in the case of youth, those 0 to 14, a difference between the two is calculated. It is this residual, a measure of spending bias in favour of the elderly, that is compared across industrialized countries. Canada's spending on old versus young falls in the middle, with Germany favouring older generations, and France and Belgium favouring younger. These findings parallel an earlier analysis of intergenerational balances in public spending, based on the Luxembourg data on industrialized countries[52] that also find Canada in the middle.

Welfare state capitalism is premised on promoting equality of opportunities through access to education (mobility), health care (ability to contribute without risks to security of ill health or injury), and income assistance (such as welfare and entitlement benefits including pensions, employment insurance, and workers' compensation). However, social policy in post–Second World War welfare states was never intended to be a major means of redistribution of income, wealth, or power. Promoting equalities of opportunities can only be secured with close to full employment, and where a strongly progressive income tax exists. Without these conditions in place, fiscal pressures make the welfare state difficult to sustain,[53] so we start believing that targeting is the answer and offers greater efficiency.[54] It is as if all of society is urged to move into the marketplace regardless of their family circumstances, no matter their health problems or disabilities, and regardless of the diminishing capacity of the market to reward them with a living wage. The centrality of gender to the quest for efficiency in targeting is vital in considering IGILs for the essential reason that, on average, women outlive men. The challenges of the market in providing living wages became apparent in the 1996 Census where employment income was found to have dropped dramatically in Canada in the 1990s, with the labour market being capable of handling fewer and fewer full-time, full-year workers.[55] This may be an example of population aging laying bare the weaknesses of existing social arrangements in covering market failures, as mentioned earlier, rather than being the causal source of the problems.

To consider what the retreat from universality in social policy means for IGILs, we must first consider what targeting or selectivity does and what implications for intergenerational solidarity they hold.[56] First, the quest for so-called efficiency often means that benefits are more difficult to obtain, hence a lowered 'take-up' rate, resulting in increased economic vulnerability for those who no longer receive benefits and increased social inequalities. Second, targeting benefits may directly increase social inequalities, including generational inequalities, because those who are least able to make moral claims for benefits are those most in need, that is, families in poverty, the disabled, the working poor, those who are no longer searching for work, the sick, disabled, or poor elderly, and the homeless.[57] Pensions, on the other hand, are more likely to be seen as political entitlements and reduced with less enthusiasm, hence the presumption that entitlements are age-based. These tendencies, taken together, can create the perception of intergenerational unfairness, reflecting not generational or demographic changes, but policy shifts.[58] Adding to the perception of unfairness, these shifts play out on gendered terrain, with women, such as lone parents, less often able to make entitlement claims, and more often cast into the categories of 'needy,' where their claims receive greater scrutiny.[59]

Third, the argument that targeting helps those who need help most opens the door to paternalistic and often costly judgments of who *deserves* help (and it quickly becomes 'help' rather than entitlement). Do the elderly, for example, have their pensions reduced less because of presumed need or because of fear of their voting power? By contrast, lone mothers on social assistance have great need, but very limited political clout. Politicians and policy makers may also identify readily with pensioners since their parents, and often they themselves, are pensioners or soon-to-be pensioners. Most politicians hope they will avoid lone motherhood and certainly social assistance. Given the gender structure of legislatures across Canada, lone motherhood is not a risk for the overwhelming majority, and among those few who are lone parents, social assistance is not much of a risk either.

Fourth, with targeting, benefits often depend on means tests of some kind, increasingly involving multiple generations in families under the presumption that families are the first line of support for their members. Eligibility for family benefits might be conditional on children staying in school, for instance, or not committing crimes, necessitating a familial intergenerational contract. Eligibility for seniors benefits for home care may be contingent on the willingness of adult children to take on some caregiving, regardless of the preferences of either the senior or the adult children. Among the childless elderly, or those with distant adult children, or children who simply cannot help out, much as they might wish to, disadvantage may be the result, a kind of penalty for not having access to intergenerational resources.

Recent social policy tendencies in Canada are shifting the grounds of relations and responsibilities among generations in both society and in families in profound ways.[60] Hidden intergenerational dependencies that may not have existed previously are becoming apparent. For example, involuntary early retirement by either lay-off just prior to pension eligibility, or with severance packages, forces some in their fifties into unpensioned retirement,[61] excluding them by fiat from both the public transfer system, and from the possibility of meaningful labour market activity because they are not expected to be looking for work. This is a social phenomenon comparable to what workers may have experienced at the time of industrialization.[62] It is intergenerationally important in that highly capable people in mid-life are without work and without pensions, and thus unable to contribute societally (to taxes or productivity) or to family resources for the benefit of older or younger generations. Similar patterns are occurring with respect to unemployed youth, who rely increasingly on their families in the absence of paid work. In Japan, as well as in some other industrialized countries,[63] a concept of gradual retirement exists whereby retirement timing norms are adjusted by policies on retirement and pensions to the changing place of work in society.

Health care infrastructure as well as the legacy of good health and longevity are vital but overlooked intergenerational public societal transfers. John Helliwell[64] argues that health care in Canada is a 'public good' often omitted from generational accounts and heritage, as are education and the inheritance of natural resources and a good environment. He suggests that 'investments in knowledge may well have much higher rates of return, seen from the perspective of the next generation, than any of the more obvious monuments to the energy and self-importance of the current generation.' P. De Broucker and L. Lavallée[65] echo this with respect to education and literacy. On Canadian health care as intergenerational transfers, Helliwell[66] compellingly argues: 'The important point to make, however, is not the dollar value to attach to ... the Canadian health care system, but that it matters to Canadians in the current generation, and is likely to matter to their successors. It is also likely, that if the Canadian system had not been established when it was, and if the spread of private insurers had followed the style and pattern seen in the United States, that there would by now be no realistic chance of starting again and getting to where we are now. This type of branching, where an opportunity not taken may be lost forever, poses great problems for the generational accounts.'

Karl Mannheim[67] wisely counselled that inherited infrastructure and potentiality for new generations are vital components of intergenerational legacies and transfers. When these diminish, argues Mannheim, the inherited legacy is lessened, regardless of the direct or indirect public transfers.

Publicly funded health care in Canada, in disproportionately benefiting the very old and very young, entails transfers from the middle generation. Social transfers are always demographically lumpy,[68] as are market benefits. None, however, are as demographically lumpy as health benefits are.

An essential contradiction/tension in the intergenerational health legacy is that the very success of healthy aging and longevity, inherited from our parents and grandparents, which both enables us to live longer and live longer in good health, is argued to challenge the public health care system and is targeted by health care reformers as a justification to sharply reduce public funds for health care.[69] Dilemmas abound here. Without good health care and an equitable society, people are less likely to live to old age, and more likely to be in poorer health at all ages. Yet, longevity of greater numbers of Canadians is posed as a problem and challenge to the continuation of the health care system in Canada. Success is thought to be the undoing of what gave rise to it. The rhetoric of population aging as a problem for Canadian health care is not well based on existing research, as shall be shown.

Another key tension/contradiction is seniors at the forefront of the movement for quicker access to health care, even if privatized. Yet today's seniors were the architects of Medicare in Canada and most vividly store the motivations for developing that system. They were the ones losing farms and jobs as a result of the costs of ill health or injury. In Alberta, a laboratory for health care restructuring, this contradiction reaches fruition with seniors pushing for access to private services for hip replacement and cataract surgeries.[70] Younger generations are the inheritors/beneficiaries of the creations, ideas, wisdom, and political struggles of older generations, part of the accumulated social and economic heritage. Younger generations tend to lose most in the future in the erosion of public health care in Canada. This process is well under way, countering the effects of debt reduction for younger generations, mentioned earlier.

Two central dimensions of this tension are detectable in Alberta.[71] First, there is the sense among some seniors who tend to be affected, on average, more than younger people by cuts to public health care, that they have less time to wait in longer queues in the public health care system since they have less time left. A man of 81 expresses this eloquently: 'Six months wait for me is a larger portion of the time I have left than for someone younger.' [72] Second, structural 'reform' takes advantage of the greater apprehensions among seniors about longer queues in the public system (queues created largely by health care cutbacks). The most significant private health care growth sector in Alberta, for instance, has been the development of eye clinics specializing in cataract surgery, services that disproportionately serve the older population.

Seniors in Canada, even in 1989 before serious health care cutbacks had begun, were less enthusiastic than younger Canadians to increase health care funding.[73] Although the greatest proportion of Canadians of all ages indeed thought that government spending on health care was too low, seniors were considerably less likely than Canadians overall to think that health care was underfunded. This may reflect a greater conservatism among seniors, on average, who seem to be more supportive in the 1990s of 'reforming' health care under the impetus of fiscal necessity than are younger Canadians.

Several findings of the mid-1990s' National Forum on Health[74] are relevant to intergenerational interlinkages and legacies: 'At a time when other traditional expressions of Canadian values have been placed under demonstrable stress, health and health care have increased in importance and prominence as a shared common value. In fact the health system has always engendered strong support among Canadians.'

The Canadian health care system as both intergenerational legacy and national(izing) symbol emerges in the exploration of values by the National Forum on Health: 'People are proud of the existing system and see it as a source of collective values and identity,' even as they worry about problems with health care.[75]

Tensions and contradictions are also apparent from the National Forum's research on values. Pride and confidence are expressed in the current health care system, yet concerns about costs and apprehension about change are also part of Canadians' concerns: 'Cynicism about change is high and the public rejects many of the premises for "reform." They believe cost problems are rooted in mismanagement and abuse, and would prefer to see these issues dealt with first. This being said, people still prefer using new public resources to preserve the integrity and core values of the system.'[76]

Images of deception recur among Canadians about the need and basis for health care 'reform' by those who seek change. Also apparent is a sense of giving up on an inherited benefit for which previous generations fought and from which future generations would benefit: 'Many people told us of their concern that health care would not remain the same in the future. A significant number believed that it was not as good as it had been because of government cuts in health care spending, longer waiting lists for doctors or procedures and the number of doctors leaving for the United States ... When participants in our research spoke about the future of the system, almost all did do in bleak terms.'[77]

The disjuncture between present health care restructuring in Canada and the deeply held values that underlie the publicly funded system, created by older generations, is clear. With 1996 data from Alberta, the province that experienced the sharpest health care cuts, seniors tend to agree less than younger people with the federal government's penalizing Alberta for contravention of the Canada Health Act by having private clinics.[78] Lowest agreement that 'budget cuts are reducing the quality of health care in Alberta' are found among seniors, however.[79] Yet 74 per cent of Albertans overall think that the government should make a significant reinvestment in Alberta's health care system.[80] Seniors have concerns about health care cuts, yet seem more flexible on contravention of the principles of Canadian health care. At the same time, seniors are less likely to acknowledge reductions in health care quality, and believe, along with the majority of all ages, that government should spend more on health care. Seniors epitomize perplexing dilemmas for policy with respect to the public intergenerational linkage of health care.

Health care in Canada has several additional IGILs dimensions. Demographic aging, for example, has been found to be much less significant in health care cost increases than the rates at which people in different age groups utilize health care.[81] Hospital usage has increased from 1961 to 1991–2 among the elderly and decreased among the young. Controlling differential hospitalization by age, to test the effects on health care of demographic aging alone, reveals that only a small amount of hospital use increases by those aged 75 and over, differentially women, is the result of demographic change. Morris L. Barer,

Robert G. Evans, and Clyde Hertzman[82] conclude: 'The effects of aging per se on health care costs have been quite limited ... these consistent research findings, like a lighthouse in the fog, have remained obscured by the persistent claims that the aging of the population will bankrupt our health care system.'

The social redistribution components of Canadian health care are not mixed.[83] There is risk reduction, a traditional insurance function where pooled contributions help indemnify against risk for individuals at any given moment. There is also a wealth transfer component whereby public programs, based on social welfare principles, are financed by proportional or progressive taxation. Public health insurance then redistributes resources, as health benefits from higher to lower income households. Research has shown that Canadian health care has been highly effective in this redistribution,[84] but its intergenerational transfer potential has yet not been examined: 'The study has not specifically described the magnitude of intergenerational transfer from tax-paying labour force participants to elderly economic families with a high incidence of health care use (this work is in progress). However, this intergenerational transfer is understood to be substantial'[85]

Mustard and colleagues elaborate: 'While cross-sectional analyses can be used to produce a simulation of life course benefit incidence using an approach similar to the estimation of a total fertility rate in demographic studies, the validity of this methodology is critically dependent on an assumption of constant age-specific health care utilization over time. Empirical evidence suggests this assumption is untenable in the case of health care.'[86]

Trends towards deeper polarization by income in Canada than has been known since the Second World War[87] have resulted in a questioning of the broad-based, middle-class consensus that used to characterize Canada.[88] 'Polarization and the related developments in the labour market represent powerful changes, with important implications for poverty, inequality and the wider sense of social solidarity in Canadian life.'[89] Class, combined with age, may be another dimension through which to analyse the tensions and contradictions posed by seniors and aging to current policy agendas.[90]

Significant policy transformations and proposals for 'rebalancing' federal/provincial relations may have consequences, thus far unknown, for class/age polarization and IGILs. The Canada Health and Social Transfer (CHST), which combines health, post-secondary education, and social welfare federal transfer, is one such policy change.

Block funding to the provinces has been reduced sharply since 1996. With CHST, the provinces work out, each independently, how to allocate funds among the three sectors. Seniors' claims to health care then compete with claims of aspiring university students and with those of low-income lone parents and the disabled. The resulting dilemmas resonate with those already mentioned about productivity and efficiency as the new ideals, determinants of investment in public goods.[91] If there is little 'payoff' for the provinces in terms of enhanced employment or GDP in funding long-term care for the elderly, might it not be tempting to take monies away from the compelling needs of seniors to fund post-secondary education? Public health care in Canada as the symbolic unifying 'railway' of twentieth-century Canada may be coming to an end, as people scramble to have comparable access to health services across provinces and across generations.

A second major policy shift is the proposed Social Union, the implications of which have yet to be fully realized or examined. Early analyses suggest potential implications for IGILs. Any federal initiative, such as the proposed home care initiative, would require majority approval of the provinces, and even then, each province could design a program of its own, to suit its own perceived needs.[92] While increasing flexibility and local management, this could produce very different approaches to home care among provinces, in a service differentially used by older generations, with different costs to users depending on where they live. Similar patchworks are observable in the application of the new parental leave allowances that came into effect as of January 2001. Implications could emerge for the balance of family care versus paid care for frail elders as well as the potential to move an elderly relative across provinces to live with relatives, with potential consequences for intergenerational dependencies.

The widely held perception that older people today are better off and therefore no longer in need of public transfers as in the past raises another perplexing dilemma. An analysis of the experiences of the major cohorts of the twentieth century in Canada finds that age is less important than cohort in shaping later life circumstances.[93] The current generation of elders is, on average (with wide variability, particularly by gender, family status, and region) better off than elders in the past, because of the benefits to which they had access while younger, including the benefits of a public health care system in Canada. Future generations of elders will not have the same opportunities and could have, in fact, greater needs for public transfers.

In analyses based on Statistics Canada LifePaths models of all generations in the Past century, it is found that 'heterogeneity swamps generation.'[94] Generation per se matters less than socioeconomic differences. Intragenerational polarization is more important than intergenerational polarization. With health care changes, particularly the increasing targeting of non-medical benefits by age group, the sweeping of seniors into a single similar circumstance may disadvantage further those who are already disadvantaged seniors, widening the polarization within the older generation.

There are also profoundly underconsidered other public infrastructural IGILs such as education. Post-secondary tuition is an example. Recent trends in university enrollments in Canada[95] have implications for IGILs in two ways: (1) increasing tuition fees and decreasing part-time course availability in universities lead to transfers from older part-time to younger full-time students; (2) that increasing tuition fees have no discernible effect on levels of full-time enrollment may indicate that parents are making bigger direct transfers to their children's education, perhaps compromising their own old age security for the sake of their children's opportunities.

The intergenerational effects of welfare reform in the United States, specifically the repeal of a 60-year-old commitment to welfare entitlement for poor families and its replacement with a block grant for temporary assistance for 'needy families,' has been examined.[96] Grandparents are found to be picking up the slack in contributing to grandchildren's upbringing, and increasingly in raising the children as their own. Meredith Minkler cites a dramatic 44 per cent increase in the numbers of dependent children living with grandparents or other older relatives in the 1990 U.S. Census. 'Skipped generation families' are a rapid growth phenomenon, suggesting that familial intergenerational 'filling in' of the cracks created by abrogation of social policy is direct. Whether such a substitution effect is apparent in Canada needs to be researched. This is an example of an underanalysed substitution of private for public IGILs and has potentially important, but as yet unknown, policy implications.

Lastly in this discussion of public IGILs is the transfer of debt from the public purse to private pockets. This is most vivid in the transfer of the entirety of the Canada Pension Plan funds into a privately run investment portfolio,[97] U.S. Federal Reserve Board Chair Alan Greenspan dismissed the idea that putting government pension funds into the stock market can ensure a good retirement for today's baby boomers, a point directly relevant to IGILs: 'Any increase in returns realized by Social Security must be offset by a reduction in returns earned on private portfolios, which represent, to a large extent, funds also held for retirement. It's a shuffling of claims and doesn't increase the real resources.'[98]

Yet, it is fear that the Canada Pension Plan might dry up before future generations can collect that helped mute objections in Canada to the government's strategy for investing the CPP in the market. That little was said about it publicly prior to the decision to place the funds on the market might also be a factor in muting public concerns. The consequence of this decision which time will show as wise or not, is indeed a reshuffling of claims, as Greenspan argues, but also of risks from public to private. Jill Quadagno[99] reveals the multiple ways in which risks have shifted from the state to markets in the United States, leaving vulnerable individuals and families without protections against unexpected risks, and as importantly, without compensation or even acknowledgment, of subsequent structural absences in opportunities. Concepts of demographic dependency, never analytically very useful for policy as already discussed, evaporate as all generations become subject to the vagaries of the market for their day-to-day livelihood.

In another sense, too, debt and risk have been downloaded in Canada from public responsibility to individual responsibility. As many governments in Canada boast about reducing deficits and debts, largely through unprecedented cutbacks in social programs and public spending, the personal debt load of individual Canadians has never been higher. Although more research is needed,[100] it would seem that public debt is being downloaded to individuals, directly and indirectly, with unknown consequences for IGILs at present and in the future. Downloading of risk is evident in individuals' greater exposure to market risks through pension plans, savings, and other mechanisms. The indirect downloading comes with individuals 'making up' for income lost in reduced earnings, reduced family incomes, and increasing job insecurity by incurring personal debt, often high-interest credit card debt, which paradoxically contributes to the very economic growth said to be spurred by reduction of public debt.

What can be concluded about public IGILs along the five dimensions? With respect to aperture, several summary conclusions can be drawn: (1) More than transfers and accounting matter: (2) We must move beyond the iconography of actuarial justice: (3) Shifting terrains of public policy expose and transform relations of market and of what is public and what is an entitlement for lifelong contributions. (4) The nature of redistribution and philosophies behind it, for example, the move away from universality in favour of targeting and the separation of entitlements from needs, have divided Canadians by generation as well as by class and gender. (5) Investments in infrastructures such as health care, knowledge, technology, literacy, and education are key components of public IGILs with currency not only in intergenerational exchanges/transfers but in timeliness of creation and in symbols of Canadian values. On direction of transfers/exchanges, we find older generations among both receivers and givers in public IGILs. In public debt reduction, cost to older generations is large, while cost to younger generations is smaller, affording them more benefits. Compared with other industrial countries, Canada is not tilting its public transfers towards older generations. Canadian health care direct transfers are from middle to older and younger generations. Canadian health care is also an infrastructural legacy from old to young. Contradictions exist in that older generations are pushing harder for private health care alternatives. This is occurring out of impatience with health care cutbacks but also, perhaps, because they are willing to pay as a kind of intergenerational transfer to those who have less.

With respect to the cohort/period conundrum, we find that generation and cohort are confounded in many existing analyses of public IGILs. Generation is a neglected dimension of social stratification but at the same time overemphasized in policy and by public discourse. Assessments of losses/gains within generations is as vital to policy as analyses of generations. Multilayered interlinkages are found. Simple public accounting of inputs and outputs is insufficient for analysing public IGILs. The public and the private are both shifting: Public IGILs are being privatized in both market and family. Hidden generational dependencies exist such as for unemployed older and younger people who fall largely outside of existing public transfer systems and depend increasingly on their families. Tensions between perceptions and realities are apparent.

Perceptions of transfers as just, equitable, and unifying, forces are often undervalued in policy development. Policy itself creates and maintains the sense of generation as identity and entitlement signifier. Policy creates tensions through recent shifts to divide entitlements from needs.Tensions in perceptions relate to social cohesion as people may feel that they are less connected to each other's interests, and as the concept of investment in the overall public good diminishes, replaced by a strong sense of being 'on one's own.'

What is known about public IGILs in relation to policy? Generation has recently emerged as a social category and identity, shaping both social cohesion (and its diminishment) and public policy options. Most research occurs on public transfers, an impartial capturing of IGILs. Policy, including privatization and targeting, tends to increase social and individual focus on generation. Older generations receive many entitlement benefits but bear costs of debt reduction and health care reform more. Declining employment income and security has accelerated concerns about public transfers and their capacities to serve as risk insurance, which differs by generation.

Several questions arise from this overview of research on public IGILs, the answers to which could be important in illuminating future policy actions. What happens when public transfers are reduced or eliminated? What substitutes at the individual and societal levels? What are the implications for IGILs? Tracing the causal pathways among different types of transfers is needed, not simply an accounting of ratios by inputs/outputs. This necessitates longitudinal data such as that being proposed by the recent Statistics Canada/Social Science and Humanities Research Council of Canada collaborative initiative. Extensions of analyses of IGILs beyond monetary transfers in the public realm is vital and should include social exchanges such as kind of help, shared housing, volunteerism.[101] Is the future like the present or past? To answer, the period, cohort, and generation effects must be analytically separated. What can be known about social IGILs and impacts on generations of recent and current policy shifts? How does gender relate to IGILs? What implications does changing retirement age and patterns have for Canadian public IGILs?

Family IGILs

Family IGILs are, surprisingly, almost entirely left out of the story of intergenerational accounting. There have been two exceptions: A focus on caregiving and care receiving that has dominated the research literature, and to a lesser extent, an interest in bequests, largely among economists, but recently among social historians. The focus in family research has been on intergenerational relations, largely between parents and children, sometimes adult children in relation to supports they provide to elderly relatives and that are provided to them by older relatives.

Given the prevalence of belief in a supportive, multigenerational 'traditional family' in times past, not nearly as much is known about intergenerational relations in families past or present as might be expected.[102] Much of what is known is also incomplete, inaccurate, or mythologized.[103] Findings from a study of pre-Confederation New-foundland are telling since Newfoundland is widely perceived as the most traditional and family-oriented of societies in North America, with presumed extended family support for the dependent, especially the aged.[104] As a society perceived as isolated from collective institu-tions of elder support, such as pensions and long-term care, which characterize more modern societies, pre-Confederation Newfoundland offers an ideal circumstance to test family IGILs in the idealized past. The findings are surprising:

• Little evidence of extended multigenerational families.
• Most aged lived alone or with spouses.
• When multigenerational households existed, they were either living together out of dire need, or supports were being provided *by* the elders.

Intergenerational relations in families involve, as Tamara Hareven[105] argues, 'the reconstruction of a multi-tiered reality' which moves away from grand theories of nature and of universalisms about family and into the social construction of families in interaction with changing societies. There is little 'settled certainty'[106] about intergenerational relations in families in the past. In practice and perspective, temporari-ness (and temporality), dynamism, social contexts, as well as families and individuals as actors/agents in creating their own stories charac-terize intergenerational relations.[107] Precarious moments in the trans-fer and transformation of power from one generation to the next emerge, moments in which it is possible to see clearly that generation is not age, and not cohort. People are products of their times and con-tribute, or not, to children, elders, and society only insofar as they are able, whatever culture or the times dictate. Neither norms nor incen-tives guarantee familial supports.

Relations of young and old examined in family contexts enable exploration of the contradictions in the status of the old in relation to the young. For example, very rapid social change, as Canada has expe-rienced recently, could cause supports to the old to increase as they become more valued links to a receding and longed-for past. So societ-ies that revere the old may not be always as traditional as has been presumed. This contrasts sharply with modernization theory which holds that the old lose status as their knowledge becomes less relevant under conditions of rapid change. This issue is one to which we return when discussing work IGILs and particularly presumed, but not supported in population-based research, perceptions of older workers' abilities. Ideals of respect for elders can modify in the face of practicalities. 'It is one thing to revere what one knows only as an abstraction, to venerate the elderly when one knows none. It is quite another thing to venerate an elderly relation who has become unable to care for himself, requires constant attention and has moved in.'[108]

How much do we know about IGILs in families? Again, not as much as we might wish. This is particularly true for policy illumination.[109] The growth in three-generation families has received attention. However, research in France has shown that among women born in 1930, 26 per cent were in four-generation families at the age of 60,[110] a proportion which is expected to increase. More than 90 per cent of the women who are in four-generation families at age 50 are in such families when they die. Similar research has not been done in Canada as yet. Images come to mind of smiling family photos with four and five generations together, but a crucial policy research question is how those who provide care and support, differentially middle-aged women, can cope with so many generations at one time? And what supports are needed to facilitate family caring, as well as to provide alternatives to those who cannot or may not wish to provide family care to elders. IGILs examined by numbers of generations in our families might yield a very different picture than what we have now of familial IGILs. The limits of caregiving and care-receiving in families and in society are examined in recent research.[111]

Older couples' unions apparently develop in response to perceived implications for intergenerational relations.[112] Couples in France who form unions when they are both over the age of 50, seem to prefer what they call 'semi-cohabitation,' in which both partners keep their own homes but spend three or four nights a week together. This enables couples to maintain their familiar homes and not disrupt relationships with adult children and grandchildren, but at the same time to establish new ways to live in unions. Here, the pattern of IGILs becomes more intricate as we learn about the multilayered interlinkages in families between old and young. Concern about generational interrelationships leads older generations to invent new family forms.

TABLE 2.4
Incidence (%) of low income[a] – Selected family types Canada,
1980–1996

Family Types	1980	1985	1990	1996
Married couple only				
1 earner	11.9	13.8	11.6	12.8
2 earners	1.6	3.2	3.4	4.0
Two parents with children				
1 earner	16.6	21.1	23.2	25.0
2 earners	5.8	7.8	6.5	6.6
3+ earners	3.6	5.0	2.6	3.4
Lone parent				
Male	25.4	26.9	25.5	31.3
Female	57.3	61.1	59.5	60.8
Elderly unattached				
Male	60.7	50.2	41.0	33.3
Female	71.6	64.1	53.8	53.4

[a]Low-income cut-offs used here are based on an analysis of 1992
family expenditure data collected by Statistics who usually spend
54.7 per cent or more of their income on food, shelter, and clothing
are considered below the low-income cut-off differentiated by size
of area and family.
Source: Statistics Canada, *Income Distributions by Size in Canada,
1996*, cat. no. 13-207-XPB, (Ottawa: Statistics Canada, 1997),
Table IV, pp. 34–5.

The biggest overall research finding with respect to family incomes
is that togetherness matters, as is apparent in Table 2.4. Being in a family, regardless of age, helps to insulate against poverty.[113] It is important to keep this firmly in mind when the image is invoked of rich
seniors in recreational vehicles, spending their children's inheritance
on snowbird winters in Arizona, Florida, or Mexico. Although families
aged 65 and over tend to have the lowest incidence of low income
among families, this changes markedly when one looks at non-family
elderly, particularly women. While it is true that there has been a
much-touted decline in low income among seniors in Canada since
1980, this has been most marked among married seniors. Among single (unattached) seniors, the news is much less good and much less

Figure 2.1   Incidence of low income families and unattached, 1980–1996

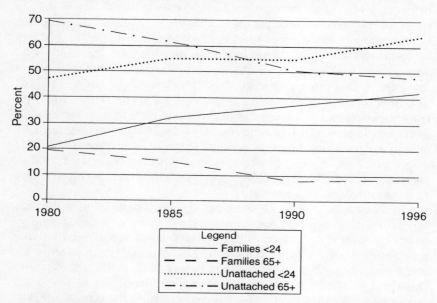

Source: Susan A. McDaniel, 'Intergenerational Transfers, Social Solidarity, and Social Policy: Unanswered Questions and Policy Challenges,' *Canadian Public Policy / Canadian Journal on Aging* (joint issue) (1997): 1–21.

discussed. Almost as large a proportion of unattached women over 65 (53.4 per cent) as female lone parents (60.8 per cent) are low income in 1996.[114] Figure 2.1 reveals the extent of difference in income levels among those in families and the unattached.

Families today cling together out of need, as they did in the past. The cluttering of parental nests with adult youth who never leave home, or who leave and then return, so-called 'boomerang children,' is now commonplace, almost normative for middle-class families.[115] Those with English mother tongue are significantly more likely to refill the parental 'nest' than are those with French or 'other' mother tongues, according to recent research.[116] Given that 'returning home is no longer atypical in Canada and is becoming one of the common pathways in the transition to adulthood,'[117] there may be some questioning of individual autonomy in present-day Canada by both younger and older generations.

Profound differences by socioeconomic status in the risk-insulating opportunity to return home when things go awry in the labour market or in marriage/relationships, may indicate 'that returning home is a behaviour available to more privileged young Canadians.'[118] This may be indicative of a kind of prolonged adolescence for 'rich kids who won't grow up.'[119] Barbara Mitchell and Ellen Gee,[120] however, see it differently: 'Our interpretation is that the possibility of returning home in young adulthood represents a new way for social classes to reproduce themselves. With low rates of economic growth, economic recessions and high youth unemployment, young adults are differentially able to use returning home as a means to buffer/overcome diminished opportunity structures.' The family of origin then becomes a kind of social safety net and/or mobility springboard in the absence of other options and avenues for mobility.

Families have built-in generations; the very definition of families involves multiple generations and reciprocity, as well noted by Tindale, Norris, and Abbott (in this volume). It is not surprising then that the family life courses of both young adults and their parents are undergoing change, given the linked nature of their lives.[121] Relationships and IGILs in families transcend market forces. The extra-market relationships in family rely on a covenant of care, the cement of community, and the basis of nationhood.[122] Were all relationships premised on the contractual relations of the market, suggests John O'Neill, society as we know it would cease to exist. Rethinking familial intergenerational relations as interdependent, non-passive, indeed positively extra-economic, opens analytical possibilities for redefining much of our thinking about elders and youths.[123] It may be the embeddedness of individuals in continuous relational generations, not birth cohorts, which provides the basis by which they get ahead in life.[124] Some evidence of this is beginning to emerge from the Longitudinal Survey of Children and Youth,[125] although much more will emerge with more panels from this survey becoming available.

That immediate family matters so much to the prevention of poverty and the reduction of risk, despite or maybe because of dependency, leads to another possibility. We know that higher (or growing) inequalities in socioeconomic status in societies lead to overall lower life expectancies. Relative deprivation matters to well-being. Is it worse or better, for example, to be poor in a poorer multigenerational family than to be poor in a better-off multigenerational family? What happens when inequalities are increasing, as they now are in Canada? We know very little about how this plays out in families. Transfers among generations in families are little understood.[126] We do know that inequalities before government transfers (such as pensions or social assistance), are much higher than after transfers, and that the gap has widened as late.[127] This is good news on the effectiveness of Canada's social transfer system, until it is remembered that it is being rapidly eroded.

The largest factor in family market income inequalities is increasing within age group differences, as found in a Statistics Canada study.[128] Increasing polarization of income in each age group matters more than population aging or shifting age structure. This is also borne out by the 1996 Census[129] which reveals that the growing numbers of baby boomers in the highest earnings group (those age 45–54) worked to offset an even greater drop in earnings over the 1990–5 period than actually occurred (the drop would have been 6 per cent overall instead of the actual 2.6 per cent decline). Population aging therefore helped to prevent a further earnings drop in the early 1990s. This is not demographic aging as apocalypse, but its opposite. An assessment of the relative contributions of family type by age-to-income inequalities finds that the net largest contributor is lone-parent families with a head under age 45.[130] Family type and gender of family head matter more than age or demographic change, a research finding that underlines the relative unimportance of generation in Canadian inequalities.

A long understood old age security motive for fertility in less developed countries has been found recently to apply in the United States.[131] Substantial poverty among the unmarried elderly in the United States is partially alleviated by financial and functional assistance of co-resident family members in the mid-1980s. Poverty among the non-familial (twice as many unmarried elderly and three times as many disabled, unmarried elderly) would be much greater without co-resident kin and functional assistance by family members. Even in families where the relations are not strictly generational, there is an IGILs component, lessening public dependency. Family members huddle together against risk, pooling resources.

The paradox is that even with a strong long-term, more collective citizen-like outlook than we currently have in Canada, increasing numbers of seniors and soon-to-be seniors are being forced by the need for cash flow, sometimes because of their growing responsibilities for their adult children or grandchildren, into becoming stakeholders (a word which speaks loudly about the diminishment of collective, civic interest in favour of self-interest) in pressuring for short-term gains. As money flows out of savings accounts, trust companies, and credit unions and into mutual funds, stock and bond markets, more in all generations become stockholders (stakeholders), and interested in good short-term returns. Pension funds are the largest existing pool of capital. Unions, teachers, nurses, and professors who may be very concerned about job security, about future savings, and about boomerang children who have trouble locating secure jobs in the reconstructing and globalizing work world are staking a hold in that world themselves in important ways, but without any real control. The upheaval in markets and pension funds as well as the sharp decline in the Canadian dollar have revealed to many how vulnerable seniors are to the market and how their fates are increasingly closely related to what happens on international financial markets. This has had the effect of pitting the day-to-day security of seniors against the public interest, despite what they may feel their personal commitment to be. Inflation aversion is but one example of how this plays out; avoiding inflation at the potential cost of jobs for working age people.

The question then becomes who is looking after the longer-term public interest? Government is not as much as previously, at least in the social realm; business is not; and increasingly we ourselves cannot because of pressures of the immediate demands of work and family, pressures that have escalated recently, or because of declining resources at the family level, or because our self-interest prevents us from public interest. A paradox indeed that at the very historical moment when the public interest needs tending most, there are few tenders, but there may be an unexpected bright light buried here. The uncertainty of capital markets, or public pensions, or Canadian publicly funded health care, may make one fall to the multigenerational family as insurance or a co-pooling of risks. Thus a commonality of interests among multiple generations in families may be found in the shared uncertainty of globalized capital and immigration markets.[132] However, this will not be a viable option for many, of course, whose extended families are simply unable to help. So, we have another complex stitch on the quilt of multiple and layered IGILs.

By adding private intergenerational exchanges to public intergenerational transfers in a study of parent–child supports, Stone, Rosenthal, and Connidis[133] make an important contribution to existing research on IGILs. These researchers enticingly suggest that intergenerational inequities provide a foundation of social cohesion: 'The prolonged building up of obligations over a lifetime of familial exchanges is a reflection of sustained dependency upon others for help. If social cohesion is strongly supported by the bonding and psychic rewards that come from discharging those obligations, then the build-up of obligations for reciprocal giving based on dependency is a foundation of social cohesion. Unless we are careful to view these processes from a life-course perspective, there is a tendency to incorrectly perceive that they create intergenerational inequities that social policy needs to try to reduce.'[134]

This certainly is in happy contrast with the prevalent, and this writer thinks wrong, notion that 'what did you ever do for me?' thinking on generational accounting will undermine social cohesion.

What can be concluded about family IGILs along the five dimensions? Widening the aperture is revealing. Our abiding myths about past families are not supported; they were not more caring and sharing among multiple generations than we are. There is a strong focus on caregiving and care-receiving in the social literature on family IGILs; on bequests and economic 'altruism' in the economics literature, but these two sets of literatures about family intergenerational relations/transfers are never brought together. Family is larger than household; much IGIL activity takes place across households. A three-generation model of IGILs in families may be becoming too narrow with four- or five-generation families now more common. With respect to the direction of transfers/exchanges among generations, myths fall when research is assessed. In the past, intergenerational transfers often were from old to young instead of from young to old as is often presumed. In fact, there are no 'laws' that characterize family IGILs and their directionality. The status of older generations in families can increase or decrease with social change, contrary to the assumption that with modernization, the status of the elderly always declines. IGILs in families that favour adult children with middle-class parents are almost normative in Canada in the 1990s. Looking at the cohort/period dimension reveals surprises. In the past, generational relations were not related to cohort as much as ability to help and need for help. Social circumstances of generations in relation to each other determines more about family IGILs than cultural ideals or birth cohort. Generations change but built-up obligations connect generations as they change, irrespective of cohort membership, thus promoting social cohesion.

Family IGILs are found to be multilayered. In the past, multigenerational living (beyond parents and children) was uncommon because life expectancies were lower and because families clung together more out of need than preference. Actuarial justice is less a factor in family IGILs than is practicality and giving out of concern or attachment. Hidden inventiveness in older and younger generations in creating new family forms is a response to IGILs. Familial IGILs may be the new social safety nets, except that they may work only for those with families that are able to help. Contradictions emerge with respect to family IGILs. Embeddedness in familial IGILs, for example, may enhance life opportunities. Tensions in perceptions and realities with respect to family IGILs are apparent in the literature although it is found that there is nothing new in the gap between perceptions and realities. Perceptions about growth in individuality may not be borne out in the strength, resourcefulness, and social cohesion found in familial IGILs.

What is known about family IGILs in relation to policy? First and fundamentally, togetherness in families matters, but the push towards intensified family IGILs may be necessity and circumstance instead of preference. Families may huddle together in generations to pool resources and insure against risks. Unattached elders in Canada are not well-off despite gains among married elders relative to younger generations. Intergenerational dependency in families may provide a 'leg-up' in mobility to those fortunate enough to come from well-off families. Within age group differences exceed those between age groups; generation per se is not a polarizing force. Population aging has offsetting effects for recent earnings drops in Canada. The IGILs component even in families is not strictly generational but occurs among non-kin and among people in similar demographic generations but at different life-course stages.

What needs to be known about family IGILs for policy illumination? Many analytical questions remain to be both asked and answered. How many generations exist in families in Canada? How frequent are the various sizes of generational families? What kinds of IGILs do different types have? Capturing new forms of IGILs in families and new forms of caring/sharing in response IGILs among different generations is needed. More information should be sought on IGILs of unattached elders. Is it sufficient to consider the 65 and over age group, or 75 and over, or 80 and over as relatively homogeneous in developing policies? Little policy attention has been given to unattached elders, particularly women, whose poverty is almost as high as that of lone mothers. With public transfers diminishing, will IGILs in families increase polarizations and inequalities over time?

Work IGILs

What do we know about work and intergenerational interlinkages? In brief, not as much as we should either to understand the complex mosaic of IGILs or to frame appropriate policy responses. To quote one analyst, we can be certain of four things:

1 There will be fewer workers supporting each retiree.
2 Costs for each retiree will be greater.
3 Average life lived after retirement will be greater, both because life expectancy is increasing but mainly because early retirement will continue.
4 We are not doing well in getting from here into the future.[135]

The last point is important enough to emphasize because of its direct policy pertinence. It may not be the trends in population aging or in IGILs, but what we are not doing about them or not doing in time, that is the challenge.

'The economists and managers are the servants of God. Like the medieval scholastics, their only job is to uncover the divine plan [of the market and market forces].'[136] The concept that the future is inevitable and that policy interventions are unwise and unimportant seems to have taken hold in many circles. Indeed, worship of the market has been rapidly gaining ascendency over any alternative perspective, including the possibility at times of useful policy interventions.

Work insecurity is characteristic of our times. Job insecurity is not new, it is the breadth and depth of the insecurity many Canadians are facing in the 1990s and it is who is at risk that is new, at least in the post–Second World War period. Lay-offs had been almost unknown among those aged 50 and over, but in the 1990s, the rate of lay-offs in this age group increased sharply, reaching deeply into the ranks of older white-collar managers and professionals, including public sector workers. And many of these lay-offs were permanent or of much longer duration than among younger workers. The concept emerges of unpensioned (unpensionable) 'retirement' whereby older workers have no work, few prospects of finding permanent work, and yet have no access to pensions or public support against this risk. Findings from a comparative study of Canada and the United States by Lipset and Meltz (personal communication) show that Canadians are much more worried about losing their jobs than are Americans. Anne Showstack Sassoon[137] points out some of the social implications of this change in work security: 'Changes in the labor market include the increasing insecurity of large sections of the population in Western Europe and North America, the shortening of working lives ... and the phenomena of polarization between work-rich but time-poor households and work-poor households but (usually for women) also time-poor households in countries like Britain and the United States.'

The ways in which work changes have resulted in shifting IGILs is interesting and unexpected. Real earnings among younger workers have declined, particularly among men. Of course, this is among those younger workers who have work, a smaller proportion because of persistently high youth unemployment. Among older workers who keep jobs, there have been increasing earnings. Patterns of inequality within age groups have also shifted, with the widest inequality increase among younger workers, but sharply growing inequalities have occurred among older workers as well, particularly among men.[138]

Inequalities in market income may be important,[139] but in the 1990s a declining portion of our income comes from the market, both for the well-off and the less well-off. The 1996 Census[140] shows that employment income declined as a proportion of total income ($0.75 in 1996 compared with $0.86 in 1970). If more people, particularly older people, depend to a greater extent on transfers and/or investments, either directly through savings or indirectly through investments of their pension or other funds, a paradox emerges. Seniors, in many ways, are leaders in concern about the longer term and public good. Their belief in hard work for the sake of future generations, in self-sacrifice, and in building infrastructure such as public education and public health, are well known. Robert Collins, in a 1997 book called, *You Had to Have Been There: An Intimate Portrayal of the Generation that Survived the Depression, Won the War and Re-Invented Canada*, has this to say about his own older generation (which he calls generation M): 'We are bewildered, saddened, angered by the state of our country, the threat of a breakup, the lawlessness on its streets, the flagrant lack of discipline in its schools, the rash of personal bankruptcies, the staggering level of household debt (reportedly) nearly 88 per cent of personal income. What happened to the postwar Canada we lavished with so many hopes and dreams 50 years ago?'[141]

Shifts away from unionization and from seniority policies in workplaces have meant shifts in IGILs among workers of different generations. Seniority policies tend to make an implicit transfer from middle to older workers, presuming lesser productivity with aging, which may or may not be true. This transfer is lessened with reduced emphasis on seniority as a principle of work. Thus older workers benefit less than they did previously.

The growing tendency to shift risks to individual workers and away from employers and governments is a transfer from older to middle or younger workers, as well as from the better-off to less well-off. This is counter to the previously described shift in some ways. Risks and responsibilities become greater among the middle-aged employed group, while older workers face fewer years of increased individual responsibility and benefit from the pooled and 'insured' risks of earlier periods. This is but one example of how the inadequacies of existing arrangements to cover market failures, mentioned earlier in this chapter, are brought out by, but not caused by, population aging.

Beliefs about older workers and what they can and cannot do can be an impediment to hiring, promotion, and retention. In one part of a larger study on the aging workforce, this issue is examined.[142] The findings are surprising. It is only on learning new technical skills and on flexibility and willingness to change that people rate younger workers as superior. On all other fronts, older workers are thought to be equal to, or better than, younger workers. On dependability, dedication, and willingness to work hard, older workers are thought to be much superior. Interestingly, more women than men do not see age as a factor at all in their perceptions of who has the superior skills. It is not ageist attitudes among the population that are causing current shifts in intergenerational rewards in work. The common perception that technology transfer occurs from younger to older is, surprisingly, not borne out by research,[143] although many of us may have contrary experience. This is an area in which more research is needed and is being done.[144]

Tensions between perceptions and realities on intergenerational issues are apparent in the quest for education by both older and younger people to better their opportunities. The young are disadvantaged by their lack of experience, and older workers by that very experience and its presumed cost to the employer. Intergenerational mobility and its promise as an abiding motivation for hard work, too, is slipping away as youth find it harder to meet their parents' achievements, let alone exceed them.[145]

So, in exploring existing research on IGILs in work, we find once again surprises in the existing research literature. In this summary of work IGILs, we have widened the aperture to include more than inter-generational transfers and more than public IGILs. In doing so, we have seen that what is assumed about work and IGILs may not be so. The contradictions of an economy doing well and the degree to which shifts in burdens are occurring in the Canadian workplace, disadvantaging young and older workers differentially is apparent. In terms of *direction* of transfers or exchanges, we note unexpected transfers from old to young at work, privatization of risks that diminish these transfers from old to young, but lessening seniority that increase risks for older workers and reduce them for younger. In relation to *cohort/period*, it is apparent that those most vulnerable may be those who planned lives to include lifetime work, and had a new reality thrust on them. This disillusioning experience of precipitously unemployed mid-life, white-collar workers has been argued to be analogous to the experience of displaced workers at the time of industrialization.[146] In terms of multi- and interlayered IGILs, it must be noted and will be stressed in summing up the connections, that workers experiencing these profound shifts in IGILs in the realm of work are not confined to that realm in their experiences of the shifts. They literally bring the risks and responsibilities home to their families.[147] And, they bring their disillusionments and increased stresses of too much or too little work to society, possibly putting greater tensions on the taut social fabric.[148] The *tension* that emerges in this examination of work IGILs between perceptions and realities potentially calls into question the values by which we have been taught to make our lives: hard work, sacrifice for a better future, and most importantly, hope for a happy retirement as a reward for a lifetime of work. The pattern of significant findings is as intricate for work as for public and family IGILs.

What policy and policy research issues/questions specifically emerge from the existing literature on work IGILs? The labour market is not separable from other aspects of social life. Indeed, the world of work is central to how we live, how we support ourselves, and who we see ourselves, as being. The labour market, as Nobel laureate Robert Solow [149] informs us, is 'unlike any other markets in that it cannot be understood without taking account of the fact that participants on both sides, have well-developed notions of what is fair and what is not.' To the extent that life opportunities are structured, and/or seen to be structured in the realm of work by age or generation rather than by merit and capacity to contribute, concepts of fairness could change. Judith Maxwell[150] and Jane Jensen[151] express concerns about what these changes mean for the development of human capital into the future and for maintenance of social cohesion.

Keith G. Banting, Charles M. Beach, and Gordon Betcherman[152] argue that human resource development is vital to any society. It could usefully be added that priority to human resource development may be even more vital in an aging society with rapidly shifting IGILs.

Specifically in terms of policy ideas, an explicit acknowledgment of the current intergenerational workplace shifts would be a vital first step in devising programs and policies that focus on retention of fairness and value for work done, regardless of age. The presumption that jobs exist for any and all who may wish them may simply no longer be tenable.[153] Privatization of retraining programs and of risk may be undermining to individuals out of work because of age (either youth or older age), who alone with their families bear the responsibility. Establishment of bridging jobs, and of risk insurance programs for those not yet eligible for pensions but in 'forced' retirement would be possible avenues to explore.

Connections and Interconnections

Eggebeen and Hogan[154] connect cuts to public transfers with implications for private transfers by arguing that private transfers act as safety valves for individuals whose needs are not met by public assistance. This is rare research and there is nothing like it in Canada thus far.

Interconnections among public, work, and family IGILs are many and complex, and mostly unexplored. We know that public transfers most often assist women when family falls apart or fails to help, and men when work ends through either unemployment or retirement. Men's and women's relations to public IGILs then are different and affected differently by redistribution of needs-based and entitlements-based public transfers. As a result, their interlinkages with generations in families and at work are different.

What's Next in Research?

Current social and economic changes are calling into question the nature of the contracts, both public and private among generations. This, argue Walker and Minichiello[155] presents important new research opportunities in sociology of aging: 'The issue of relations between generations is emerging as a significant one in sociology of aging ...

The main reasons for this interest, which echo some of the early socio-logical inquiries of Mannheim (1952/1968), are that the sociodemo-graphic changes are having a profound impact on the duration and intensity of intergenerational relations between kin and, at the macro level, fiscal austerity is raising questions about the social contract between the generations that underpins all welfare states.'

Exciting new possibilities for policy-relevant research in both demography and sociology of aging are opened by examining intergen-erational interlinkages. For example, the relationships of sociodemo-graphic changes in families, living arrangements, migration, immi-gration/emigration, and shifting age structures with durations, inten-sity, and nature of intergenerational relationships in families, work, and the public sphere call out for exploration. The coming generation of seniors in Canada, for example, are unusual in many more important ways than the size of their cohort. They are more ethnically diverse than any previous generation of seniors, will live with more genera-tions alive when they are seniors, and very importantly, will be the first generation of seniors to have experienced the kinds of family and gen-der role changes that have characterized the latter half of the twentieth century. The question then, and it is an important one, is how will these changes impact the experiences of old age and the interlinkages of this cohort of seniors with other generations? Will they have focused on work to the exclusion of family? Will family support be vital in the absence of other alternatives? What will be the variability of IGILs and how will they differ from those of past cohorts of seniors?

Links and interconnections of private and public transfers and rela-tionships need a great deal more research attention. What is the degree of substitutability of private transfers and exchanges for public? What are the hidden implications of such substitutions? The implications for social contracts among generations in all spheres of shifts from public to private intergenerational transfers and potential dependencies are in need of exploration.

The behaviours and living arrangements of seniors may have impli-cations for their adult children or for society. Yet, patterns of living among seniors have not been examined much in research in terms of intergenerational dimensions. Presumptions are made that implica-tions might exist but the nature and directions of the concerns, and whether they are well-based is not known. Are there public transfer implications if adult children discourage aging widowed mothers from beginning new relationships?

How do growing inequalities by age and class work through generations of families? How do they work in society? The relative contribution of generational inequalities to social cohesion is not fully known, although research suggests, as already noted, that the contribution is not large. The important research question to ask is whether and how generation works with or against other dimensions of societal cleavage such as class, gender, ethnicity, and/or immigration recency.

Conclusion: What Are the Policy Implications?

Much remains to be done with respect to policy in the area of intergenerational interlinkages. First, and most fundamentally, a mindset or paradigm shift seems vital. Much of our thinking about population aging and intergenerational relations is based on the illusion that generations do not peacefully coexist. Further, it is supposed, à la Jonathan Swift, that life is built on a perpetuity of youth, health, and vigour which, as Swift wisely counsels, no man [sic] could ever be so foolish to hope, no matter how extravagant his wishes might be. If our system of social and economic policies presume perpetual youth as a natural state, then old age will be treated as a crisis of cost, a non-good in the public sense. The policy question is then posed as how to meet a crisis of aging, with the support of younger generations.

Instead, in Swiftian terms, the preferred question might be how to pass this perpetual life in joy, comfort, and goodwill towards other generations in the wish that they might be as fortunate. Population aging and the opportunities provided by longer, deeper, and more intricate IGILs may be a sign of our collective success in building a caring society where people can live in relatively good health for a very long time. The opportunity of connecting the past to the future by the bridge of multiple generations may be a crucial sign of policy success. How to do it with greater dividends in terms of health, happiness, and well-being is an essential policy question.

The relation of social cohesion to IGILs is another policy question. Is social cohesion increased as a result of exchanges and interlinkages of generations in families, work, and the public sphere? Are generations thrust together in the absence of other options? What are the short- and longer-term implications for Canadian society and for the economy?

The ways in which policy changes and shifts intersect with intergenerational transfers and relationships is not known. Do policy shifts create or exacerbate intergenerational dependencies and interconnections?

What are the solidarity potentialities of IGILs? Has the policy and media attention to generation been displacing of attention to other social problems such as child poverty?

With a broad aperture on IGILs, transfers in opposing directions are apparent as well as transfers of risks, with attendant policy needs developing.

Notes

1 Thanks to SSHRCC and the Policy Research Secretariat (no. 825–98–5008) for funding, to colleagues in the Project on Trends (Demographics – Aging) for their support and collegiality, and to David Cheal in particular, to Kerri Calvert (Sociology Information Centre, University of Alberta), Hervé Gauthier (Institut de la statistique du Québec), and Evelyne Lapierre-Adamcyk (Département de démographie, Université de Montréal), for helpful reference suggestions, to Stephanie Knaak for editing assistance, and to the anonymous reviewers and the SSHRCC review board for their useful suggestions. Responsibility for the chapter's content is the author's own.
2 See Susan A. McDaniel, 'Intergenerational Transfers, Social Solidarity, and Social Policy: Unanswered Questions and Policy Challenges,' *Canadian Public Policy / Canadian Journal on Aging* (joint issue, 1997): 1–21; Susan A. McDaniel, 'Intergenerational Equity: Policy and Data Implications,' in Miles Corak, ed., *Labour Markets, Social Institutions, and the Future of Canada's Children* (Ottawa: Statistics Canada, 1998), 171–4; Alan Walker, *The New Generational Contract* (London: UCL Press, 1996); Michael C. Wolfson, Geoff Rowe, Xiaofen Lin, and Stephen F. Gribble, 'Historical Generational Accounting with Heterogeneous Populations,' in Miles Corak, ed., *Government Finances and Generational Equity* (Ottawa: Statistics Canada, 1998), 107–25.
3 See David Cheal, 'Introduction' in this volume; David Cheal, 'Aging and Demographic Change,' *Canadian Public Policy / Analyse de Politiques*, Special Supplement on the Trends Project 26 (August 2000): S109–S122.
4 See Louis Chauvel, *Le destin des générations: Structure sociale et cohortes en France au XXe siècle* (Paris: Presses Universitaire de France, 1998).
5 See Susan A. McDaniel, 'Women's Changing Relations to the State and Citizenship: Caring and Intergenerational Relations in Globalizing Western Democracies,' *Canadian Review of Sociology and Anthropology* 39, no. 2 (2002): 125–50.
6 See Chauvel, *Le destin des générations*, 15–19.

7 See Cheal, 'Aging and Demographic Change'; Cheal in this book; see also Tindale, Norris, and Abbott, in this book.
8 Tindale, et al., in this book, provide a good summary of the literature.
9 Ibid.
10 See the following, all in this book: Cheal, 'Introduction'; Connidis, 'The Impact of Demographic and Social Trends on Informal Supports for Older Persons'; Prager, 'Aging and Productivity: What Do We Know?'; Tindale et al. 'Catching Up with Diversity in Intergenerational Relationships'; Marty Thomas and Rosemary Venne, 'Work and Leisure: A Question of Balance.'
11 Laurent Martel and Jacques Légaré, 'L'orientation et le contenu des relations réciproques des personnes âgées,' *La revue canadienne du vieillissment / Canadian Journal on Aging* 19, no. 1 (2000): 80–105; Susan A. McDaniel, 'What Did You Ever Do for Me?' Intergenerational Interlinkages in a Reconstructing Canada,' in Ellen M. Gee and Gloria Gutman, eds., *The Overselling of Population Aging: Apocalyptic Demography and Inter-generational Challenges* (Oxford University Press, 2000), 129–52; Susan A. McDaniel, 'Pensions, Privilege and Poverty: Another "Take" on Intergenerational Equity,' in *Le Contrat social à l'épreuve des changement démographiques* (Montreal: INRS Urbanisation, 2001).
12 See Claudine Attais-Donfut, *Les solidarites entre les générations. Vieillesse, famille, état* (Paris: Nathan, 1995) for other examples.
13 See Jacques T. Godbout and Alain Caillé, *L'espirit du don* (Montreal: Boreal, 1972); Jacques T. Godbout and Johanne Charbonneau, *La circulatior du don et la parenté: Une roué qui tourne* (Montreal: INRS-Urbanisation, 1996); Jacques Grand'Maison and Solange Lefebvre, *La Part des Ainés* (Montreal: Éditions Fides, 1994).
14 Hanna van Solinge, Harry van Dalen, Pearl Dykstra, Evert van Imhoff, Hein Moors, and Leo van Wissen, *Population, Labour and Social Protection in the European Union: Dilemmas and Prospects* (The Hague: Netherlands Interdisciplinary Demographic Institute, 1998), 29.
15 See, e.g., Louise Garant and Mario Bolduc, *L'aide par les proches: mythes et réalités. Revue de littérature et reflections sur les personnes âgées en perte d'autonomie, leurs aidants et aidantes naturels et le lien avec les services formels* (Quebec: Ministère de la Santé et des Services Sociaux, 1990); Hervé Gauthier, 'L'interdépendence des générations dans une contexte de vieillissement démographique: application aux déspenses sociales,' in *D'une génération à l'autre: évolution des conditions de vie*, vol. 1 (Quebec: Bureau de la statistique du Québec, 1997), 205–47.
16 See Hervé Gauthier, 'Le contrat sociale au Quebec et au Canada: se

prepare-t-on vraiment a faire face au vieillisement demographique previsible?' in *Le Contrat social à l'épreuve des changement démographiques* (Montreal: INRS-Urbanisation, 2001).

17 See, e.g., Christiane Delbès and Joelle Gaymu. 'Les solidarités au seuil de la vieillesse au début de la retraite en France,' in *Le Contrat social à l'épreuve des changement démographiques* (Montreal: INRS-Urbanisation, 2001); Isabelle Delisle, 'Les solidarités intergenerationnelles,' *L'infirmière canadienne* 95 (1999): 37–40; Agnes Pitrou, *Les solidarités familiales: Vivre sans famille?* (Paris: Privat, 1992); Madeleine Rochon, 'Participation des personnes agées au financement des déspenses de santé at des déspenses sociales et vieillissement démographique,' *Cahiers québécois de démographie* 29 (1999): 299–39.

18 See Organization for Economic Cooperation and Development, *Maintaining Prosperity in an Aging Society* (Paris: OECD, 1998) for a similar conclusion.

19 See McDaniel, 'What Did You Ever Do for Me?' 129–52.

20 This particular myth is demolished by Prager, in this book.

21 See Susan A. McDaniel, *Canada's Aging Population* (Toronto: Butterworths, 1986); Susan A. McDaniel, 'Demographic Aging as Paradigm in Canada's Welfare State,' *Canadian Public Policy* 13, no. 3 (1987): 330–6.

22 See David Cheal, 'Introduction' in this book.

23 See David Foot, 'Public Expenditures, Population Aging and Economic Dependency in Canada, 1921–2021,' *Population Research and Policy Review* 8, no. 1 (1989): 97–117.

24 See Eric Moore and Mark Rosenberg, with Donald McGuiness, *Growing Old in Canada: Demographic and Geographic Perspectives* (Toronto and Ottawa: ITP Nelson and Statistics Canada, 1997).

25 See Martin Dooley, 'Women, Children and Poverty in Canada,' *Canadian Public Policy* 29, no. 4 (1994): 430–43; Jacques Roy, *Les personnes âgées et les solidarités: La fin des mythes* (Montreal: Les Presses de l'Université Laval, 1998).

26 See McDaniel, *Canada's Aging Population*, 'Demographic Aging,' and 'What Did You Ever Do'; Gauthier, 'Le vieillissement démographique' and 'Le contract social au Québec.'

27 See McDaniel 'Demographic Aging.'

28 See James Schulz, *The Economics of Aging* (Belmont, Calif.: Wadsworth, 1988).

29 See F.L Cook, V.W. Marshall, J.G. Marshall, and J. Kaufman, 'The Salience of Intergenerational Equity in the United States and Canada,' in T.R. Marmor, T.M. Smeeding, and V.L. Greene, eds., *Economic Security and Intergenerational Justice: A Look at North America* (Washington, DC: The Urban Institute, 1994). See also Stephane Dufour, Dominic Fortin, and Jacques Hamel, 'Sociologie d'un conflit de générations: les "baby boomers" et les "baby busters",' *International Journal of Canadian Studies*, no. 9 (Winter: 1993): 9–22.

30 See Ellen M. Gee and Susan A. McDaniel, 'Social Policy for an Aging Society,' in Victor Marshall and Barry McPherson, eds., *Aging: Canadian Perspectives* (Peterborough, Ont.: Broadview, 1994), 219–31.

31 See Moore et al., *Growing Old in Canada*, 10.

32 See Phillip G. Clark, 'Public Policy in the United States and Canada: Individualism, Family Obligation, and Collective Responsibility in the Care of the Elderly,' in Jon Hendricks and Carolyn Rosenthal, eds., *The Remainder of Their Days: Domestic Policy and Older Families in the United States and Canada* (New York: Garland, 1993b), 145–67.

33 See McDaniel, 'Intergenerational Transfers.'

34 Connidis, in this book, makes good analytical use of some of these data.

35 McDaniel, 'Intergenerational Transfers.'

36 See Tindale et al., in this book.

37 See Bryan S. Turner, 'Ageing and Intergenerational Conflicts: A Reply to Sarah Irwin,' *British Journal of Sociology* 49, no. 2 (1998): 299–304. See also Claudine Attias-Donfut, *Les solidarités entre les Générations. Vieillesse, famille, état* (Paris: Nathan, 1995); Louis Chauvel, *Le destin des generations*.

38 See McDaniel, 'Intergenerational Transfers'; Leroy Stone, Carolyn Rosenthal, and Ingrid Connidis, *Parent-Child Exchanges of Supports and Intergenerational Equity* (Ottawa: Statistics Canada, 1998).

39 See Janine Brodie, *Politics on the Boundaries: Restructuring and the Canadian Women's Movement* (North York, Ont.: Robarts Centre for Canadian Studies, University of Toronto, 1994).

40 See, for example, Norah Keating, Janet Fast, Judith Frederick, Kelly Cranswick, and Cathryn Perrier, *Eldercare in Canada: Context, Content and Consequences* (Ottawa: Statistics Canada, 1999).

41 See Maureen Baker, 'Reinforcing Obligations and Responsibilities Between Generations: Policy Options from Cross-National Comparisons' (Ottawa: Vanier Institute of the Family, Discussion Paper, 1996); Janine Brodie, 'Meso-Discourses, State Forms and the Gendering of Liberal-Democratic Citizenship,' *Citizenship Studies* 1, no. 2 (1997): 223–42; Keating et al., *Eldercare in Canada*; Susan A. McDaniel, 'Untangling Love and Domination: Challenges of Home Care for the Elderly in a Reconstructing Canada,' *Journal of Canadian Studies* 14 no. 3 (1999): 191–213; McDaniel, 'Women's Changing Relations to the State,' 'What Did You Ever Do for Me?'

42 See Morley Gunderson and Doug Hyatt, 'Intergenerational Considerations of Workers' Compensation Unfunded Liabilities,' in Miles Corak, ed., *Government Finances and Generational Equity* (Ottawa: Statistics Canada, 1998), 21–37.

43 See Cameron A. Mustard, Morris Barer, Robert G. Evans, John Horne, Teresa Mayer, and Shelley Derksen, 'Paying Taxes and Using Health Care

Services: The Distributional Consequences of Tax Financed Universal
Health Insurance in a Canadian Province' (Ottawa: Conference on the State
of Living Standards and the Quality of Life in Canada, 30–1 Oct. 1998).

44 See Guy Standing, 'The Folly of Social Safety Nets: Why Basic Income Is
Needed in Eastern Europe,' *Social Research: An International Quarterly of the
Social Sciences* 64, no. 4 (1997): 1339–79.

45 Paul Bernard, 'La cohésion sociale: critique dialectique d'un quasi concept,'
*Lien social et politique – RIAC: Les mots pour le dire, les mots pour le faire: le nou-
veau vocabulaire du social* 41 (spring 1999); Jane Jenson, *Mapping Social Cohesion: The State of Canadian Research* (Ottawa: Canadian Policy Research
Networks, 1998).

46 See John Ralston Saul, *Reflections of a Siamese Twin: Canada at the End of the
Twentieth Century* (Toronto: Viking, 1997).

47 See John Myles, 'Public Policy in a World of Market Failure,' *Policy Options /
Options Politiques* 17, no. 6 (1996): 14–19; John Myles, 'Restructuring the
Intergenerational Contract: How Nations Are Reforming Old Age Security,'
paper presented at the American Sociological Association, San Francisco,
1998.

48 See Marcel Merette 'The Effects of Debt Reduction on Intergenerational
Equity and Growth,' in Miles Corak, ed., *Government Finances and Generational Equity* (Ottawa: Statistics Canada and Human Resources Development Canada, 1998), 87–106,103.

49 Ibid.

50 See Victor Marshall, 'Generations, Justice and Equity Concerns in Social Policy,' paper presented at the American Sociological Association, San Francisco, 1998; Lars Osberg, 'Meaning and Measurement in Intergenerational
Equity,' in Miles Corak ed., *Government Finances and Generational Equity*
(Ottawa: Statistics Canada, 1998), 131–9; Fred C. Pampel, *Aging, Social Inequality and Public Policy* (Thousand Oaks, Calif.: Pine Forge Press, 1998).

51 See Fred C. Pampel, 'Population Aging, Class Context, and Age Inequality
in Public Spending,' *American Journal of Sociology* 100, no. 1 (1994): 153–95.

52 See John Coder, Lee Rainwater, and Timothy Smeeding, 'Inequality among
Children and the Elderly in Ten Modern Nations: The United States in
International Context,' *American Economic Review* 79, no. 2 (1989): 320–4.

53 See Jane Lewis, 'Gender and Welfare Regimes: Further Thoughts,' *Social
Politics* 4 (Summer 1997): 160–77.

54 See Brodie, *Politics on the Boundaries*; Charles Handy, *The Hungry Spirit:
Beyond Capitalism, a Quest for Purpose in the Modern World* (New York: Random House, 1997).

55 See Bruce Little, 'Economic Well-Being Plunged in '90s, Study Finds,' *Globe

and Mail, 28 Oct. 1998, B7; Statistics Canada, '1996 Census: Sources of Income, Earnings and Total Income, and Family Income' *Daily*, 12 May 1998, B7.

56 See Baker, *Reinforcing Obligations*.

57 See Philip G. Clark, 'Moral Discourse and Public Policy in Aging: Framing Problems, Seeking Solutions and Public Ethics, *Canadian Journal on Aging* 12, no. 4 (1993): 485–508.

58 See Gauthier, 'Le contrat social.'

59 See Brodie 'Meso-Discourses'; Lewis, 'Gender and Welfare Regimes'; McDaniel, 'Untangling Love and Domination,' 'Women's Changing Relations to the State and Citizenship,' and 'Pensions, Privilege an Poverty.'

60 See V.L. Bengtson, and W.A. Achenbaum, eds., *The Changing Contract across Generations* (New York: A. de Gruyter, 1993); Clark, 'Public Policy in the United States and Canada'; Robert Glossop, 'Bailing Out on Future Generations,' *Transition*, March 1996, 12–13.

61 See Susan A. McDaniel, 'Family/Work Challenges among Older Working Canadians,' in Marion Lynn, ed., *Voices: Essays on Canadian Families* (Toronto: Nelson, 1996), 195–214.

62 See Karl Ulrich Mayer, 'The Paradox of Global Social Change and National Path Dependencies: Life Course Patterns in Advanced Societies,' in Alison E. Woodward and Martin Kohli, eds., *Inclusions/Exclusions* (London: Routledge, 1998); Karl Ulrich Mayer, 'State and Life Course in Advanced Societies,' (paper presented at American Sociological Association meetings, San Francisco, 1998); Susan A. McDaniel, 'Shifting Self and Social Knowledge Identities among Older Unemployed Workers in Canada in the 1990s: Parallels with the Industrial Revolution,' (paper presented at the World Congress of Sociology, Montreal, July 1998).

63 See Chikako Usui, 'Gradual Retirement in Japan,' in K. Warner Schale and Carmi Schooler, eds., *Impact of Work on Older Adults* (New York: Springer, 1998).

64 See John Helliwell, 'What Will We Be Leaving You?' 141–7.

65 See P. De Broucker and L. Lavallee, 'Intergenerational Aspects of Education and Literacy Skills Acquisition,' in Miles Corak, ed., *Labour Markets, Social Institutions, and the Future of Canada's Children* (Ottawa: Statistics Canada, 1998).

66 Helliwell 'What Will We Be Leaving You?' 145.

67 See Karl Mannheim, 'The Problem of Generations,' in Paul Kecskemeti, ed., *Essays in the Sociology of Knowledge* (London: Routledge and Kegan Paul, 1968 (first published in 1952)), 276–322.

68 See McDaniel, 'Intergenerational Transfers.'

69 See McDaniel, 'Health Care Policy in an Aging Canada: The Alberta
    "Experiment,"' *Journal of Aging Studies* 11, no. 3 (1997): 211–28; Susan A.
    McDaniel and Neena Chappell, 'Health Care in Regression: Implications
    for Canadian Seniors,' *Canadian Public Policy* 25, no. 1 (1999): 101–10.
70 See McDaniel, 'Health Care Policy in an Aging Canada.'
71 Ibid.
72 Ibid., 223.
73 See McDaniel and Chappell, 'Health Care in Regression.'
74 See National Forum on Health, *Canada's Health Action: Building on the Leg-*
    acy. Vol. 1, *The Final Report of the National Forum on Health,* and Vol. 2, *Syn-*
    thesis Reports and Issue Papers (Ottawa: Canada Communications Group,
    1997), 5.
75 Ibid., 7.
76 Ibid.
77 Ibid., 9.
78 See McDaniel, 'Health Care Policy in an Aging Canada'; McDaniel and
    Chappell, 'Health Care in Regression.'
79 See Pamela Smith, *The 1996 Alberta Survey: Public Attitudes about Changes in*
    the Health Care System (Edmonton: Population Research Laboratory, Uni-
    versity of Alberta, 1996), 2.
80 Ibid., 2, 6.
81 See Morris L. Barer, Robert G. Evans, and Clyde Hertzman, 'Avalanche or
    Glacier? Health Care and the Demographic Rhetoric,' *Canadian Journal on*
    Aging 14, no. 2 (1995): 193–224.
82 Ibid., 195.
83 See Mustard et al., 'Paying Taxes,' 1.
84 Ibid.
85 Ibid., 15.
86 Ibid.
87 See Keith G. Banting, Charlie M. Beach, and Gordon Betcherman, 'Polariza-
    tion and Social Policy Reform: Evidence and Issues,' in Keith G. Banting
    and Charles M. Beach, ed., *Labour Market Polarization and Social Policy*
    Reform (Kingston: School of Policy Studies, Queen's University, 1995), 1–20;
    Charles M. Beach and G.A. Slotsve, *Are We Becoming Two Societies?* (Tor-
    onto: C.D. Howe Institute, 1996); Judith Maxwell, 'Social Dimensions of
    Economic Growth,' *Eric John Hanson Memorial Lecture Series,* vol. 8 (Univer-
    sity of Alberta, 25 Jan. 1996).
88 See Jane Jenson, *Mapping Social Cohesion: The State of Canadian Research*
    (Ottawa: Canadian Policy Research Networks, 1998). Clarence Lochhead
    and Vivian Shalla, 'Delivering the Goods: Income Distribution and the

Precarious Middle Class,' *Canadian Council on Social Development* 20, no. 1 (1996): 15–19.

89 Banting et al., 'Polarization and Social Policy Reform,' 16.

90 See, e.g., Chantal Hicks, 'The Age Distribution of the Tax / Transfer System in Canada,' in Miles Corak, ed., *Government Finances and Generational Equity* (Ottawa: Statistics Canada, 1998), 39–56.

91 See Brodie 'Meso-Discources.'

92 See McDaniel, 'Untangling Love and Domination'; McDaniel and Chappell, 'Health Care in Regression.'

93 McDaniel, 'Health Care Policy in an Aging Canada.'

94 Michael C. Wolfson, Geoff Rowe, Xiaofen Lin, and Stephen F. Gribble, 'Historical Generational Accounting with Heterogeneous Populations,' in Miles Corak, ed., *Government Finances and Generational Equity* (Ottawa: Statistics Canada, 1998) 107–25.

95 See Statistics Canada, 'University Enrolment,' *Daily* 14 Oct. 1998.

96 See Meredith Minkler, 'Grandparents, Grandchildren and the Dilemmas of Public Policy,' paper presented at the American Sociological Association, San Francisco, 1998.

97 See Andrew Willis, 'Barclays, TD Chosen to Invest CPP Fund,' *Globe and Mail*, 18 Feb. 1999, B1.

98 'Greenspan Renounces Investing Pension Fund in Stock Market,' *Edmonton Journal*, 4 March 1999, F6.

99 See Jill Quadagno, *The Transformation of Old Age Security: Class and Politics in the American Welfare State* (Chicago: University of Chicago Press, 1988); Jill Quadagno, *Aging and the Life Course* (Boston: McGraw-Hill, 1999).

100 See Mark MacKinnon, 'What We Owe: Debt Pressure Mounts for Canadians,' *Globe and Mail*, 9 Nov. 1998, B1, B3.

101 Statistics Canada is studying volunteering at present.

102 This is supported by other chapters in this book, particularly Tindale et al., and Connidis.

103 See Attias-Donfut, *Les solidarités entre les générations*; David Cheal, 'Repenser les transferts intergénérationnels: Axes de recherche sur les relations temporelles dans les pays anglo-saxons,' in Claudine Attias-Donfut ed., *Les solidarités entre les générations. Vieillesse, famille, état* (Paris: Nathan, 1995), 259–68; Tamara K. Hareven, 'The History of the Family and the Complexity of Social Change,' *American Historical Review* 96, no. 1 (1991): 95–124; Tamara K. Hareven, 'Aging, Generational Relations: A Historical and Life Course Perspective,' *American Review of Sociology* 20 (1994): 437–61; McDaniel, 'Intergenerational Transfers'; Susan A. McDaniel, 'Public Policy, Demographic Aging and Families,' *Policy Options / Options Poli-*

tiques (Sept. 1998): 33–5; Edgar-Andre Montigny, *Foisted Upon the Government? State Responsibilities, Family Obligations and the Care of the Dependent Aged in Late Nineteenth Century Ontario* (Montreal and Kingston: McGill-Queen's University Press, 1997); Pitrou, *Les solidarities familiales*; Roy, *Les personnes âgées et les solidarités*.

104 See Susan A. McDaniel and Robert Lewis, 'Did They or Didn't They? Intergenerational Supports in Canada's Past and a Case Study of Brigus, Newfoundland, 1920–1949,' in Lori Chambers and Edgar-André Montigny, eds., *Family Matters: Papers in Post-Confederation Canadian Family History* (Toronto: Canadian Scholars Press, 1997), 475–97.

105 Hareven 'The History of the Family,' 95.

106 See Joy Parr, 'Gender History and Historical Practice,' in Joy Parr and Mark Rosenfeld, eds., *Gender and History in Canada* (Toronto: Copp Clark, 1996), 8–27.

107 See David Levine, 'Recombinant Family Formation Strategies,' *Journal of Historical Sociology* 2, no. 2 (1989): 89–115.

108 See Matthew C. Price, *Justice between Generations: The Growing Power of the Elderly in America* (Westport, Conn.: Praeger, 1997), 1.

109 See Merril Silverstein and Vern L. Bengtson. 'Intergenerational Solidarity and the Structure of Adult Child-Parent Relationships in American Families,' *American Journal of Sociology* 103, no. 2 (1997): 429–60.

110 See Sophie Pennec, 'Four-Generation Families in France,' *Population* 9 (1997): 75–101.

111 See Janet E. Fast, Norah C. Keating, Leslie Oakes, and Deanna L. Williamson, 'Conceptualizing and Operationalizing the Costs of Informal Elder Care,' NHRDP project No. 6609-1963-55 (Ottawa: National Health Research and Development Program, Health Canada, 1997); Magaret Platt Jenson Who Cares? Gender and Welkfare Regimes,' *Social Politics* (Summer), 1997; Keating et al., 'Eldercare in Canada;' McDaniel, 'Untangling Love and Domination,' 191–213.

112 See Vincent Caradec, 'Forms of Conjugal Life among the "Young Elderly,"' *Population* 9 (1997): 47–94.

113 See Garnett Picot and John Myles, 'Social Transfers, Changing Family Structures, and Low Income Among Children' (no. 82, Research Paper Series, Analytical Studies Branch, Statistics Canada, 1995); Garnett Picot, John Myles, and Wendy Pyper, 'Markets, Families and Social Transfers: Trends in Low Income among the Young and Old, 1973–95' in Miles Corak ed., *Labour Markets, Social Institutions, and the Future of Canada's Children* (Ottawa: Statistics Canada, 1998).

114 See Statistics Canada, *Income Distributions by Size in Canada, 1996* (Ottawa: Statistics Canada, 1997), 34–5.

115 See Dominique Meunier, Paul Bernard, and Johanne Boisjoly, 'Eternal Youth? Changes in the Living Arrangements of Young People,' in Miles Corak, ed., *Labour Markets, Social Institutions, and the Future of Canada's Children* (Ottawa: Statistics Canada, 1998); Barbara A. Mitchell, 'Too Close for Comfort? Parental Assessments of "Boomerang Kid" Living Arrangements,' *Canadian Journal of Sociology* 23, no. 1 (1998): 21–46; Barbara A. Mitchell and Ellen M. Gee, 'Young Adults Returning Home: Implications for Social Policy,' in Burt Gallaway and Joseph Hudson ed., *Youth in Transition to Adulthood: Research and Policy Implications* (Toronto: Thompson, 1996), 61–71; Barbara A. Mitchell, Andrew V. Wister, and Ellen M. Gee, 'Culture and Coresidence: An Exploration of Variation in Home Returning among Canadian Young Adults,' *Canadian Review of Sociology and Anthropology* 37, no. (2000); Statistics Canada, 'Young Adults Living at Home,' *Daily*, 11 March, 1999.
116 Mitchell, Wister, and Gee, 'Culture and Coresidence.'
117 Mitchell and Gee, 'Young Adults Returning Home,' 20.
118 Ibid.
119 Meunier et al. 'Eternal Youth.'
120 Mitchell and Gee 'Young Adults Returning Home,' 21.
121 See Glen Elder, 'Time, Human Agency and Social Change: Perspectives on the Life Course,' *Social Psychology Quarterly* 57 (1994): 4–15.
122 See John O'Neill, The *Missing Child in Liberal Theory: Towards a Covenant Theory of Family, Community, Welfare and the Civic State* (Toronto: University of Toronto Press, 1994).
123 See David Cheal, 'Intergenerational Transfers and Life Course Management: Towards a Socio-Economic Perspective,' in Alan Bryman, Bill Bytheway, Patricia Allatt, and Teresa Bell, eds., *Rethinking the Life Cycle* (London: Macmillan, 1987), 141–247.
124 See L.A. Serbin and D.M. Stack, 'Longitudinal Studies of Intergenerational Continuity and the Transfer of Psychosocial Skills: An Introduction,' *Developmental Psychology* 34, no. 6, (1998), 1159–61; Silverstein and Bengston, 'Intergenerational Solidarity.'
125 See Statistics Canada, 'How Children Get Ahead in Life,' *Daily*, 5 Nov. 1998.
126 Susan A. McDaniel, 'Caring and Sharing: Demographic Change and Shifting State Policies,' in Monica Verea, ed., *Women in North America at the End of the Millennium* (Mexico City: Universidad Nacional Automona de Mexico, 1997); McDaniel, 'Health Care Policy in an Aging Canada'; McDaniel, 'Public Policy, Demographic Aging and Families'; Stone et al., *Parent-Child Exchanges.*
127 Statistics Canada, '1996 Census: Sources of Income, Earnings and Total Income, and Family Income,' *Daily*, 12 May, 1998.

128 See Myles Zyblock, 'Why is Family Market Income Inequality Increasing in Canada? Examining the Effects of Aging, Family Formation, Globalization and Technology,' (Working Paper no. W-96-11E, Applied Research Branch, Human Resources Development Canada, 1996).
129 Statistics Canada, '1996 Census: Sources of Income.'
130 See Myles Zyblock and Iain Tyrell, 'Decomposing Family Income Inequality in Canada, 1981–93,' *Canadian Business Economics* 6, no. 1 (1997): 108–19.
131 M.S. Rendall and R.A. Bahcieva, 'An Old-Age Security Motive for Fertility in the United States,' *Population and Development Review* 24, no. 2 (1998): 293–9.
132 See, e.g., Verena Haldemann, 'La solidarite entre generations: Haitiennes agees a Montreal,' *Sociologie et societiés* 27, no. 2 (1995): 43–56.
133 Stone et al. 'Parent–Child Exchanges.'
134 Ibid., 18.
135 Matthew Price, *Justice between Generations: The Growing Power of the Elderly in America* (Westport, Conn.: Praeger, 1997), 142.
136 John Ralston Saul, *The Unconscious Civilization* (Concord, Ont.: House of Anansi, 1995), 121.
137 Anne Showstack Sassoon, 'Comment on Jane Lewis: Gender and Welfare Regimes, Further Thoughts,' *Social Politics* (Summer 1997): 178–81, 179–80.
138 Ross Finnie, 'Stasis and Change: Trends in Individuals' Earnings and Inequality in Canada, 1982-1992,' *Canadian Business Economics* 6, no. 1 (1997): 84–107; Garnett Picot, 'What Is Happening to Earnings Inequality in Canada in the 1990s?' *Canadian Business Economics* 6, no. 1 (1997): 65–83.
139 Picot, 'What Is Happening.'
140 Statistics Canada, '1996 Census: Sources of Income, Earnings and Total Income, and Family Income,' *Daily,* 12 May 1998.
141 Robert Collins, *You Had to Be There: An Intimate Portrait of the Generation that Survived the Depression, Won the War, and Re-Invented Canada* (Toronto: McClelland and Stewart, 1997), 3.
142 See Susan A. McDaniel, 'The Family Lives of the Middle-Aged and Elderly,' in Maureen Baker, ed., *Families: Changing Trends in Canada*, 3rd ed. (Toronto: McGraw-Hill Ryerson, 1995), 194–210; McDaniel 'Family Work/Challenges.'
143 P. Beaudry and D. Green, 'Cohort Patterns in Canadian Earnings and the Skill Biased Technical Change Hypothesis,' Discussion Paper no. 97-03, Department of Economics, University of British Columbia, 1996.
144 See, e.g., Peter Dickinson, and George Sciadas, 'Canadians Connected,' *Canadian Economic Observer*, Feb. 1999, 3.1–3.22.
145 See Picot and Myles, 'Social Transfers'; Picot et al., Markets, Families and Social Transfers.' Zyblock, 'Why Is Family Income Inequality Increasing?'

146 McDaniel, 'Shifting Self and Social Knowledge Identities among Older Unemployed Workers in Canada in the 1990s: Parallels with the Industrial Revolution,' paper presented at the World Congress of Sociology, Montreal, July 1998.

147 See Susan A. McDaniel, 'Toward Healthy Families,' in National Forum on Health, ed., *Determinants of Health: Settings and Issues*, vol. 3 (Sainte-Foy, Que.: Editions Multimodes, 1998d), 3–42.

148 McDaniel, 'Caring and Sharing: Demographic Change and Shifting State Policies'; McDaniel, 'Intergenerational Transfers.'

149 Robert Solow, *The Labor Market as Social Institution* (Cambridge, Mass.: Basil Blackwell, 1990), 3.

150 Maxwell 'Social Dimensions.'

151 Jane Jenson *Mapping Social Cohesion: The State of Canadian Research* (Ottawa: Canadian Policy Research Networks, 1998).

152 Banting et al., 'Polarization and Social Policy Reform.'

153 Herve Gauthier, 'Le contrat social au Quebec.'

154 See D.J. Eggebeen and D.P. Hogan, 'Giving between Generations in American Families,' *Human Nature* 1 (1990): 211–32.

155 See Alan Walker and Victor Minichiello, 'Emerging Issues in Sociological Thinking: Research and Teaching,' in Victor Minichiello, Neena Chappell, Hal Kerdig, and Alan Walker. *Sociology of Aging: International Perspectives* (Melbourne: International Sociology Association Research Committee on Aging Walker and Minichiello, 1996), 1–7, 3.

3. Aging, Language, and Culture

Douglas Thorpe

Introduction: What 'Aging' Means

The demographic evidence has become compellingly familiar: graphs showing a steadily falling birth rate (below the replacement level at the turn of the millennium); graphs showing a steadily increasing life expectancy; and graphs showing the inevitable consequence – the aged cohort forming an ever-growing share of the Canadian population. When I retire twenty years from now I will join a group that will comprise over a fifth of all Canadians, a proportion more than double that which existed when my father retired.

Familiar, and indisputable, as the evidence is, its significance is more elusive. How do we account for the complex of fears that the aging of Canadian society seems to have occasioned? While the numbers are neutral and verifiable, the fears are deeply rooted in our history, our culture, and our language. Before we can interpret the numbers and project into the future, we must acknowledge how all of our interpretation and analysis is both enabled and constrained by the language at our disposal. Before we can assess what should concern us about an aging population, we have to unpack the notion of an aging population. The most fundamental task of all is to understand *aging* itself. There is a profound ageism at work in our thinking, speaking, and writing. To be blind to it may compromise any attempt to understand the social phenomenon we hope to study. To understand the implications of our understanding of aging is far harder than viewing a bar graph; it involves reading the riddle of the human life course.

The ancient Greek story of Oedipus contains, in the form of a famous riddle, one version of the human life course. The Sphinx had for years terrorized Thebes by killing all who could not guess the answer to this riddle: What walks on four legs in the morning, two legs at noon, and three in the evening? Oedipus's ability to give the correct answer – man – is what wins him fame and power and ironically dooms him to disaster. In Sophocles' tragic version of the story, *Oedipus the King*, Oedipus's success with the riddle is several times referred to, although the riddle itself is never actually told. This silence is crucial, as it reinforces the play's emphasis on Oedipus's tragic lack of self-knowledge. Although he has solved the riddle he has failed to realize its significance. His success has blinded him to his tie to common humanity: like all people he will grow, reach maturity, and then decline. The riddle is in fact an omen of his tragic fate. Once Oedipus has fully realized the riddle's meaning he will be assimilated to its final image. Maimed by a physical blindness that actualizes his moral blindness, he will walk about with the aid of a cane, the third leg of the riddle.

The Oedipus story has been much retold, its moral adapted to the imaginative needs of various cultures at succeeding points in history. Does the riddle itself help account for the supposed universal significance of the story? Does its simple three-stage version of the life course, easily adapted by Sophocles to the requirements of a patriarchal tragic plot (young man of promise rises to pinnacle of power only to fall to depth of misery) speak to all cultures' understanding of what makes us human and mortal? Is the final stage of life inevitably tied to notions of loss, weakness, suffering, and powerlessness?

That the term 'aging' itself, both as adjective and as noun, is the term by which this final stage is described is seen everywhere. Consider this recent definition from the legal scholar Richard Posner: 'Aging is most usefully viewed as a process one element of which is an inexorable decline across a broad range of bodily (including both physical and mental) capabilities: call this "bodily decline."'[1] Standard sources in the medical field adopt a similar emphasis. The chapter on normal aging in the recent volume *Ageing: The Facts*, co-authored by three members of the faculty of Medicine at the University of Cambridge begins: 'Whatever steps we take to stay "young," the combined effects of biological ageing and adverse environmental influences eventually declare themselves. As mature adults, around the age of 25, we experience maximum physical, sexual, and reproductive capacity. Decline thereafter is so gradual that for many years we are unaware of "getting older" unless greatly stretched.'[2]

Once the 'maximum' is attained, apparently, the vocabulary of aging is brought to bear on the subject. Popular usage follows a similar pattern. From the vantage point of youthful competence and accomplishment, the future portends a loss of function, however subtle at first, and this can be thought of only as aging. Consider the hockey player Ken Dryden's self-appraisal in the spring of 1979:

> For nearly the first time in my career, for the first time in my life, I am feeling old. I am thirty-one years old. I feel good. I feel the same: no more aches than I ever had, no special diet to follow, no regimen of extra sleep. My body seems to move the way it always has, the game moves no faster for me than it did. But suddenly age is the dominant fact of my life. After years of ignoring time, I have become sensitive to it. I look around the dressing room at younger players who look like me and older ones who have aged. I slap my stomach and say, 'Ahh, I feel great,' and I never did that before.[3]

The teammates who have 'aged,' of course, continue to play the sport at a highly elite level, but the level of accomplishment is irrelevant here. Regardless of age and regardless of ability, one's first consciousness of decline, or even of the possibility of decline, is invoked with the vocabulary of aging.

Competing Models of the Life Course

One phase of the aging process seems to stand in for the entire phenomenon, as if it is only in decline that we are aging. Viewed holistically, the life course comprises birth, growth, maturation, fertility, and reproduction as well, but for some reason our culture keeps the vocabulary that describes such things separate from the process of aging. Such separation makes it hard to track the continuities in our development, to see, for example, that the changes one experiences at retirement age are potentially a form of growth, comparable to, and continuous with the growth in childhood. Furthermore, aspects of growth and decline, discovery and loss, easily cohabit the same developmental stage. A three-year-old has both the body shape and the flexibility that allows her to touch the top of her head to the floor while standing with her legs straight. This ability does not survive into the school years, but rarely is such a change chronicled as a loss, or labelled as an instance of 'aging.' Nicholas Coni, William Webster, and Stephen Davison's chapter entitled 'The Biology of Ageing,' for example, pays no heed to childhood development, the earliest descriptors being applied to the period of early adulthood, and then only to provide a point of reference by which to measure loss of function later in life. The potential for a discourse of aging to emerge that would describe, with openness and balance, all the conditions of our lives, seems hampered by this long-standing identification of aging with decline. In this sense, we continue to inhabit the tragic fate of Oedipus, thinking that time cannot touch us, living a riddle whose meaning we persistently misconstrue.

The symbolic resonance of the Oedipus story is seen in another important theme. The Sphinx's riddle did not impose any chronological markers on the stages of the life course. The transformation in Oedipus's situation brings him to his final state almost instantly, with the dramatic brevity so admired by Aristotle. The fact that Oedipus is likely in his forties when this happens is somehow irrelevant to the story. The final stage of Oedipus's life is more a moral condition, an exemplum, than any kind of chronological category. Sophocles himself lived to about 80, yet there is little reason to suspect that his audience saw him as a more or less representative figure than his maimed, forty-something hero.

Many traditional representations of the life course distinguished discrete stages of development without necessarily assigning a number to them. The Seven Ages of Man speech in Shakespeare's *As You Like It* is a case in point. In examples, where a period of years is assigned to a stage, as in some of the illustrations Thomas R. Cole reproduces in his *The Journey of Life*, they appear to be devised for the sake of visual symmetry, or, as in the case of the German nursery rhyme he cites, for a kind of metrical regularity and simplicity.[4]

Our modern tendency to map and quantify the life course into developmental stages is a result of the rise of the social sciences as influential disciplines of knowledge. However, the dedication of these sciences to quantitative method has never been uncomplicated. It is worth remembering that the discipline of statistics, developed first in Germany in the eighteenth century, originally involved a verbal description of the conditions of the state (hence the term). It was only in the nineteenth century that numerical methods came to appropriate both the term and the discipline of statistics. Government legislation, in time, came to be based on statistical research, despite many contemporary critiques that argued that statistics was not itself a science, but merely a way of representing and arranging facts that scientists could then use. The social authority of statistics has been well described by Mary Poovey:

> By 1834, when the New Poor Law was passed, the machinery of government in Britain was indissolubly tied to the collection of numerical information, even though the methodological problems that persisted in the statistical variant of the modern fact had yet to be solved.
>
> To all intents and purposes these problems were never solved, because from a philosophical perspective they were unsolvable. As long as one assigned the phenomena of nature – or, even more questionably, an abstraction like the economy or society – the kind of prominence that Bacon had done, it was impossible to devise any method *except a mathematical one* for moving from observed particulars to general principles. As we will see, the kind of mathematical models that Quételet adumbrated in concepts like the 'average man' and the law of large numbers heralded the advent of an entirely new epistemological paradigm, which now dominates the late twentieth-century world.[5]

In 1833 the Cambridge geologist Adam Sedgwick defined science as 'the consideration of all objects, whether of pure or mixed nature, capable of being reduced to measurement and calculation.'[6] Such measurement and calculation, extended into the social world of humanity, gave fresh sanction to the social sciences.[7] 'Demography' enters the English language in 1880 (modelled on the French 'démographie,' which had been used in *Journal des Économistes* in 1878) to denote the statistical mapping of a community's vital information (such as births and deaths).

These new explanatory models proved their utility to policy makers, lobbyists, and social reformers generally. It has proven all too easy, however, to overestimate the force and coherence of such models. Even as their heuristic value is demonstrated, we are conscious of the possibility of other competing constructions of the life course. Our modern category of adolescence, a term popularized by G. Stanley Hall in 1904, need not correspond to either of Shakespeare's neighbouring stages: The 'whining schoolboy' or 'the lover / Sighing like furnace.'[8] Clearly, the same biological process is at work in both cases, yet the conceptual mapping of that process points irrevocably to cultural difference, the shifting imaginative needs of different disciplines in different generations. As the McGill anthropologist Margaret Lock has shown in her comparative study of North American and Japanese women experiencing menopause, a common physiological change is experienced in a profoundly different way, a difference that is itself hard to fathom as the two languages name and describe the change so differently.[9] Thus, while the English term 'menopause' names the physiological change explicitly, the Japanese term *kōnenki* has a looser, and more figurative application. Though it is the term by which the English term 'menopause' is usually translated, to a Japanese speaker the term can mean something as non-physiological as 'the turn in life' or 'the critical age.' This initial linguistic difficulty is compounded by cultural differences in the way patients report physical symptoms and how those symptoms get associated and accounted for.

How We Measure Aging: Problems with Demography

One might be tempted to think that statistical evidence could ground our understanding of the life course in more neutral ways, less susceptible to cultural inflections. In recent years, however, several scholars have pointed out how problematic such grounding is. W. Penn Handwerker's critique of demographic transition theory, for example, forcefully argues that the traditional analytic techniques of demography are useless unless they work with the culture's way of knowing itself: 'The effect of a given variable must be contingent on the manner in which it is conceptualized, and the manner in which it is conceptualized must be relative to specific culture regions and culture-historical periods.'[10]

It is not just that culture determines the community being studied, but that the scholar's own culture shapes the way research issues are formulated: 'Without cultural specification, the concept of a cost-benefit analysis will be vacuous, for choices can be irrational only for the person observing the choices made by others, and then only when the observer starts from the wrong premise.'[11] A different kind of critique is Dorothy Stein's essay entitled *People Who Count: Population and Politics, Women and Children*. Stein alerts us to the politically charged atmosphere in which decisions informed by demography are made. Instead of tying the falling birth rate and the aging population into a pattern of industrial economic development, we should conceptualize the issue rather in environmental terms, asking how much life the planet can sustain. Women will control their fertility accordingly. It is not, then, that 'would-be parents lower the number of children they calculate they need in order to supply the family labour and old age support they want.'[12] Given that the logic of economic development has not worked as planned in the developing world, and that our economic development is seriously stressing the environment, shifts in fertility behaviour must happen for reasons that make sense in the context of social and cultural goals. Stein concludes: 'Both aid and domestic policies should be focused on "social development": the promotion of health, education and well-being in the most disadvantaged women and children of both rich and poor countries, rather than on conventional economic growth, which is unsustainable and threatens the well-being of the whole planet.'[13]

Roger Schofield and David Coleman note the inherent limitation of demography itself, but see an expansive utility for it as a tool used by other disciplines:

> The subject matter of demography may be imagined as being arranged within a sphere with a hard mathematical core and a softer socio-economic and biological rind. The core represents the specific technical property of demography; the mathematical theory which deals with statics and dynamics of population ... But this hard core of demography does not touch the surface of the real world directly, except through measurement and reconstruction. It does so only when the population is made specific. An outer structure of theory and fact is then necessary to explain and predict that population's response, through the specific agencies of independent biological, social and economic causes and consequences of population trends ... This permits the risks of the fundamental human events of birth and death to be analysed interchangeably by ideas which may draw on sociology, geography, history, biology and other subjects.[14]

In short, the numerical methods of demography have given it a currency and a portability, yet its value is only known when the numbers are assimilated into a critical discourse with its own structures of evidence and argument. The numbers are not self-evident; we need words to tell us what the numbers mean. Seen this way, the discipline of demography is not far removed from humanities disciplines such as history and literature. They all inhabit the domain of language and an ageist discourse thus infects them all.

Before any significance can be assigned to the position of the old we need at the very least to question whom do we consider old. Statistical analysis most commonly uses the age of 65 as the threshold. It is the growth of the 65-and-up cohort that highlights most accounts of the aging of our society. But why 65? The number became enshrined initially in the 1880s in Germany when state-sponsored pensions first became an item of public policy. The figure was chosen for reasons of expediency; the small numbers of people affected made the program both less controversial and more affordable for the government. To an extraordinary extent, however, the marker of 65 has become naturalized to the extent that people come to assume that those over the limit have experienced biological changes that impair their ability to work productively. At 65, people are shifted into a cohort that consumes pensions and health care but no longer produces.[15] This bureaucratization of the stages of life is clearly arbitrary and indefensible. If the notion of 'stages of life' is to have any meaning, it must designate qualities of experience, functioning, and consciousness. These qualities are best seen in how the individuals themselves judge that experience. Inevitably there will be much variation – just as not all children develop and mature in the same way, so not all old people age in the same way. Any statistical measure will be at best a crude simplication of that collective experience and, at worst, a gross distortion. Nevertheless, if we must have statistical measures, let us qualify them appropriately. As the 1993 report of the National Advisory Council on Aging states: 'Indeed, the distinction between middle age and old age is now blurred; most seniors belong to what gerontologists Bernice and Dail Neugarten have termed the "young-old"; that is, retirees who are healthy, active, independent, and well-integrated in their families and communities.'[16] Similarly, medical textbooks discussing the diseases of the elderly increasingly now see 75 as a more appropriate demarcation than 65. To put it another way, many people who are today classed as old (being over 65) enjoy a health and activity level that many middle-aged working people in the nineteenth century would have struggled to match. Why, then, are we still using a nineteenth-century measure to try to understand and sort out an experience that has changed?

The difficulty of properly construing the numbers needs always to be borne in mind, as there have been some strangely persistent misunderstandings of statistical evidence. The often-cited increase in life expectancy over the past century frequently translates into the assumption that people now live much longer than people did before. While it is relatively easy to debunk such an assumption one should not underestimate its pervasiveness. It surfaces, for example, in the 1990 Canadian Supreme Court decision on mandatory retirement, when Justice La Forest notes that when Bismarck established 65 as the retirement age in nineteenth-century Germany, '65 would certainly have been considered "old," the life expectancy in Germany then being 45.'[17] In fact, the figure 45 represents not a preponderence of people dying in their forties (and hence making a 65-year old appear anomalous), but a figure reached when the normal full lifespan is offset by the appalling number of people dying in early childhood.

Lifespan (i.e., the extent of a life lived to its full extent, unmarred by accident or 'premature' death) has increased slightly, but not to the extent that would force a revolution in our thinking. Recall the words from Psalm 90: 'Seventy years is the span of our life, eighty if our strength holds; at their best they are but toil and sorrow, for they pass quickly and we vanish.' The estimate of years is not far off the modern figures; the very old have always been with us. What has changed in the past century is their emergence into a numerical prominence, an emergence that followed inevitably from a falling birth rate and the increased numbers of people surviving childhood. The old cease to be just symbolic figures, whether of honoured wisdom or of ridiculed decrepitude, and become a class, a social body about which scientists and policy makers alike must increasingly be concerned.

How We Understand Aging: Qualitative Language

As the demographic balance between the generations shifts, our language struggles to adapt its inherited vocabulary to emerging conditions. Peter Laslett, in his book entitled *A Fresh Map of Life*, pleads for a new understanding of a four-stage view of the life course, while acknowledging the conceptual pitfalls encountered in doing so. There has always been a friction between attempts to objectify the conditions of life, and people's subjective experience of those conditions. Language, at once potentially both reductive and creative, contains within it layers of embedded conceptual history, a density that may resist the hoped-for precision of science. In literary uses of language, writers have always been sensitive to the ironies and instabilities inherent in the terms we use to measure stages of life. Consider the following example from Elizabeth Barrett Browning's *Aurora Leigh* (1856), a long narrative poem chronicling a woman's growth into personal and poetic fulfilment. In this passage the 20-year-old Aurora tells her male cousin:

A woman's always younger than a man
At equal years, because she is disallowed
Maturing by the outdoor sun and air,

And kept in long clothes past the age to walk.
Ah well, I know you men judge otherwise!
You think a woman ripens as a peach,
In the cheeks, chiefly.[18] (II.329–35)

With wonderful economy, this passage touches on a number of issues of interest to us. First, it registers how any notion of the life course must be inflected by gender. Maturation is a qualitative process, measured not chronologically but by certain passages. A Victorian woman still unmarried at age 30 was already an 'old maid,' a status Aurora does much to ironize. Through her poetry, Aurora pursues a notion of fulfilment not tied to the marriage plot that her male cousin naturally assumes for her. Intriguingly, for a young woman to marry means both to fulfil herself in the eyes of the culture, but also to abandon a rival model of fulfilment, one based on vocation and accomplishment. The vocational model has, of course, traditionally been a male one, and Aurora's comments to her cousin in part manifest the emerging feminist agenda of the late nineteenth century. The passage is gendered also in the sense that it draws attention to the way in which men and women interpret the life course differently. Men assume that a woman's life course is dominated by fertility – the biological imperative – that she ripens as a peach to be plucked when it is in season. Both the vocational plot and the marriage plot are well-established traditional literary paradigms of development. In *Aurora Leigh* we see them adapted, brought to the friction point, in an attempt to express changing social conditions.

The example gives us another way of understanding the concept 'life expectancy.' This phrase has a certain statistical utility, but we can also use the phrase to denote the sense in which we expect a certain pattern to our lives.[19] One's 'life expectancy' at age 20 in 1856 is thus both a certain quantity of years that one can reasonably predict and a likely pattern of development within that period. Clearly, a man's expectation differed from a woman's in both senses. In the twenty-first century we are still grappling with the adjustments occasioned by women following the vocational narratives formerly reserved for men, but following them differently, given, say, the continued possibility of childbirth as an event both fulfilling and complicating at the same time.

The emergence of a numerically prominent elderly class, then, is no simple phenomenon. It can indeed be measured statistically. However, then it must be evaluated and described by a language and using a conceptual system that is struggling to adapt itself to the pace of demographic change. 'Life expectancy' is both a measure of that change and a particular interpretive strategy that we apply to it.

The suspicion remains that in interpreting and re-interpreting modern conditions we may not be very far removed from the position of Oedipus thousands of years ago. His blindness to his own position was at once exemplary and anomalous. While the chain of events and coincidences that doomed Oedipus was preposterously unlikely and unforseeable, his fate nevertheless captured, for the ancient Greeks, the essential inability to determine or even predict the course of our lives. Oedipus continues to hold the stage, commentators say, because we find our own forms of blindness exemplified in him.

What forms of blindness are characteristic of the era of science, an era increasingly confident in its ability to explore and explain both the human body and human nature? As Thomas R. Cole and Peter Laslett and many others have argued, the study of aging poses a special challenge to that confidence, in that it forces us, yet again in a new way, to confront our own mortality. To study the decline that aging is deemed to embody is to acknowledge our limits. To understand that decline, perhaps even to predict and monitor it with greater precision, is not to evade it. Modern medicine, with its ever-expanding powers of prevention and cure, has at best ameliorated, and at worst merely protracted the inevitable process of the final stages of life. In the end, we are thrown back on whatever emotional, cultural, and intellectual resources we have to understand what those stages mean to us. Our understanding is thus formed of both the quantitative measures that we are increasingly instructed by and the qualitative searching that has its roots in a time long before demography.

Historical Emergence of Our Understanding

A society that put its trust in scientific measurement and explanation, that celebrates the health and vigour of youth, and that pursues utility and productivity, is a society especially challenged by aging and mortality.

There is nothing new about the fear of death. Over a century ago William Hazlitt said: 'No young man ever thinks he shall die.' A culture that defines itself as a culture of youth will have a blind spot on the topic of death. I would argue that our fears are shaped by the same material and social changes from which emerged the class of the elderly.

Foremost among these social changes is the Industrial Revolution. Among many other developments, the Industrial Revolution redefined the workplace, demanding a mobile, trainable workforce. The need for such a workforce tended to uproot traditional communities and reform occupational cultures. Although it is now seen as too simplistic to say that the Industrial Revolution destroyed the extended family,[20] family structures were subjected to new forms of strain. Intergenerational conflict, long present in disputes over property, inheritance, and marriage settlements, came increasingly to involve various possibilities of government intervention and/or institutionalized support.[21] As governments in turn adopted a corresponding level of involvement, such conflict became increasingly a matter of public policy deliberation. Edgar-André Montigny notes in writing about late nineteenth-century Canada:

> Though the majority of the nineteenth-century aged population did not require government support, the assumption that all aged people were poor, ill, and dependent fuelled panic over population aging and the burden such trends represented to public resources. The belief that each additional old person in the population would require care and support from the state convinced officials in the 1890s that it was necessary to reduce the level of state responsibility for the aged in order to prevent a fiscal catastrophe in the future. Arguing that it could not provide care for every old person in the province, the government reduced or eliminated public support for the minority of the aged population that was truly dependent.[22]

Such an analysis shows the power that normative images have to control public perception. Government support waxed and waned with the shifting fiscal health of the government's resources. The identification of the aged as potential red ink on the government's books proved persistent. By 1927, when Canada joined most Western countries in institutionalizing old age pensions, the decision was driven by several versions of political and economic expediency.[23]

To the culture of industrial capitalism, the aged were doubly perceived as a burden. Not only did they require care when past the point of supporting themselves, but while still on the job they were perceived as obstructing an enterprise dedicated to speed, competition, and technological innovation. Karl Marx concludes in *Capital*: 'The supreme ideal of capitalist production is – at the same time as it increases net produce in a relative way – to reduce as much as possible the number of those who live on wages, and to increase as much as possible the number of those who live on net produce.'[24] Although this conclusion is not age-specific, that the productive value of labour supersedes any notion of the social utility of labour and labour's service to social need means that the older worker is exposed to the criterion of bald economic productivity. Even though the confirming evidence was decidedly mixed, capitalists came to identify productivity with a young workforce. William Graebner notes: 'The choice was usually between a stable, conservative work force that blended youth with age and produced moderate short-term efficiency, and a more mobile, potentially more radical and militant work force made up largely of highly productive younger workers. The choice was between two kinds of efficiency – productive and social – and between two attitudes toward future profits, one more immediate than the other.'[25] The pressure to create retirement plans for workers sprang from this same desire for productivity, an agenda that governments, in time, came to endorse as retirement was deemed to be an effective counter to the social problem of high unemployment.[26]

The ideology of competition received considerable intellectual sanction through the spread of Charles Darwin's theory of survival of the fittest. The very survival of the species, and even of subgroups within the species, according to Darwin depends on its adaptability in the hunt for scarce resources, and its resulting success in breeding. Furthermore, the fate of any individual is of negligible importance; the reproductive success of the group is paramount. Darwinism not only offered an influential explanation of the origins of human beings, its offshoot Social Darwinism gave sanction to particular social practices. The 'science' of eugenics is a notorious example, but there was scarcely any branch of learning untouched by Darwin's views. The eminent Victorian psychiatrist Henry Maudsley, for example, writing in *Physiology and Pathology of Mind* (1867), describes the mentally ill as follows: 'They are the waste thrown up by the silent but strong current of progress; they are the weak crushed out by the strong in the mortal struggle for development; they are examples of decaying reason thrown off by vigorous mental growth, the energy of which they testify.'[27]

Belief in survival of the fittest justifies ostracizing or incarcerting the unfit. This sketch of the mentally ill is uncomfortably close to our culture's stereotype of the unproductive older worker. The belief in progress is buttressed by a pervasive fear of the risk of degeneration. Notions such as 'decaying reason' are thus invested with deep moral significance, complicating the culture's ability to recognize and respond appropriately to the phenomenology of mental decline in the elderly.

The Authority of Medicine

Over such phenomena, clinical medicine became an ever more power- ful social authority. The late nineteenth century witnessed a far-reach- ing medicalization of the study of human behaviour, aging included. The human body and the human psyche both became sites of medical discourse and medical management. This discourse is captured in a highly specialized diagnostic vocabulary, not so far removed from the perceptual habits of popular culture today. Clinical precision emerges against a background of traditional knowledge and cultural norms. To take again the example of declining mental function in the elderly, note the medical historian German Berrios's view: 'Anecdotal cases of senile dementia abound in fictional and historical literature, but the concept of "senile dementia," as currently understood, was formed during the latter part of the nineteenth century. Indeed, it could not have been otherwise, as the neurobiological and clinical language that made it possible only became available during this period.'[28] Curi- ously, as Berrios's first sentence shows, there is a natural tendency to back-date the applicability of newfound diagnostic tools. People in ancient times most likely did suffer from symptoms that we are com- fortable in labelling as 'senile dementia,' but such revisions of the his- torical record are quite problematic. The term 'senile dementia' does not merely denote a set of symptoms, it also signals the operation of an entire diagnostic apparatus with a social authority specific to the mod- ern world. For all we know, many such symptoms would not at an ear- lier time even been recognized as symptoms, as objects of medical scrutiny. The assumption of a particular scientific vocabulary heralds specific forms of medical intervention in our lives.

The proliferation of diagnostic vocabulary recorded clinicians' ever- increasing ability to perceive symptomatic differences and distinguish them reliably. The ability to see such differences, however, depends in large part on habits of thought and culturally conditioned expectations of human behaviour. The story of the first diagnosis of Alzheimer's disease is an instructive example of this phenomenon. At present, Alzheimer's is probably the disease most readily identified as repre- senting declining function in the elderly, yet it might never have been diagnosed had it not been for its appearance among younger patients. The German clinician Alois Alzheimer described a problematic set of symptoms in a 51-year-old woman. Within five years a number of such cases were linked together and Alzheimer's colleague Emil Kraepelin assigned the disease its now-famous name.

What had initially puzzled Alzheimer was that the symptoms were those of senile dementia, yet they were presenting in people in their forties and fifties. Alzheimer began his review of a few such cases by noting that the obvious diagnosis is impossible: 'After all, we are dealing with the case of a 56-year-old woman and of Perusini's 46-year-old man, in whom nobody would have made a clinical diagnosis of senile dementia.'[29] He remarked a bit later of a third such patient: 'The clinical analysis of this case raises several difficulties. Senile dementia was never considered because of the onset at the age of 54.'[30] Symptoms regarded as common, and hence diagnostically unremarkable, in an elderly patient, become an anomaly and a challenge to science in a middle-aged person. These cases sharpened researchers' attention to dementia as a degenerative brain disorder, which now affects how we judge dementia in old people as well. As Berrios argues: 'Alzheimer's disease has become the prototypical form of senile dementia; indeed, the study of its history might throw light on the formation of the concept of dementia.'[31] To put the matter another way, had medicine not seen the anomalous image of a younger person showing signs of mental decay, such symptoms might have continued to be accepted as a normal and natural feature of the aging process.

Diagnostic practice is heavily influenced by an age-biased discrimination. The willingness of medicine to intervene and treat physical symptoms is likewise influenced by a normative view of bodily and mental function for the person's age. In the figurative sense of 'life expectancy,' alluded to above, one's expectation of the duration of good health and normal function determines one's willingness to regard particular lapses of function as treatable. As Kathryn Hunter argues, much can be learned by attending to the 'narrative structure of medical knowledge'.[32]

Ironically, the very success of modern medicine (in tandem with improvements in nutrition, education, and public health) has enhanced our expectation of life, creating new emotional and intellectual burdens, the ethical implications of which we are still sorting out. In some ways, we now regard life as an entitlement, and the health care profession as its trustee. Nowhere, perhaps, is this seen more clearly than in the dramatic reduction in infant and child mortality rates. For our culture, the loss of a child is one of the most intolerable forms assumed by the thought of death. It is experienced as an injustice, as a violation of the order of nature. This perception sets us apart from the culture of past generations, and it has enormous implications for our attitude to the aging process. In previous centuries, the death of children was a common experience, and while still an occasion for grieving, it was to a certain extent accepted as part of the course of nature. The French social historian Phillipe Ariès shows that such acceptance was an instance of 'tame death.' Death took people of all ages indiscriminately, and often without warning, prompting attitudes of fatalistic resignation. People commonly died in their homes, surrounded by family, including children, who were not sheltered from the experience. In our age, the scene of death has been revised in two crucial ways: most people die in hospitals, and it is old people who are doing the dying.

The collective imagination of our culture is thus challenged. The fear of death, the disturbing fact of our mortality that has troubled our philosophies and religions for millennia is now focused on the image of the elderly. We shun the elderly because we see in them the face of our own mortality. We take the birth of our children for granted, while the various infirmities of adulthood and middle age we hand over to the doctors in full expectation of treatment and cure. Violations of this pattern are met with shock and disbelief. In some cases, families find it hard to let a terminally ill loved one die, preferring to prolong some version of life indefinitely through medical intervention. We are disinclined to accept the cause of death from, in the old phrase, 'natural causes,' preferring to isolate some systemic breakdown – or mistake.

The Culture of Youth and Utility: The Case for Retirement

At the same time that old people have become more exclusively the visible symbols of our mortality, they have also come to represent the unproductive. To a remarkable extent, medical authority has played a role in this development too. Consider the case of the distinguished Canadian doctor Sir William Osler. After years of practice in Canada, Osler was lured south of the border, eventually spending sixteen years as the first professor of medicine in the new medical school at Johns Hopkins University. The masculine character of this life of achievement is partly seen in his late marriage (at age 43) and entry into parenthood (at age 47). For women, as Aurora Leigh reminded us, maturity is partly measured by the ripeness of fertility. On resigning his position at Hopkins, Osler's farewell address amplifies his view that a man is best judged by the work of his active youth. Osler proclaims the 'comparative uselessness of men above forty years of age' and 'the uselessness of men above sixty years of age.'[33] At best, an aging teacher may continue to profess, but his days of discovery and fresh insight are over. Osler extends this view of the life course to consider the aging of institutions. In a remarkable passage Osler cites two rare medical conditions, infantilism and progeria, and assigns them metaphorically to colleges that have not nourished and replaced their human resources properly:

> A rare, but still more extraordinary, bodily state is that of progeria, in which, as though touched with the wand of some malign fairy, the child does not remain infantile, but skips adolescence, maturity and manhood, and passes at once to senility, looking at eleven or twelve years like a miniature Tithonus 'marred and wasted,' wrinkled and stunted, a little old man among his toys. It takes great care on the part of anyone to live the mental life corresponding to the phases through which his body passes. How few minds reach puberty, how few come to adolescence, how fewer attain maturity! ... Progeria is an awful malady in a college. Few faculties escape without an instance or two, and there are certain diets which cause it just as surely as there are waters in some of the Swiss valleys that produce cretinism. I have known an entire faculty attacked. The progeric himself is a nice enough fellow to look at and to play with, but he is sterile, with the mental horizon narrowed, and quite incapable of assimilating the new thoughts of his day and generation.[34]

Progeria is, of course, an extremely rare condition. Nevertheless, through metaphoric extension Osler makes it a normative picture of an environment that fails to nourish the culture of youth. The post-Darwinian fear of degeneration haunts the passage, as does the belief that progress depends on investing in the heat of youth. Osler's argument inevitably points to a call for mandatory retirement, and he playfully toys with Anthony Trollope's suggestion (see below) that there should be mandatory euthanasia at age 66. Ironically, Osler himself, ended up belying his own argument. He was resigning from Hopkins at age 56 to take up the position of Regius professor of medicine at Oxford University. He lived to age 70, remaining productive long past the age he had marked as the age of complete uselessness.

Despite many such instances of continued productivity after the age of 65, our culture continues to associate institutional health with growth and youthful vigour. The whole institution of retirement, embraced initially as an economic and social expedient, has to a remarkable extent, been accepted and naturalized as an inevitable feature of the life course. A revealing indication of this mixture of expediency and natural expectation can be found in the text of the 1990 Supreme Court of Canada's decision upholding mandatory retirement. The challenge to mandatory retirement was made by several faculty members of Canadian universities, and was based on the argument that mandatory retirement violated the prohibition in Canada's Charter of Rights and Freedoms against discrimination on the grounds of age. The Justices denied the appeal, with the majority judgment written by Justice La Forest. This text, supplemented by two dissenting judgments, runs to over 100 pages. Although much of the discussion revolves around central legal issues (e.g., are universities extensions of government? does the Charter protection extend to private agreements? is retirement enforceable by law?), the most interesting aspect of the judgment is the attempt to weigh competing notions of value. How does one weigh the purported damage to the individual that enforced retirement creates against the purported social value of the institution of retirement itself?

At one level, the judgment upholds retirement by some notion of fair exchange. The cessation of work, agreed to through collective bargaining after all, is seen as part of the agreement at the time of appointment, a fair trade, as it were, for the benefits of tenure, job security, and academic freedom. Upholding this arbitrary, yet standard career limit, forecloses any discussion of the highly variable competence at certain ages that Osler, among many others, had noticed. As La Forest states:

> In a tenured system, then, there is always the possibility of dismissal for cause but the level of interference with or evaluation of faculty members' performance is quite low. The desire to avoid such evaluation does not, as I see it, relate solely or even principally to administrative convenience. Rather, the desire is to maximize academic freedom by minimizing interference and evaluation. Elimination of mandatory retirement would adversely affect this for there could well be an increase in evaluation and attempts to dismiss for cause, though it must be said that evidence on this point is unavoidably lacking.[35]

In short, we seem to have a general suspicion, based on prevailing notions of the aging process, that performance declines significantly with time. No one has substantiated this claim, however, and both individuals and institutions prefer the arbitrary yet enforceable limit as the path of least resistance. Even though the Court concedes that for some individuals the retirement half of this bargain is experienced as harsh and unfair, on the whole, the measure is seen as a benefit that spares many faculty members from a humiliating scrutiny of possible declining function. Accepting the research done in some previous cases, the Court acknowledges that 'while the aging process varies from person to person, the courts below found on the evidence that on average there is a decline in intellectual ability from the age of 60 upwards.'[36] Contrast this view with one of the dissenting views, that of Justice L'Heureux-Dubé:

> There is no convincing evidence that mandatory retirement is the quid pro quo of the tenure system. The value of tenure is threatened by incompetence, not by the aging process. The presumption of academic incapacity at age 65 is not well founded. The discrepancies between physical and intellectual abilities amongst different age groups may be more than compensated for by increased experience, wisdom and skills acquired over time. There is therefore no pressing and substantial objective addressed by the mandatory retirement policy ... Since retirement was set at 65, advances in medical science and living conditions have significantly extended life expectancy and improved the quality of life. An 'elite' group of people can afford to retire, but the adverse effects of mandatory retirement are most painfully felt by the poor. Women are particularly affected as they are less likely to have adequate pensions. There is no reasonable justification for a scheme which sets 65 as an age for compulsory retirement.[37]

Refreshingly, this judgment steers clear of the stereotype that aging necessarily involves decline, although it does so in part through another one of those hazy interpretations of the trend towards higher average life expectancy. It is not clear what people living a few years longer, on average, than they did earlier in the century has to do with the likely competence of a 65-year-old. If anything, medicine's progress in eliminating many of the causes of death among younger people has simply increased the proportion of people surviving into the time of life when they become more prone to debilitating, wasting diseases that medicine has not yet solved. The justices, it appears, could not agree about whether the evidence made it reasonable to expect this process to affect senior academics in any significant way while they are still on the payroll.

Given the judgment that mandatory retirement was on balance in the individual's interest, and the view that the medical evidence was at best inconclusive, there remained only the issue of the public interest. On this issue, the majority judgment was quite succinct:'Mandatory retirement is rationally connected to the objectives sought. It is intimately tied to the tenure system which undergirds the specific and necessary ambience of university life and ensures continuing faculty renewal, a necessary process in enabling universities to be centres of excellence on the cutting edge of new discoveries and ideas. It ensures a continuing, and necessary, infusion of new people. In a closed system with limited resources, this can only be achieved by departures of other people.'[38]

Are the connections made here transparently 'rational'? The clichés of the modern anxiety about progress and competition are there ('centres of excellence,' 'cutting edge,' 'faculty renewal'), offset by a respectful regard for the cloistered 'ambience of university life.' The metaphor of infusion associates aging with anemia, with connotations of related Victorian suspicions of failing animal heat. Implicit in both the language and the thought of the passage is the fear that without mandatory retirement universities face degeneration and sterility. The final sentence, in a different key, reminds us that economic expediency is never forgotten. Echoing Marx, the justices acknowledge that a university is like a capitalist enterprise in trying to minimize those who are just collecting a wage, and maximize those whose labour is productive and of surplus value.

There is cause for concern in this judgment, and not just for those whose situation anticipates those whose appeal was thereby denied. The text of the judgment both interprets the law, as we would expect it to, but it also rationalizes the decision in ways that show how our collective thinking about the aging process lacks consensus. Views of the life course are naturalized, with or without evidence, using explanatory models haphazardly understood.

Creative Writers on Aging

Creative writers, as Berrios notes, have been describing the phenomenology of aging for centuries, and literature has enormous potential to counter the various forms of social and instutional marginalization that have become prevalent in our time. The dramatic shifts, both in our lived experience and in our cultural habits of explanation, pose a fresh challenge to our writers and thinkers. Can we reclaim the later stages of life from this chronicle of decline and morbidity, using a language that does not deny the real suffering that many old people experience, but yet celebrates the vitality of a life that is growing naturally into a new phase? The answers to such a question are problematic. Creative writers have enormous freedom, yet they cannot by themselves reinvent the language, nor are they untouched by the cultural patterns that we have seen in the writings of legal scholars, doctors, politicians, and social scientists. Works of literature are, in this sense, products of their world, although they have the potential to pose challenging reorderings of that world.

The Case of Victorian Britain

Consider the literature of late Victorian Britain, literature contemporary with many of the social changes already described. As we have seen, Elizabeth Barrett Browning was able to critique the gender bias at work in her culture's view of the human life course, although *Aurora Leigh* ends fairly conventionally, reinforcing the expectations of a standard romance plot. The culture's stigmatization of the old maid was a forbidding imaginative barrier. Her male contemporaries were no less troubled by aging. At one extreme we could put Oscar Wilde's 1891 novel *The Picture of Dorian Gray*, in many ways a book representative of its culture. The fear of moral degeneration is powerfully caught in a revision of the Faust legend: a young man loses his soul in exchange for perpetual youth. The loss is registered in the uncannily shifting face found in a painted portrait of Gray. Disturbingly, the painted face records both Gray's descent into evil as well as his continued aging. Yet the aging is far in excess of what one would expect given the actual time elapsed in the plot. The physical signs of aging are accelerated and intensified to suggest the essential moral deterioration within. The wrinkled malevolent sneer that expresses the real Gray is a disturbing index of late nineteenth-century culture's anxiety about physical and moral decline. Fear of the aged in time breeds hostility and forms of social marginalization.

Roughly a decade earlier, something of that same fear was expressed in Robert Louis Stevenson's essay 'Crabbed Age and Youth.' Stevenson characterizes age as a steady erosion of vitality, both physical and intellectual: 'Now I know that in thus turning Conservative with years, I am going through the normal cycle of change and travelling in the common orbit of men's opinions. I submit to this, as I would to gout or gray hair, as a concomitant of growing age or else of failing animal heat ... and can no more resist this tendency of my mind than I could prevent my body from beginning to totter and decay.[39]

Although Stevenson is in his late twenties when he writes this, he had been plagued with ill health for most of his life, and there is an urgency about his celebration of youth that barely masks an anxiety about premature death, coupled with a strong fear of waning sexual performance. At its most benign, old age appears to Stevenson as a period of leisure and serene enjoyment, in which the passionate excesses of youth have been shed and something of the free play of childhood is rediscovered: 'To love playthings well as a child, to lead an adventurous and honourable youth, and to settle when the time arrives, into a green and smiling age, is to be a good artist in life.'[40] Stevenson thus reaches for a vision of pastoral simplicity to counter the real sense of antagonism towards old age that the rest of the essay expresses. A culture of youth needs a vision of retirement, one that literally greens the greyness away to mask its own hostilities.

Wilde and Stevenson are young men in their twenties and thirties when they write these words, a time in life when, as Hazlitt says, they can scarcely imagine their own mortality. To this reputed blind spot, one can add the suspicion of masculinist bias. If men tend to identify themselves by their work, so that the active working life becomes the locus of self-fulfilment, then a period that they fear will portend the decline and even cessation of this activity will seem unreal at best, and at worst like some fundamental loss of selfhood. This view animates Anthony Trollope's novel *The Fixed Period* (1881–2), the novel Osler refers to in his farewell address. This novel imagines a dystopic world in which men are retired from their occupations at age 65, sent to an island retreat for a year of philosophic contemplation, and then put to death by chloroform. As one contemporary reviewer drily remarked: 'It is a social institution for which the world was not quite ripe.' When readers suspected satire, Trollope repeatedly affirmed the seriousness of his purpose. By a bizarre irony, Trollope died within a year of completing the novel, at the age of 66, and that death ended a life now legendary for its organization and productivity. Trollope wrote some fifty novels, sticking to a rigid writing schedule built around his full-time career as a civil servant. A life of such productive toil was to have no succeeding phase.

The Case of Late Twentieth-Century Canada

Literary traditions, like people, follow a certain life course, and it has become common to speak of Canadian literatures, both in French and in English, 'coming of age' at a time concurrent with the baby boom so much discussed by demographers. After years of derivative work that struggles to shed the mantle of a colonial mentality, Canadian literature comes of age when it finds its own subjects and its own voice and language. While this coming of age is forward-looking in itself, finding one's voice also means capturing one's past. Two well-known works achieve this double task by creating memorable old characters, characters whose advanced years allow an entire cultural tradition to speak itself. Antonine Maillet's successful 1971 play *La Sagouine* gives us sixteen monologues from a vital 72-year-old woman. She is marginalized not only by age and ill health, but also by her speech, a somewhat idiosyncratic Acadian survival of the sixteenth-century settlers' French. Putting that voice and those experiences at centre-stage, and using them as a filter for a great deal of social and cultural history, was a remarkable accomplishment, in some ways as remarkable as Michel Tremblay's putting the language of Quebec working-class city streets on the stage around the same time.

Seven years prior to the first performance of *La Sagouine*, Margaret Laurence created a formidable protest against the marginalization of the aged with *The Stone Angel*. The aged Hagar Shipley tells her own story, and two pages in is already deftly connecting the constraints of her physical situation with the constrained subject position it embodies: 'The door of my room has no lock. They say it is because I might get taken ill in the night, and then how could they get in and tend me (*tend* – as though I were a crop, a cash crop). So they may enter my room any time they choose. Privacy is a privilege not granted to the aged or to the young. Sometimes very young children can look at the old, and a look passes between them, conspiratorial, sly and knowing. It's because neither are human to the middling ones, those in their prime, as they say, like beef.'[41] The cruel irony of aging is that this very insight, this knowingness so evident to the reader, is in danger of erasure. The loss of physical privacy is a metaphor for the loss of subjectivity, the dignity of a private view. The middling ones speak and act for them, as parents do for their children.

The reader may note a further irony implicit in the narration, in that Hagar is being imagined and made to speak this way by a 38-year-old Margaret Laurence. Indeed, many of the most memorable portraits of old age in literature have been written not from the inside but by some combination of keen observation, imaginative sympathy, and youthful interest and respect. In Constance Rooke's anthology *Night Light: Stories of Aging*, for example, the twelve authors represented have an average age of 47. The youngest is 31 while only Isaac Singer, at 71, is over 60. Similar spreads are found in other such anthologies (see Maura Spiegel and Richard Tristman, Wayne Booth, Margaret Fowler and Priscilla McCutcheon), which should, at the very least, make us wonder how much of the collective portrait of old age is an extension of the emotional and intellectual vantage point of middle age. Projections of both fear and desire may cloud the best-intended portrait, and we should in some measure always be sceptical of views from the outside. Margaret Laurence, facing death at age 60, reflected to herself in her journal: 'One always hears or reads that someone has "died peacefully." How can anyone except that person really know?'[42]

Such scepticism about the ability to know the consciousness of people facing the end parallels a prevailing postmodern scepticism about the capacity of any one form of language to capture consciousness. In literature this scepticism has led to experiments in fractured and multiple narration, making it harder for a Hagar or a Sagouine to hold an entire narrative together. One can contrast *The Stone Angel* with a kind of symbolic successor, Carol Shields's novel *The Stone Diaries* (1993) to see the difference. In some ways Shields's book is a more thorough rendering of all the stages of one woman's long life (the novel has a table of contents that mimics standard delineations of the life course), but her protagonist is not able to tell her story herself; the story is rather told about and through her, using a variety of discourses to do so. One can also see how Antonine Maillet's work has developed by contrasting *La Sagouine* with her 1992 novel *Les Confessions de Jeanne de Valois*, in which the 90-year-old protagonist is explored through a mingling of voices and genres similar to that used by Shields.

History does afford many examples of creative people working productively well into old age, and the demographic shift we are experiencing is bound to increase their numbers, giving some promise of the emergence of a distinctive collective voice. Happily, there is no mandatory retirement for creative writers.

Scholarship and the Aged Subject

There is cause for hope in the sheer volume of attention paid to aging in the scholarly literature in the past twenty years or so. Medical research has clarified much about the biology of aging, usefully summarized in such sources as Nicholas Coni, William Davidson, and Stephen Webster's *Ageing: the Facts* and Maddox's *The Encyclopedia of Aging*. A more specialized source, especially of interest given the prevalence of the association of aging with mental decline, is James E. Birren, R. Bruce Sloane and Gene Cohen's *Handbook of Mental Health and Aging*. Many social scientists have done valuable work in assessing current problems and tracking the effects of social change. Convenient surveys can be found by Victor W. Marshall, J.G. Marshall, and Barry McPherson, Susan A. McDaniel and Ingrid Connidis.

Within the humanities, some good historical work has been done, although it is often specific to past periods, as in Georges Minois and William Graebner, and much of it is written about the experience in Europe and the United States. The far-reaching cultural history found in the work of Thomas Cole and Peter Laslett has been extremely useful in opening up new ground. Recent anthologies such as Mike Featherstone and Andrew Wernick, Anne M. Wyatt-Brown and Janice Rossen, Kathleen Woodward, and Thomas R. Cole and Sally Gadow herald a period of fresh re-examination of the images and ideas our culture both inherits and passes on.

There is, however, mandatory retirement in academe (the Supreme Court case of 1990, after all, concerned retiring faculty). Furthermore, as universities struggle for what they call 'renewal,' strong incentives are increasingly created for early retirement. This means, in part, that the aged voice is often missing in academic writing and debate. Most scholarship on aging issues is written by people in their forties and fifties. Whether there is an ageist bias endemic to modern scholarship is thus a question difficult to answer but necessary to pose.

The old can, of course, seek out various forms of affiliation and solidarity with the culture of youth. Yet, as Barbara Macdonald forcefully argues in an address to the 1985 Conference of the National Women's Studies Association (U.S.), such contact can all too easily slip into an all too familiar scenario of patronization:

> We take in the fact that you come to us for 'oral histories,' for your own agendas, to learn *your* feminist or lesbian or working-class or ethnic histories, with not the slightest interest in our present struggles as old women. You come to fill in some much-needed data for a thesis, or to justify a grant for some 'service' for old women that imitates the mainstream and which you plan to direct, or you come to get material for a biography of our friends and lovers. But you come not as equals, not with any knowl-

edge of who we are, what our issues may be. You come to old women who have been serving young women for a lifetime and ask to be served one more time, and then you cover up your embarrassment as you depart by saying that you felt as though we were your grandmother or your mother or your aunt. And no one in the sisterhood criticizes you for such acts.

But let me say it to you clearly: We are not your mothers, your grand-mothers, or your aunts. And we will never build a true women's move-ment until we can organize together as equals, woman to woman, without the burden of these family roles.[43]

One of the risks of youthful attention to the old, then, is that we come to regard the elderly subject as exemplifying nothing but age, and being qualified to speak only from the vantage point of advanced years. Even when listened to avidly, old people can experience a diminished subjectivity.

Despite Macdonald's anger, women researchers have generally been more sensitive to issues of age, and we are all profoundly indebted to feminist critique of the experience of aging. Books by Simone de Beau-voir, Germaine Greer, Betty Friedan, and Carolyn G. Heilbrun are among the very best of the recent meditations on the phenomenology of aging. They have brought to the problem a keen sensitivity to the problem of marginalization, an awareness of how mainstream culture both patronizes and silences certain subjects.

While women's voices have had considerable presence in the study of aging, the same cannot yet be said for Aboriginal voices. Such voices must be heard if Canada is to move towards an understanding of what aging means to us collectively, as a people, for three main rea-sons: (1) many Aboriginal communities are bucking the overall demo-graphic trend by experiencing high birth rates, which means they will form a higher proportion of the Canadian population in the future; (2) the continuing threat of cultural assimilation poses unique inter-generational pressures, as assimilation often sees young people aban-doning the ways of their parents and grandparents; and (3) Aborig-inal culture itself, with its emphasis on the social cohesion found in the teachings of elders, provides a cultural model that can be of use to all of us.

One feature of this situation is the challenge Aboriginal authors face when, in an attempt to resist the cultural obliteration that assimilation threatens, they work in the language of assimilation. Richard Wag-amese's 1994 novel *Keeper'n Me* is a good example. The book blends two voices: the young man raised rootless in the city, and the old man, called Keeper, whose monologues show not only the traditional wisdom but an astute and witty irony:

> Me, I'm just an old man that's been down many trails. How they say in them movies? The ones that got lotsa Mexicans bein' Indyuns? I lived many winters? Heh, heh, heh. Guess that's true, only me, I don't talk so romantic anymore 'less some of them rich Americans are ready to dish out cash to hear a real Indyun talk 'bout the old days.
>
> Funny thing is, like I told the boy, the old days never really gone. Not for us ... The boy knows this. He come here lookin' around too not so long ago. Funny-lookin' sight he was then, too. Fresh outta the city, not even knowin' he was an Indyun, especially not an Anishanabe. Learned lots though. But he was a real tourist that one. Could got lost in a bathtub then. Heh, heh, heh. But he learned and that's why I told him to write all of this down ... Lots of people out there gotta know what happened, how you found your way and what it takes to be an Indyun these days. Real Indyun, not that Hollywood kind. That's what I told him. He's a good boy, you'll see. Me, I'll just come along for the ride, make sure he's doin' right. Besides, lotta stuff's my story too and maybe if you listen hard, pay close attention, you'll see that they're your stories too. Our stories all work like that. It's TRA-DISH-UNN. Heh, heh, heh.[44]

The old man is the source of the stories, but the young man will write them out. The question of whether an oral tradition can be preserved in written form without losing much of itself has been extensively debated. Young Aboriginal authors are keenly conscious of both the difficulties and the obligations of their position, as we hear in the conclusion of Louise Halfe's 1998 poetic sequence *Blue Marrow*:

> Did our Grandmothers know we would be scarred by the fists and boots of men? Our songs taxed, silenced by tongues that speak damnation and burning? Did they know we would turn woman against woman? Did they know some of us would follow, take mates of colour and how the boarding of our worlds would pulse breathing exiles connected to their womb? Did they know only some would dig roots, few hands calloused from tanning? Did they know only a few would know the preparation of moose nose, gopher, beaver-tail feasts? Did they know our memory, our talk would walk on paper, legends told sparingly? Did they know of our struggling hearts?[45]

That this painful depiction of cultural silencing is itself written in English is eloquent. Despite the many successes Aboriginal authors have achieved writing in English recently, the loss of mother-tongue represents a serious challenge to a community struggling to honour its elders while embracing the necessities of change. Of the hundreds of First Nations languages that existed prior to European contact, only three – Dene, Cree, and Ojibway – are not extinct or endangered.

Within the Aboriginal scholarly community there is a similar acknowledgment of the cognitive dissonance between traditional teaching and the institutions of Western thought. When we see how the English language is marked by a deeply rooted ageist discourse, perhaps it is time to look to other cultural models. As Battiste and Henderson argue, these models do not need to be invented:

> Indigenous educators ... need to balance traditional Indigenous ways of knowing with the Eurocentric tradition. They must respect and understand the other ways of knowing. They must embrace the paradox of subjective and objective ways of knowing that do not collapse into either inward or outward illusions, but bring us all into a living dialogical relationship with the world that our knowledge gives us ... The educational system and Indigenous teachers do not need to invent a new way of transmitting Indigenous knowledge and heritage. All they need to do is to develop concepts that more faithfully reflect our traditional educational transmission processes. Educators need to understand the traditional methods. This requires creating and supporting training centers that are controlled by Indigenous elders and educators. These centers must strengthen educators' capacity to document, protect, teach, and apply the traditional transmission of heritage and must be operated in the language of the people.[46]

Given the growing prominence of the Aboriginal community, in both our demographic mix and in public discourse, the voices of the elders may turn out, as Keeper said, to be telling our stories too.

Conclusion: Policy Implications

The challenge is both to allow the aged subject to speak, and to acknowledge our kinship with old age through the shared experience of aging, a process that comprises both growth and decline. We must shed the prejudice, felt both in popular usage and in academic discourse, that to be a student of aging is to study old people. The failure to acknowledge the old is both a blindness to social conditions and a lapse in self-knowledge. Oedipus's lack of self-knowledge was in part a judgment on his belief in his own invulnerability; his ignorance of the circumstances of his birth a sign that he did not see himself as part of the natural cycle of life and death. Oedipus is punished in a way that fuses him with the image of the final stage of life, echoing the answer to the Sphinx's riddle. To make that myth current may involve reminding ourselves of the forms our own ignorance takes. Consider Muriel Rukeyser's witty recasting of the Oedipus story:

Myth

Long afterward, Oedipus, old and blinded, walked the roads. He smelled a familiar smell. It was the Sphinx. Oedipus said, 'I want to ask one question. Why didn't I recognize my mother?' 'You gave the wrong answer,' said the Sphinx. 'But that was what made everything possible,' said Oedipus. 'No,' she said. 'When I asked, What walks on four legs in the morning, two at noon, and three in the evening, you answered, Man. You didn't say anything about woman.' 'When you say Man,' said Oedipus, 'you include women too. Everyone knows that.' She said, 'That's what you think.'[47]

Rukeyser writes this in her late fifties. She sees Oedipus's doom not as some instance of blind fate, as in many standard readings, but as a judgment on his double mistake: he presumptuously allows man to stand for woman, and he fails to recognize his own mother. The restoration of this doubly excluded female subject position is Rukeyser's project, achieved in part by the simple revision of allowing the Sphinx to speak. This ancient female monster, a propounder of riddles, and an object of male dread, and, in Oedipus's case, apparent conquest, is an evocative figure. In some oblique way, the myth acknowledges the power of knowledge, a power that often threatens. Oedipus vanquishes the Sphinx, while mistaking her meaning. The classical heritage that spawned the Oedipus myth eventually yielded to a Christian tradition whose myth of the fall inextricably tied knowledge to sin, and saw suffering and mortality as the joint consequence of this tie.

   Although our literature often celebrates the wisdom of age, we often hear a troubled anxiety about that knowledge, fearing perhaps that age will bring confirmation of unpleasant truths, a shattering of the self-serving illusions of youth. Goethe, in his mammoth tragic drama *Faust*, has Mephistopheles say as much:

I see my discourse leaves you cold;
Dear kids, I do not take offense;
Recall: the Devil, he is old,
Grow old yourselves, and he'll make sense![48]

Goethe was 80 years old when he wrote this. The lines are a living testament to the continuing creative power in old age, and yet at the same time a sharp satirical reminder of the ageism so prevalent in our culture's experience of language. To adopt this language, mindful of its limitations, and to remake it so as to define new social relations – that is the challenge we face.

There are many policy implications to this argument. The comprehensive view of the life course I am calling for would resist an easy demarcation of the stages of life. Public policy which assumes such a demarcation, such as mandatory retirement, needs to be reconsidered. Policies must avoid stigmatizing the elderly as unproductive. More flexible notions of productivity are called for. Educational programs are needed to foster a healthier and more inclusive understanding of the human life course and its developmental implications. Ultimately, we need to remake our language to help uncover the operations of prejudicial thinking.[49] Such change is hard to legislate, although it will emerge in the wake of other forms of social change. Perhaps the most essential step towards this change will be the collective acknowledgment that aging is not a problem that we study in others, but an experience and a consciousness that we all inhabit.

Notes

1 See Richard A. Posner, *Aging and Old Age* (Chicago: University of Chicago Press, 1995), 18.
2 See Nicholas Coni, William Davison, and Stephen Webster, *Ageing: The Facts*, 2nd ed. (Oxford: Oxford University Press, 1992), 54.
3 See Ken Dryden, *The Game: A Reflective and Thought-Provoking Look at Life in Hockey* (Toronto: Macmillan, 1983), 13.
4 Thomas R. Cole, *The Journey of Life: A Cultural History of Aging in America* (Cambridge: Cambridge University Press, 1992). For visual symmetry, see illustrations or p. 14ff; for the nursery rhyme, see p. 11.
5 See Mary Poovey, *A History of the Modern Fact: Problems of Knowledge in the Sciences of Wealth and Society* (Chicago: University of Chicago Press, 1998), 317.

6 Quoted in Poovey, *A History of the Modern Fact*, 312.
7 On the pre-nineteenth-century roots of the social sciences, see Richard Olson, ed., *The Emergence of the Social Sciences, 1642–1792* (New York: Twayne, 1993).
8 See William Shakespeare, *As You Like It*, in G. Blakemore Evans, Harry Levin, Herschel Baker, Anne Barton, Frank Kermode, Hallett Smith, Marie Edel, and Charles H. Shattuck, eds., *The Riverside Shakespeare* (Boston: Houghton Mifflin, 1974) 2.7. 145–8.
9 See Margaret Lock, *Encounters with Aging: Mythologies of Menopause in Japan and North America* (Berkeley: University of California Press, 1993).
10 See W. Penn Handwerker, ed., 'Culture and Reproduction: Exploring Micro/Macro Linkages,' *Culture and Reproduction: An Anthropological Critique of Demographic Transition Theory,* (Boulder and London: Westview Press, 1986), 11. For a discussion on how demographic factors must be considered in relation to a framework of social trends, see Connidis, in this book.
11 Ibid., 11–12.
12 See Dorothy Stein, *People Who Count: Population and Politics, Women and Children* (London: Earthscan Publications, 1995), 10.
13 Ibid., 230.
14 See David Coleman and Roger Schofield eds., 'Introduction: The State of Population Theory,' *The State of Population Theory* (Oxford: Blackwell, 1986), 5.
15 For a fuller discussion of aging and productivity see Prager, in this book.
16 See The National Advisory Council on Aging, *The NACA Position on the Image of Aging* (Ottawa: National Advisory Council on Aging, 1993), 10.
17 Supreme Court of Canada. *McKinney* v *University of Guelph. 1990.* Available online: http://www.droit.umontreal.ca/doc/.../1990/vol3/html/ 1990scr3_0229.html 5.
18 See Elizabeth Barrett Browning, *Aurora Leigh*, ed. Kerry McSweeney (Oxford: Oxford University Press, 1993), II.329–35.
19 For a discussion of current issues relating to our valuation of work and its place in our sense of the lifecourse, see Venne and Thomas in this book.
20 The point is well argued in Jill Quadagno, *Aging in Early Industrial Society: Work, Family, and Social Policy in Nineteenth-Century England* (New York: Academic Press, 1982).
21 For a discussion of recent research on intergenerational issues, see Susan McDaniel in this book.
22 See Edgar-André Montigny, *Foisted Upon the Government? State Responsibilities, Family Obligations, and The Care of the Dependent Aged in Late Nineteenth-*

Century Ontario (Montreal and Kingston: McGill-Queen's University Press, 1997), 146.

23 On the decision generally, see Lynn McDonald nd Richard A. Wannew, *Retirement in Canada* (Toronto: Butterworths, 1990). For the role of J.S. Woodsworth, see Grace MacInnis, *J.S. Woodsworth: A Man to Remember* (Toronto: Mcmillan, 1953).

24 See Karl Marx, *Capital*, ed. David McLellan (Oxford: Oxford University Press, 1995), 390.

25 See William Graebner. *A History of Retirement: The Meaning and Function of an American Institution, 1885–1978* (New Haven: Yale University Press, 1980), 40.

26 See, e.g., ibid., 226.

27 Quoted in Daniel Pick, *Faces of Degeneration: A European Disorder, c. 1848–c. 1918* (Cambridge: Cambridge University Press, 1989), 208.

28 See German E. Berrios, *The History of Mental Symptoms: Descriptive Psychopathology since the Nineteenth Century* (Cambridge: Cambridge University Press, 1996), 195.

29 See Alois Alzheimer, 'On Certain Peculiar Diseases of Old Age' (1911), repr. in *History of Psychiatry* 2 (1991): 71–101. Translated and with an Introduction by Hans Förstl and Raymond Levy, 75.

30 Ibid., 79.

31 See Berrios, *The History of Mental Symptoms*, 195.

32 See Kathryn Montgomery Hunter, *Doctor's Stories: The Narrative Structure of Medical Knowledge* (Princeton: Princeton University Press, 1991).

33 See Sir William Osler, 'The Fixed Period,' in Charles G. Roland, ed., *Sir William Osler 1849–1919: A Selection for Medical Students* (Toronto: Hannah Institute for the History of Medicine, 1982), 14–15.

34 Ibid., 12–13.

35 Supreme Court, *McKinney* v *University of Guelph.* 1990, 30–1.

36 Ibid., 33.

37 Ibid., 10.

38 Ibid., 4.

39 See Robert Louis Stevenson, 'Crabbed Age and Youth,' *Familiar Studies of Men and Books; Virginibus Puerisque; Selected Poems* (London and Glasgow: Collins, 1956), 261–2.

40 Ibid., 266.

41 See Margaret Laurence, *The Stone Angel* (Toronto: McClelland and Stewart, 1964), 6.

42 Quoted in James King, *The Life of Margaret Laurence* (Toronto: Alfred Knopf, 1997), 387.

43 See Barbara Macdonald, 'Outside The Sisterhood: Ageism in Women's Studies,' *Women's Studies Quarterly* 17, no. 1/2 (1989): 8.
44 See Richard Wagamese, *Keeper'n Me* (Toronto: Doubleday, 1994), 1–4.
45 See Louise Bernice Halfe, *Blue Marrow: Poems* (Toronto: McClelland and Stewart, 1998), 89.
46 See Marie Battiste and James (Sa'ke'j) Youngblood Henderson, *Protecting Indigenous Knowledge and Heritage: A Global Challenge* (Saskatoon: Purich Publishing, 1999), 94–5. See also Marie Battiste, ed., *Reclaiming Indigenous Voice and Vision* (Vancouver: UBC Press, 2000).
47 See Muriel Rukeyser, *A Muriel Rukeyser Reader*, ed. Jan Heller Levi (New York: W.W. Norton, 1994), 252.
48 See Johann Wolfgang von Goethe, *Faust: A Tragedy*, trans. Walter Arndt, ed. Cyrus Hamlin (New York: Norton, 1976), 171.
49 To remind us that not all relations between children and their parents follow the same pattern, Tindale, Norris, and Abbott, in this book, offer the notion of 'reciprocity' as an alternate conceptual model.

4. The Impact of Demographic and Social Trends on Informal Support for Older Persons

Ingrid Arnet Connidis

Introduction: Social Issues

Recent writings illustrate well that an alarmist view of population aging (discussed in Chapter 1) misrepresents its consequences for social policy, health care, pension costs, and family ties.[1] In all of these areas, the 'overselling' of population aging[2] has meant taking too deterministic and negative a view of its impact, distracting from our efforts to understand the real significance of an aging population.

A number of demographic and social trends are colliding with a shift in policy directives away from publicly funded formal support to greater reliance on community-based and informal support. While the shift is driven primarily by a desire to reduce deficits and debts, there has been a corresponding growth in the position that government policy must aim for intergenerational equity to ensure fairness and to avoid intergenerational conflict (discussed in Chapter 2).[3] This position typically relies on analyses of government transfers to conclude that there is a current imbalance favouring the old. Unfortunately, the bigger picture of intergenerational exchanges that occur at the informal level, particularly in families, and at the societal level, in terms of access to the labour market, is not central to the intergenerational equity debate.[4] Yet, study after study documents the considerable contribution that older persons make to younger generations, both over the long term and in their older age, through their contributions as citizens and as family members.[5]

To counter the tendency to ignore informal support, this chapter examines several parameters of family life and labour-force participation in Canada. Shifts in demographic trends such as fertility and in social trends such as marriage, divorce, and labour-force participation, set some boundaries in the availability of specific family relationships, in the direct sense of whether there are such ties (e.g., fertility) and in the indirect sense of accessibility to ties that are present (e.g., having a spouse versus a former spouse; having parents who are married versus parents who are not; and having competing commitments to family and jobs). The question addressed here is: What are the implications for informal support for older persons of trends across age groups in: marital status (married, widowed, divorced/separated, never married), family size (referring to number of children, not birth rates), number of siblings, and labour-force participation (for men and women)? Changes in labour-force participation for men and women are examined because of the challenges posed by combining the responsibilities of work and family, especially but not exclusively among women.[6]

Familiarity with demographic and social trends facilitates the prediction and understanding of informal support from families.[7] However, shifts in divorce laws, the mandatory age of retirement, federally funded benefits for various groups of older persons, health care benefits, and gender relations are examples of how factors other than demographics are critical to understanding why both demographic and social changes occur, how they influence each other, and their implications.[8] Thus, as well as presenting trends, context must be provided by reviewing related literature. Furthermore, because data on demographic and labour-force participation trends tend to focus on either the individual or household, rather than on multigenerational families,[9] the perspective of the extended family must be incorporated into our discussion.

Finally, an underlying premise of this chapter is that particular demographic changes do not determine a given outcome in familial relationships. Because family members negotiate their ties with one another in light of their current situation, one cannot assume, for example, that decreased fertility necessarily signals a significant decline in support for older persons. Instead, it may mark a change in how children meet the needs of their older parents and in how older persons negotiate other relationships such as those with their siblings. Demographic and social trends are a reflection of how individuals have negotiated their relationships with others and attempted to exercise agency over their lives, in the context of current circumstances and demands, including current public policy.[10] In turn, today's parameters of family and work life are themselves a set of circumstances to be negotiated by individuals in their relationships with family members and with others in their social world.

I will first present demographic trends (marital status, number of children, the combination of marital status and number of children, and the availability of siblings) by gender, over time and across age groups where possible. Then, trends in labour-force participation for men and women are presented. This is followed by a detailed discussion of the implications of the trends observed for future informal support, research, and public policy which highlights the significance of gender.

Demographic Trends

Examining the availability of different family ties to specific age groups over time provides the basis for estimating the *potential* for familial support. While our immediate interest here is potential support for older people, this question is best addressed by looking at trends in family composition for multiple age groups. For example, as well as knowing whether the availability of children to older parents has changed over time (fertility trends), one must also know about the situation of these parents' children (the proportion who themselves have children, are in the labour force, are lone parents, and so on). Therefore, examining trends across time for several age groups, not just for older cohorts, is crucial.

The examination of demographic and social trends related to family life is based on census data on fertility (the number of children ever born) and labour-force participation for the years 1961, 1971, 1981, 1991, and on marital status for 1961, 1971, 1981, 1991, and 1996. Data on siblings come from the 1990 General Social Survey.[11] Generally, data are presented by 10-year age groups, starting with ages 25 to 34 and ending with 85 years and over. In addition, the public-use microdata file for 1991 is used to examine the combination of family size, marital status, and age group. Analyses of these data concern women only because fertility data involve women only but, nonetheless, they create a more complete picture of family composition across age groups.

Data presented by age group across time can be studied in three ways. To focus on the changed experiences of a given age group over time, comparisons of the same age group at different points in time are best; for example, comparing those who are age 65 to 74 for the four or

TABLE 4.1
Percentage of married women and men by age: Canada, 1961–1996

Age (years)	Women					Men				
	1961	1971	1981	1991	1996	1961	1971	1981	1991	1996
25–34	86	82	76	70	66	76	76	69	61	58
35–44	88	85	81	78	75	87	85	83	79	75
45–54	82	80	81	77	75	87	85	85	83	80
55–64	69	67	70	77	71	83	82	83	83	82
65–74	50	47	43	54	55	75	75	76	80	79
75–84	29	25	26	29	30	60	61	70	71	71
85+	11	11	7	9	10	38	42	25	49	51

Source: Statistics Canada: 1961–1996 Census of Canada.

five census years that are examined. One can also look at these data by cohort by tracking a given age group (e.g., those age 25 to 34 in 1961) over the next three decades (those age 35 to 44 in 1971, those age 45 to 54 in 1981, those age 55 to 64 in 1991). Finally, age differences for any one of these years can be examined.

Marital Status

Given that a spouse is the most likely provider of support to older married persons,[12] marital status is an important parameter of familial support. In turn, the observed effects of widowhood and divorce of both older parents and their adult children on support exchanges (discussed further later) make the availability of a spouse among younger cohorts relevant to informal support for older persons. From 1981 to 1996, the percentage of older persons who were married (see Table 4.1) increased, primarily because the percentage who were widowed (see Table 4.2) has decreased as a result of longer life expectancy. This trend applies to both men and women, but the gender difference in rates of widowhood persists, with women much more likely than men to be widowed. Among those age 75 or more, the most common experience for women is to be widowed while for men it is to be married. Among younger age groups (under 55), there has been a steady decline in the percentage who are married, particularly among those age 25 to 34, reflecting, in part, later age at marriage.

As Table 4.3 shows, growing numbers of older persons enter old age

TABLE 4.2

Percentage of widowed women and men by age: Canada, 1961–1996

Age (years)	Women						Men				
	1961	1971	1981	1991	1996		1961	1971	1981	1991	1996
25–34	1	1	0	0	1		0	0	0	0	0
35–44	2	2	2	1	1		1	1	0	0	0
45–54	8	7	6	4	3		2	2	1	1	1
55–64	20	18	16	14	12		5	4	3	3	3
65–74	39	39	44	34	32		14	9	12	9	8
75–84	61	63	63	59	58		29	25	19	19	18
85+	78	78	83	79	79		53	48	66	42	39

Source: Statistics Canada: 1961–1996 Census of Canada.

TABLE 4.3

Percentage of divorced and separated men and women by age: Canada, 1961–1996

Age (years)	Women						Men				
	1961	1971	1981	1991	1996		1961	1971	1981	1991	1996
25–34	1	6	8	7	7		0	4	5	4	4
35–44	1	6	10	12	13		1	5	7	8	10
45–54	1	6	8	13	15		1	5	6	9	11
55–64	1	5	6	10	12		1	5	6	8	10
65–74	0	3	4	6	8		0	4	4	6	7
75–84	0	2	3	3	4		0	3	3	4	5
85+	0	1	1	1	2		0	2	0	3	4

Source: Statistics Canada: 1961–1996 Census of Canada.

divorced, but the proportions who do so remain quite small. Except for the youngest women, there is a steady increase in the percentage divorced from 1961 to 1991 for all age groups. Among those age 65 to 74 in 1996, 8 per cent of women and 7 per cent of men were divorced or separated. One might think that these quite low numbers mask much higher rates of divorce because those who remarry are recorded as married. Yet, in 1990, only 12 per cent of men and 8 per cent of women age 55 and over were involved in a second or subsequent partnership.[13] Nonetheless, as of 1990, one in five Canadian women and

TABLE 4.4
Percentage of single men and women by age: Canada, 1961–1996

Age (years)	Women						Men				
	1961	1971	1981	1991	1996		1961	1971	1981	1991	1996
25–34	13	12	16	23	27		23	20	26	34	39
35–44	9	7	7	9	11		12	10	10	12	16
45–54	10	7	5	6	7		10	9	7	7	8
55–64	9	10	8	6	5		11	9	8	7	6
65–74	10	11	9	7	6		11	11	8	7	6
75–84	10	11	9	9	8		11	10	8	7	6
85+	11	11	9	10	10		10	9	9	9	7

Source: Statistics Canada: 1961–1996 Census of Canada.

slightly more men aged 50 to 59 had divorced at least once. As well, we can see that the percentage who are divorced is up for the younger age groups (e.g., in 1996, 13% of women age 35 to 44 and 15% of women age 45 to 54), among whom there is still additional 'opportunity' for divorce for those who are still married.

Singlehood among Canadians has been quite constant with evidence of a recent shift. The 1961 to 1996 data (see Table 4.4) show a steady trend upward in the percentage of persons age 35 to 44 and 45 to 54 who remained single, peaking in 1991, and then declining in 1996 but to a level higher than all previous years except 1991. While some of these individuals may yet marry, it is likely that most will remain single, especially those aged 45 to 54.

When compared with the rest of the country, the proportion of Quebecers who are married has historically been smaller. This difference has been compounded in recent years by the greater increase in cohabitation, and subsequent decline in marriage, in Quebec more than in other provinces. Thus, while 14 per cent of all Canadian couples were in common-law unions as of 1995, 25 per cent of couples in Quebec were.[14] In Quebec, 11 per cent of the 1991 population age 15 and over was in a common-law union, compared with 5 per cent in Ontario.[15] The greater propensity to cohabit does minimize somewhat the difference between Quebecers and other Canadians in the likelihood of being part of a couple. However, Quebecers are twice as likely as Ontarions to never marry and, while divorce rates in Québec have mirrored the national trend upward, they have gone to even higher lev-

TABLE 4.5
Number of children ever born to ever-married women
age 45 and over: Canada, 1961–1991

No. of children	Year			
	1961	1971	1981	1991
0	14%	13%	12%	10%
1	14	13	12	11
2	18	21	22	27
3	15	17	17	22
4	10	11	14	13
5+	28	25	23	17

Source: Statistics Canada.

els.[16] As well, both divorce and widowhood are less likely to be followed by remarriage in Quebec.[17] On balance, this means that older Quebecers are less likely than other Canadians to have a partner.

Family Size

Estimating how many Canadians are childless cannot be based solely on fertility data (usually based on ever-married women only) or on data regarding marital status (on the assumption that never-married women do not have children). As well, how one looks at census data is critical. For example, regarding the issue of family size, there is a tendency to focus on the Canadian birth rate figure of 1.7 and assume that the average Canadian family has one or two children. As the data here show, the number of children born to ever-married women presents quite a different picture of declining birth rates. Particularly when considering older persons, it is important to look at fertility in terms of family composition: How many children do people have? This requires going beyond the total fertility rate and the nuclear household.

Table 4.5 reports data on the number of children ever born to ever-married women, the only data collected in Canada until 1991 when never-married women were also included. The key trends are (1) a *decline* in the percentage having zero, one, and five or more children; (2) an *increase* in the proportion having two or three children; and (3) a *substantial proportion* of families with as many as four 4 or more children (30% of the ever-married women age 45 and over in 1991).

TABLE 4.6
Number of children ever born to ever-married women 45 and over by age group: Canada, 1991

No. of children	Age group						
	45–54	55–64	65–69	70–74	75–79	80–84	85+
0	7%	9%	10%	12%	15%	21%	15%
1	10	8	10	12	14	19	19
2	37	22	20	24	24	21	19
3	25	23	20	18	15	16	17
4	12	15	15	14	12	8	10
5+	8	24	25	20	20	16	20

Source: Statistics Canada.

Examining the distribution by age group for a particular year (1991, see Table 4.6) indicates cohort differences. For the youngest cohort (age 45–54), the modal numbers of children are two (37%) and three (25%), childlessness is *least likely* (7%), and is lower than for preceding cohorts, and large families with five or more children are the second least likely (8%). Thus, in terms of a family profile, two or more children will remain typical for some time. Regarding surviving children, General Social Survey data from 1990 show that 79 per cent of all men and 76 per cent of all women age 75 and over have at least one child.[18]

While Quebec had the lowest fertility rate in the country for some time, in 1997 this position belonged to Newfoundland, followed by New Brunswick and Nova Scotia.[19] Still, Quebec's fertility rate of 1.52 was lower than that for the country overall. The Quebec rate would probably have been even lower without that province's financial assistance program, which has encouraged some women there to have second and third children.[20]

Family Composition: Combining Marital Status, Family Size, and Age

While the preceding observations are informative about shifts in marital status and in family size over time, they fail to create a portrait of family composition that reflects the combined realities of marital status and family size. To provide a more complete profile of family composi-

TABLE 4.7
Marital status by fertility for women aged 45 and over:
Canada, 1991

No. of children	Marital status			
	Single	Married	Divorced	Widowed
0	91%	9%	11%	13%
1	3	10	10	13
2	3	29	28	20
3	1	23	20	19
4	–	13	14	13
5+	3	16	16	22

Source: Statistics Canada: 1991 Census of Canada,
Public Use Microdata File: Individual File, 0.1% sample.

tion, the public use microdata file for 1991 is used to construct tables that combine family size, marital status, and age group. Because family size is included, the data are for women only (using the number of children ever born). Unlike the data on family size presented thus far, these tables also include fertility information for single (never-married) as well as ever-married women.

Using the information provided in these tables, we can compute the proportion of women who are both unmarried and childless, with the caveat that data on family size are children ever born. Therefore, among the older age groups particularly, some mothers will have experienced the death of at least one of their children. However, Ellen Gee's report[21] that 24 per cent of women age 75 and over are childless is close to the percentage of childless women in this age group (22.5) using data from the public use microdata file. Thus, while the distribution of older women's current family size (one, two, three, four, five or more children) may differ from the data based on children ever-born, calculations of childlessness are very close to actual experience.

In Table 4.7, a cross-tabulation of marital status by number of children for women age 45 and over in 1991 is presented. Including the single alters the overall distribution of family size, with a total of 15 per cent of women of post-childbearing age in 1991 childless. However, having two or three children remains the modal experience among women age 45 and over. Focusing on the single, approximately 9 per cent have one or more children while among ever-married women the vast majority do so (ranging from 87% among the widowed to 90% among the married). Using the data for single, divorced, and widowed women who have no children, almost 10 per cent (9.56%) of women age 45 and over have neither a spouse nor child.

The same data are provided by 10-year age group in Table 4.8. Comparing the results for single women in these tables, we can see a steady decrease in the percentage of single women who are childless as age goes down. While 97 per cent of single women age 75 to 84 in 1991 are childless, this drops to 87 per cent of those age 45 to 54 and 79 per cent of those age 35 to 44. While the figures for the youngest group may change, the number of additional births to these women is not likely to significantly alter the percentage who are childless, given that most women have their children before the age of 35.

Combining the data for single, divorced, and widowed women, the percentages by age group who are both unmarried and childless are as follows: 9 per cent of those age 35 to 44; 8 per cent of those age 45 to 54 (some parents of the baby boom); 7 per cent of those age 55 to 64 (parents of the baby boom); 10 per cent of those age 65 to 74; and 18 per cent of those age 75 and over. These shifts over time reflect primarily the increase in widowhood with age. However, as the previous data on marital status over time showed, divorce is a growing reason for being unmarried in younger age groups and, hence, eventually in older ones as well. At the same time, our age-group comparisons of family size by marital status suggest that the gap between older and younger cohorts in the likelihood of having neither a spouse nor children is offset somewhat by the greater likelihood of parenthood among younger single persons.

Critical to informal support is whether single women keep their children. Apparently most do according to 1990 data on co-resident children: 14 per cent of single women age 50 to 54 have one co-resident child and one-fifth of single women age 30 to 44 have one or more co-resident children.[22] The combination of fewer ever-married women having no children and more never-married women having one child means that for several upcoming cohorts of older women, rates of childlessness will go down. In contrast, single men are very unlikely to report having a child or keeping a child as a single parent.[23]

In sum, the majority of ever-married women continue to have two or more children. The trends we have observed indicate that upcoming cohorts of the elderly and middle-aged, particularly the parents of the baby boom, will be less likely to have shortcomings in their support

TABLE 4.8
Marital status by fertility, controlling for age group: Canada, 1991

Age (years)	No. of children[d]	Marital status				N	Total (%)
		Single[a]	Married[b]	Divorced[c]	Widowed		
35–44	0	79.3	10.7	13.1	4.3	328	17
(33%)	1	14.2	13.1	22.2	34.8	282	14
	2	4.1	46.1	38	21.7	804	41
	3	1.8	22.7	19	17.4	398	20
	4+	0.6	7.4	7.7	21.7	137	7
	N	169	1536	221	23	1949	
	Total (%)	100 (9)	100 (78)	100 (11)	100 (1)		100
45–54	0	86.9	6.3	13.6	13.3	167	13
(23%)	1	1.2	10.3	10.5	5	125	10
	2	6	37.6	35.8	26.7	459	35
	3	1.2	25.5	22.2	25	310	23
	4+	4.8	20.3	17.9	30	256	19
	N	84	1011	162	60	1317	
	Total (%)	100 (6)	100 (77)	100 (12)	100 (5)		100
55–64	0	87.7	8.8	5.8	11.5	138	13.2
(18%)	1	7	7.3	12.5	8.8	84	8
	2	1.8	22.6	19.2	16.9	213	20.3
	3	–	24.3	20.2	18.2	227	21.7
	4+	3.5	37	42.3	44.6	385	36.8
	N	57	738	104	148	1047	
	Total (%)	100 (6)	100 (70)	100 (10)	100 (14)		100
65–74	0	93.3	12.5	11.8	7.5	143	16.3
(15%)	1	1.7	13.1	3.9	9.2	92	10.5
	2	–	21.4	25.5	21.5	177	20.2
	3	3.3	18	13.7	21.8	158	18
	4+	1.7	35.1	45.1	39.9	307	35
	N	60	473	51	293	877	
	Total (%)	100 (7)	100 (54)	100 (6)	100 (33)		100
75+	0	98	17	11.1	17	140	23
(11%)	1	–	13	16.7	18	96	15
	2	–	27	22.2	20	127	20
	3	–	15	16.7	16	91	15
	4+	2	28	33.3	29	167	27
	N	43	180	18	380	621	
	Total (%)	100 (7)	100 (29)	100 (3)	100 (61)		100

[a]Single: never married
[b]Married: includes common law
[c]Divorced: includes women who were separated and/or divorced at the time of the survey
[d]No. of children: includes all children ever born alive to women aged 15+
Source: Statistics Canada: 1991 Census of Canada, Public Use Microdata File, Individual File, 0.1% sample.

116   Ingrid Arnet Connidis

TABLE 4.9
Percentage of ever-born siblings by age: Canada, 1990

No. of siblings	Age (years)							
	25–34	35–44	45–54	55–64	65–69	70–74	75–79	80+
0	2	5	5	5	6	4	4	4
1	14	13	16	12	11	8	8	7
2	21	19	15	11	13	11	11	9
3	19	15	14	13	9	12	10	14
4	15	11	10	11	12	10	13	10
5+	30	38	40	48	51	56	53	57

Source: Statistics Canada: 1990 General Social Survey.

network as a result of either childlessness or having only one child. Furthermore, the consequences of marital status for fertility are changing so that being single does not mean being childless for a substantial minority of women. Thus, overall, the proportion of women who will enter old age childless will not increase in the next few decades. Nonetheless, our analysis indicates that nearly one in five women age 75 and over have neither a partner nor a child. Finally, our data on family size indicate that, for the upcoming cohorts of adult children, there will continue to be the possibility of sharing responsibility for parental support with at least one other sibling.

Availability of Siblings

Siblings are not typically included in examinations of informal support but there is evidence of supportive ties between siblings, and changing circumstances such as divorce and smaller family size may alter sibling relationships in the future.[24] As the data in Tables 4.9 and 4.10 show, siblings are available as a potential source of support to the majority of Canadians. The 1990 General Social Survey provides cross-sectional data by age group on both ever-born siblings and living siblings. For ever-born siblings (see Table 4.9), while the percentage of adults with five or more siblings is down, the percentages with one to four siblings is up. The percentage with no siblings has gone down slightly, a function of the baby boom reflected in the youngest two age groups.

Regarding surviving siblings, the 1990 General Social Survey defines

TABLE 4.10
Percentage of living siblings by age: Canada, 1990

No. of siblings	Age (years)							
	25–34	35–44	45–54	55–64	65–59	70–74	75–79	80+
0	0	1	2	3	4	7	14	26
1	15	15	19	14	17	17	22	20
2	22	21	17	16	18	20	20	23
3	20	16	16	16	13	17	16	12
4	15	12	10	13	14	10	9	9
5+	29	36	37	38	34	29	18	14

Source: Statistics Canada: 1990 General Social Survey.

living siblings broadly to include step-, half-, and adopted siblings. Table 4.10 shows quite a different picture for the older age groups because of the death of siblings, but three-quarters of those age 80 and over still have at least one living sibling and over half have more than one. Thus, there are more older persons with a surviving sibling than with a spouse. On balance, these data show the availability of siblings as a potential source of support to most Canadians, including the very old.

Labour-Force Participation

Clearly, labour-force participation competes with the time available for informal support, making shifts over time in rates of working outside the home an important family and policy issue. Among women, increases in paid labour over the past 30 years have been steady and dramatic (see Table 4.11), especially for those women most likely to be meeting the needs of children and / or their older parents. Seventy-nine per cent of women age 25 to 44 in 1991 were in the labour force, over two and a half times the rate (30–31%) of the same age group in 1961. The pace of increased paid labour seems to be slowing down for those age 55 to 64. The decline in employment for the cohort age 45 to 54 in 1981 (55%) ten years later (42%) suggests that this may partly be the result of lay-offs.

The patterns are different for men where labour-force participation has been uniformly high over time (Table 4.12), with most men age 25 to 54 in the labour force. However, participation has declined among

118   Ingrid Arnet Connidis

TABLE 4.11
Percentage of female labour force participation by
age: Canada, 1961–1991

Age (years)	Year			
	1961	1971	1981	1991
25–34	30	42	66	79
35–44	21	41	63	79
45–54	33	41	55	72
55–64	24	33	40	42
65–69	12	12	10	10
70+	4	5	4	4

Source: Statistics Canada: 1961–1991 Census of
Canada.

TABLE 4.12
Percentage of male labour force participation by age:
Canada, 1961–1991

Age (years)	Year			
	1961	1971	1981	1991
25–34	94	93	96	95
35–44	94	93	95	94
45–54	92	91	93	92
55–64	82	80	75	65
65–69	48	37	26	16
70+	18	15	10	8

Source: Statistics Canada: 1961–1991 Census of
Canada.

men age 55 and over. Voluntary early retirement accounts for some of
this change, but involuntary retirement and unemployment following
lay-offs account for a growing number of early exits from the labour
force.[25] In sum, paid labour has gone up dramatically for women of all
ages over the past few decades. At the same time, among older men,
there is a decline in labour-force participation. This may also prove to
be true for those cohorts of women for whom labour-force participation rates have been high at younger ages.

The Implications of Demographic and Social Change for Informal Support and Public Policy

Continuity and Change

The data provided here indicate that the past 30 to 35 years have been marked by significant change and surprising continuity in family trends. When we look at family trends in terms of family composition and not simply rates and averages, it is clear that most older people have – and will continue to have – a substantial number of children and of siblings as potential sources of support. As well, the proportion of older persons who are married has actually gone up. However, divorce rates are also up, and future cohorts of older persons will include more individuals who are dealing with the longer-term consequences of divorce, single parenthood, remarriage, and step-parenting. In the longer-term future, remaining single will be more common and will no longer be equated with being childless. A related trend has been the increase in cohabitation in younger cohorts. This alternative to marriage has consequences beyond the union itself, being less stable over time and resulting in fewer children than is true of marriage.[26]

Quebec set the pace for cohabitation and remains the province with the highest rate of cohabitation in the country.[27] In addition to the difference in sheer numbers, the implications of cohabitation are also different for Quebecers. Quebec's Civil Code accords fewer rights to cohabiting couples than is true of common law, making cohabitation less like marriage in that province. The rationale behind this difference is captured in a statement by Quebec's Department of Justice:[28] 'The law has regulated one union; in the eyes of the law, if you wish to avoid the inconveniences of marriage, then naturally you will enjoy none of its privileges.' At the same time, the fertility rate of common-law unions in Quebec is closer to that of marriages than is true in other provinces,[29] suggesting a greater parallel between cohabitation and marriage there than in the rest of Canada.

As cohabitation becomes a more frequent basis for forming unions and for having and raising children, we must anticipate its longer-term consequences. The greater likelihood of dissolution following a common-law than marital union, coupled with the laxer requirements to provide ongoing support upon separation, makes cohabitation a less secure basis for companionship and financial security in older age. In turn, while the implications for children of such breakups may mirror those of divorce, this remains an open question that requires further study.

The most striking change in the trends studied here is the increase in paid labour among women of all ages. More recently, a notable shift has been the decline in paid labour among older men, a trend that may be occurring for women also but which is harder to detect given the recentness of increases in labour-force participation rates for these women. As well, more older persons will be experiencing the divorce of their children, the birth of grandchildren to single mothers, changes in gender relations among their children, and the paid employment of their daughters as well as their sons. What are the implications of these changes across age groups for informal support? While there is reassurance in knowing that most older persons will continue to have a spouse, children, and siblings, one cannot assume that stability in the availability of these ties ensures stability in the support that these ties provide, given the changes that have occurred.

Data from the public use microdata file show that almost one in five women age 75 and over have neither a spouse nor a child. The remainder of this discussion focuses on the impact of gendered family relations, higher rates of divorce, and labour-force activity on informal support and public policy.

Gendered Family Relations and Social Policy

As others have argued well,[30] assumptions about informal support and the role of women in providing it are central to a variety of state policies including pensions, child care, home care, and community-based services. Thus, discussions of informal support must address the current debate about intergenerational equity and the bigger policy picture, not just policies directed specifically at aiding older persons. The workplace, education, taxation, and benefit entitlements are all appropriate policy targets for redressing current gender (and other) inequities in the responsibility to provide family care.[31] Gender differences also apply to the availability of particular sources of informal support. Men are far more likely to have a spouse in older age and, thus, more likely to receive help from one. However, social change may create different supportive relations between spouses in the future.

Perhaps because the gendered nature of family ties has been slow to change, despite marked changes in other spheres of social life, there is a tendency to focus on policies that facilitate caregiving by women. In turn, research is inclined to implicitly adopt this status quo position by focusing on the availability of women to provide support as a key determinant of whether we have a crisis on our hands. It is also often assumed that a shortage of women to provide support means, by definition, that older persons will be left stranded. Yet, men do provide support when women are not available,[32] although their motivation for providing support and the type of support that they provide may differ from the motivations and approaches of women. For example, regarding motivations to help parents, research suggests that the support offered by daughters is influenced by their affection for their parents while assistance from sons is driven more by a sense of responsibility.[33]

Variations in the gender composition of sibling networks and care provided to parents are telling about both parent–child and sibling relations. In their study of families with sons only, Matthews and Heidorn[34] report that the care provided to parents in such families tends to involve masculine or gender-neutral tasks, to be downplayed by the sons who provide it, to be the outcome of parent–child negotiations rather than negotiations between siblings, and to be geared towards maintaining a parent's independence. While a typical response to such findings would be that parents are missing the more personal forms of care provided by daughters, the authors make the provocative suggestion that 'a feminine style of parent care may in fact be more harmful to parents than a masculine one' because the feminine style is more likely to be overly supportive, undermining the parent's independence.[35] Thus, the key is not necessarily to ensure that sons help in the same way that daughters do but, rather, simply that they become engaged in help even when daughters are present. This requires an equalizing of legitimate excuses[36] in which the facts of labour-force participation or parenting or geographic distance are no more compelling reasons for limited availability as care-providers for daughters or sons. The potential net effect of such a shift would be less help from daughters but more help from sons.

The Impact of Divorce

Our findings show that divorce is not an issue for many current older persons. However, as cohorts with higher divorce rates move into older age, we will confront a new situation of unattached older persons. Divorce may differ from widowhood in its impact, especially in its financial implications for divorced women who, currently at least, do not enjoy the same entitlements as do widowed women. However, if divorce is a long-term status (which is more likely than for widowhood), divorced women may also be long-term labour-force participants familiar with self-sufficiency. This is a somewhat optimistic scenario, given the poor economic situation of many divorced mothers but may apply to some groups. Research on social support shows that the divorced and single rely more than the married on formal support and paid help and less on family.[37] Thus, the absence of a spouse does not necessarily mean relying more on other family members.

The divorce of parents alters the exchanges between them *in both directions*. Generally, divorced parents provide less support to their children than do married parents,[38] whether the divorce occurs while the children are still young[39] or after they have grown up.[40] Divorce when children are young has the most detrimental, long-term consequences for the relationship between fathers and sons.[41] Even when parents divorce later in life, relationship quality, contact, and assistance between parents and children suffer.[42]

In turn, divorce rates in the younger generation may lower the amount of support from children to their older parents[43] and heighten the demand for support from the older to the younger generation as adult children seek financial help, a place to live, and child care. The refilling of the empty nest[44] exemplifies the extension of parenting and the need for public policy-makers to appreciate that supports offered to older persons will benefit younger family members as well. Grandparents, especially maternal grandmothers, are key child-care providers for their grandchildren following the divorce of their children.[45] Here again, we have evidence of older parents providing support to their adult children, in this case, by looking after their grandchildren – an extension of parental responsibility into old age. However, the suggestion that more involvement in caring for grandchildren is a good method for improving the lives of older persons[46] seems somewhat misguided given evidence of the considerable ambivalence felt by grandmothers about taking on major responsibility for their grandchildren.[47] This ambivalence has two sources; the contradiction between grandmothers' expectations of rest in old age and their experience of extensive caregiving to grandchildren, and between their desire to help their grandchildren and their reluctance to acknowledge their child's ineptness as a parent.

The impact of divorce on siblings, a tie available to a majority of Canadian adults, seems to be opposite to its effect on parent–child ties. Siblings who are single, divorced, and childless view siblings as more critical members of their support network,[48] and they are also more likely to offer help to them.[49] As well, it seems that gender is not as central a factor to help exchange between siblings as it is to parent–child exchanges.[50] Thus, it appears that evidence of supportive sibling relationships[51] applies across gender and marital status groups, suggesting that sibling relationships may grow in significance as divorce threatens spousal and parent–child exchanges. Professionals engaged in service delivery of various kinds to older clients should therefore include siblings in their assessment of family-service liaison contacts.

The Impact of Labour Force Participation

The pervasive effect of labour-force participation on families means that we must not underestimate the extent to which family life may be quite different for future cohorts of older persons, despite apparent stability in some of the parameters of family life examined here. Understanding its implications requires a consideration of how various relationships may be negotiated under changing circumstances. While employment limits the time available for meeting familial responsibilities, paid work may also mean the ability to purchase support for family members. Early and, more often, unexpected exit from the labour force also affects familial ties, both directly and, indirectly, through its effect on health and finances.[52]

Increased labour-force participation among women may signal shifts in marital relations in terms of the division of labour based on gender, assumptions about what constitutes being a proper wife or husband, and access to financial resources. Such shifts may have important consequences for caregiving between spouses. For example, there may be both a greater willingness and ability to seek help from other sources, including paid help, if wives do not define their roles primarily in terms of looking after their husband.[53]

The extent of the gendered nature of family life is evident in the fact that labour-force participation among men is not treated as a family issue, paralleling the focus on mothers' work and its potential harmful effects on children without a coincident interest in the impact of fathers' work. Studies show that women in the labour force continue to give extensive care to older family members, altering their work patterns to the point of jeopardizing advancement[54] and shifting styles away from providing all care personally to managing and purchasing alternative sources of care[55] in order to do so. This is similar to the experience of younger parents, particularly mothers, who work out- side the home and pay others to meet some of their children's needs. These mothers understand that a shift in style does not signal the breakdown of the family, nor a lack of love and concern for their chil- dren. Such a shift does herald social change. Although women are not available to personally provide all the needs of their family, they are still very preoccupied with making sure that, when they do not pro- vide care, someone else does.

The management rather than hands-on style of care provision acquired while in the labour force may well extend into retirement. Future cohorts of retired women who, when they were employed, hired others to care for their children and, in some cases, their parents, may be more comfortable not only with purchasing services to care for their mother, but also to care for their spouse and for themselves. However, the management style can only be effective if necessary services and resources are available for orchestration by a care manager. In reality, they often are not, leaving many working women whose parents need care torn between working and quitting a job in order to look after a family member.[56] The challenge to public policy for both young and old alike is to ensure that there are good alternatives available for family members to organize or purchase in the public and private sectors. Legislation concerning pay and pension benefits to those employed in caregiving positions, predominantly women, would improve the avail- ability of such services, provide greater financial security in old age for the women so employed, and improve the tax base needed to fund public services.

Greater involvement in the labour force may limit the time and incli- nation of grandmothers to provide extensive child care to grandchil- dren, even in retirement when they may have their own plans. While frequency of contact with grandchildren does not vary by labour-force participation in one study,[57] retired persons were not distinguished from those who had not been labour-force participants, possibly mut- ing actual differences between them. This is a topic requiring further study.

Unanticipated, early exit from the labour force, observed here for men and women, affects the economic and health status of older per- sons, which affects in turn other family members and alters plans for old age.[58] Early exit from the labour force has been described as a new life-course phase of neither work nor retirement, marked by uncertainty and shifting identities from being retired to being unemployed or unemployable.[59] The objective (e.g., cessation of income at a point when it was expected to peak) and subjective (shifting definitions of one's status) consequences of early retirement can have significant consequences for family ties. Guillemard[60] argues that employment (i.e., access to the labour force by all age groups) must become a central focus of public policy. Farther down the road, retirement age is likely to go up in response to the shrinking labour market as baby boomers retire. This may not be a welcome change among members of cohorts who, unlike their predecessors, began their jobs fully intending to retire in their early or mid-60s (see Chapter 1).

Finally, the impact of combined familial and labour-force commitments extends beyond the confines of family and work. Some argue that more women in the workplace has undermined voluntarism and engagement in the broader community.[61] A hallmark of communities in which there is more extensive civic involvement is equality.[62] When women were typically not in the labour force, their work in the home allowed more time for voluntary commitments by both women and men. Ironically, while heralded as a route to equality, women's workplace involvement has inadvertently underscored gender inequality and the state's view of raising the next generation as a largely private family affair. Until family work becomes more egalitarian, and the state and workplace become more involved in sharing responsibility for child care with families, community volunteer efforts will continue to be threatened by women taking their place in the labour force.[63] As recipients of the volunteer efforts of others, this may leave older persons with less support from the community at large. In the longer run, failure to establish a habit of engagement while in the labour force may lead future seniors to be less active as volunteers than today's older citizens.

Conclusion: Policy Implications

In this analysis, I have taken a broader view of the family by incorporating adult sibling ties and the place of single and childless individuals in the extended family network. Yet, the data examined reflect a traditional view of family, focusing primarily on marriage and childbearing as fundamental family trends. Calls for recognizing diversity in families (see Chapter 7) have become increasingly common and usually refer to accepting structural arrangements other than the traditional nuclear family by including, for example, lone-parent families.[64] Others must also be included. For example, despite the failure of our society to support familial relationships among them, members of the gay and lesbian community often serve as excellent examples of supportive ties. This includes dealing with the challenging effects of AIDS for substantial numbers of gay couples. While Canadian legislators have been reluctant to change long-held definitions of what constitutes marriage and appropriate benefit entitlements for gay and lesbian partners, court decisions and the arbitration of collective agreements have moved in the direction of recognizing such partnerships.[65] Future research and social policy on family ties and informal support must take a more inclusive view and incorporate the familial relationships of gay and lesbian individuals, as partners, parents, siblings, and children.[66]

The fact that older gay and lesbian persons do not differ from their straight peers in levels of depression and support[67] illustrates the ability of individuals to negotiate supportive ties, even when marginalized by the larger society and, in some cases, by immediate family. At the same time, the potential precariousness of family membership is also highlighted by the situation of excluded gay and lesbian sons, daughters, and siblings, underscoring the need for effective social policy to protect all Canadians as they age. The success of many gay and lesbian relationships in providing enduring support attests to the capacity of individuals to act with agency and of the limits of social policy to determine the actions of a targeted group.[68]

Like other marginalized groups, gay and lesbian adults also suggest the potential importance of one's broader community, particularly for those who cannot necessarily turn to family for support. Indeed, what have been termed 'weak' ties with acquaintances and members of voluntary associations are more central to building and maintaining collective efforts and community cohesion than are 'strong' ties to family and close friends.[69] More generally, citizens in communities characterized by traditional views of family life and religion are less engaged in civic life than those in more progressive communities.[70] Thus, quite unexpectedly perhaps, some of the shifts that have been discussed here – more common-law unions, more divorce, and more women in the workplace – may foster more community involvement, a potential benefit to all age groups. We must consider how social policy can best respond to new situations. As Putnam[71] concludes: 'Our responsibility now is to create ... We must figure out what the new institutions will be that fit the new way we are living our lives, while re-creating genuine bonds of community.'

As we look ahead, changing circumstances in our social world can only be expected to lead to changing circumstances in family life. Increased demands for support from family members are as likely to be felt by older parents as by their adult children in the wake of a diminishing safety net, and shifting family relationships. The combination of cutbacks in state-supported policy and programs, the aging of the baby boom, unprecedented labour-force participation among women; early, sometimes unanticipated, retirement; rising rates of divorce, never marrying, and common-law unions; and smaller families make responding to trends related to the informal support of older persons critical in the short and medium run. However, as we investigate public policy options that best meet a changing situation, connecting policy planning and implementation to the daily lives of Canadians must be a priority. As Sarah Matthews[72] observes, 'Social policies that affect the elderly are not implemented anonymously, but in relationships with professionals, friends, neighbors, and family members, in everyday life. To depict the world as sharply divided between public and private is to forget that social policies are implemented by people.'

Notes

1 See Yves Carrière, 'Population Aging and Hospital Days'; Ellen Gee, 'Population and Politics'; Anne Martin-Matthews, 'Intergenerational Caregiving'; Lynn McDonald, 'Alarmist Economics and Women's Pensions'; Barbara A. Mitchell, 'The Refilled "Nest"'; Michael J. Prince, 'Apocalyptic, Opportunistic, and Realistic Demographic Discourse'; Carolyn J. Rosenthal, 'Aging Families,' in Ellen, M. Gee and Gloria M. Gutman, eds., *The Overselling of Population Aging: Apocalyptic Demography, Intergenerational Challenges, and Social Policy* (Don Mills, Ont.: Oxford University Press, 2000).
2 Gee and Gutman, eds, *Overselling of Population Aging.*
3 See Miles Corak, *Government Finances and Generational Equity* (Ottawa: Statistics Canada, 1998); Victor W. Marshall, *The Generations: Contributions, Conflict, Equity* (Ottawa: Division of Aging and Seniors, Health Canada, 1997); Susan A. McDaniel, 'Intergenerational Transfers, Social Solidarity, and Social Policy: Unanswered Questions and Policy Changes,' *Canadian Public Policy / Canadian Journal on Aging* (suppl.) (1997): 1–21.

4 See Anne-Marie Guillemard, 'Equity Between Generations in Aging Societies: The Problem of Assessing Public Policies,' in Tamara K. Hareven, ed.,
   Aging and Generational Relations: Life Course and Cross-Cultural Perspectives
   (New York: Aldine de Gruyter, 1996), 157–76; Marshall, *Generations*; Leroy
   O. Stone, Carolyn J. Rosenthal, and Ingrid Arnet Connidis, *Parent-Child
   Exchanges of Supports and Intergenerational Equity* (Ottawa: Statistics Canada,
   1998).
5 Ingrid Arnet Connidis, *Family Ties and Aging* (Thousand Oaks, Calif.: Sage,
   2001).
6 Anne Martin-Matthews, and Lori D. Campbell, 'Gender Roles, Employment and Informal Care', in Sara Arber and Jay Ginn, eds., *Connecting Gender and Ageing: A Sociological Approach* (Buckingham: Open University
   Press, 1995), 129–43; Anne Scott and G. Clare Wenger, 'Gender and Social
   Support Networks in Later Life', in Sara Arber and Jay Ginn, eds., *Connecting Gender and Ageing: A Sociological Approach* (Buckingham: Open University Press, 1995), 158–72.
7 Anatole Romaniuc, 'Reflection on Population Forecasting: From Prediction
   to Prospective Analysis,' *Canadian Studies in Population* 21, no. 2 (1994): 165–
   80.
8 Ingrid Arnet Connidis, 'Liens familiaux et vieillissement au Canada: constantes et changements des trois dernières décennies,' *Lien social et politiques*
   38 (Autumn 1997): 133–43.
9 See Victor W. Marshall, Sarah H. Matthews, and Carolyn J. Rosenthal, 'Elusiveness of Family Lives: A Challenge for the Sociology of Aging,' in G.L.
   Maddox and M. Powell Lawton, eds., *Annual Review of Gerontology and
   Geriatrics* (New York: Springer, 1993), 39–72.
10 Ingrid Arnet Connidis and Julie A. McMullin, 'Forging Macro-Micro Links:
   Structure, Agency, and the Place of Sociological Ambivalence in Multigenerational Research,' paper presented at the Ambivalence in Intergenerational Relations Workshop, sponsored by the Bronfenbrenner Life-Course
   Centre, Cornell University, Ithaca, NY, December 1998; Sarah H. Matthews
   'Undermining Stereotypes of the Old through Social Policy Analysis,' in J.
   Hendricks and C. Rosenthal, eds., *The Remainder of Their Days: Domestic Policy and Older Families in the United States and Canada* (New York: Garland,
   1993), 105–18.
11 Statistics Canada, *General Social Survey: Family and Friends* (Ottawa: Statistics Canada, 1991).
12 Ingrid Arnet Connidis, *Family Ties and Aging* (Toronto: Harcourt Brace,
   1989); Ingrid Arnet Connidis and Lorraine Davies, 'Confidants and Companions: Choices in Later Life,' *Journal of Gerontology: Social Sciences* 47, no.

3 (1992): S115–S122; Jeffrey W. Dryer, 'The Effects of Illness on the Family,' in Rosemary Blieszner and Victoria Hilkevitch Bedford, eds., *Handbook of Aging and the Family* (Westport, CT: Greenwood Press, 1995), 401–21; Margaret Hellie Huyck, 'Marriage and Close Relationships of the Marital Kind,' in Blieszner and Hilkevitch Bedford, *Handbook of Aging*, 181–20.

13 Ellen Gee, 'Families in Later Life,' in Roderic Beaujot, Ellen M. Gee, Fernando Rajulton, and Zenaida R. Ravanera, eds., *Family over the Life Course: Current Demographic Analysis* (Ottawa: Statistics Canada, 1995), 77–113.

14 Jean Dumas and Alain Bélanger, 'Common-Law Unions in Canada at the End of the 20th Century,' in Jean Dumas and Alain Bélanger, eds., *Report on the Demographic Situation in Canada 1996: Current Demographic Analysis* (Ottawa: Statistics Canada, 1997), 121–81.

15 Jean Dumas and Alain Bélanger, *Report on the Demographic Situation in Canada 1995: Current Demographic Analysis* (Ottawa: Statistics Canada, 1996).

16 Ibid.

17 Ibid.

18 Gee, 'Families in Later Life.'

19 Alain Bélanger, *Report on the Demographic Situation in Canada 1998–1999: Current Demographic Analysis* (Ottawa: Statistics Canada, 1999).

20 Dumas and Bélanger, *Report on the Demographic Situation in Canada 1995.*

21 Gee, 'Families in Later Life.'

22 Roderic Beaujot, 'Family Patterns at Mid-Life: Marriage, Parenting and Working,' in Beaujot et al., *Family Over the Life Course*, 38–75

23 Ibid.

24 Lori D. Campbell, Ingrid Arnet Connidis, and Lorraine Davies, 'Sibling Ties in Later Life: A Social Networks Analysis,' *Journal of Family Issues* 20, no. 1 (1999): 114–48; Ingrid Arnet Connidis, 'Life Transitions and the Adult Sibling Tie: A Qualitative Study,' *Journal of Marriage and the Family* 54 (1992): 972–82; Ingrid Arnet Connidis, and Lori D. Campbell, 'Closeness, Confiding and Contact among Siblings in Middle and Late Adulthood,' *Journal of Family Issues* 16 (1995): S141–S149.

25 Victor W. Marshall, 'The Next Half Century of Aging Research – and Thoughts for the Past,' *Journal of Gerontology: Social Sciences* 50B, no. 1 (1995): S1–S3; Victor W. Marshall, 'Rethinking Retirement: Issues for the Twenty-First Century,' in Ellen M. Gee and Gloria M. Gutman, eds., *Rethinking Retirement* (Vancouver: Simon Fraser University Press, 1995), 55–68.

26 Dumas and Bélanger, 'Common-Law Unions.'

27 Ibid.

28 Government of Quebec, *Vivre à Deux* (Quebec: Department of Justice, 1995), 69.
29 Dumas and Bélanger, 'Common-Law Unions.'
30 See John Myles, 'Editorial. Women, The Welfare State, and Care-Giving,' *Canadian Journal on Aging* 10, no. 2 (1991): 82–5; Hazel Qureshi and Alan Walker, 'Caring for Elderly People: The Family and the State,' in Chris Phillipson and Alan Walker, eds., *Aging and Social Policy: A Critical Assessment* (Brookfield, Vt.: Gower, 1986), 109–127; Alan Walker, 'The Relationship between the Family and the State in the Care of Older People,' *Canadian Journal on Aging* 10, no. 2 (1991): 94–112.
31 Connidis, *Family Ties and Aging*; Ellen M. Gee, 'Demographic Change and Intergenerational Relations in Canadian Families: Findings and Social Policy Implications,' *Canadian Public Policy* 16 (1990): 191–6.
32 Martin-Matthews and Campbell, 'Gender Roles, Employment and Informal Care.'
33 Merril Silverstein, Tonya M. Parrott and Vern L. Bengtson, 'Factors that Predispose Middle-Aged Sons and Daughters to Provide Social Support to Older Parents,' *Journal of Marriage and the Family* 57 (May 1995): 465–75.
34 Sarah H. Matthews and Jenifer Heidorn, 'Meeting Filial Responsibilities in Brothers Only Sibling Groups,' *Journal of Gerontology: Social Sciences* 53B, no. 5 (1998): S278–S286.
35 Ibid.
36 See Janet Finch, *Family Obligations and Social Change* (Cambridge, Mass.: Basil Blackwell / Polity Press, 1989).
37 Ingrid Arnet Connidis and Julie A. McMullin, 'Social Support in Older Age: Assessing the Impact of Marital and Parent Status,' *Canadian Journal on Aging* 13, no. 4 (1994): 510–27.
38 Teresa M. Cooney and Peter Uhlenberg, 'Support from Parents Over the Life Course: The Adult Child's Perspective,' *Social Forces* 71, no. 1 (1992): 63–84.
39 Kris A. Bulcroft and Richard A. Bulcroft, 'The Timing of Divorce: Effects on Parent-Child Relationships in Later Life,' *Research on Aging* 13, no. 2 (1991): 226–43; Peter Uhlenberg, 'The Role of Divorce in Men's Relations with Their Adult Children after Mid-life,' *Journal of Marriage and the Family* 52 (Aug. 1990): 677–88.
40 William S. Aquilino, 'Later Life Parental Divorce and Widowhood: Impact on Young Adults' Assessment of Parent Child Relations,' *Journal of Marriage and the Family* 56 (Nov. 1994): 908–22; Gayle Kaufman and Peter Uhlenberg, 'Effects of Life Course Transitions on the Quality of Relationships between

Adult Children and Their Parents,' *Journal of Marriage and the Family* 60 (Nov. 1998): 924–38.

41 Bulcroft and Bulcroft, 'Timing of Divorce'; Uhlenberg, 'Role of Divorce.'

42 Aquilino, 'Later Life Parental Divorce and Widowhood'; Kaufman and Uhlenberg, 'Effects of Life Course Transitions.'

43 Victor G. Cicirelli, 'A Comparison of Helping Behaviour to Elderly Parents of Adult Children with Intact and Disrupted Marriages,' *Gerontologist* 23, no. 6 (1983): 619–25.

44 Monica Boyd and Edward T. Pryor, 'The Cluttered Nest: The Living Arrangements of Young Canadian Adults,' *Canadian Journal of Sociology* 14 (1989): 461–77.

45 James W. Gladstone, 'Factors Associated with Changes in Visiting between Grandmothers and Grandchildren Following an Adult Child's Marriage Breakdown,' *Canadian Journal on Aging* 6, no. 2 (1987): 117–27; James W. Gladstone, 'Perceived Changes in Grandmother-Grandchild Relations Following a Child's Separation or Divorce,' *Gerontologist* 28, no. 1 (1988): 66–72.

46 Phyllis Moen and Kay B. Forest, 'Family Policies for an Aging Society: Moving to the Twenty-First Century,' *Gerontologist* 35, no. 6 (1995): 825–30.

47 Margaret Platt Jendrek, 'Grandparents Who Parent Their Grandchildren: Circumstances and Decisions,' *Gerontologist* 34, no. 2 (1994): 206–16.

48 Ingrid Arnet Connidis, and Lorraine Davies, 'Confidants and Companions in Later Life: The Place of Family and Friends,' *Journal of Gerontology: Social Sciences* 45, no. 4 (1990): S141–S149; Connidis and Davies, 'Confidants and Companions.'

49 Ingrid Arnet Connidis, 'Sibling Support in Older Age,' *Journal of Gerontology: Social Sciences* 49 (1994): S309–S317.

50 Ibid.

51 Ibid.; Connidis, 'Life Transitions and the Adult Sibling Tie'; Connidis and Campbell, 'Closeness, Confiding and Contact among Siblings in Middle and Late Adulthood'; Campbell et al., 'Sibling Ties in Later Life.'

52 Marshall, 'The Next Half Century of Aging Research – and Thoughts for the Past'; Marshall, 'Rethinking Retirement.'

53 Deborah L. O'Connor, 'Supporting Spousal Care-givers: Exploring the Meaning of Service Use,' *Families in Society: The Journal of Contemporary Human Services* 76 (May 1995): 295–305.

54 Anne Martin Matthews and Lori D. Campbell, 'Gender Roles, Employment and Informal Care'; Anne Martin Matthews, Anne and Carolyn Rosenthal, 'Balancing Work and Family in an Aging Society: The Canadian Experience,' in G. Maddox and P. Lawton, eds., *Annual Review of Gerontology and Geriatrics*, Vol. 13 (New York: Springer, 1993), 96–122.

55 Elaine M. Brody, Mortan H. Kelban, Pauline T. Johnsen, Christine Hoffman, and Claire B. Schoonover, 'Work Status and Parent Care: A Comparison of Four Groups of Women,' *Gerontologist* 27, no. 2 (1987): 201–8; Elaine M. Brody and Claire B. Schoonover, 'Patterns of Parent Care when Adult Daughters Work and when They Do Not,' *Gerontologist* 26, no. 4 (1986): 372–81.
56 Brody et al., 'Work Status and Parent Care.'
57 Peter Uhlenberg and Bradley G. Hammill, 'Frequency of Grandparent Contact with Grandchild Sets: Six Factors that Make a Difference,' *Gerontologist* 38, no. 3 (1998): 276–85.
58 Marshall, 'The Next Half Century'; Marshall, 'Rethinking Retirement.'
59 Guillemard, 'Equity between Generations in Aging Societies.'
60 Ibid.
61 Robert D. Putnam, *Bowling Alone: The Collapse and Revival of American Community* (Toronto: Simon and Schuster, 2000).
62 Robert D. Putnam, *Making Democracy Work* (Princeton, NJ: Princeton University Press, 1993).
63 Robert D. Putnam, *The Decline of Civil Society: How Come? So What?* (Ottawa: Ministry of Supply and Services Canada, 1996).
64 Moen and Forest, 'Family Policies for an Aging Society.'
65 Donald D. Carter, 'Employment Benefits for Same-Sex Couples: The Expanding Entitlement,' *Canadian Public Policy* 24 (1998): 107–17.
66 Katherine R. Allen and David H. Demo, 'The Families of Lesbians and Gay Men: A New Frontier of Family Research,' *Journal of Marriage and the Family* 57 (Feb. 1995): 111–27.
67 Rachelle Dorfman, Karina Walters, Patrick Burke, Lovida Hardin, Theresa Karanik, John Raphael, and Ellen Silverstein, 'Old, Sad, and Alone: The Myth of the Aging Homosexual,' *Journal of Gerontological Social Work* 24, no. 1/2 (1995): 29-44.
68 See Matthews, 'Undermining Stereotypes.'
69 Mark S. Granovetter, 'The Strength of Weak Ties,' *American Journal of Sociology* 78 (1973): 1368–80, 1376; Putnam, *Making Democracy Work.*
70 Putnam, *Making Democracy Work.*
71 Putnam, *The Decline of Civil Society.*
72 Matthews, 'Undermining Stereotypes.'

5. Aging and Productivity: What Do We Know?

Joel Prager

Introduction: Population Aging, Work, and Productive Capacity

Our society stands at a demographic watershed. Although the twentieth century witnessed two terrible world wars, holocausts, Spanish influenza and HIV/AIDS pandemics, it also saw the greatest recorded increase in human longevity.[1] Canada's population has certainly followed the trend. In 1851 people age 65 and over accounted for 2.7 per cent of the country's population. By 1991 that proportion had climbed to 12 per cent; it is now projected to reach 22 per cent in 2036. In 1991 Canadians age 75, 80, 85, and 90 could expect on average to live another 11, 9, 6, and 5 years respectively. Meanwhile the proportion of young people in the population has declined. In 1986 children from 0–15 years accounted for 23 per cent of the population, but only 21 per cent in 1991. From 1981 to 1991 the proportion of the population between 15 and 24 fell by 18 per cent. As a result, the median age of the population has risen from 17 (1851) to 26 (1971) to 34 (1992), and is projected to climb to 45 by 2036. Accepting the United Nations' definition of an aging society as one in which 7 per cent or more of the population is 65 or older, Canada is well on the way to becoming a 'geriatric' society.[2]

It is therefore reasonable to ask, What are the likely consequences of these marked demographic changes – changes that some demographers have called 'the plasticity of mortality at older ages'? It is not surprising that some practitioners of the 'dismal science' of economics have predicted trouble ahead, given the increasing number of older workers and large number of early retirees expected over the next two decades. While mandatory retirement at age 65 may have made sense in the first half of the twentieth century, when younger workers greatly outnumbered older workers, it might be inappropriate for the twenty-first century.[3] It is frequently forgotten why Chancellor Bismarck, who introduced the first publicly funded old age security system in the late-nineteenth century, chose 65 as the age for eligibility. Bismarck's statisticians assured him that few Prussians would reach it, and that the fortunate few who did would not live long. Bismarck did not have to worry about having an ample supply of workers to replace those who retired or expired. But Bismarck's economy, demographic pressures, and policy options reflect a different time and place. Ours is a twenty-first-century, global, high-tech economy. His was an industrializing, manufacturing one. Our workforce is increasingly getting older and appears to be shrinking; his was rapidly growing, filled with young workers. But is this really a problem? And if it is, how bad a problem is it likely to be?

Let us begin by looking at some numbers. Demographers estimate that by 2020 Canada will have one worker for every three non-workers. For Jacques Henripin, such dramatic shifts in Canada's dependency ratios will likely impose serious financial constraints in the future: 'the more a population is aged, the less it can rest.'[4] As for other economically developed countries, a recent study by the Organization for Economic Cooperation and Development (OECD) concludes:

'The ageing of populations will put pressures on governments' tax and spending systems in nearly all OECD countries, requiring major changes to existing social systems if substantial increases in public debt are to be avoided. Private savings may also fall, to the extent that the elderly save less ... Ageing populations will ... have major effects on the growth of productive potential and living standards in all OECD and non-OECD countries.

Without sustained improvements in factor productivity growth or changes in labour force participation rates, output growth in the OECD is likely to slow down over coming decades. In the absence of specific policy adjustments, ageing populations will also tend to reduce the growth of living standards in OECD as the output from any given number of workers is divided by a greater total population. Thus the direct mechanical effect of projected increases in the dependency ratio from current levels would lead to relative reductions in the levels of GDP per capita of around 10, 18 and 23 per cent for the United States, the European Union and Japan.'[5]

A recent study by the National Bureau of Economic Research is no more reassuring. All of the ten industrially advanced countries examined registered a steep decline in labour-force participation rates for those age 65 and older, and also for those between 45 and 59. This labour-force exodus resulted in 'unused productive capacity,' ranging from 67 per cent in Belgium, to roughly 40 per cent in Canada, to 22 per cent in Japan. The study concludes that unless 'generous' pension benefits (which encourage early retirement) are reversed, the 'potential productive capacity' of a country's labour force will continue to fall in the years ahead.[6]

Productivity Issues in Historical Context

Not all economists are convinced that the early retirement of older workers from the workforce is the real problem. Some worry that, in the context of technological change and increasing global competition, older workers will become a productivity liability, undermining a country's comparative advantage. William Johnston warns:

'The challenge that industrialized nations may face in preserving their competitive positions as their workforces' age may be stiffened by the high costs of older workers and older societies. Older workers typically have higher wages because of seniority systems, and their pension and health care costs escalate during the later years of their working lives. As more workers in industrialized nations retire toward the close of the century, national health and pension taxes in these nations may rise as well. Unless these rising costs are offset by productivity gains, employers and nations that have older work forces may lose their competitive leadership in industries with standardized production technologies.[7]

Alan Reynolds, Director of the Hudson Institute, strongly disagrees with this assessment. He is not at all sure that an aging population is a productivity problem. He observes that 'although the sheer numbers of workers will be growing relatively slowly in comparison with the seventies and eighties, the aging of the labor force has the potential to augment the otherwise inadequate numbers of skilled workers.'[8] Best of all, is that 'well-educated workers typically delay retirement, presumably because their work is more enjoyable, pays a higher salary, or both.'[9] For Reynolds, older workers possess years of work experience and on-the-job expertise, and are dependable employees with a proven track record of loyalty and dedication. Why should these qualities now be seen as burdens? Indeed, why should governments, employers, and economists not recognize the productive potential of older workers?

If we are to believe these economists and demographers, the new millennium is likely to bring with it serious aging and productivity problems. Concern about the size of the workforce and the decline in productivity is not, however, a new phenomenon. Economic historians, for example, have long sought to link changes in productivity, investment, capital formation, and the level of poverty with changes in the rate of population of growth. Thomas Malthus proposed that mortality controlled population pressures and the grim reaper was responsible for spurts of economic growth and development. Malthus, it should be recalled, perceived an unending, vicious cycle between population growth, food supply, and economic well-being. This was mankind's economic cross to bear. Malthus's apocalyptic forecasts of economic stagnation and the population conundrum continue to attract a significant number of supporters.

Phyliss Deane and W.A. Cole, in an updated, neo-Malthusian version of this argument write: 'The significant variable in the long preindustrial secular swings in productivity seems to have been the rate of population growth. When population rose, product per head fell: when population fell, product per head rose.' It would therefore appear that, cliche aside, the more things change, the more they remain the same.[10]

These authors, however, were primarily interested in population changes during the course of the Industrial Revolution and what they saw as the 'demographic transition' taking place; very little attention was given to the productivity growth or marginal product of relative age cohorts. The composition of the labour force and how and to what extent the variability of cohort size influences productivity rates were not examined. Instead, these researchers looked at British fertility, mortality and morbidity rates over several hundred years and correlated their impact on the rate of industrialization, productivity per capita, and per capita monetary income. Life expectancy was short, and there were few older workers in the labour force to worry about.[11]

Neoclassical economists have tried to fill this knowledge gap. They have long assumed that an inverse relationship exists between an aging workforce and labour productivity. In a classic study done more than thirty years ago examining the economics of aging, Michael Brennan and his associates argue that economists, beginning with Adam Smith, were correct in characterizing the market as both supreme and uncaring.[12] Age did not confer any special benefits in a world where efficiency, change, competition, and profit were the rules of the game. Try as they might, neither workers, be they young or old, nor governments could change the immutable economic rules that governed the universe. Older workers would inevitably become less productive and, their worth to their employers would diminish in accordance with their falling absolute and marginal output. True, the majority of older workers, they agreed, had more or less 'paid their way' when it came to pension benefits and retirement income, but they were now no longer attractive from a productivity point of view. They were past their working prime. As the old refrain goes, 'No one wants you when you're old and grey.' Metaphorically speaking, older workers had entered into a 'Darwinian' contract with their employers and the market. When these workers were no longer productive, it was time to go, time to call it quits and retire, or to be pushed out. Only those who were productive could expect to survive and have a job. Older workers had understood and accepted this.

Michael J. Brennan et al. suggest that even if some older workers were still productive and loyal to their firms when compared with their younger counterparts, there were 'other' economic factors that made their continued employment too costly for employers. They claim that 'In a dynamic economy, the demand for particular products is constantly changing and productivity methods are revised. Thus jobs are abolished in some areas or firms and created in others. All workers are subject to these forces of the market and must accept relocation ... From the employers' perspective, an older worker is more costly to hire on the open market, even if he is as productive as younger job applicants, because of his limited work horizon under the existence of prevailing retirement income systems.'[13]

A more recent version of the Brennan argument can be found in the work of the distinguished labour economist Stephen Peitchinis. For Peitchinis there is no mystery about the future productivity performance of older workers. Experience has taught us, he asserts, that as a workforce ages, productivity inevitably declines. Age may bring wisdom, but it also brings with it technical obsolescence and physical incapacity. As much as we would like to think otherwise, there is no getting around the fact that 'the relationship between an aging labour force and productivity is unalterably negative. Nothing can be done to reverse this short of inducing aging workers to take early retirement and vacate positions in the job structure for younger workers.'[14]

He identifies two reasons, both empirically derived, for the 'negative relationship' between an aging workforce and productivity. Like Brennan, Peitchinis believes that age does not bring with it technological know-how and sophistication. And in a marketplace dominated by high technology, the 'technopeasant' is expendable. We cannot halt globalization or the computer revolution. The Luddite, like the dinosaur, is extinct. Every new advance in technology, as history has shown, brings with it not only economic benefits but costs as well.[15] Technologically speaking, the overwhelming majority of older workers are over-the-hill, fossils-in-waiting, as more complex and demanding technology is introduced to the shopfloor. In the past, because of the technology available and the pace of change, younger workers were hired to supplement older workers. Now they are hired to replace them. Even today's better educated workforce is hard-pressed to keep up with the rapid technological changes taking place. Technology is not only changing the nature and organization of work, but it is eliminating many jobs and job skills, and older workers are the most vulnerable.

James Surowiecki agrees with Peitchinis. In the 'new' economy, he claims: 'Innovation replaces tradition. The present – or perhaps the future – replaces the past. Nothing matters so much as what will come next, and what will come next can only arrive if what is here now gets overturned. While this makes the system a terrific place for innovation, it makes it a difficult place to live, since most people prefer some measure of security about the future to a life lived almost in constant uncertainty.'[16]

Is it therefore fair to say that older workers are simply helpless victims caught in amoral economic forces beyond their control? Is there nothing they can do to help themselves? Or are these 'old timers' responsible for the job and productivity loss that awaits them? Are they unwilling to keep up-to-date with the rapid, indeed, revolutionary advances now taking place in computerization, just-in-time production, informatics, and digitilization? Most studies, as we shall see, suggest that, as a group, they have opted out of the economic revolution now taking place. Many economists following Peitchinis assume that older workers 'find it difficult to adapt to new instruments and processes, new forms of work organization, new expectations, and new relationships.'[17] Yet, empirically, there is little quantitative evidence to validate such a claim. What we have is assertion, not scientific demonstration.

Few dispute that we are just entering what may be called the 'new economy.' Many (but not all) contemporary observers believe that as a consequence of the 'dot.com/e-mail revolution' many, if not most of the jobs that will garner status, deference, and income in the twenty-first century will go to those who are highly trained 'symbol analysts,' that is, those workers who have mastered the 'ins' and 'outs' of software and high technology. It is these people with their special skills who will ultimately determine a firm's or a country's productivity and competitiveness; who 'wins' and who 'loses' in the global economy. According to these commentators, who will be employed, fired, forced to retire at an early age, or encouraged to remain on the job beyond the statutory retirement age will depend on the mastering of highly prized technological skills, skills which will ineluctably dominate and become synonymous with the 'new economy.'[18]

Forecasting the future is, however, a risky business at the best of times, and it is easy to confuse a trend with destiny or with caprice. Economists and demographers, not surprisingly, are masters of qualifying and hedging their assessments of things to come while trying to appear scientific and confident. Unfortunately, their track record leaves much to be desired. With this in mind, Paul Krugman warns that 'The best way to describe the flawed vision of fin-de-siecle futurists is to say that, with few exceptions, they expected the coming of an "immaculate" economy – an economy in which people would be largely emancipated from a grubby involvement with the physical world ... Most important of all, the prophets of an "information economy" seem to have forgotten basic economics. When something is abundant, it also becomes cheap. A world awash in information will be a world in which information per se has very little market value.'[19]

Still it is important to recognize that Krugman's view of the information revolution is not widely accepted. Most economists believe that the 'icon economy' confirms the importance of human capital and worker training as an investment decision. A company invests in training because it expects that the costs incurred during the training period will be repaid handsomely by future gains in productivity and profits. When an employer decides to invest in training, the question that he or she asks is: How much will it cost, and *cui bono*, who benefits, how fast, and by how much? The decision to train employees regardless of age is never made in a vacuum, and it is not gratuitous. There is always a bottom line. The pessimists argue that additional and continuous (life-long) training for older employees may not be economically sound if an older workforce is not likely to pay back the costs for training.[20]

Given that the Canadian population and workforce are aging, can we say that Canada is in danger of becoming a geriatric or wheelchair society? Does the remarkable increase in the longevity of substantial numbers of older people invalidate the long-held belief that 'mortality at older ages is intractable'? Is it reasonable to assume that unless massive immigration takes place or a catastrophe occurs (e.g., disease or world war), the demographic and productivity forecasts are inevitable and cannot be reversed?[21] Moreover, as a consequence of this demographic shift, will Canada's labour market, its modes of production and productive capacity be radically restructured, if not reinvented? Will our standard of living plummet? And will governments find themselves overwhelmed by the costs required to support a large population of senior citizens dependent on a myriad of expensive public services?

It is important to remember that these vexing questions are not entirely new even though they seem unprecedented both in scope and magnitude and in urgent need of answers. Conventional economic theory and methodology have long tried to deal with the vectors of economic and demographic change, to shed light on what is happening and likely to happen. John Maynard Keynes, perhaps the twentieth century's greatest economist, wrote not long after the First World War: 'The great events of history are often due to secular changes in the growth of population and other fundamental economic causes, which, escaping by their gradual character the notice of contemporary observers, are attributed to the follies of statesmen and the fanaticism of atheists.'[22]

Demography, it would seem, may be destiny after all. Certainly, Keynes considers it a driving force that often escapes 'contemporary observers.' In this instance, we are not, however, dealing with the overall growth of populations that, until recently, attracted the lion's share of scholarly resources and political concern. Economists and demographers feared that 'high fecundity, high fertility' would throttle productive performance and stifle economic growth. There was the spectre of 'lebensraum' wars, a 'third world' uprising, and widespread political chaos. Today, however, attention has shifted to assessing the economic and social impact of the 'birth dearth' and the explosive growth of older age cohorts, especially those over age 55, in mature, 'modern' economies. In particular, if the growth of the baby-boom generation can drastically reduce productivity, as many economists and demographers seem to believe, and demography, as some argue, is the leading cause for the 'economic events of history,' is it reasonable to assume that tipping the scale at the other end of the age pyramid will some-how leave the level of labour productivity unscathed? Does a demo-graphic problem, in short, require a demographic 'solution'? And what should that solution be – having more babies? more immigrants?

For Richard Easterlin, it is demography, and not, as others contend, the macroeconomy or technology that will decisively affect economic behaviour and the productivity of tomorrow's workforce. It is not that these other forces are unimportant – they are, but it is demography that will be *primus inter pares*. The size of the baby-boom generation, suggests Easterlin, was in large part responsible for the relatively poor performance that nearly all industrialized countries experienced over the past thirty years. High and sustained unemployment and under-employment, reduced lifetime earnings, diminished opportunities for promotion and career development, and stagnating productivity can all be traced to the absolute size of the workforce, and not to changes in the composition of the workforce, that is, the 'greying' of the work-force. The 1970s and 1980s saw the supply of workers outstripping the demand for workers. Large numbers of younger workers, and not older workers, were the real problem. The baby boomers were respon-sible for high crime, illegitimacy, and divorce rates that characterized the last quarter of the twentieth century. This group had by far the highest drug use and based on the number of felonies per capita com-mitted during this period, was also the most violent. Equally impor-tant, tough competition for jobs lowered expectations for this age cohort when it came to employment, income, and status. In addition, as a group these workers were not well trained. This explained why productivity grew slowly, despite the large number of young entrants into the labour market. As a consequence, younger workers were likely to defer marriage and have fewer children. All of these factors, Easter-lin concludes, will lead to a 'baby bust,' and as the surfeit of workers recede, both young and old, we shall once again enter an economic growth / high productivity cycle. In short, the traditional boom-and-bust business cycles do not depend, despite what economists tell us, primarily on technology, investment, and capital formation, but to a large extent on demographic forces and their impact on the total size of the workforce.[23]

Easterlin's analysis raises serious questions. Did the pre–baby boom generation do well because older workers were in short supply after the First World War and the 30 to 100 million deaths caused by the Spanish influenza pandemic of 1918? Can we assume, as Easterlin does, that the post–baby boom generation will be very productive because of its diminished size? Can we expect an optimal balance to be struck between the supply of jobs and the demand for work? Is there really an optimal labour-force size, or age-cohort distribution, or median age that can achieve maximum productivity, while at the same time avoiding rising inflation and high unemployment? If so, what is the magic number? Will skill training, education, and the rapid introduction of new, labour-saving technology not make a significant difference when it comes to accelerating productivity growth? If they do, how large will this difference be relative to the demographic changes now taking place? Easterlin, unfortunately, does not provide us with unambiguous answers to these questions.

If we turn back to Keynes and his theory about the dynamics of secular change, a careful reading reveals that Keynes does not suggest that demographic changes alone can bring about long-term ('secular') economic restructuring. Implicit in his assessment of how and why things change is technological innovation. Along with demography 'fundamental economic causes' are very important in shaping tomorrow's economy. But what are these 'fundamental causes'? For the overwhelming majority of economists the answer is technological innovation. These economists believe that Keynes was really talking about technology, and they agree with his 'demographic-technological' growth partnership as the basis of economic growth and development. William J. Baumol, Edward N. Wolff, and Anne Batey Blackman in their ground-breaking study on productivity, declare: 'For real economic miracles one must look to productivity growth. And economic miracles it has indeed provided.'[24] So if we are looking for an 'economic miracle,' we cannot simply say that demography is destiny. Suddenly, we find ourselves back in the world of 'it depends.'

The Optimists versus the Pessimists

It would be wrong to conclude that there is no consensus on the roles that demography and technical innovation play in producing long-term economic growth, in influencing labour participation and productivity rates, and how important these factors are to creating a country's standard of living. Most economists and demographers, usually fall somewhere in the middle, and rarely take an 'either/or' position. There is no established method for thinking about aging and productivity. Economists and demographers have yet to provide us with an empirically validated theory or reliable model that can guide decision-makers into choosing the 'right' programs, policies, and practices needed to prevent or mitigate a possible longevity crisis. The 'gathering storm' school believes that if governments fail to act or act too slowly we face a major economic crisis. They contend that this crisis will soon accelerate and become increasingly 'nasty and brutish,' and that it will hang over us for much of the twenty-first century, as the baby boomers begin to reach the age of retirement.

The first order of business for responsible government is to determine whether an aging workforce presents the clear and present danger of a productivity crisis. But there are two other issues, more subtle but no less demanding, that will also need to be addressed: Should change come from the top, that is should management and not government make and direct the human resource, technological, and organizational changes required in a rapidly evolving global economy? Or should companies and their managers, in close cooperation with government, concentrate on winning the active 'involvement' of their older workers by introducing changes to enhance productivity and competitiveness in the marketplace? It is not simply a question of intervention but whether appropriate interventions should be implemented from the top down or the bottom up. At the present time, we are in an academic no-man's land, and management specialists are just beginning to recognize the seriousness of the challenge to better define these problems.[25]

It should come as no surprise that both the public and private sectors have regularly turned to management consultants and academic specialists to provide them with the data, findings, and recommendations to make informed choices and policy decisions. In this section we will explore what the experts believe is happening and what remedies they think are required. Our approach will be to dichotomize the conflicting and often incompatible views on aging and productivity into two camps, the optimists and pessimists. We are convinced this can be done without simplifying clashing positions and reducing different assumptions to the point of caricature. Such a dichotomy, we further believe, may help decision-makers better understand the uneasy compromises they may be forced to make in pursuit of a desirable policy mix. Both pessimists and optimists like to think that they are arguing from what may be called 'laws of necessity' derived from immutable, universal economic laws. In truth, much of the current debate about the impact of an aging workforce on future productivity and what public policies, if any, need to be considered and introduced, are based not on solid, replicable, empirical, and inductive research, but rather on competing economic theories and 'what if' assumptions about human behaviour.

A key issue in the debate between optimists and pessimists concerns the role of government, that is, what governments can and cannot do to accelerate productivity. This problem has long been hotly debated among economists. Keynes, for example, optimistically believed that government intervention could significantly reduce the harmful affects of secular economic changes that in the past had been fatalistically accepted. His view, while accepted by a substantial number of social scientists, has not gone unchallenged. Such well-known Nobel laureates as Hayek and Mises (leaders of the 'Austrian School'), Stigler and Friedman (from the 'Chicago School'), argue that the cures through government intervention proposed by Keynes and his followers are worse than the disease. They have strongly opposed government intervention, on the grounds that there is very little governments can do to positively control the force or direction of the economy. Intervention may be well-meaning, but it is a grand delusion. Experience, they tell us, has demonstrated that 'command economies' with their bureaucratic planners sooner or later collapse, making everyone poorer and life harder. For pessimists, who not surprisingly prefer to be called 'realists,' only the genius of the market can deal with the complexity of a modern economy, and by extension, with the aging/productivity conundrum. After all, there are limits to what governments can do, and there is no shame in accepting this.

Robert Solow, who is not an economic pessimist, puts the case plainly when he confesses, 'Making productivity rise is not an easy matter. If it were, why would we have not done it already?'[26] For Solow the prospects for successful government intervention to improve productivity appear to be slim, based on past performance. Where indeed are the successes that seem to justify government intervention? If one accepts the pessimists' argument that governments cannot intervene effectively into the marketplace or bend immutable economic laws to their will, then massive, publicly financed training initiatives will not make older workers more productive or decrease the expected gaps in output per older worker. Optimists reply that knowledge is power and research can provide the answers that will ensure government policies help productivity rise. The market is not, despite what the pessimists think, a miracle worker.

Given the demographic shift now taking place and the debate over falling productivity and an aging workforce, it is easy to feel that we are drifting on an uncharted course filled with potential dangers. The optimists, however, do not see hazards ahead. They see the benefits of downsizing the labour force because it will accelerate investment in, and create a greater reliance on, labour-saving technology. Technology will make us more efficient, more productive, more competitive, and the computer revolution will provide the income and revenues needed to ensure that our senior citizens enjoy a comfortable old age. Optimists point out that time and again, apocalyptic prophets have claimed 'limits to growth' and they have been discredited. Why should we listen to them now?

The pessimists respond that there is a very high probability that technological transformation will, among other things, bring with it growth in joblessness. They claim a large number of retirees will find themselves with a great deal of time on their hands. Furthermore, the dangers of intergenerational and intragenerational rivalries will likely increase as older, poorer retirees require more public support to make ends meet and, in effect, they will become wards of the state. People who lose their jobs will find themselves treated as poor relatives; they will lack status, income, and deference. Even if productivity does not plummet, we can expect growing joblessness to accelerate tensions and impose heavy financial pressures that will, in turn, be passed onto industry and the working public. Keeping older workers in the workforce is the best way to avoid 'self-inflicted wounds' and a proven way to reduce public expenditures and taxes. It does not take a rocket scientist to discover that the longer older workers work and receive a paycheque, the more taxes they will pay and the less they will receive in benefits from government.

Older Workers and Alternative Views on Work

Optimists argue that demographic and economic changes will eventually enhance the 'civic culture' by encouraging large numbers of retirees to become volunteers and engage in a host of needed public activities and projects. 'Productive aging,' as defined by A.R. Herzog, is 'any activity that produces goods or services, whether paid or not, including activities such as housework, child care, voluntary work, and help to family and friends.'[27] Contrary to what many economists think, optimists assert that volunteer work has market value and, moreover, such activities have become a 'mainstay of society.'

Volunteers, many of whom are retirees, are actually contributing to Canada's productive output. Unfortunately, we have not yet successfully quantified the dollars-and-cents value of such 'non-dollar, non-wage' activities. One attempt by Statistics Canada to put a value on housework finds that it is worth $211 to $319 billion a year, and consumes nearly 25 billion hours of labour. The authors of that report go on to say that, taken at face value, these sums are the equivalent of between 30 and 46 per cent of gross domestic product. Furthermore, as a percentage of GDP, this 'unpaid domestic work is worth between one-half and three-quarters of what the market actually pays workers for wages and salaries.'[28] Optimists declare that this is just the tip of the iceberg, and they frequently cite a study by Kevin Coleman that examines the value of non-wage activities of older Americans as a promise of the third sector's productive potential. Coleman reports that, the 'cost-to-purchase value' of caregiving and volunteering activities was US $102 billion in 1990, nearly 2 per cent of the $5.5 trillion GDP for that year.[29] The productivity of volunteer activities translates into big dollar savings and should be recognized and included in the calculation of GDP.

Pessimists, however, question the value of such studies, and argue that they are distractions away from the problems of jobs, wages, and productivity that must sooner or later be confronted by the public, government, employers, and older workers. They suggest that most of the studies valuing non-wage, non-employment volunteer activities performed by retirees rely on dubious assumptions, free-wheeling statistical techniques and methodologies, and sleight-of-hand definitions that are too broad to be meaningful. For the pessimists it is hard to distinguish whether some voluntary activities are production or consumption functions. To be sure, private motives do translate into wealth creation, producing goods and services, profits, and wages. These are relatively easy to see, and economists have lots of experience when it comes to comparing and contrasting various factor costs and the value they add to the finished product. Difficult as it sometimes is, economists have developed techniques that measure the value of inputs and outputs. However, they have little experience when it comes to accurately quantifying the output of the volunteer sector.

So, what do these numbers really mean? How reliable are they? If an act is voluntary, why should it have a price assigned to it in the first place? If such non-paid work turns out to be detrimental or demonstrates mixed success, should it be calculated as a loss of productivity?

Should it be amortized? In short, how do we measure this non-wage productivity so that it makes economic sense? Are all volunteer activities 'productive,' or are some more productive than others? Perhaps the biggest problem that pessimists have with redefining work to include volunteer productivity is that it 'monetizes' all human non-economic activities and relations.

Pessimists focus on the potentially destabilizing impact that a large number of unemployed retirees will have, not only on the economy but on government as well. They fear that this group of non-workers will require large-scale, ongoing government intervention. Above all, these analysts expect that governments will be forced to develop programs to redistribute income. If politicians want to remain in power, they will be under enormous pressure to act aggressively to contain the economic and social fallout caused by the disruptive demographic and economic changes that Keynes talks about. Thus, the 'real' problem that awaits Canada is not the fall in productivity caused by an aging workforce, which Peitchinis, for example, calls a 'phantom problem,' but the coming challenge to put in place an affordable and financially sustainable income maintenance program that will enable retirees not to sink into poverty and despair.[30] Implicit is the idea that the productivity 'war' has already been lost, and we have little choice but to deal as best we can with the casualties.

Again, one may ask why should policy-makers accept such a bleak view of things to come? Pessimists respond that older workers are less willing to move occupationally and geographically to improve their job prospects. 'Reduced occupational and geographic mobility, impairs adjustment [to] the market and to changing conditions with negative effects on productivity and the rate of economic growth.'[31] Older workers cannot have their cake and eat it too. Simply put, if they don't move where the prospective jobs are and if they are unwilling to market themselves aggressively, then they will increasingly become *personae non grata* to prospective employers as they approach the age of retirement. Even their old jobs are no longer secure. Kremer and Maskin report that wage inequality increases with technological change as does the pressure on employers to apply tighter 'sorting' criteria for hiring, training, and firing staff. Career paths and long-term commitments between employers and employees regarding job security and seniority can no longer be taken for granted.[32] Thus, many older employees cannot stay on, and given the diminution of job prospects because of tough 'sorting' criteria, they are not eager to relocate.

Homo Economicus and Early Retirement

One may ask, Why should older workers be resistant to learning new technologies and retool to insure continued employment and high wages? Pessimists answer that this behaviour demonstrates 'enlightened self-interest' and confirms Adam Smith's premise that men and women are economic animals (*homo economicus*). While the drop in the labour productivity of older workers may be inevitable like the cycles of business, the resistance to retooling is rational when seen through the eyes of older workers close to retirement. The withdrawal from the workforce en masse and the productivity-reducing behaviour of older workers demonstrate the power of the cost-benefit analysis individual workers engage in when making decisions about retirement, labour-force participation, and pensions. Peitchinis, for example, writes:

> Superficially, these characteristics appear largely sociological and cultural. They are not. Decisions by older workers on retraining and educational upgrading, or on relocation and changing occupation, are motivated by sound economic rationale. Such decisions involve varying amounts of imputed costs. The recovery of these costs depends on the increment in pay likely to result from the decision, and length of time remaining in employment. The fewer the number of years of employment left, the higher would need be the increment in pay to justify the costs of retraining, changing employment, and relocation.[33]

Older workers are simply (and wisely) calculating means and ends, responding to the costs and incentives that they perceive will directly affect their leisure and financial goals. Just as it is unwise for employers to invest in the training of their older workers, so, too, is it unwise for older workers to invest time, money, and effort in additional training. As an economic proposition, it is a 'lose-lose' option for both parties. Recent studies done by the National Bureau of Economic Research seem to support this 'rationality/cost-benefit' thesis. For example, Andrew Samwick finds that U.S. workers will hasten retirement if their company pension will accumulate greater benefits and payouts. He reports:

> It is private pensions, not Social Security, that primarily determine the changes in retirement wealth ... [C]hanges in social security that are typical of past and proposed legislation ... have modest impacts, reducing

labor force participation by about 1 percentage point. Increasing employer-provided pension coverage by 50 percent generates a much bigger drop in labor force participation: about 5 percentage points for those between ages 50 and 70. That's roughly 27 percent of the actual reduction that occurred during 1955 to 1975 when pension coverage did grow by fifty percent.[34]

Samwick's finding that pension payouts directly affect when workers retire is supported by Thomas Courchene. Canada, implies Courchene, does not differ from the United States when it comes to the unwillingness of older workers to invest in more training or working beyond the age of retirement. If there is untapped productive potential in older workers, then we have yet to find the 'right' policy answers to encourage them to remain in the workforce and forgo the generous pension benefits that await them. 'Short of the potential breakup of the country, the reform of the retirement income system is probably the most daunting policy challenge on the horizon. Its dimensions are staggering: it is essentially a cradle-to-the-grave issue; it embodies implicit social contracts; it is a jurisdictional quagmire and it is underpinned by every conceivable equity issue. There are no right answers in this area.'[35]

It would seem that for Courchene the problem is not that an aging workforce is necessarily unproductive because older workers can no longer do the work efficiently and profitably. Rather, it is the early retirement of older workers that is the problem. By retiring early, and in large numbers, these workers will substantially reduce Canada's productivity potential. Peitchinis's and Courchene's competing explanations of why productivity will drop as our population ages put into sharp relief the policy conundrum that faces government decision-makers. Each accepts that productivity will substantially decline as the bulk of the workforce ages. But the reasons given for this impending productivity decrease diverge sharply. Each sees a different policy challenge for governments in the years ahead as this process works its way through our society and economy. For Peitchinis, governments will need to develop a whole range of income maintenance programs. For Courchene, government must reform the retirement system if older workers are to remain in the workforce beyond the legal age of retirement. Financial incentives and disincentives must therefore be introduced by Ottawa and the provinces to prevent a mass exodus of the baby boomers.

Both Peitchinis and Courchene agree that it is imperative that decision-makers not deceive themselves by believing that substantial numbers of older workers will willingly turn their backs on the generous financial and leisure benefits that come from taking early retirement. They agree that the overwhelming majority of older workers will not act against their own best interests. Most of these older workers will not want to continue working beyond the statutory age of retirement. Why should they?[36] The question then is: Can governments introduce the sweeping changes required to reform the pension system so that early and normal retirement will become too costly for most senior workers? Peitchinis and economic pessimists think that this is simply not politically prudent and that ballots will win out over economic rationality. Courchene, in contrast, believes that economic necessity will serve as the driving force and produce a radical restructuring of Canada's current safety net. Not surprisingly, the jury is out as to who is right.

Work in Global Context

An increasing number of commentators are suggesting that workforce participation, by both young and old, will be shaped by the demands of a global economy. They assert that many of today's competitive firms, and certainly most, if not all, of tomorrow's firms, will sooner or later move costly labour-intensive components of the 'value chain' into countries where labour is relatively cheap and reliable, and where the loss of efficiency and product quality are minimal. Thus far, few labour economists dispute the claim that the decline of unskilled and blue-collar workers and wages has been more or less caused by the introduction of new labour-saving technology and the demand for highly skilled and better educated workers rather than by 'beggar-thy-neighbour' trade practices and encroaching globalization.

Following this analysis to its logical conclusion, it would seem that any attempt to understand the future implications of aging and productivity must also come to grips with the dynamics of the global economy and not only pension incentives and policy disincentives. The empirical record indicates that each year increasing numbers of OECD companies are relocating their production facilities, accelerating their outsourcing, and employing ever larger numbers of semiskilled and skilled workers in developing countries countries. It is this substitutability of labour from rich to poor countries, without loss of productivity, that the critics believe will make more and more of our older workers redundant. The lower cost of production and the productivity performance of workers in developing countries are a 'wake-up' call.

Well-paying jobs, once thought to be the domain of Canada's work-force, including its older workers, are no longer secure. That some older workers are leaving the workforce, then, may not regenerate pro-ductivity growth among the remaining workers.

The OECD warns: 'It appears likely that workforce ageing will create an increased need for older workers to change jobs because more will be laid off.'[37] As we have seen, not everyone accepts these gloomy fore-casts. Thus, for some, early retirement is a vindication of the welfare state and an occasion for rejoicing: 'the ability to enjoy a period of retirement after a lifetime of work is an appropriate social goal. As ... countr[ies] became wealthier over the last half century, it is not surpris-ing that [they] used part of that wealth to fund additional leisure at the end of the work life.'[38] Why is this a bad thing? Moreover, is an aging workforce really a serious economic problem as many seem to sug-gest? Sociologist James Schulz and his colleagues do not believe so. If anything, they are convinced that the aging and productivity debate thus far has been weak, unfocused, poorly researched, misleading, and wrong-headed:

> Not only is most of the 'burden of the elderly' literature over-simplistic, it encourages us to look for solutions in the wrong places. Today as in the past, the most important determinants of the future economic welfare of people (of all ages) are longstanding factors discussed by economists and others as influencing growth: labor force participation, saving, invest-ment in human and business capital, technological change, entrepreneur-ial initiatives, managerial skills, government provision of infrastructure, and so on. Thus the debate over how best to run an economic system is not primarily an aging discussion. In fact, the aging of populations may have little to do with the outcome.[39]

Schulz and his colleagues go on to charge that before really proving that a serious problem exists, many recent writers have jumped to pro-posing solutions. The three most popular are (1) to cut public pensions (2) to target benefits to the needy aged, and (3) to encourage older peo-ple to work longer. Are these steps really necessary?

How Much Do We Know about Aging and Productivity?

It should be pointed out that there are not many rigorous studies that actually examine the relationship between aging and productivity. Indeed, researchers cannot agree on how best to measure the long-term economic impact of population and labour-force growth.[40] As we shall see, much of the conventional wisdom is often based on anecdotes, neoclassical economic theory (selectively employed), and a few dated case studies whose findings may well be the exception rather than the rule. For example, the OECD's recent study, *The Transition from Work to Retirement*, reports:

> An analysis of the labour market for older workers entails consideration of both labour demand and supply factors specific to this age group, as well as an assessment of general trends in the labour market. Demand side analysis would address the relative productivity of older workers, their associated market wage, hiring and training costs and potential sickness record – in short, a profile on their total cost to the firm. Supply side analysis would address such factors as wealth and household income, the range and nature of benefits and pensions available, and people's preferences for leisure over work. While this chapter covers both the demand and the supply elements that influence employment of older workers, it recognises that there is not a great deal of evidence on the importance of some of the demand side elements, particularly on the productivity of older workers.[41]

Looking at Canada, the University of Toronto's Institute for Human Development, Life Course and Ageing observes:

> The research questions we are pursuing remain unanswered by the existing literature ... [T]here is little or no evidence about the level of awareness of management concerning the ageing workforce issue and whether Canadian companies are adapting their workplace organization to accommodate older workers. We do not know the specific circumstances under which work organization innovations lead to en-skilling or de-skilling of older workers or a combination of these effects. Nor do we know whether there are perceived or actual advantages or impediments to the adoption of new work organization practices by older workers. There do appear to be stereotypes about the capacity of older workers to change and adapt; however, we are unable to locate any empirical studies that examine the actual experiences of older workers in relation to new forms of work organization.[42]

Frank T. Denton and Byron Spencer make a similar plea. In their recent study examining the potential cost of an aging workforce, they point out:

An important area for further study is the decline in the labour force participation of older men and the shift toward retirement. The reasons for these trends are still not sufficiently clear, although these trends have been in evidence for a long time. The movement of older men out of the work force and into the 'dependent population' is obviously a matter of some importance. For an assessment of the effects of population aging: it both increases the number of elderly dependents and reduces the capacity of the economy to support them. We would like to see a well funded program of research to investigate the relevant issues, and in particular the role played by institutional rigidities in public and private pension plans.[43]

All these unresolved questions, however, may not only be caused by a dearth of research on these issues. Our confusion, ignorance, and uncertainty may also stem from the fact that because of their complexity and a shortage of reliable data, they are very difficult to answer with any degree of confidence. As Richard Disney admits in *Can We Afford to Grow Older? A Perspective on the Economics of Aging*: 'It is difficult to answer the question about aging and productivity because it is hard to find plausible measures of productivity with which to examine the hypotheses ... [C]ohort effects, age effects, and other productivity effects may all interact, and uncovering the net effects of demographic changes is a complex task.'[44] Can we trust the numbers, if our statistical techniques are not able to satisfactorily measure the 'net effects' of an aging workforce on productivity?

It seems that the social, financial, and economic consequences of recent demographic changes are still unknown and easy to misjudge. However, governments and decision-makers cannot act in good conscience as if nothing is happening. Accountability to the public and enlightened self-interest underscore both the need and the prudence in trying to discern trends and prepare for a future that is likely to differ from the status quo and invalidate existing public policies, programs, and strategies. To this end, it is important to consider the alleged link between an aging population and declining economic productivity, as well as the policy corollary that clearing out older workers to make way for young, presumably better educated, less expensive, and more dynamic ones will help rejuvenate Canada's lagging productivity.[45] It is necessary to emphasize that the studies from which these conclusions derive are of questionable reliability. They are based mostly on survey research and (often dated) statistical analyses that focus almost exclusively on the U.S. workforce. They are inconclusive and filled with loose ends and unanswered questions. While they may help to define a future research agenda, in no way do they offer settled conclusions. It must also be stressed that the future employability and productivity of older workers is not exclusively a technological or economic problem. Perceptions, expectations, and values also come into play. Glenn Loury notes:

> Economists have tremendous influence over policy these days, and, as an economist, that generally makes me proud. But, precisely because of my discipline's considerable clout, it is important to understand its limitations ... When it comes to particulars ... the economist's view of the world can be narrow and reductive ... [T]he single-minded attention to incentives and the pursuit of self-interest that characterizes economic analysis can be a great strength – but it can also be a fatal flaw ... [This] becomes clearer when one considers that policymaking is not simply about providing technical solutions to the problems of governance. It is also about taking symbolic actions that express people's values and beliefs.[46]

A Profile of Canada's Older Workers

The proportion of older persons who remain in the workforce in Canada is significantly lower than in many other OECD countries. Smeeding and Quinn report a participation rate of 60 per cent among Canadian males 55 to 64 years old. This is similar to levels in Australia, the United Kingdom, and Germany, but lower than in the United States and Sweden (66 per cent and 70 per cent respectively), and it compares very unfavourably with the situation in Japan. The OECD recently reported participation rates of 92.1 per cent and 71.4 per cent for Japanese males age 55 to 59 and 60 to 64 respectively.[47] Many explanations have been offered for this remarkable difference in participation rates:

1 Pensions in countries other than Japan are sufficiently generous to discourage work in later years.
2 Older people in Western nations are not as healthy as in Japan and so are less able to work in later life.
3 Employment opportunities for older people are greater in Japan than in other nations.
4 Older people in Japan have more interest in working than older people in other nations.

5 Japanese society places a greater value on work and productivity than societies in other nations.
6 Policy initiatives and incentives for the hiring and retention of older workers are different in Japan than in other nations.[48]

However, none of these hypotheses is supported by current research. John Creighton Campbell argues for another possibility – differences in attitudes. In Japan older workers are not assumed to be economic burdens; instead, they are seen as assets and thus encouraged to remain in the workforce.

> Efforts to help older people work are the most unusual aspect of Japan's policy toward the elderly. Most European countries have been trying to move aging workers out of the labor force to help solve their youth unemployment. The United States has concentrated on removing legal barriers to older people retaining their jobs ... but has done relatively little to improve the ability of the elderly to work, or encourage employers to hire or keep them. Only Japan pursues a consistently positive policy of job maintenance and creation for older people, and has put employment policy near the top of the government's measures to deal with the aging society.[49]

Labour-Force Participation in Canada

Participation rates of older workers are declining in Canada and for most of the OECD countries. Smeeding and Quinn calculate an average drop of 0.6 to 1.5 percentage points per year in participation rates for all OECD countries from 1970 to 1985. During this period Canada and the United States also saw a decrease in participation rates averaging 1.0 percentage points per year.[50] Suzanne Methot reports a similar spiralling trend and notes that 'employment levels' for Canadians age 65 and over declined sharply in recent decades. 'At the same time, there have been major increases in voluntary part-time employment among those elderly Canadians who are still working. As well, only a small percentage of the population age 65 and over not in the labour force report themselves available for work.' Between 1966 and 1994, participation rates for men age 55 to 64 fell from 86.0 to 60.3 per cent. During this same period women of the same age increased their participation rate from 28.4 to 39 per cent. But a much higher percentage of the jobs held by older women were part-time: the figures were 2.3 per cent for men and 25.5 per cent for women in 1980, 2.0 and 27.2 per cent respectively in 1990.[51] The same patterns have been observed in most other OECD countries with the exception of Japan.

The continuous decline in the participation rate of older workers is usually ascribed to the increase in early retirement. Sunter and Bowlby speculate on the causes of early retirement:

> [It] is not solely the result of forced exits from the labour force. In fact, the reasons for retirement, as measured by Statistics Canada's General Social Survey, changed only marginally between the expansion years of the 1980s and the recession dominated years of the early 1990s. While the proportion of persons who retired because of early retirement incentives almost doubled, from 7 per cent to 12 per cent, the proportion reporting unemployment as their main reason for retirement rose only slightly, from 10 per to 12 per cent. Personal choice and health remained the leading reasons in the early 1990s.[52]

According to the OECD, the continuing increase in part-time work among people of normal retirement age is partly the result of a voluntary, gradual withdrawal of older workers from the labour force.[53] Those who do opt for part-time work, often referred to as 'bridge jobs,' earn lower wages. David P. Ross and Richard Shillington report that Canadians who took these bridge jobs on reaching retirement age saw their wages plummet by nearly two-thirds.[54]

A somewhat more complex pattern seems to have emerged in the United States. In 1959, roughly three-quarters of 65-year-old males were still in the workforce. The 66 per cent participation rate in 1995 was lower; but the rate had stopped falling in 1985. According to Joseph Quinn, 'the era of earlier and earlier retirement seems to have come to an abrupt halt.'[55] Meanwhile the number of older men and women working part-time does seem to have increased. Andrew M. Sum and W. Neal Fogg report that in 1987 the rate among workers age 55 to 59 was 20 per cent, two percentage points higher than in 1968.[56] By contrast, Christopher Ruhm finds that there has not been a great change in the numbers of older workers employed part-time.[57] Olivia S. Mitchell and Joseph Quinn observe that 'the vast majority of older Americans who work part-time say they are doing so voluntarily.' But they also suggest that older workers are leaving the workforce in response to financial incentives and disincentives, such as earning limits established by Social Security and pay cuts that are imposed by defined-benefit pension plans.[58]

Unemployment among Older Canadians

The unemployment rate among older Canadians varies from region to region. In Quebec and the Atlantic Provinces, the risk of being unemployed is nearly twice the national average. Possible causes are differences in the concentration of traditional versus 'modern' industries, the size of firms, the cyclical nature of the economy, education, mobility, and the dependence on social assistance. One cause can be ruled out – differences in the proportion of senior citizens relative to the total workforce; concentrations are more or less the same across the country.

Across Canada as a whole, older workers do better on average than other age groups. In 1997 the unemployment rate of workers aged 55 to 64 was 6.7 per cent; among workers age 25 to 54 it was 7.9 per cent. Older workers do better even after controlling for differences in education. In 1995 older workers without a high school diploma had an unemployment rate of 11.4 per cent; for comparable workers age 25 to 44 the rate was 16.7 per cent. Statistics Canada reports that there is 'little evidence of a narrowing or widening of the gap over the long term.'[59] It should be noted, though, that among women the unemployment rates of older versus younger workers have begun to converge of late. In 1997, for example, older women recorded a rate of 7.3 per cent, compared with 7.9 per cent for younger women. Unemployment rates differ between the two groups because older workers have greater job tenure and security; younger workers as a group are extremely vulnerable to layoffs and economic downturns. Between 1981 and 1984, for example, 7 per cent of those age 55 to 64 lost their full-time jobs to downsizing, plant closures, and dismissals; among prime-age workers the rate was 10 per cent.

It would be wrong, however, to conclude that older workers escape the effects of unemployment. Once they become unemployed, they have a much harder time than people in other age groups to find another job. Many studies show that they are prone to 'permanent layoffs.'[60] B. Casey and S. Wood report that in Britain unemployment rates are relatively high among the young and old, and lower for middle-aged workers.[61] The same relationship holds true in Canada and the United States. Only 39 per cent of older Canadians who lost their jobs between 1981 and 1984 were employed again by 1986; for workers age 25 to 54, the figure was 65 per cent. Equally important, older workers took longer on average to re-enter the workforce: 37 weeks compared with 27 for workers age 25 to 54. A 1996 study confirmed the trend. Once an older male worker was let go, there was a 63 per cent chance he would still be unemployed a year later, compared with 30 per cent for prime-age workers. The study also found that of those older workers who had been unemployed for a year, only 47 per cent were still looking for a job; 70 per cent of younger workers had not yet given up.[62]

The experience in many other OECD countries is similar. In the United States between 1985 and 1990, 14 per cent of displaced workers fell between the age of 55 and 64. Nor did seniority afford much protection. Close to 40 per cent of those who were laid off lost jobs they had held for 20 years. Only 53 per cent of these workers were able to find work by 1990; among prime-age workers the comparable figure was 72 per cent. The U.S. Bureau of Labor Statistics reported that roughly one-third of older Americans permanently dropped out of the labour force during this period – a much higher proportion than the 14 per cent average for all workers.[63]

Kelly Morrison finds that 53 per cent of Canadians who lost their jobs in the early 1990s did not see their wages drop when they found employment again. Generally speaking, high wage expectations did not play a major role in determining whether older workers were able to rejoin the workforce.[64] In this case too the experience of other OECD countries, the United States in particular, has been similar. While many displaced U.S. workers accepted lower wages when they returned to work, these older workers were more likely than younger workers to experience wage cuts – often in excess of 20 per cent. The explanations usually given are age discrimination, the loss of firm-specific skills, and lack of a post-secondary education.

The authors of a recent OECD study, *Ageing in OECD Countries: A Critical Policy Challenge*, offer several possible explanations for the reluctance to hire older workers. One is that they are less productive since, in the absence of continuous training, their skills and work experience become largely obsolete. Another suggestion is that employee productivity, which, according to a number studies, continues to increase to age 55, plummets rapidly thereafter because of declining physical and cognitive skills. Lastly, they argue that the normal positive relationship between seniority and wages makes it uneconomic for firms to employ older workers. Indeed, this is one reason why the declining participation rate of older workers has not led to a fall in the general unemployment rate. Involuntary exits or forced retirement of older workers, the authors suggest, may have 'aggravated the problem in the longer run,' by increasing the payroll taxes needed to fund retirement programs.[65]

Education and the Trend to Knowledge Work

In Canada older workers have substantially less education than their younger colleagues. A Statistics Canada survey (1991) used the ability to read medicine labels as a proxy for literacy. On this measure it found that more than 33 per cent of adults between the age of 55 and 69 were illiterate, compared with 21 per cent for those age 44 to 55 and between 6 and 9 per cent for younger workers. Older Canadians were also more numerically illiterate: 40 per cent compared with 12 per cent for younger Canadians.[66] Grant Schellenberg likewise finds that older workers are likely to be less literate and numerate than younger workers; the overwhelming majority lack secondary and post-secondary training.[67] For example, in 1994, 18.5 per cent of workers age 55 to 64 had a Grade 8 education or less, compared with 2.9 per cent for workers age 25 to 44. Morrison notes that 24 per cent of prime-age workers were likely to participate in some job-related training program, compared with 10 per cent of those age 55 to 64. The disparity in education levels is most pronounced for working women. A 1997 survey calculates that 31 per cent of employed women over 55 had not graduated from high school. The comparable figure was 12 per cent for female workers age 25 to 54.[68]

Differences in education seem to have an effect on employment. Human Resources Development Canada finds that the likelihood of layoff for older workers is inversely related to their level of education. During 1995 and 1996, 56 per cent of older workers who were displaced did not have a high school diploma, 'more than three times the proportion of older workers currently employed with a high school diploma.' Moreover, two-thirds of older workers who had no post-secondary schooling were still unemployed a year later, while only one-third of workers with a university degree were still looking for a job.[69] Education also brings an 'earnings' premium. Another Human Resources Development Canada study finds that from 1981 to 1993 mean earnings for those with post-secondary education were roughly double those for workers with only nine to thirteen years of education. The education premium was $21,300 for men and $14,900 for women. Males age 45 to 54 profited the most from an advanced education. Their average earnings premium of $30,000 was four times that of workers age 17 to 24. Older women also fared better; their earnings premium of $15,600 was 2.5 times that of women age 17 to 24.[70]

It is unclear whether a superior education really adds to workers' productivity. Education can be and often is used as a sorting device. But the predominance of educated workers may simply reflect the forces of supply and demand. If a Bachelor of Arts degree is now as common as a high school diploma, firms might as well hire university graduates. It was, however, not very long ago that many employers were not interested in employing humanities and social science graduates. Despite their university degrees, graduates were not seen as assets on the shopfloor or as having the potential to substantially contribute to companies' productivity and profits. What has changed?

The relative lack of education among older workers is particularly important given recent trends in employment opportunities. Traditional industries like manufacturing and agriculture have suffered from lack of growth, productivity decline, and greater competition and market volatility. By contrast, in the past twenty-five years, 'knowledge workers' have increased more rapidly than any other kind of worker. In 1971 they accounted for 6.3 per cent of all workers; by 1996 that number had risen to 13.1 per cent.[71] Knowledge workers increased at twice the pace of workers in the service sector. Kathryn McMullen, a researcher at the Canadian Policy Research Network, found a similar trend:

1   By the end of 1994, 43 per cent of employees in the respondent firms used computer-based technology (CBT).
2   From 1992 to 1994, the introduction of CBT resulted in the creation of largely professional and skilled technical jobs and in the elimination of unskilled jobs.
3   Both the share and skill requirements of professional and skilled technical jobs grew over this period.
4   Even within lower-skilled and unskilled occupational groups, skill requirements relating to 'problem-solving' increased.
5   Almost 80 per cent of respondents who put some CBT in place during the study period reported that the technology led to the reorganization of work processes.
6   Of the three most-frequently cited obstacles to the introduction of CBT, one was the lack of technically qualified personnel.[72]

Norman Leckie reports that the introduction of computers and new technology increased the 'cognitive complexity' of the average job by 12 per cent.[73] Such trends are all the more worrisome given the recent finding that 'up-skilling and retraining' for career and job-related purposes has largely disappeared among older workers.[74]

When it comes to obtaining more formal education, a number of studies suggest that older workers in the United States have made considerable progress when compared with previous generations. While they are less educated than young U.S. workers, they have made significant strides in graduating from high school and post secondary institutions over the past two decades. For example, in 1968 approximately two-thirds of those 55 or older had not finished high school; by 1987 only 41 per cent of older workers lacked a high school diploma. During this same period, the proportion of older workers completing secondary and post-secondary education increased from 34 to 58 per cent. The share of those with at least a year of college rose from 14 to 24 per cent, and of those holding a college degree from 7 to 12 per cent. The hourly pay and annual earnings of older workers also rose during this period. On the other hand, neither their rate of participation in the labour force nor their employment prospects increased. Both in Canada and the United States, elderly workers with little education were more likely to be laid off or drop out of the workforce than younger workers.[75] According to the Conference Board of Canada (1997), 40 per cent of Canadian adults have a post-secondary degree, compared with only 30 per cent for the United States and 20 per cent on average in the other OECD countries.[76]

Employment trends among older workers are somewhat more favourable in the United States Between 1968 and 1987 the proportion of older workers employed in traditional industries decreased from 36.5 to 30.6 per cent. Most of them went to jobs in finance, insurance, and real estate; by 1987, 41 per cent of older workers were employed in the service sector, compared with only 33 per cent in 1968. All the same, many older U.S. workers still remain in traditional industries. Nor has their shift to the service sector been painless or cheap. The U.S. Bureau of Labor Statistics reports that in the transition older workers experienced substantial wage losses, lengthier periods of unemployment, and above-average withdrawals from the workforce.[77]

The Productivity of Older Workers

Many studies are quite positive about the relationship between age and productivity. Mary Jablonski, Kent Kunze and Larry Rosenblum uses earnings as a proxy for productivity, on the neoclassical assumption that in a competitive economy dominated by profit-maximizing firms, the wage paid to particular groups of workers will equal the value of their marginal product. Since older workers have more experience and on-the-job training, they expected to find a positive relationship between age and productivity. This was borne out by the data for 1948 to 1986; adjusting for labour-force composition, education, and growth rates of output per hour, workers' productivity on average rose from when they entered the workforce until they reached their forties. Productivity did fall off again in later years, but not by much:

> Worker productivity exceeds 90 percent of peak performance (with one exception) for both men and women near age 60 and exceeds 80 percent for those age 65 or older. The modest decline in productivity for older workers is supported by the earning equations ... Better-educated older workers still earn wages above the average for the economy (and have higher than average productivity). This group includes men with at least a high school diploma and women with some college education. When such workers choose to extend their careers rather than retire ... the result is labor composition and productivity growth are higher than if retirement were chosen.[78]

A 1985 study by Yankelovich, Skelly, and White for the American Association of Retired Persons examines the attitudes of U.S. employers to workers over age 50. They maintain that the business climate changed dramatically from the 1960s and 1970s, when an egalitarian spirit predominated, emphasizing entitlement rather than meritocracy. The 1980s, they report, ushered in a 'new realism'; business leaders were actively engaged in setting 'realistic goals' and imposing 'realistic limits' in their pursuit of cost effectiveness. In this environment, older workers were more likely to come under intense scrutiny. It is all the more remarkable, therefore, that at the time of their study, older workers were perceived by the 'gatekeepers' of U.S. business not as burdens but as positive assets. Employers had high regard for their experience, knowledge, work habits, and attitudes. Older workers received the highest ratings on productivity; and employers also rated very high their commitment to quality and 'solid performance record.' While there was no evidence of discrimination against older workers, company managers were opposed to new government regulations intended to enhance their rights. Eight of ten firms interviewed agreed that most of their older employees wanted to work as long as possible. Managers insisted, however, that continued employment must depend on the employees' ability to produce and contribute to the company's goals. Older workers could not expect and would not receive special treatment; they were just like any other worker – a productive asset to be used as fully as possible. Managers believed that performance ultimately depended on the individual, not age or seniority.[79]

On the other side of the ledger, Yankelovich et al. did find that larger companies were concerned about certain weaknesses that seemed to be more common among older workers: resistance to change, fear or discomfort with new technologies, a lack of 'aggressive spirit,' inability to learn new skills quickly, and physical limitations. This was especially the case for companies that had made extensive investments in state-of-the-art technology and computers. Yankelovich et al. are unable to determine whether this perceived resistance to technology was the product of incompetence or a 'healthy scepticism'. Companies with a large proportion of older workers on the payroll were somewhat concerned about their high cost. But in general firms did not perceive cost to be a problem; the benefits of having older workers on staff more than outweighed the costs. In fact, in respect of health insurance, older workers were actually less costly than younger colleagues: 'Only 16% of gatekeepers rated a 55 year old employee as extremely or very costly to insure. By contrast, a 30 year old with two dependants was judged to be expensive by 1 in 3 (34%). This difference is even more dramatic in the large companies: gatekeepers were almost three times as likely to attribute high health insurance costs to young employees with dependants as they were to 50-plus employees, although fewer large companies (49%) consider the health care costs for older workers to be "insignificant" than do companies in general.'[80] Finally, while nearly half the companies surveyed believed that skill training for older workers would enhance their performance, less than one-third had such programs in place. Yankelovich et al. conclude that the employment future of older workers is not preordained or defined exclusively by management; they hold the keys to their own destinies.

Michael Barth et al. reports that only a few studies have examined aging and productivity across the full spectrum of industry. Few companies keep systematic productivity data on employees, and there are even fewer hard data when it comes to relating productivity with age. Managers seem to be indifferent about age-related differences in employee costs and productivity. The few industry-wide studies that exist, they report, find only a weak correlation between age and declining productivity, not sufficient to justify mandatory retirement policies. The productivity of blue-collar workers declines with age, and as a group they are more likely than white-collar workers to retire early. In their own case studies of Days Inns of America and B&Q plc (a large British housewares chain), they find that older workers prove at least as capable as younger ones, and are 'competitive with their younger counterparts on most measures of cost-effectiveness and quality.'[81]

Richard Belous of the National Planning Association reviews more than fifty case studies to determine how older workers were affected by changes in U.S. employment and pay practices during the 1980s. He finds that employers altered compensation systems to tie wages and benefits more closely to corporate economic realities and less to custom and tradition. Employment became more flexible and contingent on corporate needs. Temporary workers were no longer given long-term contracts and now faced dismissal upon the first signs of slowing sales, financial losses, or a business downturn. Contingent employment grew faster than the average for the labour force as a whole. Those firms that retained a long-term relationship with their employees still tried to make these relationships more flexible. Lifetime employment continued to decline, being replaced more and more by a 'day-laborer' model. Productivity became an increasingly high priority for corporations. For example, in 1978 productivity ranked fourth on the list of managerial priorities (the first concern was 'industry patterns'); by 1983 productivity had risen to the top. Corporations stopped basing their wage policies on the behaviour of other companies and began using internal criteria instead: changes in labour costs per unit of output and in expected profits. Employers were convinced that flexible employment and contingent employment would increase job opportunities for older workers who wanted to remain in the workforce; the resulting drop in their wages and benefits would make them more attractive to employers. Belous notes, however: 'If labor shortages are not serious, many employers may not be willing to make the added effort to make special adjustments in their recruitment programs. If recruitment programs are not directed toward special needs and concerns of older workers, their employment may not increase at many firms despite employers' interest in hiring them.'[82]

Older workers who were willing to work part-time or on a temporary basis were not considered serious obstacles to improving company productivity. Management viewed them as having a strong work ethic and good track record, and expected them to have a productive work life even beyond the normal retirement age (although management continued to worry how they would adjust to new technology).

In a 1998 study for the Towson University Center for Productive

Aging, Donna Wagner is primarily interested in discovering the factors influencing the decision to employ older workers. She finds that 70 per cent of employers surveyed did not see health-care benefit costs as a barriers; 90 per cent of companies did not believe hiring large numbers of older workers would tarnish their corporate image. Employers were more willing to employ and retain older workers and no longer assumed, as they had in the past, that productivity and age were inversely related. On the other hand, 50 per cent responded that skill levels were 'significant barriers to the use of older workers in their workforce.' Wagner adds: 'Despite the fact that America is aging and that we have a record low unemployment rate coupled with a strong economy today, too many employers still view older workers as marginal or worse, not relevant to, their companies continued economic success.'[83] Roughly half the companies interviewed planned to increase the number of older workers on their payroll. Sixty per cent claimed it was difficult to find older workers. But when pressed, only one in five firms admitted that they had a recruitment program in place for older workers, and only 10 per cent had devised a strategy for hiring older workers in the future. Wagner recommends that the U.S. Department of Labor formulate a strategy 'to increase the awareness of employers about the demographic changes taking place that will likely influence their need for older workers in the future.'[84]

In the late 1980s, Glen M. McEvoy and Wayne Cascio review 96 studies concerned with the correlation between age and productivity. These studies were published over a 22-year period in 96 behavioural science journals. They found no relation between age and job performance. Furthermore, they report that this finding is unaffected by the type of performance measure used or the type of job (professional vs non-professional) considered. They acknowledge that they concentrated particularly on cross-sectional studies and admit that they are unable to give a more precise picture about the link between aging and productivity. Longitudinal studies and more rigorous microstudies that control for demographic differences across age groups are lacking in their study sample.[85]

E.A. Hammel examines the productivity of chemists and mathematicians at the University of California. He finds ample reason to question the 'folklore' about aging and the productivity of older academics. While he does not find that older academics are more productive than younger ones, he finds no indication that age has the negative impact usually assumed.[86]

Paul R. Sparrow and D.R. Davis use a sample of 1,308 service engineers employed by a multinational office equipment company to investigate the performance effects of age, tenure, training level, and job complexity. They warn that only a small proportion of those studied were between 46 and 55 years old and that they had difficulty controlling their findings for age. They find that on average quality of performance rose in the earlier years, reached a peak at middle age, and falls thereafter. However, they also discover wide differences in performance in individual cases. There were some 'pleasant' surprises. Although age had a statistically significant effect on quality and speed of performance, its impact was 'minimal.' Nor was the relation between age and job performance significantly affected by job complexity, as they had originally expected. A lot of the difference in performance could be accounted for by training rather than age. Engineers with little or no training scored below the sample average, regardless of age.[87] Neil Charness and E.A. Bosman make a similar point. While a decline in perceptual and cognitive performance is inevitable as the workforce ages, training and 'appropriate interventions' can do much to mitigate and control their 'negative consequences.' It is therefore a 'myth' to assume that older workers will be less productive than younger ones.[88]

The Canadian Aging Research Network (CARNET) study differences in the way older and younger workers adapted to new technologies at Sun Life Assurance of Canada.[89] Sun Life was chosen because it is an industry leader, large and technologically advanced, and has an aging workforce. Researchers report that there was no difference in adaptability; both old and young favoured the introduction and application of new technology. CARNET notes, however, that concerns continued to be expressed about the ability of older workers to adjust. And, while older workers were prepared to work with the new technology brought in by the company, they nevertheless feared this new technology and its likely impact on their jobs and on their career mobility. At least half of those interviewed wanted to retire before the company's mandatory age of 65. Especially keen to take early retirement were employees with higher incomes, who had experienced the most technological change, and whose health was not good.

Not all studies are this positive about the relation between age and productivity. The U.S. Bureau of Labor Statistics examines comparative job performance between 1956 and 1964, by age, paying special attention to output per hour for workers in the footwear and furniture industries. It finds that workers age 25 to 34 were more productive than those younger than 25 or between 55 and 64. In the footwear industry men age 25 to 34 scored 100.3 on an index of output per hour, while for men age 55 to 64 this score was 92.5. Men 65 years and older did poorly in comparison; their average score was 81.1. It should be noted, however, that the same studies also find considerable variation in output rates within age groups. And, upon closer examination, the authors conclude that variation in output was not closely related to age. Many older workers, for example, generated much more output per hour than the average for those age 35 to 44. In the final analysis, average productivity did not drop much with increases in age, except for workers older than 59.[90]

E. Lazear questions interpretations like those of Jablonski et al. which attribute the higher earnings of older workers to higher productivity. He suggests that firms pay higher wages to older workers not because they are more productive, but to attract greater effort from younger workers – who will someday become older workers. In addition, paying younger workers less than their output during the early years of employment is a useful way to reduce turnover costs and encourage long tenure.[91] James L. Medoff and Katharine G. Abraham likewise deny that older workers are more productive. For these authors, the apparent correlation between age and productivity derives from the assumption that older workers are more likely to be matched to the appropriate job. More-experienced workers tend to be less productive within their grades, but are protected by supervisors with whom they have worked over the years. Another possibility is that the higher wages of older workers is the result of union insistences to reward seniority, rather than superior experience and productivity.[92]

K.J. Gibson, W.J. Zerbem, and R.E. Franken, surveying 651 Calgary firms, report that 50 per cent of respondents did not think older workers were productive or should be encouraged to remain in the workforce beyond the normal retirement age. Many believed older workers were lacking in education and appropriate training, 'stuck in their trades ... unfamiliar with new technologies ... afraid to keep up ... resistant and fearful of change ... unable to make dramatic career changes, and slow to learn.' To make matters worse, employers thought that older workers lacked the qualifications required for the job and were not good candidates for the 'recovery of training investment.' Employing younger workers was the way to go because they could be 'quickly trained and [would] remain with the company longer.'[93]

A study commissioned by the American Association of Retired Persons (AARP), *Valuing Older Workers: A Study of Costs and Productivity* (1994), reports that managers positively assessed older workers for their experience, judgment, commitment to quality, attendance, punctuality, and low turnover. But older workers did not do as well when it came to flexibility, adaptability, ability to learn new skills, and physical ability to perform their jobs. Two-thirds of managers believed that older workers, far from accepting new technology, feared it. This made them much less attractive as employees.[94]

James Kahn and Jong-Soo Lim find that from 1958 to 1991 productivity growth was increasingly concentrated in the more skill-intensive manufacturing industries. The crucial factor in productivity increases was not new investment in capital equipment, as most economists believe, but the ability of skilled workers to master the new equipment. They suggest that new technology actually lowers productivity in the absence of skilled labour.[95] They believe that this explains the finding of Timothy Dunne, John Haltiwanger, and Kenneth R. Troske that in the past twenty years the most productive plants have 'fundamentally changed the way that they produce goods in terms of the mix of workers.'[96] Given the findings of the AARP study just cited, firms working with new technology may be eager to release older workers after the age of retirement and concentrate on training younger replacements. If older workers do not possess the necessary skills, they may be encouraged to retire early.

David H. Autor et al. find that many industries, especially those heavily reliant on computers, have been rapidly upgrading the skills of their employees. This is one reason why the demand for college graduates has increased so much of late. Their findings suggest that it will be difficult for older workers lacking new technology skills to compete in the labour market.[97] Berman et al. (1998) find that in an open economy technological change raises the demand for skilled workers and raises their wages relative to less-skilled workers.[98] Machin and Van Reenen likewise observe that in Denmark, France, Germany, Japan, Sweden, the United Kingdom, and the United States, 'R&D intensity' has increased the demand for skills and the relative demand for skilled workers. Under such circumstances, subsidizing the wages of older workers to keep them in the workforce longer would seem ill-advised, expensive, and self-defeating.[99]

In some respects the situation for older workers is worsening in Japan too. The OECD reports that mandatory retirement (now set at age 60) has been increasing steadily. Seventy per cent of employees now work in firms with mandatory retirement policies, compared with 47.6 per cent in 1966. Mandatory retirement is much more prevalent in larger companies. Pressure from trade unions and government initiatives has successfully accelerated the rate at which older workers retire. But are these older workers who retire early better off financially, as one might expect? The empirical evidence indicates that the incomes of these early retirees who depend primarily on company pensions are substantially lower than those of workers who continue to work beyond the age of retirement.[100]

On the other hand, there are also some favourable developments. Some firms, especially larger ones, have begun rehiring older workers, although in lower-ranking positions and at lower wages. To keep older workers employed after the age of mandatory retirement, the Japanese government has established human resource centres – employment agencies offering work opportunities to older workers. The government also offers training subsidies for older people and employment development grants for retirees. 'Silver manpower centres' have been created to provide temporary and part- time work opportunities. Both centres are multimillion dollar operations that have met with a good measure of success. Sara Rix writes: 'Japanese efforts on behalf of older workers have clearly positive outcomes: Employers get cheaper and presumably productive labor, and workers continue to earn. To the extent that they actually extend the work-life beyond what it would have been without these efforts, the government stands to reduce growth of its pension burden.'[101]

It should be noted, however, that many of these policies were introduced when Japan's economy was still performing exceptionally well. There were plenty of jobs available, productivity was high and making impressive gains, the country was prosperous and, in the eyes of many observers, enjoying the prospect of infinite growth. Japan was a trading state *par excellence*, and it was commonplace to hear that the twenty-first century would be Japan's century! All this has drastically changed over the past decade. Japan is now slowly emerging from a long and deep recession; for most of the 1990s it struggled to prevent financial chaos and stem the tide of widespread bankruptcy; productivity plummeted and unemployment sharply increased. The country is still in the midst of a painful economic restructuring. There is concern that to stay competitive and regain lost markets Japanese firms will move more of their manufacturing capacity and capital investments offshore, thereby reducing the number of jobs and employment opportunities for older workers. Few financial commentators are confident that Japan will quickly return to its former economic glory. Given these gloomy circumstances it is unclear whether Japan can afford to favour its older workers as before.

Conclusion: So Many Questions, So Few Answers

As we have seen in the previous sections of this chapter, the question, 'What do we know about aging and productivity?' is a very complex one. There are no on-the-shelf answers we can turn to for quick, easy, and reliable solutions. What is worse, the search for answers soon saddles us with more questions. It is therefore useful to give a brief 'shopping list' of the most daunting questions in need of reliable answers.

Perhaps foremost, we should ask, Is an aging workforce a 'defining moment' in Canada's quest towards economic growth, development, and a higher standard of living? Can we expect productivity, both in an absolute and a relative sense, to plummet as our working population progressively ages? Is the recent OECD report on Canada pessimistically comparing our present and future productivity performance with the United States and our other trading partners a 'wake-up' call, a premature and unwarranted case of economic jitters, or simply a transparent example of forecasters' hubris?[102]

Does government have a special role to play in ensuring that our older workers remain in the workforce after the statutory age of retirement because of their 'untapped' potential as contributors to future productivity growth? If so, what should the objectives of any future aging and productivity initiative be? And does this 'special responsibility' entail a fundamental break with previous government strategies and policies, or does it translate into an expansion and acceleration of programs already in place?

Is age-cohort composition as opposed to skill composition of workers the main culprit for Canada's deteriorating productivity in goods and services over the past two decades? Or is the productivity of older workers closely related to an individual's values, health, intelligence, education, and work ethic? If the answer is 'yes,' in what proportion? Does the economic transformation now taking place make older workers more expendable because they are less relevant to what futurists insist is an information-driven, knowledge-based global workplace?

Would governments therefore be wiser focusing their attention and allocating their limited resources on increasing the rate of capital investment and level of training per younger worker, while simultaneously accelerating the pace of research and development, free trade, and the adoption of new technology? Instead of concentrating on the young, should governments redouble their efforts and expenditures on 're-skilling' programs for workers over 45 years of age and increase the flow of skilled immigrants into the country? Or would the wiser policy course be, as many writers recommend, to concentrate on revising the social contract by removing, among other things, many of the pension and tax incentives frequently assumed to be mainly responsible for the continuing increase in early retirement?[103] Put another way, is it a supply- or demand-side problem that needs government attention?

The Veil of Ignorance

Throughout our review of the professional literature we have both directly and indirectly tried to show what the current state of thinking is; the divisions; the empirical findings, such as they are; and where economic and demographic theories and forecasts diverge. Since public policy is not made in a test tube, answers and future policy decisions will, to a very large extent, depend on what we actually know about the impact an aging workforce is likely to have on productivity in the years ahead. From the survey of the literature it is clear that we are not able to answer many of the questions we have raised with any degree of confidence.

A great deal of work has yet to be done to understand the impact of aging on individual and aggregate productivity, especially in Canada. We have barely scratched the surface. As matters now stand, the demographic, macro- and microeconomic, and sectoral and firm-specific case studies at our disposal are few, dated, ambiguous, theoretical, and often contradictory. Bruce Little is not far off the mark when he reports that 'productivity is in the eye of the beholder,' and a 'skeptic's delight.'[104]

Few attempts, for example, have been made to quantify how an aging workforce and its productivity performance might be affected by changes in the structure of the economy.[105] Long-term forecasting about structural economic changes is dicey at the best of times, and given our poor track record to forecast the near future, such exercises appear to be an invitation for crystal-ball-gazing and academic hubris.

Jacob Viner reminded us some forty years ago, 'No matter how refined and elaborate an analysis, if it rests solely on the short view it will still be ... a structure built on shifting sand.'[106] There continues to be a tendency to define important variables away, especially among economists, and to assume a priori that future changes in the economy will more or less conform to our existing models. Paradoxically, while economists talk of globalization, the information revolution, and demographic shifts, they often think in terms of linearity, immutability, and inevitability. Is it fair to say that economists, like generals, often fight the last war? Modesty aside, it is vitally important to recognize our limitations, what we know and do not know, and what we need to know if we are to make effective and timely policy interventions.

With this in mind, we need to be careful to distinguish between truths based on fact and truths based on theory. Economists, unfortunately, have a tendency to confuse the former with the latter, and can rightly be accused of failing to appreciate that the application of our current set of productivity models requires modesty, 'delicacy and sensitivity to the touch.'[107] If we are right, then the onus is on the economics profession to take up the aging productivity challenge and do the research that until now has been neglected and, in those instances when it has been done, has lacked the 'scientific' rigour that economists like to brag about when comparing themselves with other social science disciplines.

One area that we have neglected to give the attention it deserves is the 'psychology of an aging workforce.' Social scientists have long recognized that situations perceived as real are then treated as if they are real. We are therefore not simply dealing with technology and changes in the modes of production, distribution, transportation, and communication, but with perceptions, value systems, and egos. Can we really understand the aging–productivity conundrum and what role older workers are likely to play if we discount values, perceptions, and expectations of workers and their families, employers, and stockholders? With few exceptions, we do not know whether the firms in which substantial numbers of older workers are employed have seen their productivity drop or improve, and if so, by how much. Equally important, we know little about the extent to which the displacement of older workers or the mix of employees by age have affected employee output.[108] Indeed, it is not clear whether the jobs of displaced older workers who have found employment indicate a shift in the composition of jobs as opposed to the net loss of jobs. For that matter, we do not understand the range of jobs to which skills are transferable, an important question when considering displaced workers.[109]

Lastly we do not have an idea of the costs entailed if a substantial number of older workers decide to remain or leave a particular industry or occupation. How such an exodus by older workers may affect productivity by sector, region, and nationally, is, at this time, an open question. Even if we understood those trends better, we are not able to say with any degree of confidence how older workers will fare in the years ahead. Much will depend on the future performance of the Canadian and provincial economies, both in relative and absolute terms.

It is not unreasonable to conclude, as one critic of contemporary research in the the natural sciences has put it, that we are entering a policy terrain characterized by 'the penumbra of fact and theory,' where there is great temptation 'to make the mere aroma of words do the work that neither evidence nor logic can.'[110] This negative assessment finds support from David Turner and his associates at the OECD. They report, after studying the impact that an aging labour force may have on the macroeconomy of member states, that 'a more aged workforce can either be less dynamic and innovative and hence have impact on productivity growth, or alternatively relative labour scarcity may act as a stimulus to technical progress and boost productivity growth.'[111]

Who can say then, except *ex cathedra*, that a geriatric workforce is a prelude to an economic dark age? Moreover, who can propose with relative confidence a list of policy prescriptions designed to stimulate and sustain increases in productivity when we do not fully understand what factors increase productivity, and our models and theories are not based on carefully tested hypotheses or explanations?[112] Unfortunately, the majority of studies that we currently have at our disposal are not user-friendly to those responsible for developing and implementing public policy. For governments and their policy-makers the real, unanswered question is, How well do the competing analyses of pessimists and optimists explain what Richard Disney calls the 'dynamic effects' of an aging workforce on Canada's overall productivity?

For the confused but hard-pressed decision-maker such a sharp divergence of views and policy prescriptions translates into a 'damned if you do, damned if you don't,' seat-of-the-pants way to make policy. It should come as no surprise that an aging workforce and its likely impact on Canada's future productivity performance is not only an economic question, but a political one as well. Shawn McCarthy, after reviewing the debate over the accuracy of the OECD's gloomy productivity forecasts for Canada, notes:

It's the political equivalent of Brer Rabbit's tar baby – unwary cabinet ministers can get mightily stuck as these influences vary from sector to sector and from organization to organization, as well as over time ... 'Statistical analyses differ widely in their evaluation of causes ... [A] number of very able analysts have examined these issues; but using different data and analytic techniques, they have produced conclusions that differ considerably in quantitative terms ... This is a serious obstacle because we do not know how significant was each cause in the slowdown of productivity (or equally important, in the acceleration of productivity.'[113]

The Picture Is Not That Bleak

It is easy to despair given the uncertainty that we face in what lies ahead. But it is worth remembering that there are some things we do know. To begin with, we can take some comfort in knowing that we are not completely in the dark when it comes to productivity performance and the aging of the workforce. Depending on the industry, older workers have demonstrated that they are indeed productive and have nothing to apologize about when it comes to on-the-job performance. We also know that the dire forecasts of neo-Malthusian prophets of gloom and doom have failed to hold up empirically and historically. We know that subsidizing older workers is not likely to work if the aim is to improve productivity in the short term. We also know that in Canada and in the other OECD countries the economic incentives for older workers to remain on the job beyond the age of retirement are absent. We know that most of these workers, based on a 'What's in it for me?' cost-benefit calculus, which reasonably takes into account the number of working years left, the pay increment required to justify the cost of training and relocation, the trade-off in pension benefits and tax burden, are not prepared to undergo rigorous, prolonged training, and most firms are loath to make such investments for workers who they see ready to retire in the near future.

Moreover, we know that the matching, sorting, hiring, and retraining of workers is a complex decision and not simply based on the age of the workforce. Firm size, whether it is Canadian or foreign owned, whether a shop is organized or not, the pace and sophistication of technology introduced, the type of goods produced and traded, as well as the size of the market, the extent of competition, and market share, all directly affect the allocation of investment, inputs, and employment decisions. If, for example, job growth is greatest in small manufacturing establishments, but labour productivity is much lower, we have a better idea where we should concentrate our resources. In short, we are not leaping in the dark and using our finite resources indiscriminately. It is with this in mind that Haltiwanger et al. remind us how dangerous it is to overgeneralize about the labour market. In particular, they note: 'Across workers, even controlling for demographic characteristics, wage and employment outcomes vary a great deal, and there are sizable worker flows across jobs in the economy. These worker flows are closely connected to firm outcomes, reflecting in large part the ongoing shift in resources from less productive to more productive employers.'[114]

Most important, we know that a substantial number of older workers are not leaving the workforce in one fell swoop, but instead are working part-time as part of the transition to retirement. To assume, as some writers have, that the 'irresistible force' of an aging population is colliding with the 'immovable object' of retirement programs is unwarranted.[115] So, too, is the widely held view that older workers are a homogeneous group, that is, all age cohorts act alike regardless of time, place, and circumstance. This fallacy of composition is as naïve as it is foolish. Worst of all, it risks becoming a self-fulfilling prophecy. Today's 55-year-old is likely to be very different from tomorrow's 55-year-old in education, training, experience, and expectations. This should come as no surprise. Each generation, after all, writes its own political, social, and economic history.

Lastly, but no less important, most of the studies we have reviewed find that there is little hard evidence to support the apocalyptic claim that an aging workforce has brought with it a rapid and substantial drop in productivity. If anything, there is strong consensus that the variance of output is greater within, as opposed to between, age cohorts. Cliche aside, the devil does dwell in the details.

Given the paucity of reliable studies and the inevitable cacophony of views, it is not surprising that governments find their policy options limited. They can decide to do nothing, and muddle through by accepting Adam Smith's injunction to leave it to market forces to create the optimal balance between a rapidly aging workforce and increasing labour output per worker. But, as Keynes wisely observes, in the long run we are all dead. What we do or do not do in the interim matters.

Governments can also act defensively, and try ad hoc schemes. Acting defensively, they can return to protectionist strategies that nationalists and special interests demand; they can also throw large sums of money at training programs and even change the statutory age of retirement and pension benefits. But if previous experience teaches us anything, such responses will likely fail. They will be costly, divisive, and self-defeating. They may buy time and buy off certain groups, but they will not solve the productivity conundrum. As a trading nation we will simply be less competitive and our standard of living will suffer.

There is, however, another option. Let us call it the *Research Option*. Governments can begin to fund medium- and long-term studies that systematically and comprehensively examine the impact of an aging labour force on aggregate and individual productivity. Such studies should be targeted and could look at, among other things, the effects that changes in age composition have on specific industries, sectors, regions, firm size, displacement, wages, and the like. A longitudinal study tracking workers of different age groups, their career paths, expectations, and what Joseph Quinn has called 'the micro-economics of the retirement decision' should be commissioned as well.[116]

The time seems ripe for a study that explores what Canada's workforce may look like in the next twenty years. Such a study would pay special attention to productivity and regional trends, and develop scenarios of a Canada dominated by a service and information economy and which is deep in the throes of globalization and financial liberalization.[117] The debate about the third sector and its contribution to productivity and our GDP is far from over. Funds should be allocated to develop the statistical methodologies required to better assess the transaction costs, the outputs, and market value that such volunteerism actually produces.

Of course, policy-making, like most things, is not a case of 'either or.' Governments are right to fear that heavy dependence on a research initiative might lead to a slew of esoteric studies and a new scholasticism. But that is not inevitable. It is important to bear in mind that until recently the macroeconomic impact of an aging workforce, as Richard Disney reminds us, has been ignored, mired in the 'backwaters of economics.'[118] Fortunately, at this juncture, Canada has the time to do the basic research needed to fill the information gaps, husband the necessary resources, and enable decision-makers to plan labour market and production-enhancing policies, strategies, and priorities with greater care and precision. Decision-makers recognize that in dealing with the puzzle of aging workforce–productivity they will have to develop and implement strategies and programs based on the best research available. Daniel Bell has made this point forcefully. With baroque flair, he writes: 'The ladder of the City of Heaven can no longer be a "faith ladder," but an empirical one; a utopia has to specify where one wants to go, how to get there, the costs of the enterprise and some realization of, and justification for, the determination of who is to pay.'[119]

While we are not seeking utopia, we are in need of policy solutions that work. If governments cannot rely on the 'faith ladder,' traditional economic wisdom or freedom from a future of 'nasty surprises' then finding answers to many of the questions we have posed is more than an expensive and whimsical academic exercise, but rather a policy initiative urgently needed. This is the challenge and if we do not fund the research needed to put our productivity house in order and use our greying workforce now, 'It may simply be too late to do much about it.'[120]

Notes

1 See Jeanette C. Takamura, 'Statement Prepared for the Special Committee on Aging' (Washington, DC: U.S. Senate, 1998), 1.
2 While demographers agree that our population is aging and participation rates continue to decline, differences exist over how fast Canada is aging, the composition of the labour force, and the rate of productivity growth required in the future. For recent forecasts that discuss some of these issues, see Frank T.Denton, Christine H. Feaver, and Byron G. Spencer, 'The Future Population of Canada and Its Age Distribution,' *IESOP Research Paper*, no. 3 (Hamilton: McMaster University, June 1996); and Frank T. Denton and Byron G. Spencer, 'Population, Labour Force, and Long-term Economic Growth,' *IESOP Research Paper*, no. 25 (Hamilton: McMaster University, Dec. 1997).
3 While the Charter forbids age discrimination, Canada's Supreme Court has not declared mandatory or statutory retirement unconstitutional. The Court has ruled that mandatory retirement in certain occupations, for example, for firemen, is both legal and desirable at age sixty-five because of the physical demands of the job. Other occupations and professions, yet to be decided by future litigation, may no longer be allowed to impose a mandatory retirement requirement because of the Charter's, anti-age discrimination clause. In addition, many private pension plans, especially those based on defined contributions, impose financial penalties on those who work beyond age sixty-five. For a comprehensive review of the mandatory

retirement debate, see Richard V. Burkhauser and Joseph F. Quinn, 'The Effects of Changes in Mandatory Retirement Rules on Labor Supply of Older Workers' (Boston: Boston College, Department of Economics, April 1981); and Richard V. Burkhauser and Joseph F. Quinn, 'Is Mandatory Retirement Overrated? Evidence from the 1970s,' *Journal of Human Resources* 18, no. 3 (1982): 337–58. For a more recent discussion, see Organization for Economic Co-operation and Development, 'The Transition From Work to Retirement,' *Social Policy Studies*, no. 16 (Paris: OECD, 1995); OECD, 'The Labour Market and Older Workers,' *Social Policy Studies*, no. 17 (Paris: OECD, 1995); Joseph F. Quinn, 'Retirement Trends and Patterns in the 1990s: The End of an Era?' *Public Policy and Aging Report*, Summer 1997, 10–14; Morley Gunderson, *Flexible Retirement as an Alternative to 65 and Out* (Toronto: C.D. Howe Institute, 1998); Dorothy Lipovenko, 'Job Losses Facing Early Retirement,' *Globe and Mail*, 8 Sept., 1995, A3; and Human Resources Development Canada, 'Changing Notions of Retirement: A Phased-In Approach,' *Applied Research Bulletin* 2, no. 2 (1996).

4 See Jacques Henripin, 'Financial Consequences of Population Aging,' *Canadian Public Policy* 20, no.1 (1994): 78–94.

5 See Dave Turner, Claude Giorno, Alain De Serres, Ann Vourc'h, and Pete Richardson, 'The Macroeconomic Implications of Ageing in a Global Context,' *Economics Department Working Paper*, no. 193 (Paris: OECD, 1998), 5–6. Frank T. Denton et al., however, suggest that the 'dependency issue' is not as bleak as the OECD contends. See Frank T. Denton, Christine H. Feaver, and Byron G. Spencer, 'Immigration, Labour Force and the Age Structure of the Population,' *IESOP Research Paper*, no. 24 (Hamilton: McMaster University, Nov. 1997).

6 See Jonathan Gruber and David Wise, 'Social Security and Retirement: An International Comparison,' *American Economic Review* 88, no. 2 (1998): 158–63. For a more comprehensive analysis, see Jonathan Gruber and David Wise, eds., *Social Security and Retirement in the World* (Chicago: University of Chicago Press, 1999).

7 See William Johnston, 'Global Work Force 2000; The New World Labor Market,' *Harvard Business Review*, March/April 1991, 119.

8 See Alan Reynolds, 'Restoring Work Incentives for Older Americans,' Prepared for the U.S. Senate Subcommittee on Aging Forum on Older Workers, One Hundred and Fifth Congress, serial no. 105-7 (Washington, DC: United States Senate, 1997), 18. See also Richard W. Judy and Carol D'Amico, *Workforce 2020: Work and Workers in the 21st Century* (Indianapolis: Hudson Institute, 1997).

9 Ibid., 19.

10 See Joseph J. Spengler, 'Demographic Factors and Early Modern Economic Development,' *Daedalus* 97, no. 2 (1968): 434. See also Phyllis Deane and W.A. Cole, *British Economic Growth: 1688–1959* (Cambridge: Cambridge University Press, 1967).

11 A good historical review of the demographic literature and the role that changes in population presumably play in economic growth can be found in David Landes, *The Wealth and Poverty of Nations* (New York: W.W. Norton, 1998).

12 Michael J. Brennan et al., in Leon Stein, ed., *The Economics of Age* (New York: W.W. Norton, 1967).

13 Ibid., 208.

14 Stephen G. Peitchinis, 'Economic Implications of an Aging Population on Society,' in J.S. Frideres and C.J. Bruce, eds., *The Impact of an Aging Population on Society,* (Calgary: University of Calgary Press, 1994), 99.

15 See Francis Fukuyama, 'The Great Disruption,' *Atlantic Monthly*, May 1999, 56.

16 Cited in Thomas L. Friedman, *The Lexus and the Olive Tree.* Available at www://nytimes.com/books/first/f/friedman-lexus.html, 8.

17 See Peitchinis, 'Economic Implications,' 99.

18 Not all observers accept the technological 'promise of things to come.' Among the most prominent doubters is Robert Solow, who writes: 'You can see the computer age everywhere but in the productivity statistics.' Cited in Bill Lehr and Frank Lichtenberg, 'Information Technology and Its Impact on Firm-level Productivity: Evidence from Government and Private Data Sources, 1977–1993,' CSLS Conference on Service Sector Productivity and the Productivity Paradox, Ottawa, 11–12, April 1997), 1. See also Andrew Sharpe, 'The Productivity Paradox: An Evaluation of Competing Explanations,' *Canadian Business Economics* 6, no. 1 (1997): 32–47; and Daniel E. Sichel, *The Computer Revolution* (Washington, DC: Brookings Institution, 1997).

19 Paul Krugman, 'Why Most Economists' Predictions Are Wrong,' *Red Herring*, June 1998, 1.

20 While demonstrating that trained workers are an asset to a company, Harley Frazis and his colleagues report that 'Many argue that the conditions that made mass production techniques advantageous are no longer present and companies need to "transform" themselves, or to adopt "high performance" workplace practices.' See Harley Frazis, Maury Gittleman, and Mary Joyce, *Determinants of Training: An Analysis Using Both Employer and Employee Characteristics* (Washington, DC: U.S. Bureau of Labor Statistics, 1998), 9–10.

21 Frank Denton et al. are not optimistic that mass immigration will significantly reduce the aging of Canada's labour force. They report that 'Immigration seems not to be an instrument of much use for controlling the dependency ratio ... or for offsetting the process of population aging: Huge increases in immigration would be required to achieve small gains.' See Denton et al., 'Immigration, Labour Force and the Age Structure of the Population,' 20. David Cutler and his colleagues report that between 1960 and 1985 a clear trend emerged: industrial countries that experienced a reduction in labour force growth saw a corresponding increase in productivity, whereas in countries where the labour force expanded, e.g. in the United States and Canada, productivity declined. See David M. Cutler, James M. Poterba, Louise M. Sheiner, and Lawrence H. Summers, 'An Aging Society: Challenge or Opportunity?' *Brookings Papers on Economic Activity*, no. 1 (1990): 1–73. Denton and Spencer conclude that 'On balance, the relevant literature seems to suggest that there is no reason to anticipate a reduction of productivity growth as a consequence of population aging. Furthermore, there is the possibility that slower labour force growth will itself provide an incentive to achieve faster productivity growth, since labour will be more scarce.' See Frank T. Denton and Byron G. Spencer, 'Economic Costs of Population Aging,' *IESOP Research Paper*, no. 32 (Hamilton: McMaster University, Dec., 1998), p. 53.
22 See John Maynard Keynes, *The Economic Consequences of Peace* (London: Macmillan, 1919). See also Fausto Vicarelli, *Keynes: The Instability of Capitalism* (Philadelphia: University of Pennsylvania Press, 1984).
23 See Richard Easterlin, *Birth and Fortune: The Impact of Numbers on Personal Welfare* (New York: Basic Books, 1980).
24 See William J. Baumol, Edward N. Wolff, and Sue Ann Batey Blackman, *Productivity and American Leadership: The Long View* (Cambridge, Mass.: MIT Press, 1989), 9. In a similar vein, the economic historian J. Bradford DeLong describes how technology was able to control the destabilizing effects of the population explosion experienced in the nineteenth century, both in Western Europe and North America. See J. Bradford DeLong, 'The Shape of Twentieth Century History,' *Federal Reserve Bank of Boston Regional Review*, Fall 1998.
25 See Michael Beer and Nitrin Nohria, *Old Theories in the New Economy* (Cambridge, Mass.: Harvard Business School Press, 2000).
26 See Robert M. Solow, 'On Golden Pond,' *New York Review of Books*, 6 May 1999, 18. See also Henry Hazlitt, *The Critics of Keynesian Economics* (Lanham, Md.: University Press of America, 1977).
27 Cited in Scott A. Bass, ed., *Older and Active* (New Haven: Yale University Press, 1995).

28 Private communication from Statistics Canada.

29 Bass, *Older and Active*.

30 Peter Drucker, e.g., does not see the future as a mystery. See Peter Drucker, 'The Future That Has Already Happened,' *Harvard Business Review* (Sept.– Oct., 1997, 20, where he writes: 'The dominant factor for business in the next two decades – absent war, pestilence, or collision with a comet – is not going to be economics or technology. It will be demographics. The key factor for business will not be the overpopulation of the world, which we have warned of these last 40 years. It will be the increasing underpopulation of the developed countries – Japan and the nations of Europe and North America.' However, there is strong disagreement over what exactly is the 'real' problem that policy-makers will have to face as our workforce ages. Denton and Spencer write that 'The basic challenge for the society is thus not to cope with a massive overall increase in "dependency burden" or costs, but rather how to reallocate resources to match the changing requirements of the population as its age distribution evolves over the coming decades. We have argued that society will be better positioned to maintain its social support systems if the "aging problem" is correctly understood, and if longer-term planning is brought to bear on the systems themselves, taking into account both future demands and the future productive capacity of the economy.' See Denton and Spencer, 'Population Aging and the Maintenance of Social Support Systems,' *IESOP Research Paper*, no. 9 (Hamilton: McMaster University, Sept. 1996), 12.

31 See Peitchinis, 'Economic Implications,' 100.

32 See Michael Kremer and Eric Maskin, 'Wage Inequality and Segregation by Skill,' *NBER Working Paper*, no. W5718 (Cambridge, Mass.: National Bureau of Economic Research, 1996). Erica L. Goshen and David I. Levine, however, challenge this conclusion. in 'The Rise and Decline (?) of U.S. Internal Labor Markets,' *Federal Reserve Bank of New York Research Paper*, no. 9819 (New York: Federal Reserve Bank of New York, 1998).

33 See Peitchinis, 'Economic Implications,' 99.

34 See Andrew Samwick, 'New Evidence on Pensions, Social Security, and the Timing of Retirement,' *NBER Working Paper*, no. W6534 (Cambridge, Mass.: National Bureau of Economic Research, 1998); and Leora Friedberg, 'The Effect of Old Age Assistance on Retirement,' *NBER Working Paper*, no. W6548 (Cambridge, Mass.: National Bureau of Economic Research, 1998).

35 See Thomas Courchene, 'Generation X versus Generation XS: Reflections on the Way Ahead,' in Keith G. Banting and Robin Boadway, eds., *Reform of Retirement Income Policy: International and Canadian Perspectives* (Kingston: Queen's University, School of Policy Studies, 1997), 330.

36 For a sophisticated analysis of how pension benefits, earnings, and savings
    affect retirement behaviour, see Steven F. Venti and David A. Wise, 'The
    Cause of Wealth Dispersion at Retirement: Choice or Chance,' *American
    Economic Review* 88, no. 2 (1998): 185–91. Also see Leora Friedberg, 'The
    Effect of Government Programs on the Labor Supply of the Elderly,' *Pro-
    ceedings of the 89th Annual Conference, National Tax Association* (Boston: 1996),
    203–10.
37 See OECD, 'Work Force Ageing: Consequences and Policy Responses,' *Age-
    ing Working Paper*, AWP4.1 (Paris: OECD, 1998), 145. See also Jeffrey G. Wil-
    liamson, 'Globalization, Labor Markets, and Policy Backlash in the Past,'
    Journal of Economic Perspectives 12, no. 4 (1998): 70.
38 See Richard V. Burkhauser and Joseph F. Quinn, 'Implementing Pro-Work
    Policies for Older Americans in the Twenty-First Century,' *Preparing for the
    Baby-Boomers' Retirement: The Role of Employment*, serial no. 105-7 (Washing-
    ton, D.C.: United States Senate Special Committee on Aging, 25 July 1997),
    62.
39 See James H. Schulz, Allan Barowski, and William H. Crown, eds., *Econom-
    ics of Population Aging* (New York: Auburn House, 1991), 341.
40 See Denton and Spencer, 'Population, Labour Force, and Long-term Eco-
    nomic Growth,' 53, 23.
41 See OECD, 'Transition From Work To Retirement,' 13.
42 Anonymous, *Work Organization and the Aging Workforce: A Literature Review*
    (Toronto: University of Toronto Libraries, n.d.).
43 Frank T. Denton and Byron G. Spencer, 'Economic Costs of Population
    Aging,' 57.
44 See Richard Disney, *Can We Afford to Grow Older? A Perspective on the Eco-
    nomics of Aging* (Cambridge, Mass.: MIT Press, 1996), 155.
45 There are many studies examining lagging productivity in Canada, the
    United States, and in OECD countries. For Canada, see Andrew Sharpe,
    'The Productivity Paradox: An Evaluation of Competing Explanations,'
    Canadian Business Economics 6, no. 1 (1997): 32–47; John Baldwin and Nag-
    inder Dhaliwal, 'Labour Productivity Differences between Domestic and
    Foreign-Controlled Establishments in the Canadian Manufacturing Sector,'
    Analytical Studies Branch Research Paper Series, no. 118 (Ottawa: Statistics
    Canada, 2000); Surendra Gera, Walong Gu, and Frank C. Lee 'Foreign
    Direct Investment and Productivity Growth: The Canadian Host-Country
    Experience,' *Micro-Economic Policy Analysis Branch Papers* (Ottawa: Industry
    Canada, 1998); Doug Hostland, 'Real Wages, Labour Productivity and
    Employment in Canada: A Historical Perspective,' *Applied Research Branch,
    Strategic Policy Reports*, R-96-5E (Ottawa: Human Resources Development

Canada, 1996); Diane Galarneau and Jean-Pierre Maynard, 'Measuring Productivity,' *Perspectives on Labour and Income* (Spring 1995): 26–32; Diane Galarneau and Cecile Dumas, 'About Productivity,' *Perspectives on Labour and Income*, Spring 1993, 39–48; and Bruce Little, 'Canada Seen Lagging in Productivity Race,' *Globe and Mail*, 17 Oct. 1997, B.1.

For the United States, see Stephen Roach, 'In Search of Productivity,' *Harvard Business Review*, Sept.–Oct. 1998, 153–60; J. Bradford DeLong, 'Have Productivity Levels Converged? Productivity Growth, Convergence, and Welfare in the Very Long Run,' *Department of Economics Papers* (Berkeley: University of California, Feb. 1988); J. Bradford DeLong, 'Productivity Growth and Investment in Equipment: A Very Long Run Look,' *Department of Economics Papers* (Berkeley: University of California, Sept. 1991); Moses Abramovitz, *Thinking about Growth* (Cambridge: Cambridge University Press, 1989); William J. Baumol and Kenneth McLennan, eds., *Productivity Growth and U.S. Competitiveness* (New York: Oxford University Press, 1985); Sar A. Levitan and Diane Wernecke, *Productivity: Problems, Prospects, and Policies* (Baltimore: Johns Hopkins University Press, 1984); and Richard R. Nelson, 'Research on Productivity Growth and Productivity Differences: Dead Ends and New Departures,' *Journal of Economic Literature* 19 (Sept. 1981): 1029–64.

For the OECD, see Dirk Pilat, 'Labour Productivity Levels in OECD Countries: Estimates for Manufacturing and Selected Service Sectors,' *Economics Department Working Paper*, no. 69 (Paris: OECD, 1996); and OECD, *Technology, Productivity and Job Creation*, vols. 1 and 2 (Paris: OECD, 1996).

46 See Glenn C. Loury, 'The Hard Questions: Color Blinded,' *New Republic*, 17 and 24 Aug. 1997, 12.

47 Timothy Smeeding and Joseph F. Quinn, 'Cross-National Patterns of Labor Force Withdrawal,' in Peter Flora, Philip R. de Jong, Jun-Young Kim and Julian Le Grand, eds., *The State of Social Welfare* (Aldershot, U.K.: Ashgate Publishing, 1998), 85. See also Deborah Sunter and Geoff Bowlby, 'Labour Force Participation in the 1990s,' *Canadian Economic Observer*, Oct., 1998, 3.1–3.11; OECD, 'The Transition from Work to Retirement;' and OECD, 'The Labour Market and Older Workers,' 154.

48 See Scott A. Bass, 'An Overview of Work, Retirement, and Pensions in Japan,' in Scott A. Bass, Robert Morris, and Mosato Oka, eds., *Public Policy and the Old Age Revolution in Japan* (New York: Haworth Press, 1996), 62.

49 Ibid., 67.

50 See Smeeding and Quinn, 'Cross-National Patterns of Labor Force Withdrawal,' 91.

51 See Suzanne Methot, 'Employment Patterns of Elderly Canadians,' *Canadian Social Trends*,' Autumn 1987, 8.

52 See Sunter and Bowlby, 'Labour Force Participation in the 1990s,' 3.6–3.7.

53 See OECD, 'The Transition from Work to Retirement,' 35–37. See also Peter Hicks, 'The Policy Challenge of Ageing Populations,' *OECD Observer*, no. 212 (1998): 7–9.

54 See David P. Ross and Richard Shillington, *Flux: Two Years in the Life of the Canadian Labour Market* (Ottawa: Statistics Canada, 1991).

55 See Quinn, 'Retirement Trends and Patterns,' p. 10.

56 See Andrew M. Sum and W. Neal Fogg, 'Profile of the Labor Market for Older Workers,' in Peter B. Doeringer, ed., *Bridges to Retirement* (Ithaca, NY: ILR Press, Cornell University, 1990), 53.

57 See Christopher Ruhm, 'Career Jobs, Bridge Employment, and Retirement,' in Doeringer, *Bridges to Retirement* (Ithaca, NY: ILR Press, Cornell University, 1990), 102–5.

58 See Olivia S. Mitchell and Joseph Quinn, '1994–95 Advisory Council on Social Security: Technical Panel on Trends and Issues in Retirement Saving. Final Report,' *Population Aging Research Center, Working Paper Series*, no. 95-06 (Philadelphia: University of Pennsylvania, 1995), 5.

59 See Statistics Canada, *Labour Force Update: Older Workers*, catalogue no. 71-005-XYB (Ottawa: Statistics Canada, 1998), 19.

60 See Bruce C. Fallick, 'A Review of the Recent Empirical Literature on Displaced Workers,' *Industrial and Labor Relations Review* 50(1) (1996): 5–16.

61 See B. Casey and S. Wood, 'Great Britain: Firm Policy, State Policy, and the Employment and Unemployment of Older Workers,' in F. Naschold and B. de Vroom, eds., *Regulating Employment and Welfare* (New York: de Gruyter, 1994), 95.

62 See Human Resources Development Canada, 'Job Loss and the Older Worker,' *Applied Research Bulletin* 2, no. 1 (1995): 96, 9–10. See also Darren Lauzon, 'Worker Displacement: Trends, Characteristics and Policy Responses,' *Applied Research Branch, Strategic Policy Reports*, R-95-3 (Ottawa: Human Resources Development Canada, 1995); David Gray and Gilles Grenier, 'Jobless Durations of Displaced Workers: A Comparison of Canada and the United States,' *Applied Research Branch, Strategic Policy Reports*, W-97-16E (Ottawa: Human Resources Development Canada, 1996); Garnett Picot, Zhengxi Lin, and Wendy Pyper, 'An Overview of Permanent Layoffs,' *Perspectives on Labour and Income* (Autumn 1997): 46–51; and Kenneth A. Couch, 'Late Life Job Displacement,' *Aging Studies Program Series*, no. 6 (Syracuse, NY: Center for Policy Research, Maxwell School of Citizenship and Public Affairs, Syracuse University, 1997).

63 See Bureau of Labor Statistics, 'Who's Not Working,' *Issues in Labor Statistics, Summary,* 98-4 (Washington, DC: U.S. Department of Labor, Bureau of Labor Statistics, 1998); and Steven Hipple, 'Worker Displacement in an Expanding Economy,' *Monthly Labor Review,* Dec. 1997, 26–39.

64 See Kelly Morrison, 'Canada's Older Workers,' *Applied Research Branch, Strategic Policy Reports* (Ottawa: Human Resources Development Canada, 1996).

65 See OECD, *Ageing in OECD Countries: A Critical Policy Challenge* (Paris: OECD, 1996).

66 See Human Resources Development Canada, *Adult Education and Training in Canada* (Ottawa: Human Resources Development Canada, 1994).

67 See Grant Schellenberg, *The Employment Challenge Facing Today's Experienced Workers* (Ottawa: One Voice, Canadian Seniors Network, 1997), 14.

68 See Morrison, 'Canada's Older Workers,' 20.

69 See Statistics Canada, *Labour Force Update: Older Workers,* 20.

70 See Human Resources Development Canada, 'Earnings, Education and Age ... The Low End Goes Lower,' *Applied Research Bulletin* 2, no. 1 (1995–6): 11–12.

71 Edward Prescott has argued that total factor productivity theory fails to explain international income differences and why some economies are more productive than others. See Edward C. Prescott, 'Lawrence R. Klein Lecture 1997. Needed: A Theory of Total Factor Productivity,' *International Economic Review* 39, no. 3 (1998): 547. See also William J. Baumol, N. Wolff, and Sue Anne Blackman, *Productivity and American Leadership: The Long View* (Cambridge, Mass.: MIT Press, 1989).

72 See Kathryn McMullen, 'Working with Technology: Changing Skill Requirements in the Computer Age,' Human Resources Development Canada, *Applied Research Bulletin* 2, no. 2 (1996): 2.

73 Cited in Human Resources Development Canada, 'Increasingly Complex Jobs = Higher Skills,' *Applied Research Bulletin* 2, no. 2 (1996).

74 See OECD 'The Transition from Work to Retirement,' 27.

75 See William H. Crown, ed., *Handbook on Employment and the Elderly* (Westport, Conn.: Greenwood Press, 1996).

76 See Conference Board of Canada, *Performance and Potential: Assessing Canada's Social and Economic Performance. Members' Briefing* (Ottawa: Conference Board of Canada, 1996), 14.

77 See Sum and Fogg, 'Profile of the Labor Market for Older Workers,' 47–9.

78 See Mary Jablonski, Kent Kunze, and Larry Rosenblum, 'Productivity, Age, and Labor Composition Changes in the U.S. Workforce,' in Irving Bluestone, Rhonda J.V. Montgomery and John D. Owen, eds., *The Aging of the*

American Workforce: Problems, Programs, Policies (Detroit: Wayne State University Press, 1990), 335.

79 See Yankelovich, Skelly, and White, Inc., 'Workers Over 50: Old Myths, New Realities,' in *Report Prepared for the American Association of Retired Persons* (New York: Yankelovich, Skelly, and White, 1985), passim.

80 Ibid., 11–12.

81 See Michael C. Barth, William Mc Naught, and Philip Rizzi, 'Older Americans as Workers,' in Scott A. Bass, ed., *Older and Active* (New Haven: Yale University Press, 1995), 41.

82 See Richard S. Belous, 'Flexible Employment: The Employer's Point of View,' in Peter B. Doeringer, ed., *Bridges to Retirement* (Ithaca, NY: ILR Press, Cornell University, 1990), 124.

83 See Donna L. Wagner, 'Testimony before the U.S. Senate Special Committee on Aging' (Towson, Md.: Center for Productive Aging, Towson University, 1998), 1–2.

84 Ibid., 2.

85 See Glenn McEvoy and Wayne Cascio, 'Cumulative Evidence of the Relationship between Employee Age and Job Performance,' *Journal of Applied Psychology* 74, no. 1 (1989): 11–17.

86 See E.A. Hammel, 'The Productivity of Chemists and Mathematicians at the University of California: A Cohort Analysis,' *Program in Population Research Working Paper* 11 (Berkeley: University of California, 1983).

87 See Paul R. Sparrow and D.R. Davies, 'Effects of Age, Tenure, Training, and Job Complexity on Technical Performance,' *Psychology and Aging* 3, no. 3 (1988): 307–14.

88 See Neil Charness and E.A. Bosman, 'Age-Related Changes in Perceptual and Psychomotor Performance: Implications for Engineering Design,' *Experimental Aging Research* 20, no. 6 (1994): 45–59.

89 See Human Resources Development Canada, 'The Aging Workforce – Still Capable after All These Years,' *Applied Research Bulletin* 1, no. 2 (1995): 13–14.

90 See Bureau of Labor Statistics, 'Comparative Job Performance By Age: Large Plants in the Men's Footwear and Household Furniture Industries,' *Bulletin*, no. 1223 (Washington, D.C.: U.S. Department of Labor, Bureau of Labor Statistics, 1957).

91 See E. Lazear, 'Why Is There Mandatory Retirement?' *Journal of Political Economy* 87, no. 6 (1979): 1261–84.

92 See James L. Medoff and Katharine G. Abraham, 'Experience, Performance and Earnings,' *Quarterly Journal of Economics* 95, no. 4 (1980): 703–36.

93 See K.J. Gibson, W.J. Zerbe, and R.E. Franken, 'Job Search Strategies for

Older Job Hunters' Addressing Employers,' Perceptions,' *Canadian Journal of Counselling* 26, no. 3 (1992): 168–70.

94 Cited in *Preparing for the Baby Boomers' Retirement: The Role of Employment*, serial no. 105-7 (Washington, DC: U.S. Senate Special Committee on Aging, 25 July 1997), 56.

95 See James A. Kahn and Jong-Soo Lim, 'Skilled Labor Augmenting Technical Progress in U.S. Manufacturing,' *Federal Reserve Bank of New York, Staff Reports*, no. 47 (New York: Oct. 1998).

96 See T. Dunne, John Haltiwanger, and Kenneth R. Troske, 'Technology and Jobs: Secular Changes and Cyclical Dynamics,' *NBER Working Paper*, no. 5656 (Cambridge, Mass.: National Bureau of Economic Research, 1996).

97 See David H. Autor, Lawrence Katz, and Alan Krueger, 'Computing Inequality: Have Computers Changed the Labor Market,' *Quarterly Journal of Economics* 113, no. 4 (1998): 1169–1213.

98 See Eli Berman, John Bound, and Stephen Machin, 'Implications of Skill-Biased Technological Change: International Evidence' *Quarterly Journal of Economics* 113, no. 4 (1998) 1245–79.

99 See Stephen Machin and John Van Reenen, 'Technology and Changes in Skill Structure: Evidence from Seven OECD Countries,' *Quarterly Journal of Economics* 113, no. 4 (1998): 1215–44.

100 See OECD 'The Labour Market and Older Workers,' 158.

101 Sara Rix, 'The Challenge of an Aging Work Force: Keeping Older Workers Employed and Employable,' in Scott A. Bass, Robert Morris, and Masato Oka, eds., *Public Policy and the Old Age Revolution in Japan* (New York: Haworth Press, 1996), 92.

102 See OECD, *OECD Economic Surveys: Canada* (Paris: OECD, 1998).

103 Lynn McDonald, Peter Donahue, and Brooke Moore, have challenged what may be called the 'voluntary retiree's syndrome,' by pointing out that many older Canadians are forced out of their jobs because of downsizing and 'cost-saving pension changes,' and because of this forced retirement they experience economic hardship and emotional distress. See Lynn McDonald et al., 'The Economic Casualties of Retiring Because of Unemployment,' *IESOP Research Paper*, no. 30 (Hamilton: McMaster University, 1998).

104 See Bruce Little, 'Productivity In the Eye of the Beholder,' *Globe and Mail*, 10 April 1999, D1.

105 This is not to say that social scientists and governments have been indifferent to globalization or the structural changes now taking place in modern economies. Quite the contrary; they have been very interested. There is a substantial literature on these issues which continues to grow, but not

much attention has been paid to the relationship between an aging work-force and future productivity growth. See, e.g., Robert J. Gordon, 'U.S. Economic Growth since 1870: One Big Wave?' *American Economic Review* 89, no. 2 (1999): 123–8; Dale W. Jorgenson and Kevin J. Stiroh, 'Information Technology and Growth,' *American Economic Review* 89, no. 2 (1999): 109–15; and Todd L. Idson and Walter Y. Oi, 'Workers Are More Productive in Large Firms,' *American Economic Review* 89, no. 2 (1999): 104–8.

106 Cited in William J. Baumol et al., *Productivity and American Leadership*, 9.The following studies provide a good overview of the current debate over factors seen to be responsible for productivity growth: Disney, *Can We Afford to Grow Older*; Andrew Sharpe, 'The Productivity Paradox: An Evaluation of Competing Explanations,' *Canadian Business Economics* 6, no. 1 (1997): 32–47; Edward N. Wolff, 'The Productivity Paradox: Evidence from Indirect Indicators of Service Sector Productivity Growth,' *Canadian Journal of Economics* 32, no. 2 (1999): 281–307; and Bill Lehr and Frank Lichtenberg, 'Information Technology and Its Impact on Firm-level Productivity: Evidence from Government and Private Data Sources, 1977–1993,' CSLS Conference on Service Sector Productivity and the Productivity Paradox, Ottawa, 11–12 April 1997.

107 Nicholas Georgescu-Roegen, in Leonard Silk, *The Economists* (New York: Avon Books, 1976), 239.

108 One recent study that has tried to find some answers to these questions is John C. Haltiwanger, Julia I. Lane, and James R. Spletzer, 'Productivity Differences across Employers: The Roles of Employer Size, Age, and Human Capital,' *American Economic Review* 89, no. 2 (1999): 94–8.

109 Fallick makes it clear at the outset that studying the impact of worker displacement is more complex and controversial than is usually assumed. He writes: 'There is considerable disagreement in the literature about how to formally define "displaced worker." The question of definition is not merely academic. Government programs are often justified on the grounds that society should compensate the losers for structural changes that benefit us in the aggregate, especially if those changes are due to a change in government policy. Because of a lack of consensus on the definition of displaced workers, the estimated number of displaced workers – and hence the number who may be eligible for compensatory benefits from government programs – varies tremendously.' See Fallick, 'A Review of the Recent Empirical Literature on Displaced Workers,' 5.

110 Richard Lewontin was criticizing much of the research done today in the natural sciences. However his evaluation can be extended to many of the productivity studies being churned out today. 'Science and "The Demon-

Haunted World": An Exchange,' *New York Review of Books*, 3 March 1997, 52.

111 See Dave Turner et al., 'The Macroeconomic Implications of Ageing in a Global Context,' 4, 7.

112 See Disney, *Can We Afford to Grow Older?*

113 Shawn McCarthy, 'Productivity, a Political Issue,' *Globe and Mail*, 10 April 1999, D3.

114 John C. Haltiwanger, et al., 'Productivity Differences'; see also Murray Campbell, 'Firms Question Wisdom of Ejecting the Experienced,' *Globe and Mail*, 5 July 1999, A5.

115 See Solow's critique in, 'On Golden Pond.'

116 See Joseph F. Quinn et al., 'The Microeconomics of the Retirement Decision in the United States,' Department of Economics, Working Paper, no. 203 (Paris: OECD, 1998).

117 See, e.g., Richard W. Judy and Carol D'Amico, *Workforce 2020: Work and Workers in the 21st Century*, on the approach taken by the Hudson Institute in its recent study of the prospective changes the U.S. workforce is likely to undergo over the next twenty-five years. See also Herbert S. Parnes, ed., *Work and Retirement: A Longitudinal Study of Men* (Cambridge Mass.: MIT Press, 1981).

118 Disney, *Can We Afford to Grow Older?* 155.

119 Daniel Bell, 'The End of Ideology Revisted – Part II,' *Government and Opposition* 23, no. 3 (1988): 328.

120 See Baumol et al., *Productivity and American Leadership: The Long View*, 2–3.

6. Work and Leisure: A Question of Balance

Marty Thomas and Rosemary A. Venne

Introduction: Time Use

In 1991 Juliet Schor, a Harvard University economist, published the much-reviewed and discussed *The Overworked American: The Unexpected Decline of Leisure.*[1] Schor argued that Americans were trapped in a cycle of 'work and spend' that reduced both the quantity and quality of leisure time. The idea also resonated on this side of the border. Canadians, too, it seemed, were caught in the same trap. As a result, Schor was invited to address many conferences and discuss her ideas on Canadian television and radio talk shows. In the ensuing years some scholarly work was done on the subject, but none of it received the popular press that Schor had achieved, and it was not until 1997 that a full-scale response was heard.

After five years of preparation and overcoming many challenges to get their book into print, John Robinson and Geoffrey Godbey, published *Time for Life: The Surprising Ways Americans Use Their Time.* The authors suggest that their major difficulty in getting published may have been that their conclusions were in contradiction to 'other scholarly and popular accounts' about Americans' use of time.[2] Robinson and Godbey employed a time diary approach to conclude that Americans have more, not less, free time but feel 'time crunched' largely because of the acceleration of technological change and the speed-up of social life.

Robinson and Godbey question both Schor's methodology and, by extension, her conclusion that employed Americans were working 163 more hours a year in 1987 than in 1969. They challenge Schor's contention that women are working three times the extra hours as compared with their male counterparts. Instead, Robinson and Godbey's time diary results suggest that women's work time is not significantly higher than men's and that parents are not spending less time with their children. In terms of the larger question regarding the direction of change in hours of work, they 'argue that Americans have more free time than they did 30 years ago and that time is likely to increase in the future.'[3]

Given the cross-national similarities in so many respects, the debate presents an interesting challenge: What does the picture look like in Canada? To what degree can Robinson's and Godbey's claims be supported by Canadian data? What have we learned from recent Canadian research on time use and participation surveys that can help us understand the issue of work–leisure balance? And, what does the work–leisure balance look like over the life course, and especially in terms of our aging population?

The purpose of this essay is twofold: first, to examine the current state of knowledge related to patterns of participation in work and leisure with a particular focus on the life course, and second, to discuss 'what we know' in terms of the balance between the two. Given the complexity, as well as the intersubjectivity of the topic, the discussion is rather wide-ranging. The chapter is divided into four parts. The first, 'Definitions of Leisure, Work, and Time,' identifies the phenomena under discussion. This is followed by 'Focus on Leisure,' which is a review of time use research derived mainly from the Americans' *Use of Time* Project and various analyses based on Canada's General Social Surveys (GSS) conducted by Statistics Canada in 1986 and 1992, supplemented by participation surveys in leisure and work. The third section, 'Focus on Work,' discusses the demographic implications of work in terms of our aging population; this section concludes with a normative viewpoint on the work–leisure balance. The chapter concludes with suggestions for further research and possible public policy and workplace strategies, in a final section entitled 'A Need for Balance.'

Definitions of Leisure, Work, and Time

There are not many words whose definitions are as complex as leisure, work, and time. Each term has been explored by a variety of scholars – from historians and economists to sociologists and philosophers. Books have been written and articles published, with little apparent consensus. The question remains, Is it necessary to know the meanings of leisure and work in terms of lived experience before they can be quantified and measured? The dilemma of definitional clarity becomes one that each researcher must address to meet particular research goals.

Defining leisure is a complex and problematic undertaking since there are almost as many definitions as there are scholars of the phenomenon. The abstract nature of the concept combined with its inherent value base do much to mystify the term. Josef Pieper claimed that leisure was the basis of culture; yet many people are still living with Thorstein Veblen's concept of leisure as time wasted and non-productive.[4] Furthermore, the sheer number of definitions necessitates the use of a classification system or framework. A recent and comprehensive system was offered by Gilles Pronovost and Max D'Amours[5] in which they classify 'the best known' definitions in four categories: (1) residual – available time, beyond obligatory time; (2) activity-based – associated with free-time activity (i.e., sport, cultural activity); (3) cultural definitions that emanate from two cultural orientations: (a) resulting from a critique of the influence of mass culture or (b) related to societal change in the anthropological or sociological sense; and (4) related to the reciprocal relationship with other phenomena (i.e., work, family).

Work, too is an elusive concept. On the one hand, it can be pure toil, an obligation undertaken only under duress in order to feed one's family or otherwise contribute to community and family well-being. On the other hand, it can be seen as the major activity that gives meaning to life.[6] John Kenneth Galbraith aptly summarizes the difficulty:

> There is a problem with the word 'work.' It is used to characterize two radically different, indeed sharply contrasting, commitments of human time. Work can be something one greatly enjoys, that accords a sense of fulfillment and accomplishment and without which there would be a feeling of displacement, social rejection, depression or, at best, boredom. It is such work that defines social position – that of the corporate executive, financier, artist, poet, scholar, television commentator, even journalist. But work also consigns men and women to the anonymity of the toiling masses. Here it consists of repetitive, tiring, muscular effort replete with tedium. It has often been held that the good workman enjoys his work; this is said most frequently, most thoughtfully, by those with no experience of hard, physical, economically enforced toil. The word 'work' denotes sharply contrasting situations; it is doubtful whether any other term in any language is quite so at odds with itself in what it describes.[7]

Time in everyday conversation usually refers to the 'duration of existence, a period or interval.'[8] Measuring these periods or intervals in relation to specific categories such as work or leisure time would be a seemingly simple task since all activity occurs within time. Once time is married with the terms work or leisure, however, it can undergo many transitions in definition. Time becomes subject to a system of human values, needs, and interests that influence the set of meanings identified by the term at the level of the individual. Common phrases such as 'saving,' 'losing,' or 'spending' time demonstrate the degree to which cultural values influence how time is perceived. The simple task of carving up a pie representing a day, a week, or a month becomes complicated by the perspectives and suppositions of individuals and society as a whole. On the other hand, time can be said to be the most egalitarian of all resources – everyone has the same twenty-four hours. And, it is easy to count; we now have the astounding capability to measure time to the nanosecond.

In this discussion of work, leisure, and time, we not only deal with complex phenomena that affect the daily lives of all Canadians but also how they are related to another elusive idea – the notion of balance. Canadians are inundated with media reports related to the challenges of globalization, domination of market economies – especially with our neighbour to the south, competition, and the never-ending need to be more productive in this fast-paced world. Few would argue about either the need for balance between work and family life or equity in terms of reasonable hours of work to reduce the conundrum of over-work for some while others are unemployed. But we do argue about where the balance is, what reasonable means, and how productivity can be maintained or enhanced, if work is redistributed.

Much of what we know about the distribution of work and leisure is based on time use research. Beginning in the 1970s with a focus on productivity and efficiency for factory workers, time diary studies have undergone conceptual and methodological refinement in recent years to support a good basis for (1) comparisons between groups (gender, income, and education, (2) comparisons over time, and (3) international comparisons.[9]

Focus on Leisure

In time use research, work and leisure must be concisely defined. Work is generally understood to mean paid employment, while leisure is broadly defined as activity undertaken in 'free time.' Robinson and

Figure 6.1   Interrelations across the four types of time

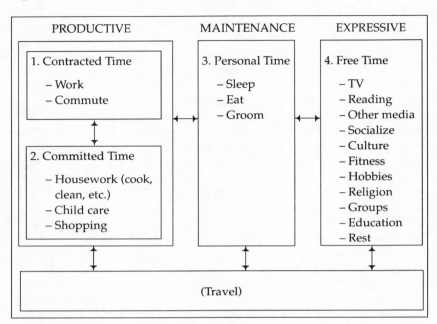

Source: John Robinson and Geoffrey Godbey, *Time for Life: The Surprising Ways Americans Use Their Time* (University Park: Pennsylvania State University Press, 1997), based on Americans' Use of Time Project.

Godbey suggest that time use falls within the following four categories: (1) paid work, (2) household and family care, (3) personal time, and (4) free time.[10] While they agree that any divisions of time are necessarily arbitrary and subject to challenge, Robinson and Godbey suggest that their model allows for a broader understanding of the determinants of time use and demonstrate that trade-offs in time use may not be limited to those within work and leisure; time may also be gained from personal care, for example. They suggest that the relationships between the types of time fall within three broad categories: (1) productive time, (2) time spent on maintenance activities, and (3) expressive time. Robinson and Godbey's model includes travel in a fourth 'floating' category that connects or acts as an adjunct to the three other types of time. With minor variations this model has been used by the Americans' *Use of Time* Project every ten years since 1965 (see Figure 6.1).

Time for Life was based on time budget data gathered every ten years from 1965 to 1985 in conjunction with the Americans' *Use of Time* Project. It provides an extensive review of time use research and includes a major review of Canadian studies.[11] The ten categories (with ninety-nine subcategories) are comprehensive, thereby offering a useful basis for comparison. Daily allocations of time are divided between non-free time (paid work, household work, child care, obtaining goods and services, and personal needs and care) and free time activity (education and training, organizational activity, entertainment and social activity, recreation, and communication).

Canadians were remarkably close to their American neighbours in how they spend their time. This is not surprising, given that Canada and the United States have very similar demographic profiles. Each country had a prolonged postwar fertility boom, which today is giving a decided middle-aged slant to the North American population profile. In both countries the baby boom, which comprises approximately one-third of the population in Canada, was preceded and followed by significant bust generations.[12] Robinson and Godbey noted many similarities in the most time-consuming of activities. Over the course of a week Canadians worked an hour less, slept about twenty minutes more and watched exactly the same number of hours of television. Some minor differences were noted. In comparison with Americans, Robinson and Godbey conclude that Canadians spent:

- More time in meal preparation, gardening, and pet care
- More time shopping
- Less time eating out
- Less time grooming
- More time on adult educational activity
- Less time on religious activity
- More time visiting, although Americans have more conversations (possible coding differences)
- Less time travelling

General Social Surveys

The second Canadian General Social Survey (GSS), conducted in 1986, collected information on time use – the first national Canadian study to focus specifically on time. The study was repeated in 1992. Cycle 2 (1986) and Cycle 7 (1992) data were collected by telephone survey of approximately 9,000 non-institutionalized Canadians 15 years of age and over. The data collection period for Cycle 2 was November and December of 1986, while Cycle 7 data were collected throughout a 12-month period starting in January 1992. The reporting in this chapter concentrates on the major conclusions related to aspects of work and leisure as reported by Andrew Harvey, Ken Marshall, and Judith Frederick for the 1986 survey (published in 1991), Frederick for 1992 (published in 1995), and other researchers who examined time use.[13] As is typical for time use research, hours are averaged over seven days. Cycle 9 data (from 1998) have recently been made available to researchers and analyses are currently under way.

Highlights from GSS Cycle 2

Canadians aged 15 and over spent:

- 7.5 hours per day on productive activity (paid work, education, and unpaid work)
- 11 hours sleeping, eating, and on other personal care activities
- 5.5 hours per day in free time activity
- Of the productive activity (7.5 hours per day),1.1 hours per day was spent on domestic activities (2.5 hours per day for women, 1.0 hours for men).

In total, paid work accounted for less than one-half of total productive activity. Thirteen per cent of Canadians 15+ engaged in educational activities (attending classes, lectures, or study). Students spent 6.2 hours per day on educational activities compared with the 6.6 hours per day workers dedicated to paid work. Just under 90 per cent of parents spent time with their children daily. Of those parents, they interacted with their children about 5.2 hours per day. More than half of all parents with children under 19 years of age and living at home spent an average of 2 hours per day on primary child care.

Not surprisingly, Canadians have more free time on weekends. Free time increases from an average of 4.7 hours on weekdays to 7.0 hours on Saturday, peaking at 7.5 hours on Sunday. Men have 0.3 hours more free time on weekdays than women, 0.7 hours more on Saturday, and just less than one hour more of free time on Sunday. Watching television took up much of the free time available, accounting for more than 40 per cent of free time activity.

Figure 6.2   Time distribution for Canadians 15 years of age and over

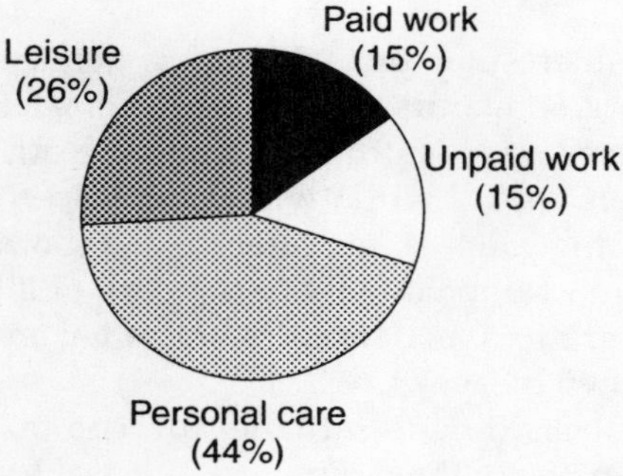

Source: Judith Frederick, *As Time Goes By: Time Use of Canadians*, Statistics Canada cat. 89-544E (Ottawa: Government of Canada Minister of Industry, 1995).

Having children limited the amount of free time available, especially for women with a partner and one or more children. They have 4.4 hours of free time per day compared with the average of 5.8 hours per day for women with a partner and no children. For their male counterparts, the average was 4.7 and 6.3 hours respectively.

Highlights from GSS Cycle 7

In 1992 a typical Canadian spent his or her day (factored over a 7-day period) in 10.5 hours of activities related to self-care, including sleeping, eating, and hygiene. This left 13.5 hours per day to divide among four primary pursuits (see Figure 6.2):

- 3.6 hours of paid work including activities related to working, such as commuting and all time spent at the workplace (inclusive of breaks and work delays, idle time before and after work, and looking for work)
- 3.6 hours of unpaid work inclusive of household chores, shopping, family responsibilities, and civic/volunteer activity
- 0.6 hours of education including homework, breaks, lectures, leisure and special interest classes, and educational travel for both full- and part-time students

- 5.7 hours of leisure including 'free time' which is not designated to any of the previously mentioned categories

Judith Frederick identified an interesting breakdown by gender: Males spent more time at paid work (4.5 hours per day) than females (2.7 hours). Almost exactly the reverse was identified for unpaid work. Females spent 4.5 hours per day on unpaid work, while males spent 2.6 hours per day. In terms of age, the 25-to-44 age category had both the most paid (4.8 hours) and the most unpaid (4.0 hours) work of all age groups. Not surprisingly this group experienced the least leisure time (see Figure 6.3 for the breakdown by age).

Statistics Canada's time use analysis describes the leisure component of the 'typical Canadian' day in one of three pursuits:

- Socializing – activities taking place both at home and away from home where social interaction is the focus of the activity
- Passive leisure – refers to activities taking place primarily at home with limited physical exertion
- Active leisure – concerns activities which take place out of the home and involve physical exertion

The 1992 snapshot of the average Canadian's day concluded that leisure time was divided in these categories:

- Socializing – 109 minutes per day
- Passive leisure – 168 minutes per day, of which 135 minutes was spent watching television
- Active leisure – 67 minutes of which 8 minutes was attending sports, movies, and other entertainment, and 59 minutes involved in active sports or leisure.

The most popular activity for Canadians was watching television; it consumed 135 minutes per day. Reading occupied approximately 30 minutes of the average Canadian's day. Civic and voluntary activity, although not considered a leisure pursuit by Statistics Canada, consumed 23 minutes of the average person's day. Survey research on behaviour in Quebec noted similar leisure patterns to the national averages with the exception that the rate of television viewing surpasses that of any other province.[14]

A recent study of voluntary activity, 'Caring Canadians, Involved Canadians,' reports that increased demands on time affected the

Figure 6.3   Time distribution for Canadians according to age groups

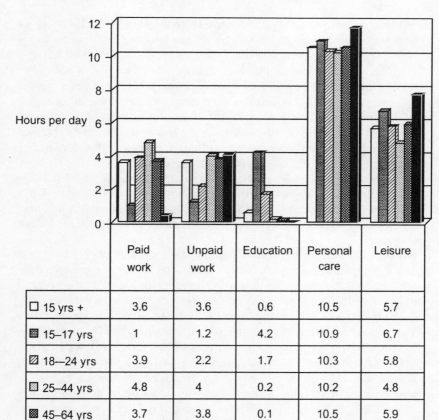

	Paid work	Unpaid work	Education	Personal care	Leisure
☐ 15 yrs +	3.6	3.6	0.6	10.5	5.7
▨ 15–17 yrs	1	1.2	4.2	10.9	6.7
▨ 18—24 yrs	3.9	2.2	1.7	10.3	5.8
▨ 25–44 yrs	4.8	4	0.2	10.2	4.8
▨ 45–64 yrs	3.7	3.8	0.1	10.5	5.9
■ 65+	0.4	4.1	0	11.7	7.7

Source: Judith Frederick, *As Time Goes By: Time Use of Canadians*, Statistics Canada cat. 89-544E (Ottawa: Government of Canada Minister of Industry, 1995).

amount of volunteer work performed by Canadians.[15] The 1987 data indicate an average volunteer contribution of 191 hours. In contrast, Canadians in 1997 were contributing an average of 149 hours of volunteer work per year. Lack of time was cited as the reason for not volunteering by three-quarters of those surveyed.

Leisure over the Life Course

- Youth, age 15 to 17 years participate in an average of 6.2 hours of leisure time per day. Young males had more leisure time than their
  female counterparts. The majority of this time was involved in passive leisure (2.6 hours) followed closely by socializing (1.9 hours).
  Active leisure comprised 1.7 hours of the day. Young males in this
  age group watched 2.6 hours of television per day, compared with
  1.7 hours per day for females. Civic and voluntary activity (not
  included in the GSS as a leisure pursuit) is noted here: males participated in 0.1 hours of civic and volunteer activity per day, females
  spent 0.4 hours in civic and volunteer activity.
- Youth age 18 to 24 years participated in an average of 5.5 hours of
  leisure time per day. Socializing for 2.3 hours makes up the bulk of
  their leisure time activity, followed by passive leisure at 2 hours and
  1.2 hours of active leisure. Civic and voluntary activity accounted for
  less than 0.3 hours per day factored over the week.
- Adults between the ages of 25 and 44 made up 42.6 per cent of the
  15+ aged Canadian population in 1992. This age group experienced
  a number of life events related to both career and family. With regard
  to leisure, this age group averaged 2.2 hours of passive activity per
  day, 1.7 hours of socializing, and 1.8 hours of active leisure pursuits.
  Variations in participation were primarily influenced by marital status, family situation, and employment status. Civic and volunteer
  activity averaged 0.3 hours per day for this age group.
- Adults age 44 to 64 years spent 3.4 hours in passive leisure. They
  participated in 1.9 hours of social activity and 1 hour of active leisure
  daily. Civic and volunteer activity averaged 0.5 hours per day.
- The 65+ category spent about one-third of their day in leisure pursuits. Over half of this time was spent in passive activities (4.8
  hours), social activities comprised 2 hours per day, and active leisure
  made up the remaining 1.3 hours. Civic and volunteer activity averaged 0.6 hours per day.

The 1997 report 'A Portrait of Seniors in Canada' by Statistics Canada described seniors as having as much as 2 hours more free time per
day than those age 15 to 64 years.[16] It would appear that the concept of
free time differs among seniors, since almost half of seniors, 47 per cent
in 1992, reported they never had 'time on their hands' and only 12 per
cent say they had time on their hands every day. Television viewing

accounted for much of the free time of older adults. In 1992 those 65 and over watched television an average of 3.3 hours per day. Television viewing was further analysed in a 1994 Statistics Canada publication in which it is noted that the number of hours of television viewing for seniors had decreased from 24.2 hours per week in 1986 to an average of 22.8 hours in 1993.[17]

Jiri Zuzanek and Bryan Smale combined three concepts: the life cycle, daily use of time, and the 'weekly rhythm' in an attempt to look at the variations in lifestyle of the weekly distribution of leisure time, paid work, and unpaid work.[18] They conclude that the recent institution of the week (in historical terms) has been both enhanced by the introduction of the full second day off to create a long weekend and eroded in that there has been a decline of religious participation and a proliferation of week-long services, Sunday shopping, and so on. Some of these changes may carry with them further challenges to a balanced family life in unintended consequences related to the quickening pace of life. Zuzanek and Smale conclude that the synchronization of services may produce as a side-effect an asynchronization and arrhythmia in family life.

Leisure Trends

Zuzanek and Smale compared the three General Social Surveys from 1981, 1986, and 1992.[19] (Note that the methodology relevant to GSS time use was changed following the 1981 survey.) The following leisure trends were identified:

- Free time decreased for employed Canadians by as much as 10 per cent from 1981 to 1992.
- Daily television watching increased from 98 minutes in 1981 to 119 minutes in 1986, then declined in 1992 to 106 minutes.
- Physical and outdoor activities increased. Men increased their participation from 23 minutes per day to 36 minutes per day from 1981 to 1992. Women increased their time from 15 to 22 minutes per day over the eleven years.
- Time spent listening to music and radio as a primary activity decreased from 6 minutes per day in 1981 to less than 3 minutes in 1992.
- Time spent reading newspapers maintained its level of 10 minutes per day from 1981 to 1992. Reading books and magazines, how-

ever, decreased from 16 minutes per day in 1981 to 13 minutes in 1992.
- Time spent on social leisure decreased by 8 per cent from 1981 to 1992.
- There was little change in participation in active leisure as defined by Statistics Canada, however, high cultural activities dropped from 1 minute per day in 1981 to half a minute per day in 1992.
- Sporting events dropped for men by 2 minutes per day over the eleven-year period, and by 0.6 minutes for women.
- Time spent on rest and relaxation decreased from approximately 18 minutes in 1981 to an average of 9 minutes per day for working men, while working women saw their resting time drop from 16 minutes in 1981 to 10 minutes in 1992.
- Time spent on hobbies for men increased from 1981 to 1992 from 9 to 13 minutes while the reverse was true for the women. Women enjoyed 16 minutes of hobby participation in 1981 and in 1992 participated in only 13 minutes per day.

D. Wayne Osgood and Hyunkee Lee looked at changes across the lifespan in the frequency of participation in a variety of leisure activities common in everyday life, and in particular, how those changes related to family and work roles.[20] Their premise is that leisure is of general sociological interest because it provides a bridge between the organization of the life course imposed by the social structure and its consequences for balanced living. Parenthood was the most important factor to affect leisure participation across four domains (marriage, living arrangements, parenthood, and work). Parents of young children had the least amount of leisure activity. Activity increased as children aged to the point where parents of teenagers engaged in leisure activities almost as often as non-parents. Full-time employment increased participation in structured activities away from home and decreased involvement in informal activities and activities in the home. Marital status and living arrangements were concluded to be largely unrelated to participation in activities.

Diane Samdahl and Nancy Jekubovich looked into 'Patterns and Characteristics of Adult Daily Leisure.'[21] Their findings suggest that leisure occurs more often in the evenings, on weekends, at home, and with family or friends. Qualitative data from their interviews reveal dynamic ways in which people structure their lives in order to influence and shape these patterns. They conclude that the work–leisure balance does not simply happen: it is planned for and arranged.

Discussion: Leisure in Canada and the United States

Canadians are remarkably similar to Americans in their use of time. While minor differences are noted, they are of limited comparative value. Furthermore, there are few notable differences for Canadians from the 1986 to 1992 GSS. Total free time for Canadians 18 years of age and over was 388 minutes per day in 1986 and 391 minutes in 1992. In terms of non-free time (work, child care, obtaining goods and services, personal needs and care) the totals in 1986 and 1992 were 1,059 minutes and 1,036 minutes respectively.

What these numbers mask in terms of the 'Schor vs Robinson and Godbey debate' is that Schor's work concentrated on Americans in the workforce while Robinson and Godbey included everyone over the age of 18. The so-called debate may simply be a case of comparing apples and oranges, complex methodology issues notwithstanding. Would the conclusions be different if there was an accounting for those who delayed entry into the workforce and, at the other end of the age spectrum, excluded the retired? In addition, Robinson and Godbey counted time actually spent working as work, whereas Schor's survey defined work as the total time spent at work, inclusive of all breaks. While this difference may be considered minor, time budget analyses (including the GSS) are recognized as having more precision than surveys.

It is clear that Canadians (and Americans) are watching a lot of television and the older they are, the more they watch. This suggests that improvement for active leisure in the form of physical activity presents a constant challenge for health planners. Although some minor reductions in TV viewing were noted, this was more than compensated for by increased computer usage.

Most recent studies report less time for leisure than in the past. This is not surprising given increased participation in work with leisure relegated to 'time left over.' Aggregate numbers mask the degree to which young parents (both female and male) face problems of reasonable time for themselves. Males across most age groups have more leisure time than women, but parents of young children (male and female) face huge challenges in their attempts to juggle responsibilities, children, and time for personal leisure. The degree to which individuals juggle daily tasks, doing two or more things at once, pose methodological problems for time use researchers given that only the 'primary' activity is recorded.

The active/passive/social classification of free time should be analy-

204 Marty Thomas and Rosemary A. Venne

sed for its relevance. The current method is often counter-intuitive. Working out on a treadmill at home, walking the dog, perhaps even reading a great book is classified as passive because these activities are based in the home and may be 'unplanned.' In reality, social activity involves interaction with others that may be home-based or away from home. The classification does not include civic or voluntary activity in its definition of active leisure.

It is also clear that much of what accounts for work and leisure relevant to time use definitions is limited when it comes to developing social policy. Most survey and time use methodology is based on one (residual – time left over) or two (activity) of the categories of leisure. The importance of the activity to the individual, with its attendant value and meaning, is lost in these definitions. The advantage in time use research is the opportunity to recode and reclassify data, and Statistics Canada has gone to great lengths to make data accessible to researchers for this purpose. The next step may be to foster collaboration between researchers from a variety of disciplines and including a variety of stakeholders who are both the developers and end-users of the research. There is a need for a combined qualitative / quantitative perspective in design and analysis. There is no question that the two paradigms foster different kinds of thinking and both are needed: qualitative research is necessary to respond to the questions of meaning/value and aid in analysis, and quantitative analysis is important in terms of generalizing results.

This section presented some snapshots of leisure trends and activity patterns. While these snapshots provide some illustration of the issue at hand, they provide few answers in terms of support for balanced leisure. Work and leisure are inexorably connected, with work dominating as the major organizer of social life. The next section focuses on work in relation to balance.

Focus on Work

As documented by the GSS, in 1992 the average Canadian spent approximately 3.6 hours per day in paid work activity (factored over seven days for all age groups).[22] This figure included students 15 years of age and over, as well as retired adults. The average day was broadly divided into paid work, unpaid work (household and family responsibilities), educational activities, personal care (sleeping, eating, washing), and leisure activities.

Work over the Life Course

- The 1992 General Social Survey identified that for youth age 15 to 17, an average of 5.3 hours per day (averaged over seven days) was devoted to education, while 0.75 hours per day were spent in paid work activities. There were significant differences between males and females. Of total productive activity, females age 15 to 17 spent 8.0 hours on total work per week (paid and unpaid), while their male counterparts spent 6.2 hours on total work activities.
- Of the youth population age 18 to 24 who attended educational institutions, males spent 6.3 hours per day pursuing their education while females spent 4.8 hours. Male students in this age category worked an average of 1.5 hours per day, while females worked an average of 1.0 hour per day. For young people age 18 to 24 years not in school, males were employed an average of 6.9 hours per day, and females employed an average of 7.3 hours per day.
- The 25-to-44 year age group were hard at work. Unmarried males employed full-time in this age group spent 6.9 hours per day at work, while married males spent from 7.1 hours (no children) to 6.6 hours (with children). Unmarried females employed full-time in this age group spent 5.9 hours per day at work, and those who were married spent from 6.8 hours (no children) to 5.3 hours (with children) at work.
- Married women aged 45 to 64, employed full-time, spent a full hour more per day at work (total of 6.4 hours per day) than unmarried women employed full-time in the same age group (total of 5.4 hours per day). The difference among married and unmarried men employed full-time was small (from 6.8 to 6.7 hours per day at work).
- Not surprisingly, seniors, age 65+ reported only 2 per cent of their day engaged in paid work activity.

Work Trends

In the early 1990s the minister of human resources development mandated a group of business, labour, and other representatives 'to study, analyze and promote discussion on the issue of working time and the distribution of work and to provide a report and recommendations to the Minister.'[23] The 1994 *Report of the Advisory Group on Working Time and the Distribution of Work*, commonly referred to as the Donner

Report, suggests that in recent years people have experienced more job loss and relocation than was the case a generation ago. The authors indicate that job turnover creates a great deal of flux in the job market especially for younger workers and those with intermittent or precarious forms of employment. The amount one works over the course of one's life has also changed. People are entering the labour force later, with less sustained work, people are experiencing more work interruptions and flux in their careers because of job loss and change; people are adding more parenting and learning time into their work life; and more people are experiencing either forced or voluntary early retirement.[24]

Thus, the portion of the life cycle devoted to paid employment was decreasing throughout the twentieth century, quite noticeably in the last quarter of the century.[25] People spent shorter portions of their life cycle in the labour force, mainly as a result of increasing educational attainment at the front end of the cycle and the trend to earlier retirement at the back end. The linear life path of school–work–leisure no longer prevails as normative. For instance, education is not just attained at the front end of the adult life cycle. Indeed, changes in career patterns have led to people returning to school to upgrade and update themselves for fast-changing careers.[26] Credentialism or rising skill requirements also account for the increasing portion of our life cycle spent in educational pursuits. Many professions now require more education or a university degree, where none was required before. Compared with a few decades ago, the transition from school to work has become a much more prolonged and complex process.[27] Credentialism is said to be the result of increased competition, generational crowding associated with the baby boomers and technological change.[28]

The Donner study compared today's younger worker with the previous generation and identified the following:

• In demographic terms, there are fewer young people today than a generation ago.
• Of those who have jobs, proportionately fewer young people are working full-time.
• Most students who are working part-time in the summer months do so because there is no full-time work available.
• Younger people are more apt to work variable hours and fewer days in the week; one-third of youth work four days or fewer, compared to 10 per cent of adults.

Compared with a generation ago, today's prime-age labour force experiences:

• Higher incidence of involuntary part-time work and underemployment
• Higher incidence of overtime and long hours
• More adults and parents working to maintain the family's standard of living

The number of women in the labour force who had preschool age children in 1971 was 31 per cent. This increased to 63 per cent in 1993. A generation ago the 'typical' Canadian family had a male breadwinner with a female homemaker running the household. Over two-thirds of families were configured this way in 1961. By 1991 this stereotype had reversed: over 60 per cent of 'nuclear' families in Canada (two parents with children) were dual-earner families. Moreover, more than 55 per cent of lone parents were also working. Compared with a generation ago, today's older workers have experienced a marked increase in both voluntary and involuntary early retirement, to the extent that many men and women retire before age 65.[29]

It has been almost eight years since the Donner Report was submitted to the federal government. Recommendations focused on the need for reduction and redistribution of work time, alternative workplace initiatives related to reduction of work time, work week and overtime proposals, paid and unpaid leaves for education, training, and family commitments. In an *Atkinson Newsletter* interview entitled 'Are Canadians Working Too Many Hours?' Dr Donner was asked what had happened to the report's recommendations. He lamented that following 'a little flurry' of interest after the report was made public, 'nothing substantial came out of it.' Donner noted the limited support from labour and the lack of champions from either the political or business community.[30]

René Morissette and Deborah Sunter identify a number of work-related trends in their report entitled 'What Is Happening to Weekly Hours Worked in Canada'.[31] They suggest that the decline in weekly hours worked up to 1960 (from 60 hours at the beginning of the twentieth century to 37 by 1960) was partly because technological advances allowed workers to produce the same amount in less time. Workers became able to trade wage advances for more leisure time. They note that as long as productivity grew fast enough to keep reduced hours cost-neutral, it was in the employer's interest to accommodate worker and union demands for more free time. Supply and demand reasons explained the stabilization in the length of the standard work week. Workers were investing in more education and needed to recoup the cost of higher education. Once employed, they were less likely to trade wage gains for shorter hours. Workers were also more interested in gaining other benefits such as health and dental coverage. The average annual vacation in 1959 was 2.7 weeks and paid holidays were limited to 7.8 days per year. This rose to 3.6 weeks of vacation and 11.1 days of holiday per year in 1979. Benefits coverage cost employers 4.6 per cent of labour income in 1961 and rose to 8.7 per cent in 1979 and 12 per cent in 1993.

The overall stability of the standard work week is deceiving in that it does not reflect the many changes in the distribution of hours. Sixty-one per cent of paid workers worked 35 to 40 hours per week in 1993, a decline from 71 per cent in 1976.[32] The increasing incidence of non-standard work weeks may be voluntary, as part-timers and casual workers meet shifting levels of demand with minimal cost to the employer. While the majority of workers continue to put in standard hours, the proportion working either shorter or longer weeks is rising. Thus, there is extensive variance in hours worked per week and that variance appears to be on the rise as an increasing portion of workers put in non-standard hours.

Discussion: Time Use in Canada and the United States

In addition to Robinson and Godbey demonstrating the similarities in time use between Americans and Canadians, they also compare American and Canadian attitudes towards time. In terms of subjective use of time, a study conducted in 1997 by Jack Harper, Denny Neider, Geoffrey Godbey, and Darlene Lamont contrasted Canadian attitudes towards time with a 1992 U.S. study by Godbey, Alan Graefe, and Anthony James.[33] The 1997 research replicated the questions from the previous, similar study. Both studies asked respondents if they had more time for recreation and leisure when compared with five years ago:

- 43 per cent of Canadians said they had less time, 35 per cent reported no change, 22 per cent reported they had more time
- 47 per cent of Americans said they had less time, 31 per cent reported no change, 22 per cent reported they had more time

- 27 per cent of Canadian women compared with 19 per cent of Canadian men were more likely to report more time for leisure
- 43 per cent of Canadians said their work was more important than leisure, compared with 35 per cent of Americans

The Canadian study (1997) found an attitude difference between younger and older Canadians. Those between 15 and 35 were more likely to report that they had less time than five years ago while those over 35 reported that they had more time than five years ago.

Zuzanek and Smale address the changes in attitudes towards time allocated to major daily activities among Canadians between 1981 to 1992. The decade saw a rise in the combined workloads of paid and unpaid work for employed Canadians. They state that this has affected the genders differently. Well over half of Canada's employed population, including 60 per cent of employed women, felt more rushed in 1992 than five years before. They conclude: 'Our analysis lends considerable support to the thesis of the polarization of different life cycle groups' access to time'.[34]

Zuzanek, Beckers, and Peters conducted a survey of Dutch and Canadian industrialized communities to confirm any gains or losses in leisure time from the 1970s to the 1990s.[35] They examined the extent to which the combined pressure of work and domestic obligations (i.e., 'time pressure' or 'time squeeze') was distributed evenly across different life cycle groups and social strata. Their findings confirm that, during the observed period, the combined workloads of paid and unpaid work have risen, and the amounts of free time have declined or remained static, for the employed populations in both countries.

A study commissioned by the Conference Board of Canada during the mid-1980s examined Canadians' attitudes towards working hours.[36] Seventeen per cent of respondents said they were interested in a reduction of work hours *with a cut in pay* and the proportion increased to 31 per cent if the respondent would 'trade all or some of your pay increase in the next two years for more time off.' More females than males were willing to reduce hours, and this was particularly true if the woman had children under 5. In order of importance, most respondents preferred the option of a reduced work week, followed by more time off every year. An interest in early retirement was a distant third choice.

A more recent study, with different assumptions and questions, found limited support (6.4%) for trading reduced hours for reduced pay.[37] Although it may seem that interest in reduced work time is on the wane, the first survey defined work time reductions much more broadly than the 1995 survey's more narrow definition. Other surveys also indicate a strong preference for flexibility in terms of workplace and work time issues.[38]

It is no surprise that the issue of work–family or work–life balance became a much-discussed, recognized, and researched issue in the 1980s and 1990s, given the various demographic and workplace changes that were confronting workers.[39] As the baby-boom generation moved into middle age, the so-called busy mid-life decades were made even busier by other significant changes. In terms of demography, major changes included the increase in dual-earner households and an increasing labour force participation rate of women. In terms of the workplace, major changes included organizational restructuring such as downsizing, the delayering effect with its associated flatter organizational structures, wider spans of control and less promotion-centred career paths, increased technological change, as well as an increase in non-standard work arrangements.[40] Employees today are taken care of by the employer less.[41] The 'new contract' requires the employee to take charge of his or her career with associated lifelong learning requirements and with much less stability compared with the lifetime one-company career patterns prevalent in the immediate post-war decades.

The issue of work–family balance (now more commonly referred to as work–life balance) often refers to the needs of employees as caretakers of young children and as caregivers to elderly relatives. As parents, the boomers have children who are facing higher tuition costs, greater demands for education (e.g., credentialism where the young are no longer 'job ready' at the end of high school), and are slower leaving home.[42] Also with the increasing life expectancy of the older generation, the baby-boom generation may be called on to provide some assistance to their elderly parents. Although as Tindale et al. point out, the notion of 'sandwich generation,' the so-called middle generation being squeezed by both children and by elderly parents, is quite overblown.[43] They contend that reciprocity is the order of the day for these intergenerational relationships as exchange patterns work both ways in aging families. Also research into 'boomerang' children or the 'refilled' nest, characterizes these generational relationships as cooperative and on the rise. The issue of work–life balance, although often discussed primarily with reference to middle-aged adults, also seems to resonate for young adults, perhaps because of the changing career patterns and resulting decreases in occupational stability. A survey of recent business school graduates found that the notion of a balanced life was front and centre for this younger generation. The graduates rated 'achieving a balance between personal life and career' first before 'building a sound financial base.'[44]

Work Patterns over the Life Course

Although the structure of the labour force has changed since the immediate postwar decades, some employers treat their increasingly diverse workforce as one monolithic group requiring one set of policies in terms of work time scheduling and benefits. This rigidity or lack of flexibility on the part of employers is perhaps most prevalent in terms of work time scheduling. Indeed, Blyton notes that until recently the pattern of working time had remained an aspect of work which had not been subject to extensive employee influence.[45] In contrast to other work areas where employees have achieved a degree of participation (e.g., how work is done), most work time patterns show continued rigidity. Slowly, with technological change, recognition of the increasingly diverse nature of the workforce, and demands from employees, alternative work time arrangements have become more prevalent, since the 1970s (e.g., with flextime, compressed work weeks, job sharing, and more recently with telecommuting).

Many researchers examine 'phased' or 'transitional' retirement programs where employees nearing retirement age gradually reduce their hours of work and receive a prorated salary for a period of several years prior to complete retirement.[46] This period of transition allows the organization to use the employees' expertise in roles such as mentors, consultants, and in special assignments. The current transition from work to retirement is often an abrupt one, mainly because of pension rules rather than individual preferences.[47]

In North America these flexible early retirement programs are not as widespread as they are in Europe. Yet there does seem to be interest in these programs on the part of employees. A survey in the province of Quebec documents public support for the concept of gradual or transitional retirement with interest greatest in those in mid-age and nearing retirement[48] (although not many firms actually offer this innovation).[49] Preference for working 3.5 days per week at age 55 with gradual reduction in hours until they are working 0.5 days per week at age 70 was at 75 per cent for those age 45 to 54 and 72 per cent for those age 25 to 44.

Another flexibility, the sabbatical leave, is found mainly in academic occupations and may not be practical for all jobs. Yet non-academic workplace sabbaticals at a number of 'high tech' firms have gathered attention since the 1970s. Bachler has documented corporate sabbatical leave programs at a number of large North American companies.[50] They are used mainly with mid- to upper-level employees for reasons of stress reduction, job retention, creativity enhancement, and as a reward. Bachler notes that some of these programs should more properly be called leaves as they are not limited to a seven-year cycle, are much shorter than the traditional year-long sabbatical, and may be on an unpaid basis.

A variation of the sabbatical is the uniquely Canadian self-funded leave plan, such as the '5 over 4 plan' whereby an employee works four years at 80 per cent of regular pay with the other 20 per cent of pay held in trust and used to fund the fifth year in which the employee does not work. This plan is different from a typical sabbatical in that funding for the fifth year comes from foregone pay in each of the previous four years. Although not very common, this self-funded leave plan has been used with teachers, nurses, and a few private sector companies and offers benefits of flexibility similar to those of the sabbatical leave.[51]

Multiple-choice flexibility systems such as those found in European firms (e.g., in the Netherlands) seem out of reach to most North American employees.[52] The multiple-choice system allows workers to choose the package of employment conditions best suited to their personal needs, within an overall framework. For example, employees may be allowed to choose between participation in extra days off, end-of-year bonuses, or study leaves. In effect, the employees gain considerable freedom to 'buy' or 'sell' their time. It is expected that employees in higher-level functions may sell time, while employees in lower-level functions will be more likely to buy time. Although North American firms seem rigid in comparison with their European counterparts, there is increasing recognition that to recruit and retain the best employees, firms need to respond to employee demands for flexibility.[53] Indeed, firms that provide the most flexibility to their time-crunched employees tend to have the lowest rates of turnover.[54]

The 'time is right' to implement voluntary work reduction programs as a viable and realistic means to achieve more balance in the distribution of work across generations.[55] Converging trends include demographic changes and increased employee interest in more flexible work time arrangements, while employers are seeking ways to reduce costs. Since middle-aged and older workers earn more, and it is precisely this group who favour work reduction, it is reasonable to expect that youth levels of unemployment and underemployment could be reduced by voluntary work reduction programs. As well, an improved achievement of the work–life balance would be expected for the middle-age group engaging in voluntary work time reduction. David Foot and Rosemary Venne argue that while even modest participation would be a success, there is every reason to believe that favourable legislation and employer support combined with widespread introduction of voluntary work reduction policies could result in gains towards equity in the distribution of work among older and younger workers.

It can be said that the main life-course transition points are changing (from school to work and from work to retirement) where learning is now occurring over the life course – the so-called lifelong learning trend.[56] The 'boxes' model of life – the individual first goes to school to prepare for work, then spends his or her years until approximately age 65 at work, and finally retires to a well-deserved life of leisure, is seriously outmoded. While the limitation is commonly recognized, our social policy is still stuck in the assumption. Policies such as work sabbaticals, work-life leaves, and tax incentives for education may be appropriate to support returning to education and training opportunities.

In terms of demography and aging, expectations that the next generation will engage in the same work and leisure behaviour as the preceding generation should be questioned. Of course, demography is not destiny.[57] In fact, if age is less important than cohort in shaping later life circumstances, as Susan McDaniel contends, then the behaviour of our future elderly is certainly less likely to be predictable based on past cohorts' behaviour.[58] McDaniel further points out that the coming generations of seniors in Canada are quite different from previous generations in terms of ethnic diversity and family and gender role changes experienced in the latter half of the twentieth century. It is true though, that once the large North American baby boom-generation reaches retirement age, there will be fewer people of traditional working age and the average age of those working will rise.[59] An Organization for Economic Cooperation and Development (OECD) report notes that if all else remains the same, there may be a shortage of young people in the future labour force. Yet, previous predictions of labour-force shortages for the late 1980s and 1990s (when the current bust generation was entering the labour force) largely did not materialize in Canada, as other factors clearly had an impact (e.g., the recession of the early 1990s and organizational restructuring such as downsizing and delayering).[60]

A related example is that expectations of continued early retirement for the present working generation may prove to be false. In fact, rising levels of education, and a greater share of workers in professional occupations (which are associated with higher participation rates) are likely to encourage people to remain longer in the labour force.[61] The OECD analysis also expects that 'current trends towards early retirement are likely to be moderated or reversed,' and this appears to be already happening in some European countries, thus throwing into question the prediction of future labour-force shortages.[62] Also in terms of policy, future decisions to remove early retirement incentives embedded in social programs or less-enticing retirement benefits may affect current trends to early retirement.[63]

With the distinction between middle age and old age being blurred, with many 65 and over belonging to the 'young-old' group of active seniors, Douglas Thorpe contends that it is time to question whom we consider old.[64] In terms of the life course, Thorpe insists that we need to resist any easy demarcation of the stages of life. If the trends towards earlier retirement are reversed during possible future labour-force shortages, Thorpe challenges that the public policies regarding mandatory retirement need to be reconsidered (perhaps with more flexible workplace policies that encourage transitional retirement, discussed earlier), and we need to question our collective ageism.

As our population ages, will we enter a more balanced life course with more free time (as Robinson and Godbey predict)? Will the feeling of time famine lessen? With respect to the greying of the population, Foot proposes that the concept of below-replacement level fertility and a stabilizing or even slowly declining population is not such a great cause for alarm.[65] Joel Prager's chapter on aging and productivity calls into question the widely held assumption of declining productivity associated with an aging workforce.[66] Indeed, Foot points out that an absence of population growth in a country can result in increased productivity, less unemployment, and reduced pressure on both urban and rural environments. If the educated young demand a greater work–life balance, will employers be forced to become even more flexible in terms of their human resource policies in order to attract and retain these valuable workers? This seems to be happening today as those employers with the most flexible policies attract the best workers.[67]

Conclusion: A Need for Balance

The stubborn questions remain to be answered. How long should the work week be? What is an optimum amount of free time for individual and family well-being? What costs and benefits would accrue to individuals, families, communities, and Canadian society in general if public policy supported reduction of work hours? And finally, is there any evidence that reduced hours would result in more jobs? There are limited answers at this point. Is it possible to frame the questions from neither the right nor the left, and not even from the top? The point-of-view of the critical stakeholder, the citizen, forces us to look at the issues differently.

An interesting story was posted on the 32 hours network listserve that put this debate over work time in context. As the story goes, Saskatchewan Deputy Minister of Labour Brian King was a panelist at a recent Ottawa conference. He was asked whether labour legislation like that found in Europe could be implemented in Canada. He responded:

> The climate is as bad as I've ever seen it for moving things in what one might call a progressive direction. In fact, if you look across Canada you'll see the race to the bottom. Several years ago I was flying down to Atlanta and I came across a business magazine which said in ads in there, 'Move to Mississippi or Alabama, we have the cheapest workers' compensation, and the lowest minimum wage, and unions are outlawed.' And I thought, Oh my God! What an awful society that would advertise that sort of thing, 'We have slaves to work for you here.' And I opened my *Globe and Mail* about six months ago, and a certain premier of a certain Atlantic province says, 'Come on down, we have the cheapest workers' compensation rates and we have minimum standards and minimum wages.'

The story illustrates the analogy of 'is the glass half full or half empty?' The answer will differ if seen from the perspective of a shareholder or CEO of a corporation, or from that of the unemployed or underemployed individual. Clearly, both perspectives are needed in the analysis and development of appropriate social policy. Also, equal weight must be given to both viewpoints – creative work to design a consultative process that will mitigate against the common views that (1) the corporations are in charge and (2) that this is a zero sum exercise with much competition for a personal rather than collective payback. The complexity of the issues surpasses the ability of our current mechanisms to measure productivity and gross domestic product. Good social policy needs to begin with some agreement on these value-laden and emotional terms (e.g., work, leisure, family, and time) prior to addressing the concept of balance.

The optimal length of weekly hours at any particular time can only be determined by experimentation. The research is not simple – the relationship between the hours of work and the intensity of effort is not mechanical. Past research on optimal work times has invariably found a lag between a change in schedule and an increase in productivity, as people work out new ways of doing things and as they gradually recover from accumulated fatigue. There also needs to be ongoing research into the relative benefits of other arrangements, such as longer vacation times or phased retirement, compared with shorter work weeks.

Many recommendations related to work reduction have been suggested, but there is a reluctance to confront the issue of structural unemployment. The moment may now be ripe in political terms to respond to Donner's recommendations. The Donner Report on working time and distribution of work listed twenty-four recommendations, of which a number refer directly or indirectly to work time. These recommendations include:

• The legislated standard work week should be no longer than 40 hours per week in any jurisdiction.
• Employees should be given the right to refuse overtime work after 40 hours work per week.
• Employers and employees should utilize time off in lieu of overtime pay after the standard work week.
• The maximum amount of overtime in excess of regular working hours should be set at 100 hours annually.

In 1996 a number of practitioners, academics, and policy-makers from Canada and the United States gathered in Iowa City to discuss the 'time famine' and the future of work. Social and economic policies were much discussed, and the Americans made it clear that they were looking to Canadians for leadership and direction. In that gathering, the 'Iowa City Declaration' was signed by the conference delegates (see Appendix, p. 245). The recommendation for dialogue is a critical first step. The call for balance in work, leisure, family, and community is particularly pertinent as our population ages and demands for balance increase.

In reference to the issue of time stress, it is clear that there is a significant time 'crunch' or stress for those in their mid-life years. As Frederick reports, almost one-third of women, with children and employed, are highly stressed.[68] Men employed full-time are likely to report high stress. The changes in terms of family structure (e.g., more dual-earner families with no stay-at-home spouse looking after the household full-time) are quite profound. Despite smaller family size, the dual-earner household reports higher stress levels and appears to have greater needs for a work–leisure balance. Also in terms of career patterns, there are quite profound changes from a generation ago.[69] Today, career patterns may require time off for the employee to upgrade and engage in lifelong learning, and these pressures associated with the new career patterns also require a greater need for balance in terms of work and leisure. Demographic changes, mainly the baby boomers passing through their busy mid-life decades, means that they face dual pressures. As parents, the boomers face dealing with children who are slower to leave home because of a longer and more complex school-to-work transition. As children of aging parents, the boomers face dealing with the increased life expectancy of the older generation at a time when the boomers are likely to be busy working in dual-earner households.

In terms of balance, will employers respond to the demands and needs of mid-life boomers with flexible policies (e.g., transitional retirement, alternative working time arrangements, and leave programs)? With respect to younger workers (who are most likely to engage in multiple careers with the need for lifelong learning), those in high-demand areas expect flexibility on the part of employers, and employers are forced to become more flexible in order to retain valuable employees. More workplace flexibility, in turn, will further contribute to breaking down the linear nature of our existing work–retirement–leisure progression, or in other words the 'boxes' model of life. Christopher Higgins et al. and Linda Duxbury et al. note that employers with the most flexible policies (e.g., those who are most attuned to their time-crunched employees' needs) tend to attract the best workers.[70]

Although population aging may seem straightforward (each year we get a year older) the changes discussed here mean that any demographic analysis needs to take these other factors into account in a 'multidimensional' demographic analysis. In other words, the behaviour of today's soon-to-be retired employees may not be predictive of subsequent generations' work–leisure behaviour. Thus, the work–leisure balance is more of an issue today in terms of population aging because of demographic changes and shifting workplace realities.

Notes

1 See Juliet Schor, *The Overworked American: The Unexpected Decline of Leisure* (New York: Basic Books, 1991).
2 See John Robinson and Geoffrey Godbey, *Time for Life: The Surprising Ways Americans Use Their Time* (University Park: Pennsylvania State University Press, 1997), Preface.
3 Ibid., 5.
4 See Josef Pieper, *Leisure: The Basis of Culture* (New York: New American Library, 1963); and Thorstein Veblen, *The Theory of Leisure: An Economic Study of Institutions* (New York: B.W. Huebsch, 1899).
5 See Gilles Pronovost and Max D'Amours, 'Leisure Studies: A Re-examination of Society,' *Leisure and Society* 13, no. 1 (1990): 39–62.
6 See Donald Reid, *Work and Leisure in the 21st Century: From Production to Citizenship* (Toronto: Wall and Emerson, 1995), 10.
7 See John Kenneth Galbraith, *The Good Society: The Humane Agenda* (Boston: Houghton Mifflin, 1996).
8 See *Random House Webster's Dictionary*, 3rd ed. (New York: Ballantine, 1998), 747.
9 See Michael Ornstein and Tony Haddad, *About Time: Analysis from a 1986 Survey of Canadians* (Toronto: Institute for Social Research, York University, 1993).
10 See Robinson and Godbey, *Time for Life*.
11 See Jack Harper, Denny Neider, Geoffrey Godbey, and Darlene Lamont, *The Use and Benefits of Local Government Parks and Recreation Services – A Canadian Perspective* (Winnipeg: University of Manitoba Health, Leisure and Human Performance Research Institute, 1997); and Geoffrey Godbey, Alan Graefe, and Anthony James, *The Benefits of Local Recreation and Park Services: A Nationwide Study of the Perceptions of the American Public* (Arlington, Va.: National Recreation and Parks Services, 1992).

12 See David K. Foot with Daniel Stoffman, *Boom, Bust and Echo: How to Profit from the Coming Demographic Shift* (Toronto: Macfarlane, Walter, and Ross, 1996); David Foot and Daniel Stoffman, *Entre le Boom et l'Écho: comment mettre à profit la realité démographique* (Montreal: Librairie Renaud-Bray, 1996); Doug Owram, *Born at the Right Time: A History of the Baby Boom Generation* (Toronto: University of Toronto Press, 1996); Francois Ricard, *La génération lyrique, essai sur la vie et l'oeuvre des premiers-nés du baby-boom* (Montreal: Éditions du Boréal, 1992).

13 See Andrew Harvey, Ken Marshall, and Judith Frederick, *Where Does Time Go?* Statistics Canada Catalogue no. 11-612E, N.4 (Ottawa: Government of Canada, Minister of Industry, Science, and Technology, 1991); and Judith Frederick, *As Time Goes By: Time Use of Canadians*, Statistics Canada Catalogue no. 89-544E (Ottawa: Government of Canada, Minister of Industry, 1995).

14 See Gouvernement de Québec, *Évolution de l'emploi du temps au Québec 1986–1992* (Quebec: Gouvernement de Québec, 1996); and Gouvernement de Québec, *La Pratique des activités de loisir culturel et scientifique des Québécois* (Quebec: Gouvernement de Québec, 1995).

15 See Michael Hall, Tamara Knighton, Paul Reed, Patrick Bussiere, Don McRae, and Paddy Bowen, *Caring Canadians, Involved Canadians: Highlights from the 1997 National Survey of Giving, Volunteering, and Participating*, Statistics Canada Catalogue, no. 71-542-XPE (Ottawa: Government of Canada, Minister of Industry, 1998).

16 See Government of Canada, *A Portrait of Seniors in Canada*, 2nd ed., Statistics Canada Catalogue no. 89-519-XPE (Ottawa: Government of Canada: Minister of Industry, 1997).

17 See Government of Canada, *Television Viewing 1993*, Statistics Canada Catalogue no. 87-208 (Ottawa: Minister of Industry, Science and Technology, 1994).

18 See Jiri Zuzanek and Bryan Smale, 'Life Cycle Variations in Across the Week Allocation of Time to Selected Daily Activities,' *Society and Leisure* 15, no. 2 (1992): 559–86.

19 See Jiri Zuzanek and Bryan Smale, 'More Work-Less Leisure? Changing Allocations of Time in Canada, 1981–1992,' *Society and Leisure* 20, no. 1 (1997): 73–106.

20 See D. Wayne Osgoode and Hyunkee Lee, 'Leisure Activities, Age, and Adult Roles across the Lifespan,' *Society and Leisure* 16, no. 1 (1993): 181–208.

21 See Diane Samdahl and Nancy Jekubovich, 'Patterns and Characteristics of Adult Daily Leisure,' *Society and Leisure* 16, no. 1 (1993): 129–49.

22 See Frederick, *As Time Goes By*

23 See Advisory Group on Working Time and the Distribution of Work, *Report of the Advisory Group on Working Time and the Distribution of Work* (Ottawa: Human Resources Development Canada, 1994), 67.

24 See Advisory Group on Working Time and the Distribution of Work, *Report of the Advisory Group,'* 21.

25 See Deborah Sunter and René Morissette, 'The Hours People Work,' *Perspectives on Labour and Income* 6, no. 3 (1994): 8–12.

26 See David K. Foot and Rosemary A. Venne, 'Population, Pyramids, and Promotional Prospects,' *Canadian Public Policy* 16, no. 4 (1990): 387–98.

27 See Harvey Krahn, Clay Mosher, and Laura Johnson, 'Panel Studies of the Transition from School to Work: Some Methodological Considerations,' in Paul Anisef and Paul Axelrod, eds., *Transitions: Schooling and Employment in Canada,* (Toronto: Thompson Educational, 1993), 169–87. See also Geoff Bowlby, 'The School-to-work Transition,' *Perspective on Labour and Income* 12, no. 1 (2000): 43–8.

28 See Bruce O'Hara, *Working Harder Isn't Working* (Vancouver: New Star Books, 1993). See also Ken Bennett, 'Recent Information on Training,' *Perspectives on Labour and Income* 6, no. 1 (1994): 22–4.

29 See Dave Gower, 'Measuring the Age of Retirement,' *Perspectives on Labour and Income* 9, no. 2 (1997): 11–17. See also Patrick Keiran, 'Early Retirement Trends,' *Perspectives on Labour and Income* 13, no. 4, (2001): 7–13.

30 See *Atkinson Newsletter* (Toronto: Atkinson Foundation, Oct. 1999).

31 See René Morissette and Deborah Sunter, 'What Is Happening to Weekly Hours Worked in Canada?' *Analytical Studies Branch Research Paper Series,* no. 65 (Ottawa: Statistics Canada, 1994).

32 See Sunter and Morissette, 'The Hours People Work,' 8–12.

33 See Jack Harper et al., *The Use and Benefits of Local Government Parks,* and Geoffrey Godbey et al., *The Benefits of Local Recreation.*

34 See Zuzanek and Smale, 'More Work – Less Leisure?'

35 See Jiri Zuzanek, Theo Beckers, and Pascale Peters, 'The Harried Leisure Class Revisited: Dutch and Canadian Trends in the Use of Time from the 1970s to the 1990s,' *Leisure Studies* 17 (1998): 1–19.

36 See Prem Benimadhu, *Hours of Work: Trends and Attitudes in Canada* (Ottawa: Conference Board of Canada, 1987).

37 See Marie Drolet and René Morissette, 'Working More? Working Less? What Do Canadians Prefer?' *Analytical Studies Branch Research Paper Series,* no. 104 (Ottawa: Statistics Canada, 1997).

38 See Linda Duxbury and Christopher Higgins, *Work-Life Balance in Saskatchewan: Realities and Challenges* (Saskatoon: Government of Saskatchewan, 1998); Linda Duxbury, Christopher Higgins, Catherine Lee,

and Shirley Mills, *Balancing Work and Family: A Study of the Canadian Federal Public Sector* (Ottawa: Carleton University, 1991); and Christopher Higgins, Linda Duxbury, and Catherine Lee, *Balancing Work and Family: A Study of Canadian Private Sector Employees* (London, Ont.: National Centre for Management Research and Development, University of Western Ontario, 1992).

39 See Gilles Guérin, Sylvie St-Onge, Victor Haines, Renée Trottier, and Manon Simard, 'Les pratiques d'aide à l'équilibre emploi-famille dans les organisations du Québec,' *Relations industrielles* 52, no. 2 (1997): 275–303.

40 See Foot and Venne, 'Population, Pyramids, and Promotional Prospects,' and, Harvey Krahn, 'Non-standard Work on the Rise,' *Perspectives on Labour and Income* 7, no. 4 (1995): 5–42. See also Anne Bourhis and Thierry Wils, 'L'éclatement de l'emploi traditionnel: Les défis posés par la diversité des emplois typiques et atypiques,' *Relations industrielles* 56, no. 1 (2001): 66–91.

41 See Gerard Egan, 'Hard Times Contract,' *Management Today,* Jan. 1994, 48–50.

42 See Monica Boyd and Doug Norris, 'The Cluttered Nest Revisited: Young Adults at Home in the 1990s,' *Center for Study of Population, Working Paper* (Tallahassee: Florida State University, 1995).

43 See Joseph Tindale, Joan Norris, and Krista Abbott, Chapter 7 in this book.

44 See *CA Magazine,* 'They Prefer a Balanced Life,' Oct. 1999, 9.

45 See Paul Blyton, *Changes in Working Time: An International Review* (London: Croom Helm, 1985).

46 See Judith Bardwick, *The Plateauing Trap* (New York: Amacom, 1986); Hilda Kahne, *Reconceiving Part-time Work: New Perspectives for Older Workers and Women* (Totowa, NJ: Rowman and Allanheld, 1985); Barney Olmsted and Suzanne Smith, *Creating a Flexible Workplace: How to Select and Manage Alternative Work Options*, 2nd ed. (New York: Amacom, 1994); Tania Saba, Gilles Guérin, and Thierry Wils, 'Les pratiques efficaces pour gérer les travailleurs vieillissants: le cas des professionnels syndiqués au Québec,' in Rick Chaykowski, Paul-André LaPointe, Guylaine Vallée, and Anil Verma, eds., *La représentation des salariés dans le contexte du libre échange et de la déréglementation: Sélection de textes du XXXIII Congrès de l'ACRI,* 1997.

47 See Organisation for Economic Co-operation and Development, *Ageing in OECD Countries: A Critical Policy Challenge* (Paris: OECD, 1996), 79.

48 See Louise Gendron, 'Bye bye boulot,' *L'Actualité,* July 1997, 14–24.

49 See Diane Bellemare, Lise Poulin Simon, and Diane-Gabrielle Tremblay, 'Vieillissement, emploi, préretraite: les facteurs socio-économiques influant sur la gestion de la main-d'oeuvre vieillissante,' *Relations industrielles* 50, no. 3 (1995): 483–515.

50 See Christopher Bachler, 'Workers Take Leave of Job Stress,' *Personnel Journal* 74, no. 1 (1995): 38–48.

51 See Ray Murill and Sheldon Wayne, 'Buy Your Leave,' *Benefits Canada*, Dec. 1986, 33–43.
52 See Anon, 'Time for Sale,' *Better Times*: The Newsletter of 32 HOURS – Action for Full Employment and the Shorter Work Time Network of Canada, Sept., 1999, 9.
53 See Barney and Smith, *Creating a Flexible Workplace*; and Barney Olmsted and Suzanne Smith, *Managing in a Flexible Workplace* (New York: Ama Com, 1997).
54 See Duxbury et al., *Balancing Work and Family*; and Higgins et al., *Balancing Work and Family*.
55 See David K. Foot and Rosemary A. Venne, 'The Time Is Right: Voluntary Reduced Worktime and Workforce Demographics,' *Canadian Studies in Population* 25, no. 2 (1998): 114.
56 See OECD, *Ageing in OECD Countries: A Critical Policy Challenge*, 11.
57 See also David Cheal and Joel Prager chapters in this book. For an opposite point of view, see T. John Samuel, *Quebec Separatism Is Dead: Demography Is Destiny* (Ottawa: John Samuel and Associates, 1994).
58 See Susan McDaniel, in this book.
59 See OECD, *Ageing in OECD Countries*, 14.
60 See John Naisbitt and Patricia Aburdene, *Re-inventing the Corporation* (New York: Warner Books, 1985).
61 See Richard Judy and Carol D'Amico, *Workforce 2020: Work and Workers in the 21st Century* (Indiana: Hudson Institute, 1997), 100.
62 See OECD, *Ageing in OECD Countries*, 14.
63 Ibid.; and Judy and D'Amico, *Workforce 2020*.
64 See Douglas Thorpe, this book.
65 See Foot with Stoffman, *Boom, Bust and Echo*,' 204.
66 See Prager, in this book.
67 See Duxbury and Higgins, *Work-Life Balance in Saskatchewan*; Duxbury et al., *Balancing Work and Family*; and Higgins et al., *Balancing Work and Family*.
68 See Frederick, *As Time Goes By*.
69 See Michael Driver, 'Demographic and Societal Factors Affecting the Linear Career Crisis,' *Canadian Journal of Administrative Studies* 2 (2), 1985, 245–63; Daniel Mercure, Robert-Paul Bourgeois, and Thierry Wils, 'Analyse critique de la typologie des choix de carrière,' *Relations industrielles* 46, no. 1 (1991): 120–40.
70 See Duxbury et al., *Balancing Work and Family*; and Higgins et al., *Balancing Work and Family*.

7. Catching Up with Diversity in Intergenerational Relationships

Joseph A. Tindale, Joan E. Norris, and Krista Abbott

Introduction: Intergenerational Relationships

This chapter builds on our earlier work examining reciprocity in inter-generational relationships.[1] We constructed the term 'global reciprocity' to identify the negotiation of reciprocity in intergenerational and familial exchange relations across the broad sweep of the life course. The character of such relations hinges on close bonds of identification among people who are important to each other and generally held in affectionate regard. We argue discrete events that can cause ruptures in the fabric of these relations are normally amenable to a healing process. For example, research on successful negotiation of farm transfers from one generation to the next have lent support to this understanding of global reciprocity.[2] Relationships that have been more distant or fractious through the early developmental years are less likely to mend well when faced with a serious challenge in adulthood. As a result, the exchange relations that characterize parents and their young to middle-aged adult children are more likely to be reciprocal in nature if that has been their character through the years the children were growing towards adulthood. The importance of reciprocity considered in this global sense, across the lifespan, and through the life course, is that any discussion of issues such as intergenerational conflict or caregiver burden can only be made sensibly in the context of relationship history.

The Caregiving 'Sandwich' Gets More Attention Than It Deserves

Our investigations indicate that concerns about 'caregiver burden,' the problems of the 'sandwich generation,' or the likelihood of 'intergenerational conflict' are overblown. This point is underscored in this book by Ingrid Arnet Connidis and Susan A. McDaniel as well. Making such a statement, however, does not change the fact that much of the literature on adult intergenerational relations is based on a notion of inactive seniors with a diminished resource base that necessarily leaves them in an inequitable power and resource relationship relative to their children. These parents are seen as being in need of support, and are unable to maintain equity in the relationship. Phenomena such as caregiver burden and intergenerational conflict are almost inevitable consequences. Books popularizing the burdens of the so-called sandwich generation[3] still fail to consider that the nourishment between two slices of dependent bread is yesterday's dependent youth and tomorrow's dependent senior.[4] Thus, the sandwich analogy and its associated tensions are without context: out of place and out of time and, therefore, a distortion of real intergenerational relations. More importantly, the degree to which there is an interactive support relationship between parent and child well into the seventies for most parents and thirties or forties for most children is conveniently ignored. In reality, intergenerational relationships are much less like a sandwich and much more akin to the intermingling of components in a layered food such as lasagna.

We began our examination of how reciprocity is developed and expressed across the lifespan by considering something akin to a 'baseline' relationship. Hence we thought it more likely that reciprocity would be the order of the day in stable couple relationships. That established, we have sought since then to explore how adding diversity might help us to better understand the nature of reciprocal family relations.[5] Our assumption is that global reciprocity is likely close to a 'universal,' but that its timing, substantive feel, and associated family norms would likely vary.

Our focus in this chapter is one that captures a range of family backgrounds as they can be identified by cultural differences growing out of ethnic and racial groupings. We are recognizing and addressing some dimensions of the heterogeneity that is social life in Canada. Gerontologists, especially in the United States, have been talking for years about the need to recognize heterogeneity and decrying the homogeneity of our research samples.[6] There is still much work to be done in the United States, and in Canada we have barely scratched the surface. Indeed, in Canada much of the research we read is American; thus it not only includes mostly middle-class white samples, but also it reflects the experience of another country and culture.

This chapter first establishes what we mean by reciprocity as it is developed and expressed across the span and course of intergenerational relations. We argue that a failure to take the long view across the breadth of the life course leads to interpretations of relationships that are without context and history. The resulting misunderstanding gives rise to work that mines the plight of the sandwich generation. Our understanding of intergenerational reciprocity is rooted in affection, context, and family history. We use this benchmark to begin to redress the homogeneity of our understanding of intergenerational relations in Canada. The heterogeneity and diversity that is increasingly a part of our landscape provides us with the scope to make recommendations, in part for changes in substantive policy, but also for a different way of conceptualizing the issue.

Much of the research on aging families assumes that older people are inactive and therefore the relationship between younger and older generations is inequitable. This view gives credence to the notion that aging families are characterized by intergenerational conflict. It also gives weight to the argument, made by many scholars,[7] that aging family members place burden and strain on their adult children as they take more than they give. However, we argue that there is not much evidence for either of these assumptions. The majority of families do not experience conflict-ridden intergenerational relations nor caregiver burden or strain. Rather, it is our contention that intergenerational relationships are characterized by mutual interdependence and reciprocity.

Notions of Caregiving Burden and Inequitable Intergenerational Relations

Joan Norris and Joseph Tindale,[8] and other authors in this book, have argued that the gerontological literature is dominated by a view of older parents as frail and in need of care by their adult children. They contend that the 'caregiver burden' is grossly exaggerated both within the literature and by the media (see, e.g., Wooley[9]). Similarly, Vern Bengtson, Carolyn Rosenthal, and Linda Burton claim that the caregiver burden is based on several assumptions:[10] (1) caregiver burden implies that having an elderly parent is necessarily experienced as burdensome; (2) the multiple roles that tend to be associated with caregiving create negative rather than positive situations for family members; (3) the notion of caregiving burden assumes that elderly parents are dependent recipients of care; and (4) that older parents need extensive assistance from their adult children, thus representing more burden than benefit.[11]

However, most discussions of caregiving ignore the roles that elderly parents may play in helping younger generations.[12] It is important to note that in most intergenerational families, older parents are not necessarily frail and/or inactive, passively receiving extensive amounts of assistance.[13] Rather, older parent–adult–child helping relationships are characterized by reciprocity, with mutual exchange and support occurring.[14] However, as previously stated, the contributions elderly relatives have made within their intergenerational families have not been acknowledged in the literature.[15] Indeed, as Norris and Tindale have pointed out, much of the gerontological literature views support as flowing from young to old.[16] Janice M. Keefe and Patricia J. Fancey argue that research needs to move beyond analysing relationships in which elderly parents are characterized as being dependent on their adult children.[17] In fact, it has been suggested that elderly parents are likely to give more assistance to their adult children than they are to receive help from them.[18]

Similarly, Robert Hannson and Bruce Carpenter claim that there is myth in the literature that implies that older persons are an emotional strain on their families as they take more than give, resulting in an unequal balance of reciprocity.[19] However, based on the results of their research, these authors argue that relationships within the aging family are characterized by exchange; family members continue to be heavily involved in providing social and caregiving support, with elderly parents contributing long after their children have grown up and established their own families.[20] In earlier work, we made a similar point, arguing that exchanges among adult family members change and mature along with the individuals involved.[21]

Thus, it is our contention that there is little research evidence to support the popular perception that the caregiving burden for middle-aged adult children is the necessary result of having an intergenerational family with elderly parents as members. Suzanne Kingsmill and Benjamin Schlesinger in a book designed to help people 'survive' the sandwich generation, point out that most adult children are not overwhelmed by the caregiving role because caregiving is usually not continuous, and the days that are filled with frustration, anger, and guilt are, in most cases, outnumbered by the positive days.[22] It is also important to recognize that many adult children derive satisfaction from being able to help their aging parents,[23] particularly when they are able to balance this role with a supportive work environment and good formal services.[24] Viewed this way, the caregiving experience may be seen as challenging and potentially rewarding.

Second, we find little support for the assumption that older family members are passive recipients of support and assistance, resulting in an unequal balance in intergenerational exchange. Rather, we – and, recently, other family researchers – argue that exchange patterns in aging families work both ways and can be characterized as mutual reciprocity.[25]

Notions of Intergenerational Conflict: The Example of 'Boomerang Kids'

Because the relationship between younger and older generations is seen as inequitable, there is an assumption that intergenerational conflict within the family is the result. Again, we find no solid evidence in the literature to support this assumption. For example, several studies examining adult–child–parent co-residence have demonstrated that the older parent often makes a significant contribution to the continuing shelter needs of adult children, rather than the other way around and that families can adjust to these circumstances.

According to Barbara A. Mitchell the recent trend of young adults returning to the parental home (often referred to as 'boomerang kids') has resulted in a burgeoning field of research.[26] However, there is some controversy over the consequences of this social phenomenon for families in terms of the impact co-residence has on parent–child relations and the balance of exchange.[27] Some studies suggest that adult–child–parent co-residence creates intrafamilial conflict and strained relationships, while others report positive experiences with the presence of co-residing children on family members' lives.

Much of the literature assumes that intergenerational conflict is the inevitable result of a 'boomerang kid' situation, as young adult children are assumed to take advantage of their parents, particularly in terms of the sharing of household responsibilities and finances. Because these young adult children are seen as 'not pulling their weight' within the intergenerational home, parental resentment occurs, which in turn leads to conflict-ridden relationships. However, Mitchell argues this may not necessarily be the case; a return home may result in greater intergenerational sharing and closeness that may offset any of the negative consequences that may occur as a result of intergenerational co-residence.[28] Similarly, Tindale, Mitchell, and Norris suggest that the result of parent–adult–child co-residence is commonly one that affirms parent–child attachment and that serious intergenerational conflict is the exception in these situations, not the rule.[29] Indeed, the results of Mitchell's Vancouver-based study of 218 'boomerang families' indicate that sharing a home with an adult child did not inevitably lead to a conflict-ridden living situation.[30] Rather, the majority of parents in the sample indicated that their boomerang living situation was working out 'quite well.'[31]

Lynn White and Stacey Rodgers examined the effects of co-residence on multiple dimensions of parent–child solidarity.[32] Their results indicate that although some families did experience some tension within relationships, overall, co-residence increased the exchange of resources between parents and children.[33] Similarly, Tindale, Norris, Stephaneé Kuiack, and Linnea Humphrey examined parent–child relations within a sample of Anglo-Canadian and Italian-Canadian families and found that there was a great deal of intergenerational exchange and support taking place.[34] In their 1996 study examining relationship quality between parents and their young adult children, Tindale et al., found that reciprocal support was negotiated in most families without a significant level of conflict and that most parents did get something out of having a child move back in with them; this support was most often in the form of emotional support that led to parents' satisfaction with the relationship. Based on their results, Tindale and colleagues conclude that having a boomerang living arrangement was managed quite well by most families, because of the strong and affectionate relationship underpinning the offer of room and board.[35]

Rosemary Blieszner, Paula Usita, and Jay Mancini examined the predictors of relationship quality between adult daughters and their elderly mothers.[36] Results indicate that affection and support are still very much a part of mother–daughter relations in later life. In concluding their study, Blieszner et al. argue that it is not appropriate to assume that the flow of assistance and support is unidirectional within an intergenerational relationship; rather the flow is bidirectional with a mutual exchange taking place.[37]

Lastly, based on the findings from her studies on boomerang families, Mitchell argues that we need to critically analyse the popular perception propagated by many social scientists and media sources that the increasing demographic trend of returning home represents a crisis for middle-generation families.[38] A challenge to this perception is in much of the research on intergenerational co-residence which indicates that returns to the nest are not typically characterized by dissatisfaction and conflict. According to Mitchell, cooperation rather than conflict characterizes most generational relations in the refilled nest.[39] Indeed, the literature does suggest that most couples do quite well when finding themselves in a situation of intergenerational co-residence.

Reciprocity in Intergenerational Relations

In our Introduction, we noted that reciprocity is the most appropriate characterization of intergenerational family relations. In the next section, we address what is still a prominent picture in the gerontology literature, one that depicts parent–child interactions as dominated by caregiver burden, sandwiching, and conflict.[40] We explained why we believe such a view is a distortion of typical intergenerational dynamics. At this point, we extend our main premise: reciprocity and interactive support between parents and their adult children is a more promising avenue to follow when looking at such relations.

In our book entitled *Among Generations*,[41] we cite Monica Boyd and Edward T. Pryor to show that the proportion of young adult children co-residing with their parents is substantial and increasing.[42] Here, we turn again to Boyd, this time with Doug Norris, to update the point.[43] They suggest, since Boyd's first article, that the proportion of young adults living at home has increased (44% of women in 1981 to 47% in 1996 and 55% of men in 1981 to 56% in 1996). They are older (men and women over the age of 25 increased from 33% in 1981 to 40% in 1996), and the numbers of those married or living common law have increased proportionately as well.

Considering those adult children (20 years of age or older) living at home during the period 1981 to 1996, the proportion who were married or living common law increased from 52 per cent of women and 64 per cent of men in 1981 to 69 per cent for women and 78 per cent of men by 1996.[44] These figures suggest a continued growth in the proportion of young adults choosing to co-reside with their parents. Indeed, in an examination of 1990 General Social Survey data, Stone and Rosenthal created social network profiles of older Canadians.[45] In their largest network cluster, labelled 'very large: balanced,' 21 per cent of the men and 25 per cent of the women lived with a spouse and their children. They identify these families as being ones where the children have not yet left home. The figures cited by Boyd and Norris could have been even higher were it not that, in the fifteen years between 1981 and 1996, population aging continued apace with the result that the mean age of those in the cohort 20 to 34 also increased.[46] While it is true that increasing proportions of these young adults co-resided with parents, it remains true too that the older a young adult is, the greater the likelihood that he or she will have moved out of the parental home. Thus, increases in the average age of this cohort indicate that, had population aging remained constant between 1981 and 1996, the proportional increase in co-residence would have been even higher.[47]

The relations between parents and their young adult children are also becoming more complex in the range of potential configurations and circumstances. First, in both the early 1980s and 1990s Canada was in the grips of recession, and it was the first half of each of those decades that accounted for most of the change for the decade as a whole. Thus, when we are looking for reasons why adult children continue to need the support of their parents, economic fortunes continue to play a strong role. Whether this is perceived to be an acceptable reason for co-residence is a point we have addressed in previous work.[48] We noted that while it might be viewed as inappropriate in some quarters, in families where there was strong attachment, reciprocity in exchange relations such as co-residence could normally be negotiated with little serious conflict.

Second, we found that in different cultural settings, Anglo and Italian Canadians in this case, there were cultural norms prevailing among the Italian-Canadian families that made continued reliance of adult children on parents more acceptable than was the case with the Anglo-Canadian families.[49] This pattern of results was also alluded to by Boyd,[50] who notes that as Canada becomes more diverse both in family forms and the ethnic composition of those families, different norms may prevail, making extended support of children more variably an issue in need of resolution.[51] A similar phenomenon has been noted in other countries such as France.[52]

Third, using data from the General Social Survey in 1990, Boyd and Norris note that family structure makes a difference in the likelihood that young adults will co-reside with their parents.[53] While the proportion was up from 1981, the probability of co-residence was less if the parents were either widowed or divorced. If the surviving widowed parent was the mother, the likelihood of co-residence was greater than if it was the father. Similarly, when neither divorced parent had remarried, the likelihood of a child co-residing was greater with the mother. If both divorced parents had remarried, it was considerably less likely that children would co-reside with either of them.[54] This is the situation when the parents face such dislocations. However, the opposite occurs when the children are the ones experiencing either a dislocation such as divorce, or remain single. In Canada and in the United States, the rates for persons who are ever-single or divorced are each substantially higher than they were a generation ago. Couple this with the reality that adult children in these circumstances are more likely to co-reside with parents than are children living in stable partnerships and the result is that parents' long-term responsibility for children is likely to remain high.

Finally, when researchers talk about parents' provision of care for their children, we typically restrict ourselves to census families: a couple, and young dependent children. If any children are co-residing single adults, they too are included. However, Nancy Zukewich Ghalam argues that the structure of the Canadian family is becoming more diverse and suggests it makes more sense when thinking of family composition to examine economic families.[55] Such families include the couple and all relatives living in the same household whether they be children or not, and regardless of whether they are related to the family by marriage or parenthood. These economic units are more common among Aboriginal and immigrant families and deserve separate research attention.[56]

Combine these factors, and there is a situation where a growing proportion of young-to-middle-aged children need substantial support from parents. Canadian families in these circumstances are becoming more diverse and complex because of the marital circumstances of both parents and children, the need to consider economic and not just census families, and the evolving cultural diversity in Canada. These factors add to the complexity of our empirical work. They also create challenge for our theorizing to the extent that many studies are atheoretical (e.g., Boyd and Norris)[57] or have relied on simple variants of exchange theory. We have briefly discussed our own framework, global reciprocity. Other hypotheses and frameworks that have been proposed in this context include integenerational stake.

The intergenerational stake hypothesis predicts that parents, versus adult children, are more likely to rate the nature of the relationship and the level of support exchanged highly because they have a stake in family continuity that their children are not yet old enough to appreciate. The finding, first discussed twenty years ago, has been validated as having robust if modest support.[58] It is, however, in the words of Victor Marshall, still 'a finding in search of an interpretation,'[59] because it remains unclear why young and old adults might have differing perceptions of intergenerational relations. A developmental interpretation is suggested by the phenomenon (i.e., with age, people become more concerned with continuity), but such a circular argument does not sit well with most life-course theorists who are concerned with contextual determinants.[60]

Other theorists have considered exchange theory from the perspective of what Adam Davey calls 'contingent need': close friends and family members involved in exchange relations receive in approximate accordance with their needs.[61] When such exchanges occur, they facilitate mental well-being among older persons.[62] Whether that contingent need is considered reciprocal is another question. The work of Dennis Hogan, David Eggebeen, and Clifford Clogg suggests that altruism and reciprocity are a part of exchange when it occurs, although such intergenerational support is not widespread because of limited means among family members.[63]

Not too dissimilarly, Mitchell and colleagues on the west coast have been exploring patterns of co-residence as one kind of parent–adult child exchange. In their earlier papers they discussed theory somewhat loosely in terms of life-course development and a sense of timing associated with patterns of co-residential support of parents to children.[64] More recently, the group associated with this research has moved to look at an exchange perspective within the life-course context.[65]

In all of this research, there is a need to place the exchange in a sociohistorical context and the life-course approach does this to some degree. There is also a need to examine the properties of the exchange and the theory of the same name generally gets that job done. More importantly though, is the question, What explains why such exchanges are different than those involved in buying groceries or a car? Could patterns of intergenerational support be perceived as equitable because of the affective components of global reciprocity, that is, the attachment nurtured when the children were still very young and very dependent? We think so. An analysis of previous attempts to come to grips with diversity reveals that the theoretical premises employed fall short, in part because these perspectives do not adequately integrate attachment and exchange.

Diversity in Patterns of Intergenerational Exchange

In late March of 1999 a newspaper story described the concern of two young parents who had sent their eight-month-old baby to Yugoslavia to spend time with both sets of grandparents.[66] The couple felt that it was important for the older generation, who were not permitted to leave Belgrade to visit Canada, to spend time with their granddaughter. At the time of this story, the baby and both sets of grandparents were living together in one Belgrade apartment, fearful of NATO bombing, and rarely going outside. The parents were desperate to get their baby back and be reassured that the grandparents were safe.

This situation, albeit dramatic, highlights the diversity among norms and patterns of interaction within Canadian families. An understanding of the intergenerational relations of such a family requires a different lens than the one we commonly use to explore concepts such as filial obligation among and between generations. Reciprocity is there, affection and identity relations are there, but the context is radically different. Most of the research which we reviewed earlier involved white, middle-class, American families. In this section, we examine what is known of families who differ from these in a variety of ways. As we know, Canadian society is rapidly becoming more diverse in its ethnic and cultural makeup.[67] What impact does this diversity have on the causes, correlates, and consequences of intergenerational helping?

Vern L. Bengtson, Elizabeth D. Burgess, and Tonya M. Parrott have argued that our understanding of aging will be enhanced only if researchers abandon their 'happily atheoretical' approach to data-gathering and adopt strong theoretical frameworks and concepts.[68] Perhaps nowhere is this more important than when one considers research on the influence of ethnicity on families. Simply cataloguing the differences between a variety of minority families and those from the majority culture does little to further knowledge or application. Examining this research for evidence of the critical concepts which we outlined in the previous section, however, can provide some insights into family functioning in the context of ethnic diversity.

Intergenerational Solidarity

Intergenerational solidarity is a frequently mentioned concept in this body of work.[69] We argue that the development and maintenance of family solidarity must be seen within a lifespan context, one recognizing the importance of early, culturally appropriate, attachment experiences, and the continuous evolution of relationships. It is little more than an interesting observation, for example, that old people in Wales receive more help from physically proximal children than do old people in the United States, if we do not try to interpret the meaning of such closeness within each culture.[70] As Merril Silverstein and colleagues point out, geographic proximity in traditional or rural cultures may be perceived to have greater significance, and therefore a greater influence on intergenerational solidarity, than in urban North American society.

Other researchers have also noted that the ethnicity of the participants in their samples has significantly affected the utility of a general model of intergenerational solidarity. Renee Lawrence, Joan M. Bennet, and Kyriakos Markides find that, in their study of Mexican American families, predictions from the model about the relationship between closeness and psychological distress were not supported when the dyad studied was an older parent and an emotionally closest, versus less close, child.[71] Stoller finds additional complexity in her study of Finnish-American retirees.[72] In this study, migrants to the sunbelt are less likely than those Finnish Americans remaining in Minnesota to name non-kin as partners in the exchange of support. Using a solidarity framework, one would expect that those in closer proximity with children (i.e., those in Minnesota), not those more distant, would be likely to rely less on friends for help. To add further to her interpretive difficulties, Stoller also finds that the Finnish Americans in Florida are less likely to rely on friends for support than are other European-American migrants.

In their 1990 response to a study which failed to support the original solidarity model, Roberts and Bengtson propose a much simplified framework.[73] The goal of this model was still to understand intergenerational association (always Bengtson's goal), but focused on three major predictors: norms of closeness, balanced exchange of support, and affection. This revised model, still untested, has elements in common with our ideas of global reciprocity. Both emphasize the importance of understanding shared attachments within families as well as the shared beliefs about the nature of reciprocal support. The Roberts and Bengtson model is unidirectional, however, focusing its attention on contact. Our model is fully recursive and attempts to predict positive relationships, in general, among adult family members. We theorize that a history of rewarding interactions creates an environment that allows family members to assimilate beliefs about meeting each others' needs. Successfully reciprocated helping strengthens relationships and reinforces a familial norm of shared support.

For families who differ according to their ethnic background, it is important to examine cultural norms surrounding affection and support that will affect the mechanisms and circumstances of exchange. Nevertheless, the basic processes will remain uniform across diverse groups. Examined in this way, the decisions of the Serbian-Canadian couple in our example, compared with – let us say – their German-Canadian neighbours, become readily interpretable. Canadian families from Eastern Europe are typically first- or second-generation immigrants, who carry with them strong norms about intergenerational support and contact. The affection which they hold for one another smoothes the way for this contact in the face of very difficult historical circumstances. Their motivations, however, differ little from their third- or fourth-generation neighbours who are able to fulfil desires for affection and support among a close-knit German-Canadian community.

Filial Obligation

A second organizing framework used to explain intergenerational support suggests that North Americans families of Asian descent will be strongly influenced by a norm of filial piety that leads automatically to positive intergenerational relationships.[74] Recently, however, researchers have pointed out that there is very little evidence for this 'model minority' idea. Tae-Ock Kauh, for example, speculates that the harmonious intergenerational relationships that she found among members of Korean-American families were maintained by low, and not high, expectations of filial obligation reported by the oldest generation.[75] Misako Ihsii-Kuntz also found that strong norms of filial obligation were not central in predicting intergenerational helping among three communities of Japanese, Chinese, and Korean Americans.[76] Instead, parental need and income levels were more important. Additionally, she found that there were marked differences among the three communities in the extent to which they did endorse the norm of obligation. Relative to the others, Korean Americans subscribed most strongly to the norm, an interesting finding when one considers that, according to Kauh's study, this group was already not as connected to the notion of obligation as the stereotype would predict.

Non Asian communities within the United States have been examined for evidence of filial norms, but with even more mixed results (see Drieger and Chappell for a review[77]). Similarly, the scant Canadian lit-

erature reveals a correspondingly complex pattern. John Bond, Carol
Harvey, and Elizabeth Hildebrand, for example, found that a homogeneous group of rural Mennonites in Manitoba actually showed *more*
intergenerational diversity in solidarity-related norms than did a heterogeneous non-Mennonite group.[78] Barbara A. Mitchell, Andrew V.
Wister, and Ellen M. Gee found that young francophone adults were
less likely than their anglophone peers to boomerang home, leading
these authors to suggest the presence of different norms surrounding
intergenerational obligation in the two groups.[79] Nevertheless, they
have no direct evidence to support this view.

How can we understand these findings? There is no straightforward
support for a norm of filial obligation in various cultures or the positive effect of such a norm on intergenerational helping. Once again, we
believe that researchers' failure to consider the relationship basis of
helping within families has created interpretive difficulties. It is essential to consider the interacting influences of traditional cultural norms,
such as filial obligation, with patterns of attachment and shared helping among generations of individual families. Eggebeen and Davey,
commenting on their study of more than 1,000 adult families, suggest
that knowing general family beliefs about 'who should do what for
whom' is relatively unimportant when attempting to predict actual
exchanges of support.[80] We would argue that researchers should examine these norms for cultural diversity – the Eggebeen and Davey study
used a homogeneous sample – but should do so in the context of specific family histories.

Other Kinds of Diversity

Researchers are just beginning to appreciate the role of other kinds of
diversity in influencing intergenerational support in aging families.
One of the most noteworthy of these 'other diversities' is that of disability. Traditionally, the focus of family research on disability has been
on young parents caring for young children with disabilities and on
middle-aged children caring for frail old parents (see our review
above)[81]. Lately, however, researchers have become more interested in
the possible influence of a pre-existing disability on intergenerational
support within aging families.[82]

As with many emerging bodies of work, this research is not strongly
grounded in any one theoretical framework; rather, a loosely constructed life-course perspective has been applied.[83] Findings suggest
that families may not feel overwhelmingly burdened by the care they

provide for disabled members nor experience significant negative psychological outcomes because of the members' diagnoses.[84] Instead, they may see improvements in their own resilience and personal mastery as they learn to support one another.[85]

Problems in coping with the care of the disabled appear somewhat more closely linked to individual and societal interpretations of disability as a life-course marker than they do to the nature of the disability itself.[86] As George has argued, however, the notion of off-time or disorderly life events as a single, significant challenge to most families appears overblown.[87] Instead, it seems that the intersection of disability with other normative and non-normative life events may have a more powerful effect on the exchange of assistance and how it affects family functioning. For example, the co-residence of adult children, a potential strain in all families – as we have argued above – can cause additional difficulties when the children are disabled. Nevertheless, it is important to point out that even these families experience many rewards in their relationships.

Once again, considering the diversity of intergenerational families leads us back to our theoretical position: families provide for their members, whatever their circumstances, in a manner that is determined, at least in part, by a history of affectionate and mutually supportive relationships. Although the work on disability does not use our model of global reciprocity, it is apparent that it is readily applicable. For example, Brigit Mirfin-Veitch, Anne Bray, and Marilyn Watson's study of disabled grandchildren and their grandparents found that these relationships were more strongly affected by the mutually supportive relationships of parents and grandparents than they were by the child's disability.[88] Furthermore, the body of research reviewed by Judith Cook et al. stressed the importance of the interacting influences such as relationship history, birth cohort, and historical period when understanding how a family provides care for adults with psychiatric disorder.[89] Adults currently in their thirties and forties, who are now experiencing the onset of a psychiatric illness, will have benefited from fuller participation in social and family life than those with an early onset illness, or from a previous cohort.

Conclusion: Policy Implications

To the degree that policy does not reflect the heterogeneity and diversity in parent–adult child relations, the gap between the haves and have-nots can be expected to expand.[90] Our work has demonstrated that intergenerational relations between parents and their young adult children are complex evolving patterns of reciprocal relations. There are contextual differentials in how young adult child autonomy is understood in different cultures, how it is addressed in different social classes, and how these family relations fit with respect to the role of the state.[91] To the degree governments in Canada see their job as being one of downsizing the state, inequality in social condition will jeopardize individual attempts to gain access to opportunity. To this end, we think policy recommendations associated with the aging of the baby boomers should be formulated within a context that can capture the heterogeneity and diversity of our population beyond age parameters. This means that the focus should:

• Not be on intergenerational conflict
• Not focus on caregiver burden or the perils of the so-called sandwich generation.

Instead, more benefit can be gained by thinking in terms of a reformulated economic life course. When John Myles and Debra Street discussed this they were doing so in the context of addressing changes in later life work and retirement.[92] However, we – and others writing in this book – think the same premise applies in the context of later life family relations. If there is a caregiver issue, it is not one of burden but one of limited supply.[93] Too few available family members, read women, to provide the care being demanded by some governments on top of the already willingly provided family care. This suggests no further dumping of care responsibilities on families. At the same time, we need to invest in equitable conditions and opportunities for young adult children. To the degree that young adults are able to establish themselves, the need to rely on parents is diminished. To the degree that parents are relieved of this concern, the better able they are to prepare for their retirement in a manner that minimizes dependency on the state. What goes around, comes around.

Notes

1 See Joan E. Norris and Joseph A. Tindale, *Among Generations: The Cycle of Adult Relationships* (New York: Freeman, 1994); Joseph A. Tindale, Barbara Mitchell, and Joan E. Norris, 'Global Reciprocity: Examining Relationship

Quality between Parents and Their Young Adult Children,' Paper Presented at the Canadian Sociology and Anthropology Association, Brock University, St Catharines, Ontario, June 1996.

2 See Janet Taylor, Joan E. Norris, and Wayne Howard, 'Succession Patterns of Farmer and Successor in Canadian Farm Families,' *Rural Sociology* 63, no. 4 (1998): 553–73.

3 See Suzanne Kingsmill and Benjamin Schlesinger, *The Family Squeeze: Surviving the Sandwich Generation* (Toronto: University of Toronto Press, 1998).

4 See Alexander Wooley, 'The Sandwich Generation: U of G Researchers Investigate Slices of Canadian Family Life,' *Guelph Alumnus* (1999), 22–7.

5 See Joseph A. Tindale, Joan E. Norris, Stephanie Kuiack, and Linnea Humphrey, 'The Need for Open Communication: A Layered Context of Parent-Adult Child Relations in a Sample of Anglo and Italian Families,' Paper Presented at the Canadian Association on Gerontology Annual Meeting, Winnipeg, Oct. 1994.

6 See Toni Calasanti, 'Incorporating Diversity: Meaning, Levels of Research, and Implications for Theory,' *Gerontologist* 36, no. 2 (1996): 147–56.

7 See Elaine Brody, *Women in the Middle: Their Parent-Care Years* (New York: Springer, 1990); Rachel Pruchno, 'The Effects of Help Patterns on the Mental Health of Spouse Caregivers,' *Research on Aging* 12, no. 1 (1990): 57–71.

8 See Norris and Tindale, *Among Generations.*

9 See Alexander Wooley, 'Sandwich Generation.'

10 See Vern L. Bengston, Carolyn Rosenthal, and Linda Burton, 'Paradoxes in Families and Aging,' in Robert Binstock and Linda George, eds., *Handbook of Aging and the Social Sciences* (San Diego, Calif.: Academic Press, 1996), 253–82.

11 Ibid.

12 Ibid.

13 See Jacques Roy, 'Solidarité horizontale chez les aînés.' *La revue canadienne du vieillissement* 17, no. 3 (1998): 311–29.

14 Ibid. See also Laurent Martel, 'L'orientation et le contenu des relations réciproques des personnes âgées,' *La revue canadienne du vieillissement* 19 (1) (2000): 80–105.

15 See Janice M. Keefe and Patricia J. Fancey, 'Work and Eldercare: The Contributions of Elderly Parents to Their Employed Children,' Paper Presented at the Annual Meeting of the Canadian Association on Gerontology, Vancouver, Oct. 1998.

16 See Norris and Tindale, *Among Generations.*

17 See Keefe and Fancey, 'Work and Eldercare.'

18 See Terry Hargrave, and William Anderson, *Finishing Well: Aging and Prepa-*

ration in the Intergenerational Family (New York: Bruner/Mazel, 1992); Norris and Tindale, *Among Generations*.

19 See Robert Hannson and Bruce Carpenter, *Relationships in Old Age* (New York: Guilford, 1994).

20 Ibid.

21 See Norris and Tindale, *Among Generations*.

22 See Kingsmill and Schlesinger, *Family Squeeze*.

23 See Sherry Dupuis and Joan E. Norris, 'The Roles of Adult Daughters in Long-Term Care Facilities: Alternative Role Manifestations,' *Journal of Aging Studies* 15, no. 1 (2001): 27–54.

24 See Nancy Guberman and Pierre Maheau, 'Le rapport entre l'adéquation des services de maintien à domicile et la trajectoire de travail des personnes soignantes,' *La revue canadienne du viellissement* 19, no. 4 (2000): 380–408.

25 See Norris and Tindale, *Among Generations*; Claudine Attias-Donfut, 'Famille: Les solidarités entre générations,' *Les données sociales* (Paris: Institut national de la statistique et des études économiques, 1996), 317–23.

26 See Barbara Mitchell, 'Too Close for Comfort? Parental Assessments of "Boomerang Kid" Living Arrangements,' *Canadian Journal of Sociology* 23, no. 1 (1998): 21–46.

27 Ibid.

28 See Mitchell, 'Too Close for Comfort?'

29 See Tindale, Mitchell, and Norris, 'Global Reciprocity.'

30 See Mitchell, 'Too Close for Comfort?'

31 Ibid.

32 See Lynn White and Stacy Rodgers, 'Strong Support but Uneasy Relationships,' *Journal of Marriage and the Family* 59, no. 1 (1997): 62–76.

33 Ibid.

34 See Tindale et al., 'Need for Open Communication.'

35 See Tindale et al., 'Global Reciprocity.'

36 See Rosemary Blieszener, Paula Usita, and Jay Mancini, 'Diversity and Dynamics in Late-Life Mother-Daughter Relationships,' *Journal of Women and Aging* 8, no. 3–4 (1996): 5–24.

37 Ibid.

38 See Barbara Mitchell, 'The Refilled Nest: Debunking the Myth of Families-in-Crisis,' Paper presented at the 9th Annual John K. Freisen Conference and Lecture, Simon Fraser University, Vancouver, 14-15 May 1998.

39 Ibid.

40 See Isabelle Delisle, 'Les solidarités intergénérationnelles,' *L'infirmière canadienne* 95 (1999): 37–40.

41 See Norris and Tindale, *Among Generations*.

42 See Monica Boyd and Edward T. Pryor, 'The Cluttered Nest: The Living Arrangements of Young Canadian Adults,' *Canadian Journal of Sociology* 14, no. 4 (1989): 461–77.
43 See Monica Boyd and Doug Norris, 'Leaving the Nest? The Impact of Family Structure,' *Canadian Social Trends* 38 (1995): 14–17; Boyd and Norris, 'The Crowded Nest: Young Adults at Home,' *Canadian Social Trends* 52 (1999): 2–5.
44 Boyd and Norris, 'The Crowded Nest,' 3.
45 See Leroy Stone and Carolyn Rosenthal, 'Profiles of the Social Network of Canada's Elderly: An Analysis of 1990 GSS Data,' in Howard Litwin, ed., *The Social Networks of Older People* (Westport, Conn.: Praeger, 1996), 77–97.
46 See Boyd and Norris, 'Crowded Nest.'
47 Ibid.
48 See Norris and Tindale, *Among Generations.*
49 Tindale et al., 'Need for Open Communication.'
50 See Monica Boyd, 'Birds of a Feather: Ethnic Variations in Young Adults Living at Home,' *Working Paper Series* (Center for the Study of Population and Demography, Florida State University, 1998), 98–140.
51 See Boyd and Norris, 'Crowded Nest.'
52 See Agnès Pitrou, 'De la transformation des classes d'âges à l'évolution des rapports sociaux,' *Sociologie et sociétés* 27 (1995): 27–42.
53 See Boyd and Norris, 'Leaving the Nest?'
54 Ibid., 15–16.
55 See Nancy Zukewich Ghalam, 'Living with Relatives,' *Canadian Social Trends* 42 (1996): 20–4.
56 Ibid., 22.
57 See Boyd and Norris, 'Crowded Nest.'
58 See Rosean Giarrusso, Michael Stallings, and Vern Bengtson, 'The "Intergenerational Stake" Hypothesis Revisited: Parent-Child Differences in Perceptions of Relationships 20 Years Later,' in Vern Bengston, K. Warner Schaiem and Linda Burton, eds., *Adult Intergenerational Relations: Effects of Societal Change* (New York: Springer, 1995), 227–63; Marshall Fine, Joan E. Norris, and Greta Hofstra, 'Intergenerational Family Relations: Two Disciplines Meet Two Generations,' *Journal of Family Social Work* 5, no. 4 (2001): 17–38.
59 See Victor Marshall, 'Commentary: A Finding in Search of an Interpretation: Discussion of the Intergenerational Stake Hypothesis Revisited,' in Bengtson et al., *Adult Intergenerational Relations,* 277–97.
60 See Alice Rossi, 'Commentary: Wanted: Alternative Theory and Analysis Modes,' in Bengtson et al., *Adult Intergenerational Relations,* 264–76.

61 See Adam Davey and Joan E. Norris, 'Social Networks and Exchange
    Norms Across the Adult Life Span,' *Canadian Journal on Aging* 17, no. 3
    (1998): 212–33.
62 See Adam Davey and David Eggebeen, 'Patterns of Intergenerational
    Exchange and Mental Health,' *Journal of Gerontology: Psychological Science*
    53B, no. 1 (1998): P86–P95.
63 See Dennis Hogan, David Eggebeen, and Clifford Clogg, 'The Structure of
    Intergenerational Exchanges in American Families,' *American Journal of
    Sociology* 98, no. 6 (1993): 1428–58.
64 See Jean Veevers, Ellen Gee, and Andrew Wister, 'Homeleaving Age
    Norms: Conflict or Consensus?' *Aging and Human Development* 43, no. 3
    (1996): 277–94; Barbara Mitchell and Ellen Gee, '"Boomerang Kids" and
    Midlife Parental Marital Satisfaction,' *Family Relations*, 45, no. 4 (1996): 442–
    8; Ellen Gee, Barbara Mitchell, and Andrew Wister, 'Returning to the Paren-
    tal "Nest": Exploring a Changing Canadian Life Course,' *Canadian Studies
    in Population* 22, no. 2 (1995): 121–44; Andrew Wister, Barbara Mitchell, and
    Ellen Gee, 'Does Money Matter? Parental Income and Living Satisfaction
    among "Boomerang" Children during Coresidence,' *Canadian Studies in
    Population* 24, no. 2 (1997): 125–45.
65 See Jean Veevers and Barbara Mitchell, 'Intergenerational Exchanges and
    Perceptions of Support within "Boomerang Kid" Family Environments,'
    Aging and Human Development 46, no. 2 (1998): 91–108.
66 See Barbara Aggerholm, 'Kitchener Couple Worry about Safety of Baby,
    Parents in Belgrade,' *Kitchener-Waterloo Record*, 29 March 1999, A3.
67 See Tina Chui, 'Canada's Population: Charting into the 21st Century,' *Cana-
    dian Social Trends* 42 (1996): 3–7.
68 See Vern L. Bengtson, Elizabeth O. Burgess, and Tonya M. Parrott, 'Theory,
    Explanation, and a Third Generation of Theoretical Development in Social
    Gerontology,' *Journal of Gerontology: Social Sciences* 52B, no. 2 (1997): S72–
    S88.
69 See Delisle, 'Les solidarités intergénérationnelles'; Attias-Donfut, 'Famille:
    Les solidarités entre générations.'
70 See Merril Silverstein, Vanessa Burholt, G. Clair Wenger, and Vern Beng-
    ston, 'Parent-Child Relations among Very Old Parents in Wales and the
    United States: A Test of Moderization Theory,' *Journal of Aging Studies* 12,
    no. 4 (1997): 387–409.
71 See Renee H. Lawrence, Joan M. Bennet, and Kyriakos Markides, 'Per-
    ceived Intergenerational Distress among Older Mexican Americans,' *Jour-
    nal of Gerontology* 47, no. 2 (1992): S55–S65.
72 See Eleanor P. Stoller, 'Informal Exchanges with Non-Kin Among Retired

Sunbelt Migrants: A Case Study of a Finnish American Retirement Community,' *Journal of Gerontology: Social Sciences* 53B, no. 5 (1998): S87–S98.
73 See Robert E. Roberts and Vern L. Bengston, 'Is Intergenerational Solidarity a Unidirectional Construct? A Second Test of a Formal Model,' *Journal of Gerontology: Social Sciences* 45, no. 1 (1990): S12–S20.
74 See Misako Ishii-Kuntz, 'Intergenerational Relationships among Chinese, Japanese, and Korean Americans,' *Family Relations* 46, no. 1 (1997): 23–32.
75 See Tae-Ock Kauh, 'Intergenerational Relations: Older Korean-Americans' Experiences,' *Journal of Cross Cultural Gerontology* 12, no. 3 (1997): 245–71.
76 See Ishii-Kuntz, 'Intergenerational Relationships.'
77 See Leo Driedger and Neena Chappell, *Aging and Ethnicity: Toward an Interface* (Toronto: Butterworths, 1987).
78 See John Bond, Carol Harvey, and Elizabeth Hildebrand, 'Familial Support of the Elderly in a Rural Mennonite Community,' *Canadian Journal on Aging* 6, no. 1 (1987): 7–18.
79 See Barbara Mitchell, Andrew Wister, and Ellen Gee, 'Culture and Coresidence: An Exploration of Home Returning among Canadian Young Adults,' Paper presented at the 14th World Congress of Sociology, Montreal, 28 July 1998.
80 See David J. Eggebeen and Adam Davey, 'Do Safety Nets Work? The Role of Anticipated Help in Times of Need,' *Journal of Marriage and the Family* 60, no. 4 (1998): 939–50.
81 See Gillian King, Susanne King, Peter Rosenbaum, and Richard Goffin, 'Family-Centered Caregiving and Well-Being of Parents of Children with Disabilities: Linking Process with Outcome,' *Journal of Pediatric Psychology* 24, no. 1 (1999): 41–53.
82 See Sharon R.Livingstone, Joseph A. Tindale, and Anne Martin-Matthews, 'Balancing Work and Family: Perspectives of Employed Individuals Providing Care to Adults with Special Needs,' Paper Presented at the Annual Meeting of the Canadian Association on Gerontology, Halifax, October 1998.
83 See Judith A. Cook, Bertram J. Cohler, Susan A. Pickett, and Jeff A. Beeler, 'Life-Course and Severe Mental Illness: Implications for Caregiving within the Family of Later Life,' *Family Relations* 46, no. 4 (1997): 427–36.
84 See Susan A. Pickett, Judith Cook, Bertram Cohler, and Mitchell Solomon, 'Positive Parent/Adult Relationships: Impact of Severe Mental Illness and Caregiving Burden,' *American Journal of Orthopsychiatry* 67, no. 2 (1997): 220–30.
85 See Edie Mannion, 'Resilience and Burden in Spouses of People with Mental Illness,' *Psychiatric Rehabilitation Journal* 20, no. 2 (1996): 13–23.

86 See Sharon Livingstone and Joseph A. Tindale, 'Growing Old with a Developmental Disability,' *Canadian Nurse* 96 (2000): 28-31; Susan A. Pickett, James R. Greenley, and Jan S. Greenberg, 'Off-Timedness as a Contributor to Subjective Burdens for Parents of Offspring with Severe Mental Illness,' *Family Relations* 44, no. 2 (1995): 195–201.
87 See Linda George, 'Missing Links: The Case for a Social Psychology of the Life Course,' *Gerontologist* 36, no. 2 (1996): 248–55.
88 See Brigit Mirfin-Veitch, Anne Bray, and Marilyn Watson, '"We're Just that Sort of Family": Intergenerational Relationships in Families Including Children with Disabilities,' *Family Relations* 46 (July 1997): 305–11.
89 See Cook et al., 'Life-Course and Severe Mental Illness.'
90 See Mitchell, 'Too Close for Comfort?'; Carolyn J. Rosenthal, 'Le soutien des familles canadiennes à leurs membres vieillissants: Changements de contexte,' *Lien social et politiques* 38 (Autumn 1997): 123–31.
91 See Agnès Pitrou, 'Vieillesse et famille: qui soutient l'autre?' *Lien social et politiques* 38 (Autumn 1997): 145–58.
92 See John Myles and Debra Street, 'Should the Economic Life Course Be Redesigned? Old Age Security in a Time of Transition,' *Canadian Journal on Aging* 14, no. 2 (1995): 335–59.
93 See John Myles, 'Women, the Welfare State, and Caregiving,' *Canadian Journal on Aging* 10, no. 1 (1991): 82–5.

Appendix: Iowa City Declaration

Post-industrial society in North America is experiencing a time famine. Yet, while many working people have inadequate time to pursue family, personal, and community life, others have become economically redundant in the continuing waves of corporate downsizing. The maldistribution of work and free time, with attendant inequality of incomes, has created a growing social problem. We believe that this problem may effectively be addressed by a general reduction in working hours.

The forty-hour workweek became the legal standard for U.S. hourly workers in 1940. Labor productivity has increased by many times since then. Increased labor productivity, unless accompanied by shorter hours, tends to displace workers from employment in productive enterprise. The result is higher unemployment or increasing employment in low-wage occupations.

Responsible social policy requires correction of these trends. Responsible employment requires that the jobs allow adequate time for employees to cultivate rich and fulfilling lives outside their work environment. Responsible direction of national economies requires attention to the widening income gap in society. Responsible practice in international trade requires that nations refrain from dumping domestic unemployment on their trading partners by maintaining a schedule of work hours in excess of levels appropriate for their stage of industrial development.

We North Americans, gathered in Iowa City, therefore urge the national governments of Canada and the United States to put in place before the year 2000 the legal arrangements to ensure that a thirty-two hour workweek will become the norm for full-time workers in the first decade of the new millennium.

While a reduced workweek is the focus of this appeal, we also recognize that longer vacations, sabbaticals, job sharing, and other forms of hours reductions or alternative schedules are desirable objects. In the process of reducing work hours, it is important to protect and enhance the basic wage and benefit structure for workers in advanced economies, including those employed as part-time, contingent, temporary, or contract workers. We invite support for those objectives from representatives of the labor movement, the business community, public officials, religiously committed persons, socially or environmentally conscious groups, and others concerned with humanity's future.

Adopted in Iowa City, Iowa, on 10 March 1996

Bibliography

Abramovitz, Moses. *Thinking about Growth*. Cambridge: Cambridge University Press, 1989.

Advisory Group on Working Time and the Distribution of Work. *Report of the Advisory Group on Working Time and the Distribution of Work*. Ottawa: Human Resources Development Canada, 1994.

Aggerholm, Barbara. 'Kitchener Couple Worry about Safety of Baby, Parents in Belgrade.' *Kitchener-Waterloo Record*, 29 March 1999, A3.

'All Our Tomorrows: A Survey of the Economics of Ageing: *Economist*, 27 Jan. 1996.

Akyeampong, E.B. 'Older Workers in the Canadian Labour Market.' *The Labour Force*, 85–120. Ottawa: Statistics Canada, 1987.

Allen, Katherine R., and David H. Demo. 'The Families of Lesbians and Gay Men: A New Frontier of Family Research.' *Journal of Marriage and the Family* 57, no. 2. (1995): 111–27.

Alzheimer, Alois. 'On Certain Peculiar Diseases of Old Age.' (1911). Repr. in *History of Psychiatry* 2 (1991): 71–101. Trans. and with an Introduction by Hans Förstl and Raymond Levy.

American Demographics Editors. 'What If ... ?' *American Demographics*, Dec. 1997, 39–41.

Andersen, Otto. 'Occupational Impacts on Mortality Declines in the Nordic Countries.' In Wolfgang Lutz, ed., *Future Demographic Trends in Europe and North America*, 41–54. London: Academic Press, 1991.

Aquilino, William S. 'Later Life Parental Divorce and Widowhood: Impact on Young Adults' Assessment of Parent-Child Relations.' *Journal of Marriage and the Family* 56 (Nov. 1994): 908–22.

Ariès, Philippe. *The Hour of Our Death*. Trans. Helen Weaver. New York: Alfred Knopf, 1981.

Atkinson Newsletter. Toronto: Atkinson Foundation, Oct., 1999.

Attias-Donfut, Claudine. 'Famille: Les solidarités entre générations.' In *Les données sociales*, 317–23. Paris: Institut national de la statistique et des études économiques, 1996.

– ed., *Les solidarités entre les générations. Vieillesse, famille, état*. Paris: Nathan, 1995.

Autor, David H., Lawrence Katz, and Alan Krueger. 'Computing Inequality: Have Computers Changed the Labor Market.' *Quarterly Journal of Economics* 113, no. 4: (1998): 1169–1213.

Bachler, Christopher. 'Workers Take Leave of Job Stress.' *Personnel Journal* 74, no. 1 (1995): 38–48.

Bagnell, Priscilla von Dorotka, and Patricia Spencer Soper. *Perceptions of Aging in Literature: A Cross-Cultural Study*. Westport, Conn.: Greenwood Press, 1989.

Baker, Maureen. 'Reinforcing Obligations and Responsibilities between Generations: Policy Options from Cross-National Comparisons,' Discussion Paper for the Vanier Institute of the Family, Ottawa, 1996.

Baldwin, John R., and Naginder Dhaliwal. 'Labour Productivity Differences between Domestic and Foreign-Controlled Establishments in the Canadian Manufacturing Sector,' *Analytical Studies Branch Research Paper Series*, no. 118. Ottawa: Statistics Canada.

Banting, Keith G., Charles M. Beach, and Gordon Betcherman. 'Polarization and Social Policy Reform: Evidence and Issues.' In Keith G. Banting and Charles M. Beach, eds., *Labour Market Polarization and Social Policy Reform*, 1–20. Kingston: School of Policy Studies, Queen's University, 1995.

Bardwick, Judith. *The Plateauing Trap*. New York: Amacom, 1986.

Barer, Morris L., Robert G. Evans, and Clyde Hertzman. 'Avalanche or Glacier? Health Care and the Demographic Rhetoric.' *Canadian Journal on Aging* 14, no. 2 (1995): 193–224.

Barth, Michael C., William McNaught, and Philip Rizzi. 'Older Americans as Workers.' In Scott A. Bass, ed., *Older and Active*, 35–70. New Haven: Yale University Press, 1995.

Bass, Scott A. 'An Overview of Work, Retirement, and Pensions in Japan.' In Scott A. Bass, Robert Morris, and Masato Oka, eds. *Public Policy and the Old Age Revolution in Japan*. New York: Haworth Press, 1996.

– *Older and Active*. New Haven: Yale University Press, 1995.

Bass, Scott A., Francis G. Caro, and Yung Ping Chen, eds. *Achieving a Productive Society*. Westport, Conn.: Auburn House, 1993.

Bass, Scott A., Robert Morris, and Masato Oka, eds. *Public Policy and the Old Age Revolution in Japan*. New York: Haworth Press, 1996.

Battiste, Marie, ed. *Reclaiming Indigenous Voice and Vision*. Vancouver: UBC Press, 2000.

Battiste, Marie, and James (Sa'ke'j) Youngblood Henderson, eds. *Protecting Indigenous Knowledge and Heritage: A Global Challenge.* Saskatoon: Purich Publishing, 1999.

Baumol, William J., and Kenneth McLennan, eds. *Productivity Growth and U.S. Competitiveness.* New York: Oxford University Press, 1985.

Baumol, William J., Edward N. Wolff, and Sue Anne Batey Blackman. eds., *Productivity and American Leadership: The Long View.* Cambridge, Mass.: MIT Press, 1989.

Beach, Charles M., and G.A. Slotsve. *Are We Becoming Two Societies?* Toronto: C.D. Howe Institute, 1996.

Beaudry, P., and D. Green. 'Cohort Patterns in Canadian Earnings and the Skill Biased Technical Change Hypothesis.' Discussion Paper no. 97-03, Department of Economics, University of British Columbia, 1996.

– 'Immigration Policy and Sociodemographic Change: The Canadian Case.' In Wolfgang Lutz, ed., *Future Demographic Trends in Europe and North America,* 359–77. London: Academic Press, 1991.

Beaujot, Roderic. 'Family Patterns at Mid-Life (Marriage, Parenting, and Working).' In Roderic Beaujot, Ellen M. Gee, Fernando Rajulton, and Zenaida R. Ravanera, eds., *Family over the Life Course: Current Demographic Analysis,* 38–75. Ottawa: Statistics Canada, 1995.

Beer, Michael, and Nitrin Nohria. *Old Theories in the New Economy.* Cambridge: Harvard Business School Press, 2000.

Bélanger, Alain. *Report on the Demographic Situation in Canada, 1998–1999: Current Demographic Analysis.* Ottawa: Statistics Canada, 1999.

Bell, Daniel. 'The End of Ideology Revisited – Part II.' *Government and Opposition* 23, no. 3 (1988): 321–31.

Bellemare, Diane, Lise Poulin Simon, and Diane-Gabrielle Tremblay. 'Vieillissement, emploi, préretraite: les facteurs socio-économiques influant sur la gestion de la main-d'oeuvre vieillissante.' *Relations industrielles* 50, no. 3 (1995): 483–515.

Belous, Richard S. 'Flexible Employment: The Employer's Point of View.' In Peter B. Doeringer, ed., *Bridges to Retirement,* 111–29. Ithaca, NY: ILR Press, Cornell University, 1990.

Bengtson, Vern L., and W. A. Achenbaum, eds. *The Changing Contract across Generations.* New York: Aldine de Gruyter, 1993.

Bengtson, Vern L., Elizabeth O. Burgess, and Tonya M. Parrott. 'Theory, Explanation, and a Third Generation of Theoretical Development in Social Gerontology.' *Journal of Gerontology: Social Sciences* 52B, no. 2 (1997): S72–S88.

Bengtson, Vern L., Carolyn Rosenthal, and Linda Burton. 'Paradoxes in Families and Aging.' In Robert Binstock and Linda George, eds., *Handbook of*

Aging and the Social Sciences, 4th ed., 253–82. San Diego: Academic Press, 1996.

Benimadhu, Prem. *Hours of Work: Trends and Attitudes in Canada*. Ottawa: Conference Board of Canada, 1987.

Bennett, Ken. 'Recent Information on Training.' *Perspectives on Labour and Income* 6, no. 1 (1994): 22–4.

Berman, Eli, John Bound, and Stephen Machin. 'Implications of Skill-Biased Technological Change: International Evidence.' *Quarterly Journal of Economics* 113, no. 4 (1998): 1245–79.

Bernard, Paul. 'La cohésion sociale: critique dialectique d'un quasi concept.' *Lien social et politique* 41 (Spring 1999): 47–59. Also published as a Canadian Policy Research Network discussion paper, under the title, 'Social Cohesion: A Critique.'

Berrios, German E. *The History of Mental Symptoms: Descriptive Psychopathology since the Nineteenth Century*. Cambridge: Cambridge University Press, 1996.

Betcherman, Gordon, and Norman Leckie. 'Age Structure of Employment in Industries and Occupations.' *Applied Research Branch, Strategic Policy Report* no. R-96-7E. Ottawa: Human Resources Development Canada, 1995.

Bird, Richard. 'Few Jobs in High Tech.' *Policy Options*. Sept. 1984, 23–7.

Birnbacher, Dieter. *La responsibilité envers les générations futures*. Paris: Presses Universitaires de France, 1994.

Birren, James E., R. Bruce Sloane, and Gene D. Cohen, eds. *Handbook of Mental Health and Aging*. 2nd ed. San Diego: Academic Press, 1992.

Blieszener, Rosemary, Paula Usita and Jay Mancini. 'Diversity and Dynamics in Late-Life Mother-Daughter Relationships.' *Journal of Women and Aging* 8, no. 3–4 (1996): 5–24.

Bliss, Michael. *William Osler: A Life in Medicine*. Toronto: University of Toronto Press, 1999.

Blondal, Sveinbjorn, and Stefano Scarpetta. 'The Retirement Decision in OECD Countries.' *Economic Department Working Papers*, no. 202. Paris: OECD, 1998.

Bluestone, Irving, Rhonda J.V. Montgomery, and John D. Owen, eds. *The Aging of the American Workforce*. Detroit: Wayne State University, 1990.

Blyton, Paul. *Changes in Working Time: An International Review*. London: Croom Helm, 1985.

Bodipo, Alejandro, and David Wessel. 'U.S. Productivity Surges 4 Per Cent in First Quarter.' *Globe and Mail*, 12 May 1999, B11.

Bond, John, Carol Harvey, and Elizabeth Hildebrand. 'Familial Support of the Elderly in a Rural Mennonite Community.' *Canadian Journal on Aging* 6, no. 1 (1987): 7–18.

Booth, Charles. *The Aged Poor in England and Wales: Condition.* London: Macmillan, 1894.

Booth, Wayne, ed. *The Art of Growing Older: Writers on Living and Aging.* New York: Poseidon Press, 1992.

Bourhis, Anne, and Thierry Wils. 'L'éclatement de l'emploi traditionnel: Les défis posés par la diversité des emplois typiques et atypiques.' *Relations industrielles* 56, no. 1 (2001): 66–91.

Bowlby, Geoff. 'The School-to-Work Transition.' *Perspectives on Labour and Income* 12, no. 1 (2000): 43–8.

Boyd, Monica. 'Birds of a Feather: Ethnic Variations in Young Adults Living at Home.' Working Paper Series, Center for the Study of Population and Demography. Tallahassee: Florida State University, 1998.

Boyd, Monica, and Doug Norris. 'The Cluttered Nest Revisited: Young Adults at Home in the 1990s.' Center for Study of Population, Working Paper. Tallahassee: Florida State University, 1995.

– 'The Crowded Nest: Young Adults at Home'. *Canadian Social Trends*, no. 52 (1999): 2–5.

– 'Leaving the Nest? The Impact of Family Structure.' *Canadian Social Trends*, no. 38 (1995): 14–17.

Boyd, Monica, and Edward T. Pryor. 'The Cluttered Nest: The Living Arrangements of Young Canadian Adults.' *Canadian Journal of Sociology* 14, no. 4 (1989): 461–77.

Brennan, Michael J., et al. In Leon Stein, ed., *The Economics of Age.* New York: W.W. Norton, 1967.

Brodie, Janine. 'Meso-Discourses, State Forms, and the Gendering of Liberal-Democratic Citizenship.' *Citizenship Studies* 1, no. 2 (1997): 223–42.

– *Politics on the Boundaries: Restructuring and the Canadian Women's Movement.* Toronto: Robarts Centre for Canadian Studies, University of Toronto, 1994.

Brody, Elaine M. *Women in the Middle: Their Parent-Care Years.* New York: Springer, 1990.

Brody, Elaine M., Morton H. Kleban, Pauline T. Johnsen, Christine Hoffman, and Claire B. Schoonover. 'Work Status and Parent Care: A Comparison of Four Groups of Women.' *Gerontologist* 27, no. 2 1987, 201–8.

Brody, Elaine M., and Claire B. Schoonover. 'Patterns of Parent-Care when Adult Daughters Work and when They Do Not.' *Gerontologist* 26, no. 4 (1986): 372–81.

Browning, Elizabeth Barrett. *Aurora Leigh.* Ed. Kerry McSweeney. Oxford: Oxford University Press, 1993.

Bulcroft, Kris A., and Richard A. Bulcroft. 'The Timing of Divorce: Effects on

Parent-Child Relationships in Later Life.' *Research on Aging* 13, no. 2 (1991): 226–43.

Bureau of Labor Statistics. 'Are Workers More Secure?' *Issues in Labor Statistics, Summary*, 98–5. Washington, DC: U.S. Department of Labor, Bureau of Statistics, 1998.

– 'Comparative Job Performance by Age: Large Plants in the Men's Footwear and Household Furniture Industries.' *Bulletin*, no. 1223. Washington, DC: U.S. Department of Labor, Bureau of Labor Statistics, 1957.

– 'Employment Growth among Sectors in The United States, Japan, and Europe Based upon Educational Attainment.' *Issues in Labor Statistics, Summary*, 98–7. Washington, DC: U.S. Department of Labor, Bureau of Labor Statistics, 1998.

– 'Older Workers' Injuries Entail Lengthy Absences from Work.' *Issues in Labor Statistics, Summary*, 96–6. Washington, DC: U.S. Department of Labor, Bureau of Labor Statistics, 1996.

– 'Who's Not Working.' *Issues in Labor Statistics, Summary*, 98–4. Washington, DC: U.S. Department of Labor, Bureau of Labor Statistics, 1998.

Burkhauser, Richard V., Debra Dwyer, Maarten Léndeboom, Jules Theeuwes, and Isolde Woiltez. 'Health, Work, and Economic Well-Being of Older Workers Aged 51 to 61: A Cross-National Comparison Using the United States HRS and The Netherlands CERRA Data Sets.' *Aging Studies Program Papers*, no. 11. Syracuse, NY: Center for Policy Research, Maxwell School of Citizenship and Public Affairs, Syracuse University, 1997.

Burkhauser, Richard V., and Joseph F. Quinn. 'The Effects of Changes in Mandatory Retirement Rules on Labor Supply of Older Workers.' Boston: Boston College, Department of Economics, April 1981.

– 'Implementing Pro-Work Policies for Older Americans in the Twenty-First Century.' *Preparing for the Baby-Boomers: The Role of Employment*, serial no. 105–7. Washington, DC: U.S. Senate Special Committee on Aging, 25 July, 1997.

– 'Is Mandatory Retirement Overrated? Evidence from the 1970s.' *Journal of Human Resources* 18, no. 3 (1982): 337–58.

Calasanti, Toni. 'Incorporating Diversity: Meaning, Levels of Research, and Implications for Theory.' *Gerontologist* 36, no. 2 (1996): 147–56.

Campbell, Lori D., Ingrid Arnet Connidis, and Lorraine Davies. 'Sibling Ties in Later Life: A Social Networks Analysis.' *Journal of Family Issues* 20, no. 1 (1999): 114–48.

Campbell, Murray. 'Firms Question Wisdom of Ejecting the Experienced.' *Globe and Mail*, 5 July 1999, A5.

Caradec, Vincent. 'Forms of Conjugal Life among the "Young Elderly."' *Population* 9 (1997): 47–94.

Carrière, Yves. 'Population Aging and Hospital Days: Will there Be a Problem?'
    In Ellen M. Gee and Gloria M. Gutman, eds., *The Overselling of Population
    Aging: Apocalyptic Demography, Intergenerational Challenges, and Social Policy,*
    26–44. Don Mills, Ont.: Oxford University Press, 2000.
Carter, Donald D. 'Employment Benefits for Same-Sex Couples: The Expand-
    ing Entitlement.' *Canadian Public Policy* 24, (1998): 107–17.
Casey, B., and S. Wood. 'Great Britain: Firm Policy, State Policy, and the
    Employment and Unemployment of Older Workers.' In F. Naschold and B.
    de Vroom, eds., *Regulating Employment and Welfare.* New York: Walter de
    Gruyter, 1994.
Centre for the Study of Living Standards. *Productivity: Key to Economic Success.*
    Ottawa: Atlantic Canada Opportunities Agency, 1998.
Charness, Neil, and E.A. Bosman. 'Age-Related Changes in Perceptual and
    Psychomotor Performance: Implications for Engineering Design.' *Experimen-
    tal Aging Research* 20, no. 6 (1994): 45–59.
Chauvel, Louis. *Le destin des générations: Structure sociale et cohortes en France au
    XXe siècle.* Paris: Presses Universitaires de France, 1998.
Cheal, David. 'Aging and Demographic Change.' *Canadian Public Policy* 26
    (suppl. 2) (2000): S109–S122.
– 'Intergenerational Transfers and Life Course Management: Towards a
    Socio-Economic Perspective.' In Alan Bryman, Bill Bytheway, Patricia
    Allatt, and Teresa Bell, eds., *Rethinking the Life Cycle,* 141–247. London: Mac-
    millan, 1987.
– 'Repenser les transferts intergénérationnels: Axes de recherche sur les rela-
    tions temporelles dans les pays anglo-saxons.' In *Les solidarités entre les
    générations. Vieillesse, famille, état.* Ed. Claudine Attias-Donfut, 259–68. Paris:
    Nathan, 1995.
Cheal, David, and Karen Kampen. 'Poor and Dependent Seniors in Canada.'
    Ageing and Society 18, no. 2 (1998): 147–66.
Chui, Tina. 'Canada's Population: Charting into the 21st Century.' *Canadian
    Social Trends,* no. 42 (1996): 3–7.
Cicirelli, Victor G. 'A Comparison of Helping Behavior to Elderly Parents of
    Adult Children with Intact and Disrupted Marriages.' *Gerontologist* 23, no. 6
    (1983): 619–25.
Clark, Philip G. 'Moral Discourse and Public Policy in Aging: Framing Prob-
    lems, Seeking Solutions and "Public Ethics."' *Canadian Journal on Aging* 12,
    no. 4 (1993): 485–508.
– 'Public Policy in the United States and Canada: Individualism, Family Obli-
    gation, and Collective Responsibility in the Care of the Elderly. In Jon Hen-
    dricks and Carolyn Rosenthal, eds., *The Remainder of their Days: Domestic*

Policy and Older Families in the United States and Canada, 145–67. New York: Garland. 1993.

Clark, Robert L., Ed. *Retirement Policy in an Aging Society.* Durham: Duke University Press, 1980.

Cloutier, Renée. 'Nouvelles solidarités: extension du sens du mot famille.' *Critere* 33 (1982): 207–18.

Coder, John, Lee Rainwater, and Timothy Smeeding. 'Inequality among Children and the Elderly in Ten Modern Nations: The United States in International Context.' *American Economic Review* 79, no. 2 (1989): 320–24.

Cole, Thomas R. *The Journey of Life: A Cultural History of Aging in America.* New York: Cambridge University Press, 1992.

Cole, Thomas R., and Sally Gadow. *What Does It Mean to Grow Old? Reflections from the Humanities.* Durham: Duke University Press, 1986.

Cole, Thomas R., Robert Kastenbaum, and Ruth E. Ray, eds. *Handbook of the Humanities and Aging.* 2nd ed. New York: Springer, 2000.

Cole, Thomas R., and Mary G. Winkler, eds. *The Oxford Book of Aging: Reflections on the Journey of Life.* Oxford: Oxford University Press, 1994.

Coleman, David, and Roger Schofield, eds. *The State of Population Theory.* Oxford: Blackwell, 1986.

Collins, Robert. *You Had to Be There: An Intimate Portrait of the Generation that Survived the Depression, Won the War, and Re-Invented Canada.* Toronto: McClelland and Stewart, 1997.

Conference Board of Canada. *Performance and Potential: Assessing Canada's Social and Economic Performance, Members' Briefing.* Ottawa: Conference Board of Canada, 1996.

Coni, Nicholas, William Davison, and Stephen Webster. *Ageing: The Facts.* 2nd ed. Oxford: Oxford University Press, 1992.

Connidis, Ingrid Arnet. *Family Ties and Aging.* Toronto: Butterworths, 1989.

– *Family Ties and Aging.* Thousand Oaks, Calif.: Sage, 2001.

– 'Liens familiaux et vieillissement au Canada: constantes et changements des trois dernières décennies.' *Lien social et politiques* 38 (Autumn 1997): 133–143.

– 'Life Transitions and the Adult Sibling Tie: A Qualitative Study.' *Journal of Marriage and the Family* 54 (1992): 972–82.

– 'Sibling Support in Older Age.' *Journal of Gerontology: Social Sciences* 49 (1994): S309–S317.

Connidis, Ingrid Arnet, and Lori D. Campbell. 'Closeness, Confiding, and Contact Among Siblings in Middle and Late Adulthood.' *Journal of Family Issues* 16 (1995): 722–745.

Connidis, Ingrid Arnet, and Lorraine Davies. 'Confidants and Companions:

Choices in Later Life.' *Journal of Gerontology: Social Sciences* 47, no. 3 (1992): S115–S122.

– 'Confidants and Companions in Later Life: The Place of Family and Friends.' *Journal of Gerontology: Social Sciences* 45 (1990): S141–S149.

Connidis, Ingrid Arnet, and Julie A. McMullin. 'Forging Macro-Micro Links: Structure, Agency, and the Place of Sociological Ambivalence in Multigenerational Research.' Paper presented at the Ambivalence in Intergenerational Relations Workshop sponsored by the Bronfenbrenner Life-Course Center, Cornell University, Ithaca, NY. December 1998.

– 'Social Support in Older Age: Assessing the Impact of Marital and Parent Status.' *Canadian Journal on Aging* 13, no. 4 (1994): 510–27.

Cook, F.L., V.W. Marshall, J.G. Marshall, and J. Kaufman. 'The Salience of Intergenerational Equity in the United States and Canada.' In T.R. Marmor, T.M. Smeeding, and V.L. Greene, eds., *Economic Security and Intergenerational Justice: A Look at North America*, 91–132. Washington, DC: Urban Institute, 1994.

Cook, Judith A., Bertram J. Cohler, Susan A. Pickett, and Jeff A. Beeler. 'Life-Course and Severe Mental Illness: Implications for Caregiving within the Family of Later Life.' *Family Relations* 46, no. 4 (1997): 427–36.

Cooney, Teresa M., and Peter Uhlenberg. 'Support from Parents over the Life Course: The Adult Child's Perspective.' *Social Forces* 71, no. 1 (1992): 63–84.

Corak, Miles, ed. *Government Finances and Generational Equity*. Ottawa: Statistics Canada, Catalogue no. 68–513–XPB, 1998.

– *Labour Markets, Social Institutions and the Future of Canada's Children*. Ottawa: Statistics Canada, Catalogue no. 89–553–XPB, 1998.

Couch, Kenneth A. 'Late Life Job Displacement.' *Aging Studies Program Series*, no. 6. Syracuse, NY: Center for Policy Research, Maxwell School of Citizenship and Public Affairs, Syracuse University, 1997.

Coupland, Nikolas, Justine Coupland, and Howard Giles. *Language, Society and the Elderly: Discourse, Identity and Ageing*. Oxford: Blackwell. 1991.

Courchene, Thomas. 'Generation X versus Generation XS: Reflections on the Way Ahead.' In Keith G. Banting and Robin Boadway eds., *Reform of Retirement Income Policy: International and Canadian Perspectives*, Kingston: Queen's University, School of Policy Studies, 1997.

Cranswick, Kelly. 'Canada's Caregivers.' *Canadian Social Trends*, no. 47 (1997): 2–6.

Crompton, Susan. 'You Wear It Well: Health of Older Workers.' *Perspectives on Labour and Income* (Autumn 1996): 31–6.

Crown, William H., ed. *Handbook on Employment and the Elderly*. Westport, Conn.: Greenwood Press, 1996.

Cutler, David M., James M. Poterban, Louise M. Sheiner, and Lawrence H.

Summers. 'An Aging Society: Challenge or Opportunity?' *Brookings Papers on Economic Activity*, no. 1 (1990): 1–73.

D'Amours, Martine, Frédéric Lesemann, Stéphane Crespo, and Julie Beausoleil. *La sortie anticipée d'activité des travailleurs et travailleuses de 45 à 64 ans*. Montreal: Institut national de la recherche scientifique, 1999.

Darveau, Jean-Guy. *Familles et grands-parents*. Quebec: Conseil de la famille, 1994.

Davey, Adam, and David Eggebeen. 'Patterns of Intergenerational Exchange and Mental Health.' *Journal of Gerontology: Psychological Science* 53B, no. 1 (1998): P86–P95.

Davey, Adam, and Joan Norris. 'Social Networks and Exchange Norms Across the Adult Life Span.' *Canadian Journal on Aging* 17, no. 3 (1998): 212–33.

David, Hélène. 'Rapports sociaux et vieillissement de la population active.' *Sociologie et sociétés* 27, no. 2 (1995): 57–68.

– 'Le vieillissement au travail et en emploi.' *Lien social et politiques* 38 (Autumn 1997): 51–61.

Deane, Phyllis, and W. A. Cole. *British Economic Growth: 1688–1959*. Cambridge: Cambridge University Press, 1967.

Deats, Sara Munson, and Lagretta Tallent Lenker. *Aging and Identity: A Humanities Perspective*. Westport, Conn.: Praeger, 1999.

de Beauvoir, Simone. *The Coming of Age*. Trans. Patrick O'Brian. New York: Putnam's Sons, 1972.

De Broucker, P., and L. Lavallée. 'Intergenerational Aspects of Education and Literacy Skills Acquisition.' In Miles Corak, ed., *Labour Markets, Social Institutions, and the Future of Canada's Children*, 129–44. Ottawa: Statistics Canada, Catalogue no. 89-553-XPB, 1998.

Delbès, Christiane, and Joëlle Gaymu. 'Les solidarités au seuil de la vieillesse au début de la retraite en France.' *Le contrat social à l'épreuve des changement démographiques*. Montréal: INRS-Urbanisation, 2001.

Delisle, Isabelle. 1999. 'Les solidarités intergénérationnelles.' *L'infirmière canadienne* 95 (1999): 37–40.

Delisle, Marc-André. *Aspects démographiques, économiques et sociologiques du vieillissement*. Sainte-Foy, Que.: Les Éditions la Liberté, 1996.

– 'Les changements dans les pratiques de loisir des Québécois âgés 1979–1989.' *Canadian Journal on Aging* 12, no. 3 (1993): 338–59.

DeLong, J. Bradford. 'Have Productivity Levels Converged? Productivity Growth, Convergence, and Welfare in the Very Long Run.' *Department of Economics Papers*. Berkeley: University of California, February 1988.

- 'How "New" Is Today's Economy?' *Department of Economics Papers*. Berkeley: University of California, August 1998.
- 'Productivity Growth and Investment in Equipment: A Very Long Run Look.' *Department of Economics Papers*. Berkeley: University of California, September 1991.
- 'The Shape of Twentieth Century History.' *Federal Reserve Bank of Boston Regional Review* (Fall 1998).
Demers, Marie. 'Age Differences in the Rates and Costs of Medical Procedures and Hospitalization during the Last Year of Life.' *Canadian Journal on Aging* 17, no. 2 (1998): 186–96.
Denton, Frank T., Christine H. Feaver, and Byron G. Spencer. 'The Future Population of Canada and Its Age Distribution.' *IESOP Research Paper*, no. 3. (June) Hamilton: McMaster University. 1996.
- 'The Future Population of Canada: Its Age Distribution and Dependency Relations.' *Canadian Journal on Aging* 17, no. 1 (1998): 83–109.
- 'Immigration, Labour Force and the Age Structure of the Population.' *IESOP Research Paper*, no. 24. Hamilton: McMaster University, (Nov.) 1997.
Denton, Frank T., and Byron G. Spencer. 'Economic Costs of Population Aging.' *IESOP Research Paper*, no. 32. Hamilton: McMaster University, Dec. 1998.
- 'Population Aging and the Maintenance of Social Support Systems.' *IESOP Research Paper*, no. 9. Hamilton: McMaster University, Sept. 1996.
- 'Population, Labour Force, and Long-term Economic Growth.' *IESOP Research Paper*, no. 25. Hamilton: McMaster University, Dec. 1997.
Desjardins, Bertrand. *Population Ageing and the Elderly*. Ottawa: Statistics Canada, 1993.
Dickinson, Peter, and George Sciadas. 'Canadians Connected.' *Canadian Economic Observer*, Feb. 1999, 3.1–3.22.
Disney, Richard. *Can We Afford to Grow Older? A Perspective on the Economics of Aging*. Cambridge, Mass.: MIT Press, 1996.
Doeringer, Peter B., Ed. *Bridges to Retirement*. Ithaca, NY: ILR Press, Cornell University, 1990.
Dooley, Martin. 'Women, Children and Poverty in Canada.' *Canadian Public Policy* 29, no. 4 (1994): 430–43.
Dorfman, Rachelle, Karina Walters, Patrick Burke, Lovida Hardin, Theresa Karanik, John Raphael, and Ellen Silverstein. 'Old, Sad, and Alone: The Myth of the Aging Homosexual.' *Journal of Gerontological Social Work* 24, no. 1/2 (1995): 29–44.
Driedger, Leo, and Neena Chappell. *Aging and Ethnicity: Toward an Interface*. Toronto: Butterworths, 1987.

Driver, Michael. 'Demographic and Societal Factors Affecting the Linear Career Crisis.' *Canadian Journal of Administrative Studies* 2, no. 2 (1985): 245–263.

Drolet, Marie, and René Morissette. 'Working More? Working Less? What Do Canadians Prefer?' *Analytical Studies Branch Research Paper Series*, no. 104. Ottawa: Statistics Canada, 1997.

Drucker, Peter. 'The Future that Has Already Happened.' *Harvard Business Review*, Sept.–Oct. 1997, 20–4.

Dryden, Ken. *The Game: A Reflective and Thought-Provoking Look at a Life in Hockey.* Toronto: Macmillan, 1983.

Dryer, Jeffrey W. 'The Effect of Illness on the Family.' In Rosemary Blieszner and Victoria Hilkevitch Bedford, eds. *Handbook of Aging and the Family.* Westport, Conn.: Greenwood Press.

Dufour, Stephane, Dominic Fortin, and Jacques Hamel. 'Sociologie d'un conflit de générations: les "baby boomers" et les "baby busters".' *International Journal of Canadian Studies* (Winter 1993): 9–22.

– *Report on the Demographic Situation in Canada, 1995: Current Population Analysis.* Ottawa: Statistics Canada, 1996.

Dumas, Jean, and Alain Bélanger. 'Common-Law Unions in Canada at the End of the 20th Century.' In Jean Dumas and Alain Bélanger, eds., *Report on the Demographic Situation in Canada 1996: Currrent Demographic Analysis*, 121–81. Ottawa: Statistics Canada, 1997.

Dunne, Timothy, John Haltiwanger, and Kenneth R. Troske. 'Technology and Jobs: Secular Changes and Cyclical Dynamics.' *NBER Working Paper*, No. 5656. Cambridge, Mass: National Bureau of Economic Research, 1996.

Dupuis, Sherry, and Joan E. Norris. 'The Roles of Adult Daughters in Long-Term Care Facilities: Alternative Role Manifestations.' *Journal of Aging Studies* 15, no. 1 (2001): 27–54.

Duxbury, Linda, and Christopher Higgins. *Work-Life Balance in Saskatchewan: Realities and Challenges.* Regina: Government of Saskatchewan, 1998.

Duxbury, Linda, Christopher Higgins, Catherine Lee, and Shirley Mills. *Balancing Work and Family: A Study of the Canadian Federal Public Sector.* Ottawa: Carleton University, 1991.

Dwyer, Jeffrey W. 'The Effects of Illness on the Family.' In Rosemary Blieszner and Victoria Hilkevitch Bedford, eds., *Handbook of Aging and the Family*, 401–21. Westport, Conn.: Greenwood Press, 1995.

Easterlin, Richard. *Birth and Fortune: The Impact of Numbers on Personal Welfare.* New York: Basic Books, 1980.

Egan, Gerard. 'Hard Times Contract.' *Management Today*, Jan. 1994, 48–50.

Eggebeen, David J., and Adam Davey. 'Do Safety Nets Work? The Role of

Anticipated Help in Times of Need.' *Journal of Marriage and the Family* 60, no. 4 (1998): 939–50.

Eggebeen, David J., and Dennis Hogan. 'Giving between Generations in American Families.' *Human Nature* 1 (1990): 211–32.

Elder, Glen H., Jr. 'Time, Human Agency, and Social Change: Perspectives on the Life Course.' *Social Psychology Quarterly* 57 (1994): 4–15.

Fallick, Bruce C. 'A Review of the Recent Empirical Literature on Displaced Workers.' *Industrial and Labor Relations Review* 50, no. 1 (1996): 5–16.

Fast, Janet E., Norah C. Keating, Leslie Oakes, and Deanna L. Williamson. 'Conceptualizing and Operationalizing the Costs of Informal Elder Care.' NHRDP project no. 6609-1963-55. Ottawa: National Health Research and Development Program, Health Canada, 1997.

Featherstone, Mike, and Andrew Wernick. *Images of Aging: Cultural Representations of Later Life*. London: Routledge, 1995.

Fellegi, Ivan P. 'Can We Afford an Aging Society.' *Canadian Economic Observer*, Oct. 1988, 4.1–4.34.

Finch, Janet. *Family Obligations and Social Change*. Cambridge, Mass.: Basil Blackwell / Polity Press, 1989.

Fine, Marshall, Joan E. Norris, and Greta Hofstra. 'Intergenerational Family Relations: Two Disciplines Meet Two Generations.' *Journal of Family Social Work* 5, no. 4 (2001): 17–38.

Finnie, Ross. 'Earnings Dynamics in Canada: Earnings Patterns by Age and Sex in Canada, 1982–1992.' *Applied Research Branch, Strategic Policy Report*, no. R–97–11E. Ottawa: Human Resources Development Canada, 1997.

– 'Stasis and Change: Trends in Individuals' Earnings and Inequality in Canada, 1982–1992.' *Canadian Business Economics* 6, no. 1 (1997): 84–107.

Foot, David K. 'Public Expenditures, Population Aging, and Economic Dependency in Canada, 1921–2021.' *Population Research and Policy Review* 8, no. 1 (1989): 97–117.

Foot, David K., with Daniel Stoffman. *Boom, Bust and Echo: How to Profit from the Coming Demographic Shift*. Toronto: Macfarlane, Walter and Ross, 1996.

Foot, David K., with Daniel Stoffman. *Entre le Boom et l'Écho: comment mettre à profit la realité démographique*. Montréal: librairie Renaud-Bray, 1996.

Foot, David K., and Rosemary A. Venne. 'Population, Pyramids and Promotional Prospects.' *Canadian Public Policy* 16, no. 4 (1990): 387–98.

– 'The Time Is Right: Voluntary Reduced Worktime and Workforce Demographics.' *Canadian Studies in Population* 25, no. 2 (1998): 91–114.

Fougère, Maxime, and Marcel Merette. 'Population Aging, Intergenerational Equity, and Growth.' Unpublished paper, 1998.

Fowler, Margaret, and Priscilla McCutcheon, eds. *Songs of Experience: An Anthology of Literature on Growing Old*. New York: Ballantine Books, 1991.

Frazis, Harley, Maury Gittleman, and Mary Joyce. *Determinants of Training: An Analysis Using Both Employer and Employee Characteristics*. Washington, DC: Bureau of Labor Statistics, 1998.

Frederick, Judith. *As Time Goes By: Time Use of Canadians*. Statistics Canada Catalogue no. 89-544E. Ottawa: Government of Canada, Minister of Industry, 1995.

Friedan, Betty. *The Fountain of Age*. New York: Simon and Schuster, 1993.

Friedberg, Leora. 'The Effect of Government Programs on the Labor Supply of the Elderly.' *Proceedings of the 89th Annual Conference, National Tax Association*, 203–10. Boston: National Tax Association, 1996.

– 'The Effects of Old Age Assistance on Retirement.' *NBER Working Paper*, no. W6548. Cambridge, Mass: National Bureau of Economic Research, 1998.

Friedman, Thomas L. *The Lexus and the Olive Tree*. Available at: www://nytimes.com/books/firstf/friedman-lexus.html.

Fukuyama, Francis. 'The Great Disruption.' *Atlantic Monthly*, May, 1999, 55–80.

Galarneau, Diane, and Cecile Dumas. 'About Productivity.' *Perspectives on Labour and Income* (Spring 1993): 39–48.

Galarneau, Diane, and Jean-Pierre Maynard. 'Measuring Productivity.' *Perspectives on Labour and Income* (Spring 1995): 26–32.

Galbraith, John K. *The Good Society: The Humane Agenda*. Boston: Houghton Mifflin, 1996.

Garant, Louise, and Mario Bolduc. *L'aide par les proches: mythes et réalites. Revue de littérature et reflections sur les personnes âgées en perte d'autonomie, leurs aidants et aidantes naturels et le lien avec les services formels*. Quebec: Ministère de la Santé et des Services Sociaux, 1990.

Garber, Marjorie. *Coming of Age in Shakespeare*. New York: Routledge, 1997.

Gauthier, Hervé. 'Le contrat social au Québec et au Canada: se prepare-t-on vraiment a faire face au vieillisement démographique previsible?' *Le Contrat social à l'épreuve des changement démographiques*. Montréal: INRS-Urbanisation, 2001.

– 'L'interdépendance des générations dans un contexte de vieillissement démographique: application aux depenses sociales.' *D'une génération à l'autre: évolution des conditions de vie*, vol. 1, 205–47. Quebec: Bureau de la statistique du Québec, 1997.

– 'Le vieillissement démographique au Québec: un défi pour la système social.' In Jaques Véron and Marie DiGoix, eds., *Age, génération et activité: vers un nouveau contrat social?* Proceedings of the First Sauvy Conference, Paris, October 1998, 229–52.

Gauthier, Hervé, and Louis Duchesne. *Le vieillissement démographique et les personnes âgées au Québec*. Quebec: Bureau de la statistique du Québec, 1991.

Gee, Ellen M. 'Demographic Change and Intergenerational Relations in Canadian Families: Findings and Social Policy Implications.' *Canadian Public Policy* 16 (1990): 191–6.

– 'Families in Later Life.' In Roderic Beaujot, Ellen M. Gee, Fernando Rajulton, and Zenaida R. Ravanera, eds., *Family over the Life Course: Current Demographic Analysis*, 77–113. Ottawa: Statistics Canada, 1995.

– 'Population and Politics: Voodoo Demography, Population Aging, and Social Policy.' In Ellen M. Gee and Gloria M. Gutman, eds., *The Overselling of Population Aging: Apocalyptic Demography, Intergenerational Challenges, and Social Policy*, 5–25. Don Mills, Ont.: Oxford University Press, 2000.

Gee, Ellen M., and Gloria M. Gutman, Eds. *The Overselling of Population Aging: Apocalyptic Demography, Intergenerational Challenges, and Social Policy*. Don Mills, Ont.: Oxford University Press, 2000.

Gee, Ellen M., and Susan A. McDaniel. 'Pension Politics and Challenges: Retirement Policy Implications.' *Canadian Public Policy* 17 (1991): 456–472.

– 'Social Policy for an Aging Society.' In Victor Marshall and Barry McPherson, eds., *Aging: Canadian Perspectives*, 219–31. Peterborough, Ont: Broadview, 1994.

Gee, Ellen M., Barbara Mitchell, and Andrew Wister. 'Returning to the Parental "Nest": Exploring a Changing Canadian Life Course.' *Canadian Studies in Population* 22, no. 2 (1995): 121–44.

Gendron, Louise. 'Bye bye boulot.' *L'Actualité*, July 1997, 14–24.

George, Linda. 'Missing Links: The Case for a Social Psychology of the Life Course.' *Gerontologist* 36, no. 2 (1996): 248–55.

Gera, Surendra, Wulong Gu, and Frank C. Lee. 'Foreign Direct Investment and Productivity Growth: The Canadian Host-Country Experience.' *Micro-Economic Policy Analysis Branch Papers*. Ottawa: Industry Canada, 1998.

Giarrusso, Rosean, Michael Stallings and Vern L. Bengtson. 'The "Intergenerational Stake" Hypothesis Revisited: Parent-Child Differences in Perceptions of Relationships 20 Years Later.' In Vern L. Bengtson, K. Warner Schaie, and Linda Burton, eds., *Adult Intergenerational Relations: Effects of Societal Change*, 227–63. New York: Springer, 1995.

Gibson, K.J., W.J. Zerbe, and R.E. Franken. 'Job Search Strategies for Older Job Hunters: Addressing Employers' Perceptions.' *Canadian Journal of Counselling* 26, no. 3 (1992): 168–70.

Giddens, Anthony. *Modernity and Self-Identity: Self and Society in the Late Modern Age*. Stanford, Calif.: Stanford University Press, 1991.

Gladstone, James. 'An Analysis of Changes in Grandparent-Grandchild Visitation Following an Adult Child's Remarriage.' *Canadian Journal on Aging* 10, no. 2 (1991): 113–26.

- 'Factors Associated with Changes in Visiting between Grandmothers and Grandchildren Following an Adult Child's Marriage Breakdown.' *Canadian Journal on Aging* 6, no. 2 (1987): 117–27.

- 'Perceived Changes in Grandmother-Grandchild Relations Following a Child's Separation or Divorce.' *Gerontologist* 28, no. 1 (1988): 66–72.

Glossop, Robert. 'Bailing Out on Future Generations.' *Transition*, March 1996, 12–13.

Godbey, Geoffrey, Alan Graefe, and Anthony James. *The Benefits of Local Recreation and Park Services: A Nationwide Study of the Perceptions of the American Public.* Arlington, Va: National Recreation and Parks Services, 1992.

Godbout, Jacques, and Alain Caillé. *L'esprit du don.* Montreal: Boreal, 1992.

Godbout, Jacques T., and Johanne Charbonneau with Vincent Lemieux. *La Circulation du Don et la Parenté: Une Roué qui Tourne.* Montréal: INRS-Urbanisation, 1996.

Goethe, Johann Wolfgang von. *Faust: A Tragedy.* Trans. Walter Arndt. ed. Cyrus Hamlin. New York: W.W. Norton, 1976.

Gordon, Robert J. 'U.S. Economic Growth since 1870: One Big Wave?' *American Economic Review* 89, no. 2 (1999): 123–8.

Goshen, Erica L, and David I. Levine. 'The Rise and Decline (?) of U.S. Internal Labor Markets.' *Federal Reserve Bank of New York Research Paper*, No. 9819. New York: Federal Reserve Bank of New York, 1998.

Gouvernement de Québec. *Évolution de l'emploi du temps au Québec 1986–1992.* Quebec: Gouvernement de Québec, 1996.

- *La Pratique des activités de loisir culturel et scientifique des Québécois.* Quebec: Gouvernement de Québec, 1995.

- *Vivre à Deux.* Quebec: Department of Justice.

Government of Canada. *A Portrait of Seniors in Canada*, 2nd ed. Statistics Canada Catalogue no. 89-519-XPE. Ottawa: Government of Canada, Minister of Industry, 1997.

- *Television Viewing 1993.* Statistics Canada Catalogue no. 87-208. Ottawa: Ministry of Industry, Science and Technology, 1994.

Gower, Dave. 'Measuring the Age of Retirement.' *Perspectives on Labour and Income* 9, no. 2 (1997): 11–17.

Graebner, William. *A History of Retirement: The Meaning and Function of an American Institution, 1885–1978.* New Haven: Yale University Press, 1980.

Grand'Maison, Jacques, and Solange Lefebvre. *La Part des Ainés.* Montreal: Éditions Fides, 1994.

Granovetter, Mark S. 'The Strength of Weak Ties.' *American Journal of Sociology* 78 (1973): 1368–80.

Gray, David, and Gilles Grenier. 'Jobless Durations of Displaced Workers: A Comparison of Canada and the United States.' *Applied Research Branch, Strategic Policy Reports*, W-97-16E. Ottawa: Human Resources Development Canada.

'Greenspan Renounces Investing Pension Fund in Stock Market.' *Edmonton Journal*, 4 March 1999, F6.

Greenspon, Edward. 'Health Care Not the Only Casualty of Federal Cutbacks.' *Globe and Mail*, 19 December 1998, A9.

Greer, Germaine. *The Change: Women, Aging, and the Menopause*. New York: Fawcett Columbine, 1991.

Gruber, Jonathan. 'Social Security and Retirement In Canada.' *NBER Working Paper*, no. 6308. Cambridge, Mass.: National Bureau of Economic Research, 1997.

Gruber, Jonathan, and David Wise. 'Social Security and Retirement: An International Comparison.' *American Economic Review* 88, no. 2 (1998): 158–63.

– eds. *Social Security and Retirement in the World*. Chicago: University of Chicago Press.

Gruman, Gerald J. 'A History of Ideas about the Prolongation of Life: The Evolution of Prolongevity Hypotheses to 1800.' *Transactions of the American Philosophical Society*, New Series 56, no. 9 (1996): 5–102.

Guay, Jean-Herman. *Avant, pendant et après le Boom: Portrait de la culture politique de trois générations de Québécois*. Sherbrooke: Éditions Les Fous du Roi, 1997.

Guberman, Nancy, and Pierre Maheau. 'Le rapport entre l'adéquation des services de maintien à domicile et la trajectoire de travail des personnes soignantes.' *La revue canadienne du vieillissement* 19, no. 4 (2000): 380–408.

Guérin, Gilles, Sylvie St-Onge, Victor Haines, Renée Trottie, and Manon Simard. 'Les pratiques d'aide à l'équilibre emploi-famille dans les organisations du Québec.' *Relations industrielles* 52, no. 2 (1997): 275–303.

Guillemard, Anne-Marie. 'Equity between Generations in Aging Societies: The Problem of Assessing Public Policies.' In Tamara K. Hareven, ed., *Aging and Generational Relations: Life Course and Cross-Cultural Perspectives*, 157–76. New York: Aldine de Gruyter, 1996.

Gunderson, Morley. *Flexible Retirement as an Alternative to 65 and Out*. Toronto: C.D. Howe Institute, 1998.

Gunderson, Morley, and Douglas Hyatt. 'Intergenerational Considerations of Workers' Compensation Unfunded Liabilities.' In Miles Corak, ed., *Govern-*

ment Finances and Generational Equity, 21–37. Catalogue no. 68-513-XPB, Ottawa: Statistics Canada, 1998.

Haldemann, Verena. 'La solidarité entre générations: Haïtiennes âgées à Montréal.' *Sociologie et Sociétés* 27, no. 2 (1995): 43–56.

Halfe, Louise Bernice. *Blue Marrow: Poems.* Toronto: McClelland and Stewart, 1998.

Hall, G. Stanley. *Adolescence.* New York: D. Appleton, 1904.

Hall, Michael, Tamara Knighton, Paul Reed, Patrick Bussiere, Don McRae, and Paddy Bowen. *Caring Canadians, Involved Canadians: Highlights from the 1997 National Survey of Giving, Volunteering and Participating.* Statistics Canada Catalogue no. 71-542-XPE. Ottawa: Government of Canada, Minister of Industry, 1998.

Haltiwanger, John C., Julia I. Lane, and James R. Spletzer. 'Productivity Differences across Employers: The Roles of Employer Size, Age, and Human Capital.' *American Economic Review* 89, no. 2 (1999): 94–8.

Hammel, E.A. 'The Productivity of Chemists and Mathematicians at the University of California: A Cohort Analysis.' *Program in Population Research Working Paper,* no. 11. Berkeley: University of California, 1983.

Handwerker, W. Penn, ed. *Culture and Reproduction: An Anthropological Critique of Demographic Transition Theory.* Boulder, Colo.: Westview Press, 1986.

Handy, Charles. *The Hungry Spirit: Beyond Capitalism – A Quest for Purpose in the Modern World.* New York: Random House, 1997.

Hannson, Robert, and Bruce Carpenter. *Relationships in Old Age.* New York: Guilford, 1994.

Hareven, Tamara K. 'Aging, Generational Relations: A Historical and Life Course Perspective.' *American Review of Sociology* 20 (1994): 437–61.

– 'The History of the Family and the Complexity of Social Change.' *American Historical Review* 96, no. 1 (1991): 95–124.

Hargrave, Terry, and William Anderson. *Finishing Well: Aging and Reparation in the Intergenerational Family.* New York: Bruner/Mazel, 1992.

Harper, Jack, Denny Neider, Geoffrey Godbey, and Darlene Lamont. *The Use and Benefits of Local Government Parks and Recreation Services: A Canadian Perspective.* Winnipeg: University of Manitoba Health, Leisure and Human Performance Research Institute, 1997.

Harvey, Andrew, Ken Marshall, and Judith Frederick. *Where Does Time Go?* Statistics Canada Catalogue no. 11-612E, N. 4. Ottawa: Government of Canada, Minister of Industry, Science and Technology, 1991.

Hashimoto, Akiko. *The Gift of Generations: Japanese and American Perspectives on Aging and the Social Contract.* New York: Cambridge University Press, 1996.

Hazlitt, Henry. *The Critics of Keynesian Economics*. Lanham, Md.: University Press of America, 1977.

Heckman, James J. 'Lessons from the Bell Curve.' *Journal of Political Economy* 103, no. 5 (1995): 1091–1120.

Heilbrun, Carolyn G. *The Last Gift of Time: Life beyond Sixty*. New York: Balllantine Books, 1997.

Helliwell, John F. 'What Will We Be Leaving You?' In Miles Corak, ed., *Government Finances and Generational Equity*, 141–7. Catalogue no. 68-513-XPB. Ottawa: Statistics Canada, 1998.

Henripin, Jacques. 'Financial Consequences of Population Aging.' *Canadian Public Policy* 20, no. 1 (1994): 78–94.

Hicks, Chantal. 'The Age Distribution of the Tax/Transfer System in Canada.' In Miles Corak, ed., *Government Finances and Generational Equity*, 39–56. Catalogue no. 68-513-XPB. Ottawa: Statistics Canada, 1998.

Hicks, Peter. 'The Policy Challenge of Ageing Populations.' *OECD Observer*, no. 212 (1998): 7–9.

Higgins, Christopher, Linda Duxbury, and Catherine Lee. *Balancing Work and Family: A Study of Canadian Private Sector Employees*. London, Ont.: National Centre for Management Research and Development, University of Western Ontario, 1992.

Hipple, Steven. 'Worker Displacement in an Expanding Economy.' *Monthly Labor Review*, Dec. 1997, 26–39.

Hobbs, Frank B., and Bonnie L. Damon. '65+in the United States.' *Current Population Reports, Special Studies*, P23-P190. Washington, DC: 1996.

Hogan, Dennis, David Eggebeen, and Clifford Clogg. 'The Structure of Intergenerational Exchanges in American Families.' *American Journal of Sociology*, 98, no. 6 (1993): 1428–58.

Hostland, Doug. 'Real Wages, Labour Productivity, and Employment in Canada: A Historical Perspective.' *Applied Research Branch, Strategic Policy Reports*, R-96-5E. Ottawa: Human Resources Development Canada, 1996.

– 'What Factors Determine Structural Unemployment in Canada?' *Applied Research Branch, Strategic Policy Reports*, R-96-2E. Ottawa: Human Resources Development Canada, 1995.

Human Resources Development Canada. *Adult Education and Training in Canada*. Ottawa: Human Resources Development Canada, 1994.

– 'The Aging Workforce – Still Capable after All These Years.' *Applied Research Bulletin* 1, no. 2 (1995): 13–14.

– 'Changing Notions of Retirement: A Phased-In Approach.' *Applied Research Bulletin* 2, no. 2 (1996): 11–13.

266   Bibliography

– 'Earnings, Education, and Age ... The Low End Goes Lower.' *Applied Research Bulletin* 2, no. 1 (1995–6): 11–12.
– 'Increasingly Complex Jobs = Higher Skills.' *Applied Research Bulletin* 2, no. 2 (1996).
– 'Job Loss and the Older Worker.' *Applied Research Bulletin* 2, no. 1 (1995–6): 9–10.
– 'Technological and Organizational Change and Labour Demand: The Canadian Situation.' *Applied Research Branch, Strategic Policy Reports*, R-97-1E. Ottawa: Human Resources Development Canada, 1996.
Hunter, Kathryn Montgomery. *Doctor's Stories: The Narrative Structure of Medical Knowledge.* Princeton: Princeton University Press, 1991.
Huyck, Margaret Hellie. 'Marriage and Close Relationships of the Marital Kind.' In Victoria Hilkevitch Bedford and Rosemary Blieszner, eds., *Handbook of Aging and the Family,* 181–200. Westport, Conn.: Greenwood Press, 1995.
Idson, Todd L., and Walter Y. Oi. 'Workers Are More Productive in Large Firms.' *American Economic Review* 89, no. 2 (1999): 104–8.
Ishii-Kuntz, Misako. ' Intergenerational Relationships among Chinese, Japanese, and Korean Americans.' *Family Relations* 46, no. 1 (1997): 23–32.
Jablonski, Mary, Kent Kunze, and Larry Rosenblum. 'Productivity, Age, and Labor Composition Changes in the U.S. WorkForce.' In Irving Bluestone, Rhonda J.V. Montgomery, and John D. Owen, eds., *The Aging of the American Workforce: Problems, Programs, Policies,* 304–38. Detroit: Wayne State University Press, 1990.
Jendrek, Margaret Platt. 'Grandparents Who Parent Their Grandchildren: Circumstances and Decisions.' *Gerontologist* 34, no. 2 (1994): 206–16.
Jenson, Jane. *Mapping Social Cohesion: The State of Canadian Research.* Ottawa: Canadian Policy Research Networks, 1998.
– 'Who Cares? Gender and Welfare Regimes.' *Social Politics* (Summer 1997): 182–7.
Johnston, William B. 'Global Work Force 2000: The New World Labor Market.' *Harvard Business Review,* March/April 1991, 115–27.
Jorgenson, Dale W., and Kevin J. Stiroh. 'Information Technology and Growth.' *American Economic Review* 89, no. 2 (1999): 109–15.
Judy, Richard, and Carol D'Amico. *Workforce 2020: Work and Workers in the 21st Century.* Indianapolis: Hudson Institute, 1997.
Kahn, James, and Jong-Soo Lim. 'Skilled Labor-Augmenting Technical Progress in U.S. Manufacturing.' *Federal Reserve Bank of New York, Staff Reports,* no. 47. New York, Oct. 1998.
Kahne, Hilda. *Reconceiving Part-time Work: New Perspectives for Older Workers and Women.* Towona, NJ: Rowman and Allanheld, 1985.

Kalish, Richard A. 'The New Ageism and the Failure Models: A Polemic.' *Gerontologist* 19, no. 4 (1979): 398–402.

Kaufman, Gayle, and Peter Uhlenberg. 'Effects of Life Course Transitions on the Quality of Relationships between Adult Children and Their Parents.' *Journal of Marriage and the Family* 60 (Nov. 1998): 924–38.

Kauh, Tae-Ock. 'Intergenerational Relations: Older Korean-Americans' Experiences.' *Journal of Cross Cultural Gerontology* 12, no. 3 (1997): 245–71.

Keating, Norah, Janet Fast, Judith Frederick, Kelly Cranswick, and Cathryn Perrier. *Eldercare in Canada: Context, Content and Consequences.* Catalogue no. 89-570-XPE, Ottawa: Statistics Canada, 1999.

Keefe, Janice M., and Patricia J. Fancey. 'Work and Eldercare: The Contributions of Elderly Parents to Their Employed Children.' Paper presented at the Annual Meeting of the Canadian Association on Gerontology. Halifax, October 1998.

Keynes, John Maynard. *The Economic Consequences of Peace.* London: Macmillan, 1919.

King, Gillian, Susanne King, Peter Rosenbaum, and Richard Goffin. 'Family-Centered Caregiving and Well-being of Parents of Children with Disabilities: Linking Process with Outcome.' *Journal of Pediatric Psychology* 24, no. 1 (1999): 41–53.

King, James. *The Life of Margaret Laurence.* Toronto: Alfred Knopf, 1997.

Kingsmill, Suzanne, and Benjamin Schlesinger. *The Family Squeeze: Surviving the Sandwich Generation.* Toronto: University of Toronto Press, 1998.

Kohl, Richard, and Paul O'Brien. 'The Macroeconomics of Ageing, Pensions and Savings: A Survey.' Economics Department, Working Paper no. 200. Paris: OECD, 1998.

Krahn, Harvey. 'Non-Standard Work on the Rise.' *Perspectives on Labour and Income* 7, no. 4 (1995): 5–42.

Krahn, Harvey, Clay Mosher, and Laura Johnson. 'Panel Studies of the Transition from School to Work: Some Methodological Considerations.' In Paul Anisef and Paul Axelrod, eds., *Transitions: Schooling and Employment in Canada*, 169–187. Toronto: Thompson Educational Publishing, 1993.

Kremer, Michael, and Eric Maskin. 'Wage Inequality and Segregation by Skill.' *NBER Working Paper*, no. W5718. Cambridge, Mass.: National Bureau of Economic Research, 1996.

Krugman, Paul. 'Why Most Economists' Predictions Are Wrong.' *Red Herring*, June 1998, 1–4.

Kuhn, Peter, and A. Leslie Robb. 'Shifting Skill Demand and the Canada–U.S. Unemployment Gap: Evidence from Prime-Age Men.' *Applied Research*

   Branch, Strategic Policy Reports, W-97-17E. Ottawa: Human Resources Development Canada, 1996.

Landes, David. *The Wealth and Poverty of Nations*. New York: W.W. Norton, 1998.

Langlois, Simon, Jean-Paul Baillargeon, Gary Caldwell, Guy Fréchet, Madeleine Gauthier, and Jean-Pierre Simard. 1991. *Recent Social Trends in Quebec, 1960–1990*. Montreal and Kingston: McGill-Queen's University Press. [Translation of *La société québécoise en tendances, 1960–1990*. Quebec: Institut québécois de recherche sur la culture, 1990.]

Laroche, Mireille, and Marcel Merette. *Measuring Human Capital in Canada*. Ottawa: Government of Canada, Department of Finance. 1999.

Laslett, Peter. *A Fresh Map of Life: The Emergence of the Third Age*. Cambridge: Harvard University Press, 1991.

Laurence, Margaret. *The Stone Angel*. Toronto: McClelland and Stewart, 1964.

Lauzon, Darren. 'Worker Displacement: Trends, Characteristics and Policy Responses.' *Applied Research Branch, Strategic Policy Reports*, R-95-3. Ottawa: Human Resources Development Canada, 1995.

Lawrence, Renee H., Joan M. Bennett, and Kyriakos Markides. 'Perceived Intergenerational Distress among Older Mexican Americans.' *Journal of Gerontology* 47, no. 2 (1992): S55–S65.

Lazear, E. 'Why Is There Mandatory Retirement?' *Journal of Political Economy* 87, no. 6 (1979): 1261–84.

Lehr, Bill, and Frank Lichtenberg. 'Information Technology and Its Impact on Firm Level Productivity: Evidence from Government and Private Data Sources, 1977–1993.' Paper presented at CSLS Conference on Service Sector Productivity and the Productivity Paradox. Ottawa, 11–12 April 1997.

Leibfritz, Willi, Deborah Roserearem Douglas Fore and Eckhard Wurzel. 'Ageing Populations, Pension Systems, and Government Budgets: How Do They Affect Saving?' *Economics Department, Working Paper*, No. 156. Paris: OECD, 1995.

Levine, David. 'Recombinant Family Formation Strategies.' *Journal of Historical Sociology* 2, no. 2 (1989): 89–115.

Levitan, Sar A., and Diane Wernecke. *Productivity: Problems, Prospects, and Policies*. Baltimore: Johns Hopkins University Press, 1984.

Lewis, Jane. 'Gender and Welfare Regimes: Further Thoughts.' *Social Politics* (Summer 1997): 160–77.

Lewis, Jane, and H. Glennerster. *Implementing the New Community Care*. Buckingham: Open University Press, 1996.

Lewontin, Richard. 'Science and "The Demon-Haunted World": An Exchange.' *New York Review of Books*, 6 March 1997, 51–2.

Lindsay, Colin. 1996. *A Portrait of Seniors in Canada*, 2nd ed. Ottawa: Statistics Canada, 1996.

Lipovenko, Dorothy. 'Job Losses Facing Early Retirement.' *Globe and Mail*, 8 Sept. 1995: A3.

Lisac, Mark. 'Political Direction Shrouded in Illusion.' *Edmonton Journal*, 21 Jan. 1999, A14.

Little, Bruce. 'Canada Seen Lagging in Productivity Race.' *Globe and Mail*, 17 Oct. 1997, B.1.

– 'Economic Well-Being Plunged in '90s, Study Finds.' *Globe and Mail*, 28 Oct. 1998, B7.

– 'Productivity In the Eye of the Beholder.' *Globe and Mail*, 10 April 1999, D1.

Livingstone, Sharon R., and Joseph A. Tindale. 'Growing Old with a Developmental Disability.' *Canadian Nurse* 96 (2000): 28–31.

Livingstone, Sharon R., Joseph A. Tindale, and Anne Martin-Matthews. 'Balancing Work and Family: Perspectives of Employed Individuals Providing Care to Adults with Special Needs.' Paper presented at the Annual Meeting of the Canadian Association on Gerontology, Halifax, October 1998.

Lochhead, Clarence, and Vivian Shalla. 'Delivering the Goods: Income Distribution and the Precarious Middle Class.' *Canadian Council on Social Development* 20, no. 1 (1996): 15–19.

Lock, Margaret. *Encounters with Aging: Mythologies of Menopause in Japan and North America*. Berkeley: University of California Press, 1993.

Logan, John R., and Glenna D. Spitz. *Family Ties: Enduring Relations between Parents and Their Grown Children*. Philadelphia: Temple University Press, 1996.

Loriaux, Michel. 'Les conséquences de la révolution demographique et du viellissement societal.' *Sociologie et sociétés* 27, no. 2 (1995): 9–26.

Loury, Glenn C. 'The Hard Questions: Color Blinded.' *New Republic*, 17 and 24 August, 1997.

Macdonald, Barbara. 'Outside the Sisterhood: Ageism in Women's Studies.' *Women's Studies Quarterly* 17, nos. 1–2 (1989): 6–11.

Machin, Stephen, and John Van Reenen. 'Technology and Changes in Skill Structure: Evidence from Seven OECD Countries.' *Quarterly Journal of Economics* 113, no. 4 (1998): 1215–44.

MacInnis, Grace. *J.S. Woodsworth: A Man to Remember*. Toronto: Macmillan, 1953.

MacKinnon, Mark. 9 Nov., 'What We Owe: Debt Pressure Mounts for Canadians.' *Globe and Mail*, 9 Nov. 1998, B1, B3.

Macunovich, Diane J. 'An Economist's Perspective.' In Peter A. Diamond,

David Linderman, and Howard Young eds., *Social Security: What Role for the Future?* 43–65. Washington, DC: Academy of Social Insurance, 1996.

– 'Relative Cohort Size and Inequality in the United States.' *American Economic Review* 88, no. 2 (1998): 259–64.

Macunovich, Diane J., Richard Easterlin, Christine Schaeffer, and Eileen Crimmins. 'Echoes of the Baby Boom and Bust: Recent and Prospective Changes in Living Alone among Elderly Widows in the United States.' *Demography* 32, no. 1 (1995): 17–28.

Maddox, George L, ed. *Encyclopedia of Aging.* New York: Springer, 1987.

Maillet, Antonine. *Les Confessions de Jeanne de Valois: Roman.* Montreal: Leméac, 1992.

– *La Sagouine: pièce pour une femme seule.* Montreal: Leméac, 1971.

Mannheim, Karl. 'The Problem of Generations.' In Paul Kecskemeti, ed., *Essays in the Sociology of Knowledge*, 276–322. London: Routledge and Kegan Paul (first published in 1952).

Mannion, Edie. 'Resilience and Burden in Spouses of People with Mental Illness.' *Psychiatric Rehabilitation Journal* 20, no. 2 (1996): 13–23.

Marshall, Victor W. *Aging in Canada: Social Perspectives,* 2nd ed. Markham, Ont.: Fitzhenry and Whiteside, 1987.

– 'Commentary: A Finding in Search of an Interpretation: Discussion of the Intergenerational Stake Hypothesis Revisited.' In Vern L. Bengtson, K. Warner Schaie, and Linda Burton, eds., *Adult Intergenerational Relations: Effects of Societal Change*, 277–97. New York: Springer, 1995.

– *The Generations: Contributions, Conflict, Equity.* Prepared for the Division of Aging and Seniors, Health Canada, 1997.

– 'Generations, Justice and Equity Concerns in Social Policy.' Paper presented at the American Sociological Association Annual Conference, San Francisco, 1998.

– 'The Next Half-Century of Aging Research – and Thoughts for the Past.' *Journal of Gerontology: Social Sciences* 50B (1995): S1–S3.

– 'Rethinking Retirement: Issues for the Twenty-first Century.' In Ellen M. Gee and Gloria M. Gutman, eds., *Rethinking Retirement*, 51–68. Vancouver: Simon Fraser University Press, 1995.

Marshall, Victor W., J.G. Cook and J.G. Marshall. 'Conflict over Generational Equity: Rhetoric or Reality in a Comparative Context.' In Vern L. Bengtson and W.A. Achenbaum, eds., *The Changing Contract across Generations*, 119–40. New York: Aldine de Gruyter, 1993.

Marshall, Victor W., Sarah H. Matthews, and Carolyn J. Rosenthal. 'Elusiveness of Family Lives: A Challenge for the Sociology of Aging.' In George L. Maddox and M. Powell Lawton, eds., *Annual Review of Gerontology and Geriatrics*, vol. 13, 39–72. New York: Springer, 1993.

Marshall, Victor W., and Barry McPherson. *Aging: Canadian Perspectives*. Peterborough, Ont.: Broadview, 1994.

Martel, Laurent. 'L'orientation et le contenu des relations réciproques des personnes âgées. *La revue canadienne du vieillissement* 19, no. 1 (2000): 80–105.

Martel, Laurent, and Jacques Légaré. 'L'orientation et le contenu des relations réciproques des personnes âgées.' *La revue canadienne du vieillissment* 19, no. 1 (2000): 80–105.

Martin-Matthews, Anne. 'Intergenerational Caregiving: How Apocolyptic and Dominant Demographies Frame the Questions and Shape the Answers.' In Ellen M. Gee and Gloria M. Gutman, eds., *The Overselling of Population Aging: Apocalyptic Demography, Intergenerational Challenges, and Social Policy*, 64–79. Don Mills, Ont.: Oxford University Press, 2000.

Martin Matthews, Anne, and Lori D. Campbell. 'Gender Roles, Employment, and Informal Care.' In Sara Arber and Jay Ginn, eds., *Connecting Gender and Ageing: A Sociological Approach*, 129–43. Buckingham: Open University Press, 1995.

Martin Matthews, Anne, and Carolyn Rosenthal. 'Balancing Work and Family in an Aging Society: The Canadian Experience.' In George L. Maddox and P. Lawton, eds., *Annual Review of Gerontology and Geriatrics*, vol. 13, 96–122. New York: Springer, 1993.

Marx, Karl. *Capital*. Ed. David McLellan. Oxford: Oxford University Press, 1995.

Mathews, Georges. 'L'avenir démographique des régions: analyse critique et implications des plus récentes perspectives démographiques du BSQ.' *Recherches sociographiques* 37, no. 3 (1996): 411–37.

Matthews, Carol. 'A Powerful Presence: Images of the Grandmother in Canadian Literature.' *Canadian Journal on Aging* 15, no. 2 (1996): 264–73.

Matthews, Sarah H. 'Undermining Stereotypes of the Old through Social Policy Analysis: Tempering Macro- with Micro-Level Perspectives.' In J. Hendricks and C. Rosenthal, eds., *The Remainder of Their Days: Domestic Policy and Older Families in the United States and Canada*, 105–18. New York: Garland, 1993.

Matthews, Sarah H., and Jenifer Heidorn. 'Meeting Filial Responsibilities in Brothers-Only Sibling Groups.' *Journal of Gerontology: Social Sciences* 53B, no. 5 (1998): S278–S286.

Maxwell, Judith. 'Social Dimensions of Economic Growth.' *The Eric John Hanson Memorial Lecture Series*, Vol. 8. University of Alberta, 1996.

Mayer, Karl U. 'The Paradox of Global Social Change and National Path Dependencies: Life Course Patterns in Advanced Societies.' In Alison E. Woodward and Martin Kohli, eds., *Inclusions/Exclusions*. London: Routledge, 1998.

- 'State and Life Course in Advanced Societies.' Paper presented at American Sociological Association Annual Conference. San Francisco, 1998.
McCarthy, Shawn. 'Productivity: A Political Issue.' *Globe and Mail*, 10 April, 1999, D3.
McDaniel, Susan A. *Canada's Aging Population*. Toronto: Butterworths, 1986.
- 'Caring and Sharing: Demographic Change and Shifting State Policies.' In Monica Verea, ed., *Women in North America at the End of the Millennium*. Mexico City: Universidad Nacional Automona de Mexico, 1997.
- 'Demographic Aging as Paradigm in Canada's Welfare State.' *Canadian Public Policy* 13, no. 3 (1987): 330–6.
- 'The Family Lives of the Middle-Aged and Elderly.' In Maureen Baker, ed., *Families: Changing Trends in Canada*, 3rd ed., 194–210. Toronto: McGraw-Hill Ryerson, 1995.
- 'Family/Work Challenges among Older Working Canadians.' In Marion Lynn, ed., *Voices: Essays on Canadian Families*, 195–214. Toronto: Nelson, 1996.
- 'Health Care Policy in an Aging Canada: The Alberta "Experiment."' *Journal of Aging Studies* 11, no. 3 (1997): 211–28.
- 'Intergenerational Equity: Policy and Data Implications.' In Miles Corak, ed., *Labour Markets, Social Institutions, and the Future of Canada's Children*, 171–5. Statistics Canada, Catalogue no. 89-553-XPB, Ottawa: Statistics Canada, 1998.
- 'Intergenerational Transfers, Social Solidarity, and Social Policy: Unanswered Questions and Policy Challenges.' *Canadian Public Policy / Canadian Journal on Aging*, Suppl. (joint issue) (1997): 1–21.
- 'Pensions, Privilege, and Poverty: Another "Take" on Intergenerational Equity.' *Le Contrat social à l'épreuve des changements démographiques*. Montreal: INRS-Urbanisation, 2001.
- 'Public Policy, Demographic Aging and Families.' *Policy Options / Options Politiques*, Sept. 1998, 33–5.
- 'Serial Employment and Skinny Government: Reforming Caring and Sharing among Generations.' *Canadian Journal on Aging* 16, no. 3 (1997): 465–84.
- 'Shifting Self and Social Knowledge Identities among Older Unemployed Workers in Canada in the 1990s: Parallels with the Industrial Revolution.' Paper presented at the World Congress of Sociology, Montreal, July 1998.
- 'Toward Healthy Families.' *Determinants of Health: Settings and Issues*, vol. 3, by the National Forum on Health, 3–42. Sainte-Foy, Que.: Éditions Multimodes, 1998.
- 'Untangling Love and Domination: Challenges of Home Care for the Elderly in a Reconstructing Canada.' *Journal of Canadian Studies* 14, no. 3 (1999): 191–213.

- '"What Did You Ever Do for Me?" Intergenerational Interlinkages in a Reconstructing Canada.' In Ellen M. Gee and Gloria Gutman, eds., *The Over-selling of Population Aging: Apocalyptic Demography and Inter-generational Challenges*, 129–52. Don Mills, Ont: Oxford University Press, 2000.
- 'Women's Changing Relations to the State and Citizenship: Caring and Inter-generational Relations in Globalizing Western Democracies.' *Canadian Review of Sociology and Anthropology* 39, no. 2 (2002): 125–50.
McDaniel, Susan A., and Neena Chappell. 'Health Care in Regression: Impli-cations for Canadian Seniors.' *Canadian Public Policy* 25, no. 1 (1999): 101–10.
McDaniel, Susan A., and Ellen M. Gee. 'Social Policies Regarding Caregiving to Elders: Canadian Contradictions.' *Journal of Aging and Social Policy* 5, no. 1/2 (1993): 57–72.
McDaniel, Susan A., and Robert Lewis. 'Did They or Didn't They? Intergenera-tional Supports in Canada's Past and a Case Study of Brigus, Newfound-land, 1920–1949.' In Lori Chambers and Edgar-Andre Montigny, eds., *Family Matters: Papers in Post-Confederation Canadian Family History*, 475–97. Toronto: Canadian Scholars Press, 1997.
McDonald, Lynn. 'Alarmist Economics and Women's Pensions: A Case of "Semanticide."' In Ellen M. Gee and Gloria M. Gutman, eds., *The Overselling of Population Aging: Apocalyptic Demography, Intergenerational Challenges, and Social Policy* 115–29. Don Mills, Ont.: Oxford University Press, 2000.
McDonald, Lynn, Peter Donahue, and Brooke Moore. 'The Economic Casual-ties of Retiring because of Unemployment.' *IESOP Research Paper*, no. 30. Hamilton: McMaster University, 1998.
McDonald, Lynn, and Richard A. Wanner. *Retirement in Canada*. Toronto: But-terworths, 1990.
McEvoy, Glenn M., and Wayne Cascio. 'Cumulative Evidence of the Relation-ship between Employee Age and Job Performance.' *Journal of Applied Psy-chology* 74, no. 1 (1989): 11–17.
McLerran, Jennifer. 'Saved by the Hand that Is Not Stretched Out: The Aged Poor in Hubert von Herkomer's *Eventide: A Scene in the Westminster Union*.' *Gerontologist* 33, no. 6 (1993): 762–71.
McMullen, Kathryn. 'Working with Technology: Changing Skill Requirements in the Computer Age.' *Applied Research Bulletin* 2, no. 2 (1996). [Ottawa: Human Resources Development Canada.].
Medoff, James L., and Katharine G. Abraham. 'Experience, Performance and Earnings.' *Quarterly Journal of Economics* 95, no. 4 (1980): 703–36.
Mercure, Daniel, Robert-Paul Bourgeois, and Thierry Wils. 'Analyse critique de

la typologie des choix de carrière.' *Relations industrielles* 46, no. 1 (1991): 120–40.

Merette, Marcel. 'The Effects of Debt Reduction on Intergenerational Equity and Growth.' In Miles Corak, ed., *Government Finances and Generational Equity*, 87–106. Ottawa: Statistics Canada and Human Resources Development Canada, Catalogue no. 68-513-XPB, 1998.

Methot, Suzanne. 'Employment Patterns of Elderly Canadians.' *Canadian Social Trends* (Autumn 1987): 7–11.

Meunier, Dominique, Paul Bernard, and Johanne Boisjoly. 'Eternal Youth? Changes in the Living Arrangements of Young People.' In Miles Corak, ed., *Labour Markets, Social Institutions, and the Future of Canada's Children*, 157–70. Ottawa: Statistics Canada, Catalogue no. 89-553-XPB, 1998.

Minkler, Meredith. 'Grandparents, Grandchildren and the Dilemmas of Public Policy.' Paper presented at the American Sociological Association Annual Conference, San Francisco, 1998.

Minois, Georges. *History of Old Age from Antiquity to the Renaissance*. Translated by S.H. Tenison. Chicago: University of Chicago Press, 1989.

Mirfin-Veitch, Brigit, Anne Bray, and Marilyn Watson. '"We're Just that Sort of Family": Intergenerational Relationships in Families Including Children with Disabilities.' *Family Relations* 46 (July 1997): 305–11.

Mitchell, Barbara A. 'The Refilled Nest.' In Ellen M. Gee and Gloria M. Gutman, eds., *The Overselling of Population Aging: Apocalyptic Demography, Intergenerational Challenges, and Social Policy*, 80–99. Don Mills, Ont.: Oxford University Press, 2000.

– 'The Refilled Nest: Debunking the Myth of Families-in-Crisis.' Paper presented at the 9th Annual John K. Freisen Conference and Lecture. Simon Fraser University, Vancouver, May 1998.

– 'Too Close for Comfort? Parental Assessments of "Boomerang Kid" Living Arrangements.' *Canadian Journal of Sociology* 23, no. 1 (1998): 21–46.

Mitchell, Barbara A., and Ellen M. Gee. '"Boomerang Kids"' and Midlife Parental Marital Satisfaction.' *Family Relations* 45, no. 4 (1996): 442–8.

– 'Young Adults Returning Home: Implications for Social Policy.' In Burt Gallaway and Joseph Hudson, eds., *Youth in Transition to Adulthood: Research and Policy Implications*, 61–71. Toronto: Thompson, 1996.

Mitchell, Barbara A., Andrew V. Wister, and Ellen M. Gee. 'Culture and Co-residence: An Exploration of Home Returning among Canadian Young Adults.' Paper presented at the 14th World Congress of Sociology, Montreal, July 1998.

– 'Culture and Co-residence: An Exploration of Variation in Home Returning among Canadian Young Adults.' *Canadian Review of Sociology and Anthropology* 37 (2000): 197–22.

Mitchell, Olivia S., and Joseph F. Quinn. '1994–95 Advisory Council on Social Security: Technical Panel on Trends and Issues in Retirement Saving. Final Report.' Population Aging Research Center, Working Paper Series, no. 95-06. Philadelphia: University of Pennsylvania, 1995.

Moen, Phyllis, and Kay B. Forest. 'Family Policies for an Aging Society: Moving to the Twenty-First Century.' *Gerontologist* 35, no. 6 (1995): 825–30.

Montigny, Edgar-André. *Foisted upon the Government? State Responsibilities, Family Obligations, and the Care of the Dependent Aged in Late Nineteenth Century Ontario.* Montreal and Kingston: McGill-Queen's University Press, 1997.

Moore, Eric G., and Mark W. Rosenberg, with Donald McGuiness. *Growing Old in Canada: Demographic and Geographic Perspectives.* Toronto and Ottawa: ITP Nelson and Statistics Canada, 1997.

Morissette, René, and Deborah Sunter. 'What Is Happening to Weekly Hours Worked in Canada?' *Analytical Studies Branch Research Paper Series*, no. 65. Ottawa: Statistics Canada, 1994.

Morris, Robert, and Scott A. Bass, eds. *Retirement Reconsidered: Economic and Social Roles for Older People.* New York: Springer, 1988.

Morrison, Kelly. 'Canada's Older Workers.' Applied Research Branch, Strategic Policy Reports. Ottawa: Human Resources Development Canada, 1996.

Murill, Ray, and Sheldon Wayne. 'Buy Your Leave.' *Benefits Canada*, Dec. 1986, 33–43.

Mustard, Cameron A., Morris Barer, Robert G. Evans, John Horne, Teresa Mayer, and Shelley Derksen. 'Paying Taxes and Using Health Care Services: The Distributional Consequences of Tax Financed Universal Health Insurance in a Canadian Province.' Paper presented at the Conference on the State of Living Standards and the Quality of Life in Canada, Ottawa, 30–1 Oct. 1998.

Myles, John. 'Editorial: Women, the Welfare State and Care-Giving.' *Canadian Journal on Aging* 10, no. 2 (1991): 82–5.

– 'Public Policy in a World of Market Failure.' *Policy Options / Options politiques* 17, no. 6 (1996): 14–19.

– 'Restructuring the Intergenerational Contract: How Nations are Reforming Old Age Security.' Paper presented at the American Sociological Association Annual Conference, San Francisco, 1998.

Myles, John, and Debra Street. 'Should the Economic Life Course Be Redesigned? Old Age Security in a Time of Transition.' *Canadian Journal on Aging* 14, no. 2 (1995): 335–59.

Naisbitt, John, and Patricia Aburdene. *Re-inventing the Corporation.* New York: Warner Books, 1985.

National Advisory Council on Aging. *The NACA Position on the Image of Aging.* Ottawa: National Advisory Council on Aging, 1993.

– *1999 and beyond: Challenges of an Aging Canadian Society.* Ottawa: Health Canada, 1999.

National Forum on Health. *Canada's Health Action: Building on the Legacy.* Vol. 1, *The Final Report of the National Forum on Health.* Vol. 2, *Synthesis Reports and Issue Papers.* Ottawa: Canada Communications Group, 1997.

Nelson, Richard R. 'Research on Productivity Growth and Productivity Differences: Dead Ends and New Departures.' *Journal of Economic Literature* 19 (Sept. 1981): 1029–64.

Neugebauer-Visano, Robynne. *Aging and Inequality: Cultural Constructions of Differences.* Toronto: Canadian Scholars' Press, 1995.

Norris, Joan E., and Joseph A. Tindale. *Among Generations: The Cycle of Adult Relationships.* New York: Freeman, 1994.

O'Connor, Deborah L. 'Supporting Spousal Caregivers: Exploring the Meaning of Service Use.' *Families in Society: Journal of Contemporary Human Services,* May 1995, 295–305.

O'Hara, Bruce. *Working Harder Isn't Working.* Vancouver: New Star Books, 1993.

Olmsted, Barney, and Suzanne Smith. *Creating a Flexible Workplace: How to Select and Manage Alternative Work Options,* 2nd ed. New York: Amacom, 1994.

– *Managing in a Flexible Workplace.* New York: Amacom, 1997.

Olson, Richard. *The Emergence of the Social Sciences, 1642–1792.* New York: Twayne, 1993.

O'Neill, John. *The Missing Child in Liberal Theory: Towards a Covenant Theory of Family, Community, Welfare and the Civic State.* Toronto: University of Toronto Press, 1994.

Organisation for Economic Co-operation and Development. *Ageing in OECD Countries: A Critical Policy Challenge.* Paris: OECD, 1996.

– 'The Labour Market and Older Workers.' *Social Policy Studies,* no. 17. Paris: OECD, 1995.

– *Maintaining Prosperity in an Ageing Society.* Paris: OECD, 1998.

– *OECD Economic Surveys: Canada.* Paris: OECD, 1998.

– *Technology, Productivity and Job Creation,* vols. 1 and 2. Paris: OECD, 1996.

– 'The Transition from Work to Retirement.' *Social Policy Studies,* no. 16. Paris: OECD, 1995.

– 'Work Force Ageing: Consequences and Policy Responses.' *Ageing Working Paper,* AWP4.1. Paris: OECD, 1998.

Ornstein, Michael, and Tony Haddad. *About Time: Analysis from a 1986 Survey of Canadians.* Toronto: Institute for Social Research, York University, 1993.

Osberg, Lars. 'Meaning and Measurement in Intergenerational Equity.' In Miles Corak, ed., *Government Finances and Generational Equity,* 131–9. Ottawa: Statistics Canada, Catalogue no. 68-513-XPB, 1998.

Osgoode, D. Wayne, and Hyunkee Lee. 'Leisure Activities, Age and Adult Roles across the Lifespan.' *Society and Leisure* 16, no. 1 (1993): 181–208.

Osler, Sir William. 'The Fixed Period.' In *Sir William Osler, 1849–1919: A Selection for Medical Students*. Ed. Charles G. Roland. Toronto: Hannah Institute for the History of Medicine, 1982.

Owram, Doug. *Born at the Right Time: A History of the Baby Boom Generation*. Toronto: University of Toronto Press, 1996.

Pampel, Fred C. *Aging, Social Inequality and Public Policy*. Thousand Oaks, Calif.: Pine Forge Press, 1998.

– 'Population Aging, Class Context, and Age Inequality in Public Spending.' *American Journal of Sociology* 100, no. 1 (1994): 153–95.

Parnes, Herbert S., ed. *Work and Retirement: A Longitudinal Study of Men*. Cambridge, Mass.: MIT Press, 1981.

Parr, Joy. 'Gender History and Historical Practice.' In Joy Parr and Mark Rosenfeld, eds, *Gender and History in Canada*, 8–27. Toronto: Copp Clark, 1996.

Pavalko, Eliza. 'Beyond Trajectories: Multiple Concepts for Analyzing Long-Term Process.' In Melissa Hardy, ed., *Studying Aging and Social Change*, 129–7. Thousand Oaks, Calif.: Sage, 1997.

Peitchinis, Stephen G. 'Economic Implications of an Aging Population on Society.' In J.S. Frideres and C.J. Bruce, eds., *The Impact of an Aging Population on Society*. Calgary: University of Calgary, 1994.

Pelling, Margaret, and Richard M. Smith, eds. *Life, Death, and the Elderly: Historical Perspectives*. London: Routledge, 1991.

Pennec, Sophie. 'Four-Generation Families in France.' *Population* 9 (1997): 75–101.

Phipps, Shelley A. and Peter S. Burton. 'Collective Models of Family Behaviour: Implications for Economic Policy.' *Canadian Public Policy* 22 (1996): 129–43.

Picard, André. *This Gift of Death: Confronting Canada's Tainted Blood Tragedy*. Toronto: HarperCollins, 1998.

Pick, Daniel. *Faces of Degeneration: A European Disorder, c. 1848 – c. 1918*. Cambridge: Cambridge University Press, 1989.

Pickett, Susan A., Judith Cook, Bertram Cohler, and Mitchell Solomon. 'Positive Parent/Adult Relationships: Impact of Severe Mental Illness and Caregiving Burden.' *American Journal of Orthopsychiatry* 67, no. 2 (1997): 220–30.

Pickett, Susan A., James R. Greenley, and Jan S. Greenberg. 'Off-Timedness as a Contributor to Subjective Burdens for Parents of Offspring with Severe Mental Illness.' *Family Relations* 44, no. 2 (1995): 195–201.

Picot, Garnett. 'What Is Happening to Earnings Inequality in Canada in the 1990s?' *Canadian Business Economics* 6, no. 1 (1997): 65–83.

Picot, Garnett, and Z. Lin. 'Are Canadians More Likely to Lose Their Jobs in the 1990s?' *Canadian Economic Observer*, Sept. 1997, 3.1–3.4.

Picot, Garnett, and John Myles. 'Social Transfers, Changing Family Structures, and Low Income Among Children.' Research Paper Series, no. 82. Ottawa: Statistics Canada Analytical Studies Branch, 1995.

Picot, Garnett, John Myles, and Wendy Pyper. 'Markets, Families, and Social Transfers: Trends in Low Income among the Young and Old, 1973–95.' In Miles Corak, ed., *Labour Markets, Social Institutions, and the Future of Canada's Children*. Catalogue no. 89-553-XPB. Ottawa: Statistics Canada, 1998.

Picot, Garnett, Zhengxi Lin, and Wendy Pyper. 'An Overview of Permanent Layoffs.' *Perspectives on Labour and Income* (Autumn 1997): 46–51.

Pieper, Josef. *Leisure: The Basis of Culture*. New York: New American Library, 1963.

Pilat, Dirk. 'Labour Productivity Levels in OECD Countries: Estimates for Manufacturing and Selected Service Sectors.' *Economics Department Working Paper*, no. 69. Paris: OECD.

Pitrou, Agnès. *Les solidarités familiales: Vivre sans famille?* Paris: Privat, 1992.

– 'De la transformation des classes d'âges à l'évolution des rapports sociaux.' *Sociologie et sociétés* 27 (1995): 27–42.

– 'Vieillesse et famille: qui soutient l'autre?' *Lien social et politiques* 38 (Autumn 1997): 145–58.

Policy Research Committee. *Report on Growth, Human Development, and Social Cohesion*. Ottawa: Policy Research Initiative, 1996.

Poovey, Mary. *A History of the Modern Fact: Problems of Knowledge in the Sciences of Wealth and Society*. Chicago: University of Chicago Press, 1998.

Porter, Nancy. 'The Art of Aging: A Review Essay.' *Women's Studies Quarterly* 17, no. 1/2 (1989): 97–108.

Posner, Richard A. *Aging and Old Age*. Chicago: University of Chicago Press, 1995.

'Preparing for the Baby Boomers' Retirement: The Role of Employment.' Paper prepared for the U.S. Senate Special Committee on Aging, Forum on Older Workers, One Hundred and Fifth Congress, serial no. 105-7. Washington, DC: U.S. Senate, 1997.

Prescott, Edward C. 'Lawrence R. Klein Lecture 1997. Needed: A Theory of Total Factor Productivity.' *International Economic Review* 39, no. 3 (1998): 525–51.

Price, Matthew C. *Justice between Generations: The Growing Power of the Elderly in America*. Westport, Conn.: Praeger, 1997.

Prince, Michael J. 'Apocalyptic, Opportunistic, and Realistic Demographic Discourse: Retirement Income and Social Policy or Chicken Littles, Nest-Eggies, and Humpty Dumpties.' In Ellen M. Gee and Gloria M. Gutman, eds., *The Overselling of Population Aging: Apocalyptic Demography, Intergenerational Challenges, and Social Policy,* 100–14. Don Mills, Ont.: Oxford University Press, 2000.

Pronovost, Gilles, and Max D'Amours. 'Leisure Studies: A Re-examination of Society.' *Society and Leisure* 13, no. 1 (1990): 39–62.

Pruchno, Rachel. 'The Effects of Help Patterns on the Mental Health of Spouse Caregivers.' *Research on Aging* 12, no. 1 (1990): 57–71.

Putnam, Robert D. *Bowling Alone: The Collapse and Revival of American Community,* Toronto: Simon and Schuster, 2000.

– *The Decline of Civil Society: How Come? So What?* Ottawa: Ministry of Supply and Services, 1996.

Putnam, Robert D. *Making Democracy Work.* Princeton, NJ: Princeton University Press, 1993.

Quadagno, Jill. *Aging in Early Industrial Society: Work, Family, and Social Policy in Nineteenth-Century England.* New York: Academic Press, 1982.

– *Aging and the Life Course.* Boston: McGraw-Hill, 1999.

– *The Transformation of Old Age Security: Class and Politics in the American Welfare State.* Chicago: University of Chicago Press, 1988.

Quinn, Joseph F. 'The Effects of Changes in Mandatory Retirement Rules on Labor Supply of Older Workers.' Department of Economics Papers. Boston: Boston College, 1981.

– 'Employment and the Elderly.' *Gerontologist* (April 1998): 254–9.

– 'New Paths to Retirement.' In Brett Hammond, Olivia Mitchell, and Anna Rappaport, eds., *Forecasting Retirement Needs and Retirement Wealth.* Philadelphia: University of Pennsylvania Press, 1999.

Quinn, Joseph F. 'Retirement Trends and Patterns in the 1990s: The End of an Era?' *Public Policy and Aging Report* (Summer 1997): 10–14.

Quinn, Joseph, Richard Burkhauser, Kevin Cahill, and Robert Weathers. 'Microeconometric Analysis of the Retirement Decision: United States.' Department of Economics, Working Paper, No. 203. Paris: OECD, 1998.

Quinn, Joseph F., and Michael Kozy. 'The Roles of Part-Time Work and Self-Employment in the Retirement Transition: A Preliminary View from HRS.' Department of Economics Papers. Boston: Boston College, 1995.

Qureshi, Hazel, and Alan Walker. 'Caring for Elderly People: The Family and the State.' In Cris Phillipson and Alan Walker, eds., *Ageing and Social Policy: A Critical Assessment,* 109–27. Brookfield, Vt: Gower, 1986.

Random House Wester's Dictionary, 3rd ed. 1993. New York: New Ballantine Publishing Group.

Rashid, Abdul. 'Family Income: 25 Years of Stability and Change.' *Perspectives on Labour and Income* 11, no. 1 (1999): 9–15.

Reid, Donald. *Work and Leisure in the 21st Century: From Production to Citizenship.* Toronto: Wall and Emerson, 1995.

Rendall, M.S., and R.A. Bahcieva. 'An Old-Age Security Motive for Fertility in the United States.' *Population and Development Review* 24, no. 2 (1998): 293–307.

Revised English Bible, with the Apocrypha. Oxford and Cambridge: Oxford University Press and Cambridge University Press, 1989.

Reynolds, Alan. 'Restoring Work Incentives for Older Americans.' Paper Prepared for the U.S. Senate Subcommittee on Aging Forum on Older Workers, One Hundred and Fifth Congress, serial no. 105–7: 15–26. Washington, DC: United States Senate, 1997.

Ricard, Francois. *La génération lyrique, essai sur la vie et l'oeuvre des premiers-nés du baby-boom.* Montreal: Éditions du Boréal, 1992.

Richardson, Pete, ed. 'Globalisation and Linkages: Macro-Structural Challenges and Opportunities.' Economics Department, Working Paper, no, 181. Paris: OECD, 1997.

Riche, Richard W., Daniel E. Heckel, and John U. Burgan. 'High Technology Today and Tomorrow: A Small Slice of the Employment Pie.' *Monthly Labor Review,* Dec. 1983, 50–8.

Rifkin, Jeremy. *The End of Work.* New York: Putnam's 1995.

Rix, Sara. 'The Challenge of an Aging Work Force: Keeping Older Workers Employed and Employable.' In Scott A. Bass, Robert Morris, and Masato Oka, eds., *Public Policy and the Old Age Revolution in Japan,* 79–94. New York: Haworth Press, 1966.

Roach, Stephen. 'Search of Productivity.' *Harvard Business Review,* Sept–Oct. 1998, 153–60.

Roadburg, Alan. *Aging: Retirement, Leisure and Work in Canada.* Toronto: Methuen, 1985.

Roberts, Robert E., and Vern L. Bengtson. 'Is Intergenerational Solidarity a Unidirectional Construct? A Second Test of a Formal Model.' *Journal of Gerontology: Social Sciences* 45, no. 1 (1990): S12–S20.

Robinson, John, and Geoffrey Godbey. *Time for Life: The Surprising Ways Americans Use Their Time.* University Park, Pa.: Pennsylvania State University Press, 1997.

Rochon, Madeleine. 'Participation des personnes âgées au financement des dépenses de santé et des dépenses sociales et vieillissement démographique.' *Cahiers québécois de démographie* 29 (1999): 299–329.

Roebuck, Janet. 'When Does "Old Age" Begin? The Evolution of the English Definition.' *Journal of Social History* 12, no. 3 (1979): 416–28.

Romaniuc, Anatole. 'Reflection on Population Forecasting: From Prediction to Prospective Analysis.' *Canadian Studies in Population* 21, no. 2 (1994): 165–80.

Rooke, Constance, ed. *Night Light: Stories of Aging*. Toronto: Oxford University Press, 1986.

Rosenthal, Carolyn J. 'Aging Families: Have Current Changes and Challenges Been "Oversold"?' In Ellen M. Gee and Gloria M. Gutman, eds., *The Overselling of Population Aging: Apocalyptic Demography, Intergenerational Challenges, and Social Policy*, 45–63. Don Mills, Ont.: Oxford University Press, 2000.

– 'Le soutien des familles canadiennes à leurs membres vieillissants: Changements de contexte.' *Lien social et politiques* 38 (Autumn 1997): 123–31.

Ross, David P., and Richard Shillington. *Flux: Two Years in the Life of the Canadian Labour Market*. Ottawa: Statistics Canada, 1991.

Rossi, Alice. 'Commentary: Wanted: Alternative Theory and Analysis Modes.' In Vern L. Bengtson, K. Warner Schaie, and Linda Burton, eds., *Adult Intergenerational Relations: Effects of Societal Change*, 264–76. New York: Springer, 1995.

Roy, Jacques. *Les personnes âgées et les solidarités: La fin des mythes*. Sainte-Foy, Que.: Les éditions de l'IQRC, les Presses de l'Université Laval, 1998.

– 'Solidarité horizontale chez les ainés'. *La revue canadienne du vieillissement* 17, no. 3 (1998): 311–29.

Ruhm, Christopher. 'Career Jobs, Bridge Employment, and Retirement.' In Peter B. Doeringer, ed., *Bridges to Retirement*, 92–109. Ithaca, NY: ILR Press, Cornell University, 1990.

Rukeyser, Muriel. *A Muriel Rukeyser Reader*. Jan Heller Levi. New York: W.W. Norton, 1994.

Saba, Tania, Gilles Guérin, and Thierry Wils. 'Les pratiques efficaces pour gérer les travailleurs vieillissants: le cas des professionnels syndiqués au Québec dans la représentation des salariés dans le contexte du libre échange et de la déréglementation.' In Rick Chayhowski, Paul-André LaPointe, Guylaine Vallée, and Anil Verma, eds., *Sélection de textes du XXXIII Congrès de l'ACRI*. 1996.

Samdahl, Diane, and Nancy Jekubovich. 'Patterns and Characteristics of Adult Daily Leisure.' *Society and Leisure* 16, no. 1 (1993): 129–9.

Samuel, T. John. *Quebec Separatism Is Dead: Demography Is Destiny*. Ottawa: John Samuel and Associates. 1994.

Samwick, Andrew. 'New Evidence on Pensions, Social Security, and the Timing of Retirement.' NBER Working Paper, no. W6534. Cambridge, Mass.: National Bureau of Economic Research, 1998.

Sassoon, Anne Showstack. 'Comment on Jane Lewis: Gender and Welfare Regimes, Further Thoughts.' *Social Politics* (Summer 1997): 178–81.

Saul, John Ralston. *Reflections of a Siamese Twin: Canada at the End of the Twentieth Century.* Toronto: Viking, 1997.
– *The Unconscious Civilization.* Concord, Ont.: House of Anansi, 1995.
Schaie, K. Warner, and W. Andrew Achenbaum. *Societal Impact on Aging: Historical Perspectives.* New York: Springer, 1993.
Schellenberg, Grant. *The Employment Challenge Facing Today's Experienced Workers.* Ottawa: One Voice, the Canadian Seniors Network, 1997.
– *Older Workers and Canada's Aging Labour Force.* Ottawa: One Voice, Options 45+, the Canadian Seniors Network, 1994.
Schor, Juliet. *The Overworked American: The Unexpected Decline of Leisure.* New York: Basic Books, 1991.
Scott, Anne, and G. Clare Wenger. 'Gender and Social Support Networks in Later Life.' In Sara Arber and Jay Ginn, eds., *Connecting Gender and Ageing: A Sociological Approach*, 158–172. Buckingham: Open University Press, 1995.
Schulz, James. *The Economics of Aging.* Belmont, Calif.: Wadsworth, 1988.
Schulz, James, Allan Burowski, and Williana H. Crown, eds. *Economics of Population Aging.* New York: Auburn House, 1991.
Sennett, Richard. *A Corrosion of Character: Personal Consequences of Work in the New Capitalism.* London: Penguin, 1998.
Serbin, L.A. and D.M. Stack. 'Longitudinal Studies of Intergenerational Continuity and the Transfer of Psychosocial Skills: An Introduction.' *Developmental Psychology* 34, no. 6 (1998): 1159–61.
Shakespeare, William. *As You Like It.* In G. Blakemore Evans, Harry Levin, Herschel Baker, Anne Barton, Frank Kermode, Hallett Smith, Marie Edel, and Charles H. Shattuck. eds., *The Riverside Shakespeare.* Boston: Houghton Mifflin, 1974.
Sharpe, Andrew. 'The Productivity Paradox: An Evaluation of Competing Explanations.' *Canadian Business Economics* 6, no. 1 (1997): 32–47.
Shields, Carol. *The Stone Diaries.* Toronto: Random House, 1993.
Shigehara, Kumiharu. *Globalisation and Employment.* Paris: OECD, 1997.
Sichel, Daniel. *The Computer Revolution.* Washington, DC: Brookings Institution, 1997.
Silk, Leonard. *The Economists.* New York: Avon Books, 1976.
Silverstein, Merril, and Vern L. Bengtson. 'Intergenerational Solidarity and the Structure of Adult Child-Parent Relationships in American Families.' *American Journal of Sociology* 103, no. 2 (1997): 429–60.
Silverstein, Merril, Vanessa Burholt, G. Clare Wenger, and Vern L. Bengtson. 'Parent-Child Relations among Very Old Parents in Wales and the United States: A Test of Modernization Theory.' *Journal of Aging Studies* 12, no. 4 (1997): 387–409.

Silverstein, Merril, Tonya M. Parrott, and Vern L. Bengtson. 'Factors that Predispose Middle-Aged Sons and Daughters to Provide Social Support to Older Parents.' *Journal of Marriage and the Family* 57 (May 1995): 465–75.

Smeeding, Timothy M., and Joseph F. Quinn. 'Cross-National Patterns of Labor Force Withdrawal.' In Peter Flora, Philip R. de Jong, Julian LeGrand, and Jun-Young Kim, eds., *The State of Social Welfare, 1997*, 83–118. Aldershot, U.K.: Ashgate Publishing, 1998.

Smith, Pamela. 'The 1996 Alberta Survey: Public Attitudes about Changes in the Health Care System.' Population Research Laboratory Series. Edmonton: University of Alberta, 1996.

Sokoloff, Janice. *The Margin that Remains: A Study of Aging in Literature.* New York: Peter Lang, 1987.

Solow, Robert. 'On Golden Pond.' *New York Review of Books*, 6 May 1999.

– *The Labor Market as Social Institution.* Cambridge, Mass.: Basil Blackwell, 1990.

Sparrow, Paul R., and D.R. Davies. 'Effects of Age, Tenure, Training, and Job Complexity on Technical Performance.' *Psychology and Aging* 3, no. 3 (1988): 307–14.

Special Committee on Aging. 'Preparing for the Baby Boomers' Retirement: The Role of Employment.' Forum before the Special Committee on Aging, United States Senate, One Hundred Fifth Congress, serial no. 105–7. Washington, DC: U.S. Senate, 25 July, 1997.

Spengler, Joseph J. 'Demographic Factors and Early Modern Economic Development.' *Daedalus* 97, no. 2 (1968): 433–46.

Spiegel, Maura, and Richard Tristman, eds. *The Grim Reader: Writings on Death, Dying, and Living On.* New York: Doubleday, 1997.

Standing, Guy. 'The Folly of Social Safety Nets: Why Basic Income Is Needed in Eastern Europe.' *Social Research: An International Quarterly of the Social Sciences* 64, no. 4 (1997): 1339–79.

Statistics Canada. *The Consequences of Population Ageing: An International Analysis and Review.* Catalogue no. 89–569-XCB. Ottawa: Statistics Canada, 1999.

– *General Social Survey: Family and Friends – Public Use Microdata File.* Ottawa: Statistics Canada, 1990–1.

– *General Social Survey: An Overview.* Statistics Canada, Catalogue no. 89F0115XIE. Ottawa: Statistics Canada, 2001

– 'How Children Get Ahead in Life,' *Daily*, November 5, 1998.

– *Income Distributions by Size in Canada, 1996.* Catalogue no. 13-207-XPB, Ottawa: Statistics Canada, 1997.

– *Labour Force Update: Older Workers.* Catalogue no. 71-005-XPB. Ottawa: Statistics Canada, 1998.

– '1996 Census: Sources of Income, Earnings and Total Income, and Family Income.' *Daily,* 12 May, 1998.
– 'Pension Coverage among Young and Prime-Aged Workers.' *Statistics Canada Daily,* 22 Dec., 1999.
– 'University Enrolment.' *Daily,* 14 Oct., 1998.
– 'Young Adults Living at Home.' *Daily,* 11 March, 1999.
Stein, Dorothy. *People Who Count: Population and Politics, Women and Children.* London: Earthscan Publications, 1995.
Stevenson, Robert Louis. 'Crabbed Age and Youth.' *Familiar Studies of Men and Books; Virginibus Puerisque; Selected Poems.* London: Collins, 1956.
Stoller, Eleanor P. 'Informal Exchanges with Non-Kin among Retired Sunbelt Migrants: A Case Study of a Finnish American Retirement Community.' *Journal of Gerontology: Social Sciences* 53B, no. 5 (1998): S87–S98.
Stone, Leroy O., ed. *Cohort Flow and the Consequences of Population Ageing: An International Analysis and Review.* Ottawa: Minister of Industry, 1999.
Stone, Leroy O., and Carolyn J. Rosenthal. 'Profiles of the Social Network of Canada's Elderly: An Analysis of 1990 GSS Data.' In Howard Litwin, ed., *The Social Networks of Older People,* 77–97. Westport, Conn.: Praeger, 1996.
Stone, Leroy O., Carolyn J. Rosenthal, and Ingrid Arnet Connidis. *Parent-Child Exchanges of Supports and Intergenerational Equity.* Catalogue no. 89-557-XPE. Ottawa: Statistics Canada, 1998.
Sum, Andrew M., and W. Neal Fogg. 'Profile of the Labor Market for Older Workers.' In Peter B. Doeringer, ed., *Bridges to Retirement,* 64–91. Ithaca, NY: ILR Press, Cornell University, 1990.
Sunter, Deborah, and Geoff Bowlby. 'Labour Force Participation in the 1990s.' *Canadian Economic Observer,* October 1998, 3.1–3.11.
Sunter, Deborah, and René Morissette. 'The Hours People Work.' *Perspectives on Labour and Income* 6, no. 3 (1994): 8–12.
Supreme Court of Canada. *McKinney v University of Guelph* (1990). http://www.droit.umontreal.ca/doc/.../1990/vol3/html/1990scr3_0229.html.
Surman, Kerry. *Postretirement Labour Force Activity.* Kingston, Ont.: Industrial Relations Centre, Queen's University, 1989.
Suzman, Richard M., David P. Willis, and Kenneth G. Martin. *The Oldest Old.* Oxford: Oxford University Press, 1996.
Szkodzinski, Michael, and Ralph Bradburd. 'The Productivity of the American Workforce in 1998, 2025, and 2040: A Preliminary Report.' Department of Economics Papers, Williams College, 1998.
Takamura, Jeanette C. 'Statement Prepared for the Special Committee on Aging.' Washington, DC: U.S. Senate, 1998.
Taylor, Janet, Joan E. Norris, and Wayne Howard. 'Succession Patterns of

Farmer and Successor in Canadian Farm Families.' *Rural Sociology* 63, no. 4 (1998): 553–73.

Termote, Marc, and Jacques Ledent. *L'avenir démolinguistique du Québec et de ses régions*. Quebec: Le Conseil de la langue française, 1994.

'They Prefer a Balanced Life.' *CA Magazine*, Oct. 1999, 9.

Thibault, Normand, and Hervé Gauthier. 'Perspectives de la population du Québec au XXIe siècle: Changement dans le paysage de la croissance.' *Statistiques: Données sociodémographiques en bref* 3, no. 2 (1999): 1–8.

Thompson, Paul, Catherine Itzin, and Michele Abendstern. *I Don't Feel Old: Understanding the Experience of Later Life*. Oxford: Oxford University Press, 1991.

'Time for Sale.' *Better Times*: The Newsletter of 32 Hours – Action for Full Employment and the Shorter Work Time Network of Canada, 9 Sept. 1999.

Tindale, Joseph A., Barbara Mitchell, and Joan E. Norris. 'Global Reciprocity: Examining Relationship Quality between Parents and Their Young Adult Children.' Paper presented at the Annual Meeting of the Canadian Sociology and Anthropology Association, Brock University, St Catharines, Ont., June 1996.

Tindale, Joseph A., Joan E. Norris, Stephanie Kuiack, and Linnea Humphrey. 'The Need for Open Communication: A Layered Context of Parent-Adult Child Relations in a Sample of Anglo and Italian Families.' Paper presented at the Canadian Association on Gerontology Annual Meeting, Winnipeg, Oct. 1994.

Turner, Bryan S. 'Ageing and Intergenerational Conflicts: A Reply to Sarah Irwin.' *British Journal of Sociology* 49, no. 2 (1998): 299–304.

Turner, Dave, Claude Giorno, Alain De Serres, Ann Vourc'h and Pete Richardson. 'The Macroeconomic Implications of Ageing in a Global Context.' Economics Department Working Paper, no. 193. Paris: OECD, 1998.

Uhlenberg, Peter. 'The Role of Divorce in Men's Relations with Their Adult Children after Mid-Life.' *Journal of Marriage and the Family* 52 (August 1990): 677–88.

Uhlenberg, Peter, and Bradley G. Hammill, 'Frequency of Grandparent Contact with Grandchild Sets: Six Factors That Make a Difference.' *Gerontologist* 38, no. 3 (1998): 276–85.

Ulysse, Pierre-Joseph, and Frédéric Lesemann. 'On ne vieillit plus aujourd'hui de la même façon qu'hier.' *Lien social et politiques* 38 (Autumn 1997): 31–49.

Underhill, Susan, Victor Marshall, and Sylvie Deliencourt. *Options 45+: HRCC Survey*. Toronto: Institute for Human Development, Life Course and Aging, University of Toronto, 1997.

Usui, Chikako. 'Gradual Retirement in Japan.' In K. Warner Schaie and

Carmi Schooler, eds., *Impact of Work on Older Adults*. New York: Springer, 1998.

Vallin, Jacques, Stan d'Souza, and Alberto Palloni, eds. *Measurement and Analysis of Mortality: New Approaches*. Oxford: Clarendon Press, 1990.

van Solinge, Hanna, Harry van Dalen, Pearl Dykstra, Evert van Imhoff, Hein Moors, and Leo van Wissen. *Population, Labour and Social Protection in the European Union: Dilemmas and Prospects*. The Hague: Netherlands Interdisciplinary Demographic Institute, 1998.

Veblen, Thorstein. *The Theory of Leisure: An Economic Study of Institutions*. New York: B.W. Huebsch, 1899.

Veevers, Jean, Ellen Gee, and Andrew Wister. 'Homeleaving Age Norms: Conflict or Consensus?' *Aging and Human Development* 43, no. 4 (1996): 277–94.

Veevers, Jean, and Barbara Mitchell. 'Intergenerational Exchanges and Perceptions of Support within "Boomerang Kid" Family Environments.' *Aging and Human Development* 46, no. 2 (1998): 91–108.

Venti, Steven F., and David A. Wise. 'The Cause of Wealth Dispersion at Retirement: Choice or Chance.' *American Economic Review* 88, no. 2 (1998): 185–91.

Vicarelli, Fausto. *Keynes: The Instability of Capitalism*. Philadelphia: University of Pennsylvania Press, 1984.

Wagamese, Richard. *Keeper 'n Me*. Toronto: Doubleday, 1994.

Wagner, Donna L. 'Testimony before the U.S. Senate Special Committee on Aging.' Towson, Md: Center for Productive Aging, Towson University, 1998.

Walker, Alan. 'The Economic "Burden" of Ageing and the Prospect of Intergenerational Conflict.' *Ageing and Society* 10, no. 4 (1990): 377–96.

– *The New Generational Contract*. London: UCL Press, 1996.

– 'The Relationship between the Family and the State in the Care of Older People.' *Canadian Journal on Aging* 10 (1991): 94–112.

Walker, Alan, and Victor Minichiello. 'Emerging Issues in Sociological Thinking: Research and Teaching.' In Victor Minichiello, Neena Chappell, Hal Kendig, and Alan Walker, eds., *Sociology of Aging: International Perspectives*, 1–7. Melbourne: International Sociology Association Research Committee on Aging, 1996.

Waxman, Barbara Frey. *From the Hearth to the Open Road: A Feminist Study of Aging in Contemporary Literature*. Westport, Conn.: Greenwood Press, 1990.

– *To Live in the Center of the Moment: Literary Autobiographies of Aging*. Charlottesville: University Press of Virginia, 1997.

White, Lynn, and Stacy Rodgers. 'Strong Support but Uneasy Relationships.' *Journal of Marriage and the Family* 59, no. 1 (1997): 62–76.

Williamson, Jeffrey G. 'Globalization, Labor Markets and Policy Backlash in the Past.' *Journal of Economic Perspectives* 12, no. 4 (1998): 51–72.

Willis, Andrew. 'Barclays, TD Chosen to Invest CPP Fund.' *Globe and Mail*, 18 Feb. 1999, B1.

Wister, Andrew, Barbara Mitchell, and Ellen Gee. 'Does Money Matter? Parental Income and Living Satisfaction among "Boomerang" Children during Coresidence.' *Canadian Studies in Population* 24, no. 2 (1997): 125–45.

Wolff, Edward N. 'The Magnitude and Causes of the Recent Productivity Slowdown in the United States: A Survey of Recent Studies.' In William J. Baumol and Kenneth McLennan, eds., *Productivity Growth and U.S. Competitiveness*, 29–57. New York: Oxford University Press, 1985.

– 'The Productivity Paradox: Evidence from Indirect Indicators of Service Sector Productivity Growth.' *Canadian Journal of Economics* 32, no. 2 (1999): 281–307.

Wolfson, Michael C., and Brian B. Murphy. 'New Views on Inequality Trends in Canada and the United States.' *Monthly Labor Review* 121, no. 4 (1998): 3–23.

Wolfson, Michael C., Geoff Rowe, Xiaofen Lin, and Stephen F. Gribble. 'Historical Generational Accounting with Heterogeneous Populations.' In Miles Corak, eds., *Government Finances and Generational Equity*, 107–25. Catalogue no. 68-513-XPB. Ottawa: Statistics Canada, 1998.

Woodward, Kathleen. *Aging and Its Discontents: Freud and Other Fictions*. Bloomington: Indiana University Press, 1991.

– ed. *Figuring Age: Women, Bodies, Generations*. Bloomington: Indiana University Press, 1999.

Woodward, Kathleen, and Murray Schwartz, eds. *Memory and Desire: Aging – Literature – Psychoanalysis*. Bloomington: Indiana University Press, 1986.

Wooley, Alexander. 'The Sandwich Generation: U of G Researchers Investigate Slices of Canadian Family Life.' *Guelph Alumnus* (1999): 22–7.

Work Organization and the Ageing Workforce: A Literature Review. Toronto: University of Toronto Libraries, n.d.

Wyatt-Brown, Anne M., and Janice Rossen, eds. *Aging and Gender in Literature: Studies in Creativity*. Charlottesville: University Press of Virginia, 1993.

Yankelovich, Skelly, and White, Inc. 'Workers Over 50: Old Myths, New Realities.' *Report Prepared for the American Association of Retired Persons*. New York: Yankelovich, Skelly, and White, Inc., 1985.

Zukewich Ghalam, Nancy. 'Living with Relatives.' *Canadian Social Trends*, no. 42 (1996): 20–4.

Zuzanek, Jiri, Theo Beckers, and Pascale Peters. 'The Harried Leisure Class Revisited: Dutch and Canadian Trends in the Use of Time from the 1970s to the 1990s.' *Leisure Studies* 17 (1998): 1–19.

Zuzanek, Jiri, and Bryan Smale. 'Life Cycle Variations in across the Week Allo-

cation of Time to Selected Daily Activities.' *Society and Leisure* 15, no. 2 (1992): 559–86.
- 'More Work – Less Leisure? Changing Allocations of Time in Canada, 1981–1992.' *Society and Leisure* 20, no. 1 (1997): 73–106.
Zyblock, Myles. 'Why Is Family Market Income Inequality Increasing in Canada? Examining the Effects of Aging, Family Formation, Globalization and Technology.' Working Paper, no. W-96-11E. Ottawa: Human Resources Development Canada Applied Research Branch, 1996.
Zyblock, Myles, and Iain Tyrell. 'Decomposing Family Income Inequality in Canada, 1981–93.' *Canadian Business Economics* 6, no. 1 (1997): 108–119.